A HANDBOOK

ON

GOLD AND SILVER

A HANDBOOK
ON
GOLD AND SILVER

GYAN

Published by

Gyan Publishing House
5, Ansari Road
Daryaganj, New Delhi-110002
Phone: 011-47034999, 9811692060
E-mail: books@gyanbooks.com

Distribution Network
gyanbooks.com
India, USA, Canada, UK, Australia

ISBN: 978-93-7169-077-5 (PB)

First Published, 1878

2nd Impression 2025

Printed at: Gyan Press, Delhi.

A HANDBOOK ON GOLD AND SILVER

A HANDBOOK

ON

GOLD AND SILVER

BY

AN INDIAN OFFICIAL

LONDON
LONGMANS, GREEN, AND CO.
1878

INTRODUCTION.

The Silver difficulty and the universal depression of trade are but symptoms of the same economic disorder. In the British Empire the former may develop into paralysis of its Asiatic limb; the latter into disease menacing its heart, viz., a waning prosperity of British manufactures, and a deteriorating condition of the agricultural classes.

The crisis requires wise and prompt treatment; but statesmen resign their duty to political economists who love abstract reasoning, and to theorise; and to brilliant journalists who excel in discussing the events of the everyday life of nations, but who have not time, opportunity, or the commonplace power of drudgery, for digging out the facts which must guide correct opinions of what the silver question means, and the universal depression of trade implies. There is yet another class, viz., bankers and merchants engaged in commerce between the East and West, who are peculiarly fitted to form a correct practical decision on the silver question; but they are content to salute it as a big subject which must be approached through a wide investigation of facts.

In the papers which form an Appendix to the present work, an endeavour has been made to bring together the facts requisite for understanding the silver difficulty, and the general depression of trade, in their bearing more particularly on the prospects of the British Empire; to bring, in short, a big subject within the grasp of the thought and common sense of the educated part of the nation, who in this matter must lead the opinion, and shape the policy of its statesmen and legislators.

The papers in the Appendix treat of the recent financial, monetary, and commercial history of the world for the term of but one generation; yet it is a wondrous story which they unfold. The proper telling of it requires a skill in dealing with prosaic but significant facts of commerce, and a political insight, to which the present writer can lay no claim; so as to trace the course of the commercial and political movements which—beginning about the time of the gold discoveries, and the last overthrow of the French monarchy—have changed the face of the world and the map of Europe.

The repeal of the corn and navigation laws, and the gold discoveries, mark a new era of commerce, on a scale and proportions that have dwarfed all previous efforts of the world's industry and enterprise; also, with them began a wonderful development of credit and finance which has dwarfed even the gold discoveries. If California and Australia have added some 450 millions sterling of gold and silver to the wealth of the world since 1848, credit and finance have increased the debts of the world by above 6,000 millions sterling.

Commerce, and credit and finance—as we now behold them—though of twin birth, and rocked in the same cradle, went different ways. Commerce began the career of its triumphs with a shout of 'peace at any price;' credit and finance, leaving the highways of commerce, struck into the regions of politics, of the ambition and rivalry of rulers and States.

Ubiquitous finance made its influence felt in the cabinets of rulers, in the barrack, the Bank-parlour, and the homes of the poor. It stirred the ambition of kings by giving them the means of gratifying ambition—by showing how hosts of armed men would spring out of the earth at the stamping of its feet, and peaceful industries be deluded into making bloated armaments and military lines of railway. With cruel malice, it showed how the mighty hosts might be moved, and the engines of destruction employed on their bloody work, and then it betrayed the secrets of the council chamber in the homes of the poor, through a heavy grinding taxation.

All this it did with consummate skill, using as its principal yet unconscious instrument in the work of war the country which courts isolation from Europe as the apostle of peace at any price—the country which, though familiar with the hackneyed truth that history repeats itself, yet does not see that, more than any other country, it has helped to render possible, in this nineteenth century, an irruption of the barbarians, by lending freely, abroad, the capital which should have cherished its agriculture and industry at home, but which abroad has made England powerless to obtain a general disarmament, which the spirit of the England of 1815 could have secured. At this point of universal armament in Europe, outside the British isles, and of the universal depression of trade, the long-parted twin brothers, commerce and finance, have again met.

In the same period commerce completed a career of marvellous progress and prosperity. Distant lands attracted its ships, and yielded to it their materials of well-being; harbours were created, and cities sprung up on erst desolate shores; the earth gave to the myriads who sought her virgin soil in the New World and in the fifth Continent, the riches which had been denied to them in the Old. Production in every form was stimulated; science was invoked to supplement, to direct, to multiply manifold, the power of human industry, and in union with the arts to help invention in devising means for augmenting the necessaries, the comforts, the embellishments of life. Distance was annihilated by the steamer, the railway, the telegraph, to bring producers into close communication and ready interchange of traffic with the purchasers from whom they were separated by vast continents.

In short, commerce, by finding a market for every kind of merchandise, energised the forces of production, and provided liberal inducements for invention, organisation, and enterprise, to thinkers and workers, to captains and the rank and file of industry.

In so doing, however, and from the nature of its pursuits, it got imbued with a spirit of materialism; and in England it receded farther and farther from the spirit which had animated the England of the beginning of the nineteenth century.

It was conscious all along of this change; but until of late years it pointed boastfully to the material triumphs which it had achieved with the help of science, and felt that in these days we are better than our fathers were.

This self-complacency has been disturbed by the depression of trade, if it has not been utterly subdued by the wail of distress which arises on every side from suffering myriads, who cannot get work in a world in which labour is the inheritance of man.

And when, in the retrospect of the past thirty years, it recalls to mind the shout of peace at any price with which it went forth on a prosperous career, serious misgivings must disturb it when confronted, as now, with great nations ready for battle, and almost every country in Europe guarding itself against English commerce by a barrier of protective duties; misgivings whether somehow finance has not outwitted commerce, and made the handmaid of peace and civilisation the unconscious instrument in bringing about the present tension in the relations of European States, which may be only the prelude of bloodier wars than any in this century.

The prodigious borrowings by European States could not have been advanced by the lenders if commerce had not provided the means of remittance. The service has been requited by the existing general depression of trade, which arises, as to one cause, from diminished means of purchase of foreign manufactures, owing, 1st, to the pressure of heavy taxation for meeting the interest on national debts; 2ndly, to the overwhelming pressure under which exports have to be sent abroad for meeting interest payments to foreign creditors, whereby but little of other exports is available for interchange with foreign imports.

The depression of trade has been aggravated further by the depreciation of the currencies of ambitious, extravagant States, which for some time prevented a free introduction of capital into those countries, and latterly has been stimulating its withdrawal, which withdrawal involves a further export of merchandise from the indebted countries, without their being able to demand foreign imports in exchange.

These principal causes of the depression of trade have been reinforced by a third cause, viz., the depreciation of silver, which, like the other two causes, occasions an increase of exports from the countries of depreciated silver currency, in exchange, not for foreign imports, but for silver.

The solvent European States are thus flooded—England in particular—with exports from countries of depreciated currency which cannot demand other merchandise in exchange.

The remedies for England are:—

1. To demonetise silver in India.

2. To regain command over foreign markets for her manufactures:

a. By increasing the efficiency of British labour through a resolute, unflinching suppression of drunkenness.

b. By invigorating British agriculture, through the free application of capital to the land.

c. By enlarging the home market for British manufactures as a necessary consequence of the second measure, and thereby enabling the British manufacturer to sell abroad more cheaply than he can now do.

The principal means by which the second and third objects are to be attained is a revision of the land laws in a spirit of true conservatism, and with the purpose of restoring to land its former supremacy in moulding the spirit and strengthening the will of the nation, among whom commerce has had free course to work its will, during the past thirty years, and has failed in those more essential objects of national welfare which are dearest to the patriot.

CONTENTS.

APPENDICES.

A HANDBOOK
ON
GOLD AND SILVER.

CHAPTER I.

THE DEPRECIATION OF SILVER.

IN the words of a late pamphlet, the depreciation of silver has raised a question 'of world-wide importance, demanding the most careful solution, as the most important commercial problem of the day.'

Among the prominent facts are the following:—

I. The yearly production of gold and silver has been as follows, in millions sterling:—

	1848.	1876.
Gold	10	22
Silver	8	15
	18	37

The total production from 1853 to 1876 amounted to 569 millions of gold and 231 millions of silver, giving a yearly average of 24¾ millions for gold, and 10 millions for silver.

II. The price of silver has been as follows, viz.:—

From	1848 to 1852	. .	59½	to	60½*d.*	an ounce.
"	1853 " 1866	. .	61½	"	61⅛	"
"	1867 " 1872	. .	60$\frac{9}{16}$	"	60$\frac{5}{16}$	"
"	1873 " 1875	. .	59¼	"	56⅞	"
"	1876	. . . . . .			52¾	"

And the monthly fluctuations in the price have been:—

	No. of variations	Price of bar silver in London. Pence per ounce		Corresponding value of a rupee in India, in pence		Bank bills in Calcutta, on London, on demand		Rate of exchange of Council Drafts on India. Pence
		Highest	Lowest	Highest	Lowest	Highest	Lowest	
1875.								
January . .	9	57·62	57·25	22·30	22·15	22·25	22·	22·16
April . .	9	57·37	57·	22·20	22·13	22·94	21·81	21·97
July . .	8	56·	55·62	21·67	21·52	21·87	21·37	21·34
October . .	5	57·06	56·69	22·08	21·93	21·75	21·62	21·84
Total for year .	78							
1876.								
January . .	7	56·	54·87	21·67	21·23	21·37	20·81	21·29
April . .	8	54·	53·87	20·89	20·68	20·87	20·44	20·93
July . .	15	51·5	47·	19·93	18·19	19·75	18·12	18·62
October . .	14	53·62	52·	20·75	20·12	20·5	19·12	20·2
Total for year .	151							
1877.								
January . .	14	58·62	57·	22·68	22·06	22·37	21·62	22·16
April . .	12	55·	53·5	21·28	20·70	21·93	20·5	21·12
July . .	10	54·75	53·87	21·18	20·85	21·	20·60	20·83
October . .	11	55·62	54·75	21·52	21·18	21·93	21·	no allotment made
Total to 31 Oct.	98							
23 Nov. 1877	. .	54·62	54·50	. .	. .	20·94	20·87	

The variations in the price of wheat can scarcely have exceeded the variations in the price of the standard of value in 1875 to 1877; and, notwithstanding the great expansion of the Indian export trade in these years, the price of silver fell, and with it the rate of exchange declined. This shows that the depreciation of silver had stimulated the exports, and not that the exports from India, as during the cotton famine, had raised the price of silver—as they should have done if the expectation be at all reasonable, that silver will rise again through an increase of Indian exports.

III. This depreciation of silver is not a new thing. As stated in a summary by the 'Times,' in January 1875, of notes by Dr. Soetbeer on variations in the proportionate values of gold and silver, that relative value in ancient times was about 1 to 13⅓, 'and towards the end of the old Roman Empire of the west it rose to about 1 to 14½. In the middle ages, and down to the fifteenth century, the standard was about 16 of silver to 1 of gold; but after the discovery of America *the value of gold fell rapidly*, until the proportion stood at 10½ to 11 of silver to 1 of gold, which relation was maintained with but little fluctuation during the sixteenth and beginning of the seventeenth centuries. After that date gold began to rise again in value, and by the end of the century the proportion had become 1 to 15. The standard of comparative worth fluctuated backwards and forwards at about that figure during the eighteenth century, and at the close silver was about 15½. Up to 1850 silver had never fallen so low as 16, while from 1850 to 1852, owing chiefly to French coinage operations, and the absorption of silver for the double standard in that country, the price of that metal tended to advance slightly. It was never higher than 15, but still it was considerably less than 15½. After 1859 the course of the price of silver tended downwards, by almost imperceptible steps; but it was not until 1873 that the price began to be decidedly low; it then fell to 16·08 in relation to gold, and by the end of the last year had touched, in London, 16·80, or 57$\frac{1}{16}$*d.* Since the beginning of the sixteenth century gold has "appreciated," as against silver, almost 50 per cent., and nearly 7 per cent. of that appreciation has occurred since 1862; while, if we compare the favourable price of silver in 1859 with that ruling in the latter part of 1874, the value of the metal will be found to have fallen nearly 18 per cent.' With silver at 54½*d.* an ounce, the relative value is about 17·3 to 1.

IV. The course of the depreciation was the same after the discovery of America as after the gold discoveries in California and Australia. In both periods silver rose at the outset, in some gradation, only to fall eventually in a greater degree.

V. There is also a similarity in the distribution, as affecting the relative value of the precious metals in the two periods. In the second period the proportion of new gold exceeded that of silver; but in the first period 'it is stated, by other authorities,[1] that the proportion of *silver* so greatly exceeded the proportion of *gold*, in the new supplies of the precious metals in the sixteenth century, that the quantity of silver brought forward was *sixty* times greater than the quantity of gold;' and yet it was silver and not gold that appreciated at the outset. This arose from two circumstances: *first*, 'till about 1525 but little silver arrived in Europe; and though the great *silver* mine of Potosi was discovered in 1545, yet it was not until 1571, after the discovery in 1567 of the great quicksilver mine of Huancevalica in Peru, that an abundant yield was obtained from Potosi. The receipts of the precious metals in Europe, till about 1525, were confined merely to such quantities of *gold* as were obtained by force, or persuasion, or purchase from the Indian natives.' This, however, accounts for the depreciation of gold, only until the last quarter of the sixteenth century; whilst *secondly*, gold continued to depreciate after the beginning of the seventh century, though the imports of silver from America had by that time long preponderated over the supplies of new gold. Adam Smith completes the explanation; the silver produce was drained to the East, through the low price there of commodities, and 'because in China and the greater part of the other markets of India the proportion between fine silver and fine gold is but as ten, or at most as twelve to one; whereas in Europe it is as fourteen or fifteen to one. In China and the greater part of the other markets of India ten or at most twelve ounces of silver will purchase an ounce of gold; in Europe it requires from fourteen to fifteen ounces. In the cargoes, therefore, of the

[1] *History of Prices*, vol. vi. p. 361.

greater part of European ships which sail to India silver has generally been one of the most valuable articles.' This export had been in progress from the end of the seventeenth century at least. 'The export to Asia of piastres coined from American silver assumed colossal proportions, averaging, as Professor Soetbeer estimates, from 1690 to 1800 about $1\frac{1}{5}$ million sterling annually. Moreover, there was a considerable importation of gold from Asia in return to Spain and England.'[1] Thus the silver from the mines of Potosi was drained off to the East, causing a smaller depreciation of the precious metals in Europe than if a passage to the East by the Cape of Good Hope had not been discovered; for, though gold was brought back in exchange, yet the merchandise of the East also formed part of the exchange, with the result that, as in the period since 1849, 1st, the precious metals did not depreciate in the West to the extent which may have been predicated from the magnitude of the gross additional supplies of gold and silver; 2ndly, when, from the continued exports of silver to the East, the ratio of gold to silver declined in the East, and the export of gold thence to the West lessened, the price of silver declined in the West.

VI. In accordance with the foregoing are the facts of the distribution of gold and silver in the second period, viz., a second exportation of silver to the East, though the new supply of the precious metals was furnished this time by the golden sands of California and Australia. The total production of the precious metals, from 1853 to 1875, exceeded the computed amount, at the former yearly rate, by sums which, in those twenty-three years, amounted to 336 millions sterling extra of gold, and 31 millions sterling extra of silver. But in the exports to the East the proportions were inverted, viz., to 198 millions sterling of silver and only 61 millions of

[1] *Blue Book on Depreciation of Silver—Appendix*, p. 32.

gold; that is to say, the East absorbed 168 millions of the old rate of silver production, and the whole of the extra production of that metal, with only 68 millions of the extra production of gold. On the other hand, the West, by thus parting with all the new, and a great deal of old supplies of silver, was able to retain all but 61 millions of the extra production of gold, viz., 336 millions, without any injurious disturbance of prices. Or, confining the view to the thirteen years from 1853 to 1865, the extra production of gold amounted to 200 millions sterling, while the silver production showed no increase. Of this extra production, the West retained 168 millions, sending to the East only 32 millions of new gold; but it sent 151 millions of silver, which included 113 millions at the old rate of production, and 38 millions from the old stock. The bullion operations for getting together this stock of silver, old and new (by an exchange with gold), for exportation to the East, coincided with an exceptional dearness of cotton in the West, and with a consequent exceptional demand for the cotton of the East, and both these circumstances raised the gold price of silver in the West from 1853 to 1865. Relatively to commodities, both gold and silver depreciated during that period; but silver appreciated, relatively to gold, from the temporary causes just mentioned; although its depreciation in the East, relatively to commodities, was greater than the similar depreciation of gold, relatively to commodities, in the West. The high price in the West, of Asiatic productions, raised the gold price of silver in the West, while the drain to the East, of all but 17 millions of the equivalent of the extra production of 200 millions of gold and silver, caused the depreciation of silver in the East.

VII. Comparing 1873 to 1877 with 1853 to 1865, the only difference to be noted is that whereas, in the earlier period, the depreciation, relatively to commodities, was greater for silver, which, from temporary causes, had appreciated in the West relatively to gold—in the later period silver had recovered some of its depreciation and gold had increased its depreciation relatively to commodities, while silver had now permanently depreciated relatively to gold, far more than in any former period in the world's history.

VIII. Alike in the period after the discovery of America, and in that after the gold discoveries in California and Australia, the principal cause which determined the drain of silver to the East was the low price of Asiatic produce; but there was a second cause, viz., in the first period, an undervaluation of gold in the East, which caused its export to the West, in exchange for silver; and, in the second period, an over-valuation, so to speak, in the West, of the Asiatic production of cotton, which caused its export from the East in similar exchange for silver. In both periods, the second cause operated temporarily to raise the price of silver in the West; but, in the final result, the drain of silver to the East issued in its depreciation in the West.

IX. If, therefore, it be wise to infer from the experience of three centuries, that what has been will be and must be, and that the drain of silver to the East must continue, we should not stop short of the further inference that this drain will only result in a further depreciation of silver in the West.

X. We are shut up to this latter conclusion by the further fact of the great increase of paper currency since 1848. On whatever other points respecting a paper currency writers may differ, all are agreed that the portion of it which permanently circulates displaces a nearly corresponding amount of metallic currency. This is the result even where the paper currency is readily convertible into coin; and the effect is aggravated in countries with an inconvertible paper currency. In such countries, if the issues of inconvertible notes is excessive, a great portion of the metallic currency is exported; there are extreme cases, as in Italy and Russia, where, virtually, the whole of the coin of full legal tender has been exported. And again, if any of these countries resume specie payments, they can do so with a smaller amount of metallic currency, from the nation having become habituated to paper currency. From the combined influence of these circumstances, a large amount of metallic currency has been displaced by the inordinate increase of paper currency. The displacement has been general throughout the western world, and as it happens that all but two countries in the West, which have a double standard, have an inconvertible paper currency, it has come about that the portion of the metallic currency which has been expelled by a process of natural selection, is the silver coinage. But expelled whither? A portion of it has been sent to the East, but, failing the East for the portion not thus exported (which remains to be expelled from the western system of currency), the West, in the absence of means of export to Kingsley's world on the other side of nowhere, is being forced to demonetise silver.

XI. Practically, only one of the precious metals can circulate as full legal tender, in any one country, even if it has the double standard. Hence, the depreciation of silver would be of little consequence, it would indeed be unmeaning, if the country had no foreign trade. It is as international money that the depreciation acquires importance; the country which uses depreciated silver not being able to correct an adverse exchange by sending it to countries where the export would only cause a further depreciation of silver. On this point the following extract from Professor Senior's lecture, on the 'Transmission of the precious metals from one country to another,' deserves to be remembered.

'I will suppose that all the protecting duties, with which we have clogged our commerce with France, are suddenly removed, and that the removal is immediately followed by an increased importation of

French commodities to the amount of five millions sterling. And I will suppose the commercial restrictions on the part of France to remain unaltered. I will suppose, too, that the five millions in question are actually remitted in money. It must be admitted that the efflux of so large a sum from England, and its influx into France, must sink all English prices, and occasion a general rise of prices in France. Indeed, if it did not, the transaction would be one of pure benefit to England, and of pure loss to France. As money is not a source of gratification, but a mere instrument of commerce, if our prices were not affected by parting with a portion of our money, we should be insensible of our loss; or rather, we should have sustained no loss whatever, and have gained the five millions worth of French commodities without any real sacrifice; while France would have parted with those commodities, and received no sensible equivalent.

'But those who fear that a nation may be injured by parting with its money, are certainly right in supposing that the transmission of five millions in specie to France would occasion a general fall of prices in England, and a general rise in France. The steps by which these effects would be produced in each country cannot properly be stated in this part of my Lectures, but I suppose there is no one present who doubts that such would be the case.

'The consequence would be an immediate and universal increase of imports and diminution of exports in France, and an immediate and universal increase of exports and diminution of imports in England. The commerce which any country carries on with its neighbours must depend on the prices of their respective exportable commodities. When commodities of the same quality, or which may be substituted for one another, can be imported from different quarters, a slight variation of price will decide which shall be preferred. If linen of the same quality can be imported into South America indifferently from Germany and from France, and the cost of transport from each country is the same, while the price per yard is also the same, South America will probably import indifferently from each country; but if the influx of money should raise the price of linen of a given quality from two shillings to two shillings and a farthing per yard in France, while it remained at two shillings in Germany, South America would instantly desert the French market, and confine her linen trade to Germany.

'With every commercial rival with whom France was formerly on a par, she would now be at a disadvantage; and many would now meet her in markets from which she had formerly excluded them.

The same consequences, though to a less extent, would follow, even in the cases in which France had exclusive powers of production. Every commodity has among its purchasers some whose desire for it, or at least for that variable quantity of it which they consume, induces them to spend on it a given portion of their income, and no more. On the slightest rise of price, they either discontinue or diminish their consumption. A very slight rise in the price of claret would occasion some to drink less, and others to drink more. Precisely the same causes which would diminish the exports of France, would increase her imports. However earnestly a nation may endeavour to secure to its own productive classes the monopoly in what they respectively produce, it cannot really protect them against foreign competition by any measure short of the prohibition of all foreign commerce. The consumer cannot be forced to buy the dearer or inferior home-made article. If he is prohibited from importing precisely what he wants, he may still make his purchase abroad. The increased price in France of all home commodities would, of course, stimulate the consumption of foreign ones. The bills of France, on other countries, would increase; those of other countries on France would diminish; and the exchange would be against France throughout the commercial world. It is impossible that, under such circumstances, she could retain for a month the five millions which I have supposed to have been paid to her. They would flow from her in every direction.

'In fact, until she parted with the money, France would have derived, not benefit, but rather evil, from her export to England. That money is a means, not an end; that no gratification is afforded by an increase in the quantity necessary to effect a given purpose; that it is quite as pleasant to purchase a given commodity for five shillings as for fifty,—are truisms, but truisms so often impliedly denied, that they cannot be too often repeated. The rise of prices in France, while they lasted, must have been an evil. It must have deranged, so far as it went, the existing relations of society; have impoverished creditors, and those whose incomes were fixed; and, to a certain extent, unfitted money to perform its functions of a permanent expression or standard of value. If no other results were to to have followed from the sacrifice of so much French industry, France had better have given away, than have sold, her five millions' worth of silks. The sale of the silks would have become advantageous to her only when, by re-exporting their price, she had obtained from other countries commodities capable of affording her more gratification than she could have received from the industry of the silk trade, manufacturing silks or other commodities for her own home market.

'It is obvious, that all this time precisely an opposite process would be going on in England. The general fall in English prices would give a preference to our goods in every market of which they had merely an equal portion before; it would admit them to many others from which they were previously excluded. It would exclude from the English market many foreign commodities, which could now be obtained more cheaply at home. While the bills in England on foreign countries were increasing, the foreign bills on England would diminish; the exchange would be in our favour with the whole world, and the five millions would come back as rapidly as they went went out. To suppose that the level of the precious metals in the commercial world can be permanently disturbed, by taking money from one country to another, is as absurd as to suppose that the level of a pond can be altered by taking a bucket-full from one place and pouring it into another. The water instantly rushes to the place from which the bucket-full has been drawn, just as it rushes from the place into which it has been poured. Every country to which France exported any of the money she received from England would, to that extent, have more money than her habitual state of prices would allow. It would flow from her either directly to England, or to those countries which were in want of money in consequence of having previously exported it to England.

'It appears, therefore, that even in the extravagant case which I have supposed, of an export of five millions in money, the loss, if it can be called one, would be immediately repaired. The only inconvenience that we should suffer from the refusal of France to take our cottons and our hardware in return for her silks, would be that instead of the direct exchange of English for French commodities, we should give to France money; France would export that money to Germany, Holland, and Russia; and Germany, Holland, and Russia would return that money in exchange for our manufactures; that our trade would, in short, be circuitous instead of direct.

'For the sake of illustration, I have supposed a sudden and great transmission of money; effects the same in kind, though less in degree, would of course follow a more gradual one. If a balance of only one hundred thousand sovereigns a year were sent to France, similar consequences, though less palpable, would follow; either immediately, or as soon as the annual efflux of money from the one country to the other amounted to a sum sufficient to affect the prices of either country or of both.'

This is a long quotation, but the truth which it enforces is overlooked by writers on the present depreciation of silver, who would solve the controversy respecting gold and silver by retaining gold for the currency of the West, and allotting silver for the currency of the East. The argument in the extract rests entirely on the assumption of a common money between the countries engaged in foreign trade. If France had a silver currency, and England and all the other countries with which France trades had a gold currency, the illustrations and the argument in the extract would entirely fail: 1st. The five millions of silver sent by England to France could not be exported by the latter to other countries, and the passing evils which, in the illustration, France experienced until she could re-export the silver, would have been permanent. 2ndly. Prices would not have sunk in England to the extent supposed in the extract, from the export of five millions of silver, if it was not international money, and therefore was not readily convertible into English money. In other words, for the free play of the precious metals in international settlements, there must be an universal international money, whether that be gold, or, until 1867 and somewhat later, both gold and silver. Every country which receives one of the precious metals in settlement of international obligations should be free to re-export that metal in correction of an adverse exchange. But any such re-export of silver from the East to the West must be impracticable if silver be demonetised in the West. In 1876-7 there was a gross export from India to Europe of £1,229,000 in gold, but of only £146,000 in silver.

The facts and conclusions presented in this chapter are that—

I. The price of silver had fallen in 1876 to 52¾*d.* an

ounce, from 59½*d.* to 60½*d.* in 1848 to 1852; and from 1875 to 1877 the price has been as variable as that of wheat.

II. This depreciation of silver is not a new thing. The course of silver depreciation, relatively to gold, has been uniform, alike in the period after the discovery of America, when the new supplies of gold and silver diffused themselves over the world, as in the period after the gold discoveries in California and Australia; though, in this second period, the production of gold greatly preponderated over that of silver. In both periods alike, the drain of silver to the East issued, through the perverse fate of this standard of value, in its depreciation in the West.

III. In both periods alike, the price of silver was temporarily enhanced in the West, relatively to gold, from the exceptionally high price in the West, compared with the East, of a special export from the East, viz., of gold in the first period and of cotton in the second period. On the cessation of this influence, the gold price of silver declined in the West; this tendency to decline being the normal relation of silver to gold.

IV. If it be wise to infer from the experience of three centuries, that what has been will be, and must be, and that the drain of silver to the East must continue, then, as in the past, this drain can only result in a further depreciation of silver in the West.

V. Hence, it cannot be seriously maintained that the depreciation which silver has reached is not permanent, except in the sense that a lower depth remains to be sounded by the East, in its progress to financial ruin, unless, like the West, it stops the further coinage of silver.

VI. The depreciation of silver in the West would of course be immaterial to the East, if there were no trade between the two hemispheres; but an international common money is a vital necessity of foreign trade, because every country which receives one of these precious metals in international settlements should be free to re-export it, in correction of an adverse exchange.

VII. Hence, no further reason is required to show that, the West having closed its mints against the coinage of silver, the East must do so too. Argument on this point can be raised only by a denial of patent facts.

CHAPTER II.

THE BATTLE OF THE STANDARDS.

Is there a remedy for the depreciation of silver, or must the silver-using countries submit to loss, and bear it as best they may? The din of the battle of the standards prevents the immediate hearing of an answer to the question.

2. If some modification of the standard of value in silver-using countries be indispensable, we get scant encouragement from the disputants. The mono-metallists proclaim that silver is for the East, and gold for the West; by which fiat, should it prevail, they would condemn the East to the darkness of Erebus, and deepen the gloom that overhangs the finances of India and her prospects of material progress. On the other hand, the bi-metallists administer the cold pitiless comfort that silver must continue to fall until the nations join in an universal bi-metallism, in that remote, improbable future when England and Germany may give up their gold standard.

3. On one point some bi-metallists and mono-metallists of Europe, that is, the advocates of a gold standard for the West and a silver standard for the East, are agreed, namely, the inexpediency or the injustice of altering the standard of value—that is, the inexpediency or the injustice of any change of the systems which they severally maintain for their respective countries. It does not occur to these controversialists, that if both their systems be perfect, and the third system of a silver standard be bad, the deliverance of

the silver-using countries from this third system by a change of standard may be wise, just, and humane.

4. Professor Emile de Laveleye is the latest exponent of the main argument which his school of bi-metallists and the mono-metallists of Europe employ against any alteration of the standard of value. His argument is as follows:—

I. The demonetisation of the cheaper metal (as of silver in a bi-metallic system, or, as in a change from a silver to a gold standard), 'is a great injustice, since it modifies all contracts to the detriment of those whose interests are most worthy to be considered—namely, the debtors. They have at present the right of paying their debts either in gold or silver at their option; and to deprive them of that right, and oblige them to pay in gold only, at the very moment when, by the act of demonetising silver, the value of gold has been considerably increased, would be a grave hardship. It would be sacrificing the tax-payers for the benefit of the bond-holders.'

II. It would also be inexpedient. 'All countries burdened with a heavy debt which they mean to pay, like France, Italy, Austria, Russia, England, and the United States;—all mortgage debtors, all railway companies with their milliards of bonds, are interested in having bi-metallic money, because the simultaneous employment of the two metals secures an abundance of money, and acts in the long run, in the direction of a rise of prices; while the single standard system causes a scarcity of money, and acts in the direction of a fall of prices. It would be a great aggravation of the burden of debtors, if they were required to pay exclusively in gold, inasmuch as that metal would, of necessity, be made scarcer and dearer by the exclusion of silver.' (The last sentence equally applies to an alteration from a silver to a gold standard, in a country like India, which owes gold debts abroad.) 'Certain countries, such as Austria, Italy, Russia (and India), 'have a large part of their public debt placed abroad, and it is for their advantage to be able to pay it with as small an amount of products as possible,' whereas, if silver be demonetised, the value of gold will be raised and the prices of commodities will fall.

Before stating the general considerations which are opposed to this argument, the replies of certain bi-metallists to a portion of it may be quoted.

a. Mr. HENRI CERNUSCHI. 'Breach of faith! The English creditors have stipulated for payment in gold; if they are paid in silver they are aggrieved. This is a pitiful scruple: they would be aggrieved if a given sum in silver was worth less than the same sum in gold, but they are not if the two sums are exactly equivalent, and universal bi-metallism makes them equivalent. England has been in turn bi-metallic, silver mono-metallic, again bi-metallic, and lastly gold mono-metallic, without drawing on herself the reproach of having at every change committed a breach of faith. Holland, Belgium, the United States have changed their monetary metal without incurring any blame. The French *rentier* has never troubled himself whether he would be paid in gold or silver; he has always been indifferent to the colour of the metal. The English fund-holder will be so too. English interests the interests of the whole world, demand this reform, which consists in declaring the coinage of silver free, even in England; and this reform will injure nobody. To reject it there must be good reasons, not mere pretexts or pitiful scruples.'

b. Mr. SAMUEL SMITH, *President of the Chamber of Commerce, Liverpool.* 'All nations benefit by stability in monetary matters. None, except thieves and rogues, wish to borrow in one standard, and pay in another.'

c. Mr. ERNEST SEYD. 'In a bi-metallic system, the mass of debts is paid not in metal, either gold or silver, but in paper; that is, through accounts, cheques, clearing systems,—without any use of currency,—at the relative value between gold and silver which is fixed in the bi-metallic system, irrespectively of the price of the metals outside the system.'

6. Categorically stated, M. de Laveleye's argument is as follows:—

I. That in any alteration of standard, creditors suffer by a change from the dearer to the cheaper, and debtors by a change from the cheaper to the dearer metal; and that, as the interests of debtors are most worthy to be considered, the change should never be from the cheaper metal.

II. It is not to the interest of countries which owe, abroad, debts payable in gold, that the cheaper metal should be demonetised; because thereby gold would be enhanced in value, the prices of commodities would fall, and a larger amount of products would have to be exported for payment of the old amount of debt, or of the interest on it.

III. And it would also be to the advantage of all who owe debts within the country, that prices should be kept high, by not demonetising the cheaper metal, for thereby the incomes out of which debts are paid will be kept high; whereas, if prices fall, incomes will fall, but the old amount of debt will remain unaltered.

7. The first of these arguments is met, under the bimetallic system, by the passages quoted from M. Cernuschi and Mr. Seyd; but we have to consider the wider application of the three objections, to a change from a silver to a gold standard, as well as to the demonetisation of silver in the bimetallic system.

8. Conceding for the moment, that a judicious alteration of the standard must injure either the creditor or the debtor class, is it the latter or the former who should be protected from injury? Apparently, the interests of creditors should be regarded—

I. Because the creditor class is the representative of capital, which is wealth accumulated by past labour, and the motive power of the marvellous industrial progress in the world since the gold discoveries in California and Australia. Injury to creditors means destruction of part of the wealth which provides profitable employment for the debtor class.

II. If capital suffer, the rate of interest must rise; and as the largest part of the debt existing at any time in the work of production, distribution, and supply is renewed at short intervals, the enhanced rate of interest would soon reach the mass of debtors, whose last state, by reason of the destruction of capital, would be worse than the first. Nor would the richer debtors, in whose behalf, rather than in that of the poorer, the argument is employed, be in better plight: for a rise in the rate of interest lowers the price of stocks and securities; and it is not to the advantage of a government, a railway company, or other industrial enterprise, that its stocks or securities should be depreciated.

9. It is assumed in the second and third arguments, that an alteration of standard from silver to gold, or by demonetising silver in a bi-metallic system, must reduce prices. In the second of the arguments this reduction of prices is supposed to be general in all countries; in the third, the reduction spoken of refers to that in the country whose standard is altered. On the first-mentioned supposition of a general fall of prices, the fall would in a poor or indebted country be greater, among other articles, for the imports into it, than in the rich or creditor country for the imports into it; so that the old amount of indebtedness, that is, the old amount of extra or special production for payment of its yearly debt by the indebted to the creditor country, would probably not be materially affected.

10. And in this regard it should be remembered that while no government of any country would wantonly alter its standard of value, no circumstance affecting merely the country's home trade would ever influence the change. Some serious inconvenience in the country's foreign trade, or in its payment of foreign debt or tribute in a metallic standard different from its own, would be the grave and imperious necessity for change. In other words, if the standard be not altered, after it has ceased, abroad, to be money, the special difficulty in making the foreign payments (when once that difficulty has become inherent in the standard of value of the indebted country), must continue to increase with a

growing depreciation of that standard; consequently, the amount of exports from the debtor to the creditor country would continue to increase (with an accompanying fall of their price in the creditor country), without the countervailing advantage to the debtor country of a corresponding fall in the prices of the imports from the creditor country, such as, on the hypothesis considered in the preceding paragraph, would accompany an alteration of the standard in the indebted country. If two years ago the standard in India had been altered from silver to gold, at a relative value of 15½ to 1, would the amount of exports for settling India's indebtedness to England, with exchange at 1*s.* 11*d.* per rupee, be greater now than the amount which will be required two years hence, if, with a continuing silver standard, exchange were to fall to 1*s.* 6*d.* per rupee? To suppose that it would, one must disregard all experience—and the evidence at the present time—of the action of a low exchange in stimulating exports and reducing their gold price abroad.

11. Silver is money in the East, but it is no longer international money in the West, from the closure against it, to the public, of the mints in Europe and the United States. This virtual demonetisation of silver in the West, as international money, is overlooked in M. de Laveleye's objection, that for silver-using countries, or the East, to change to a gold standard would be folly, because thereby they would raise the value of gold, and in consequence would have to export to the West a larger quantity of goods to pay the old amount of indebtedness. Whatever mischief, in the direction of enhancing the value of gold in the West, was possible, has been already done by the discontinuance there of silver as international money. The prices in England of Asiatic merchandise can be reduced only in two ways, viz., 1st, by an offer by the East, of increased quantities of it, otherwise than in response to an increased demand at the

old price; 2ndly, by a scarcity of gold, which would cause a general fall of prices in the West. Now, the first of these causes must continue to act so long as the low exchange of the rupee with sterling (that is, the depreciation of silver, concurrently with its retention in India as money), operates as a bounty on exports from India. The additional exports which, under the influence of this bounty (and not in response to an increased demand from Europe, at the old price), are sent to the West, must lower the gold price of Asiatic produce in the West, and thereby compel India to send larger quantities of goods for the old amount of indebtedness. Thus, the disadvantage which is apprehended from an alteration to a gold standard besets an adherence to the silver standard; and the evil is progressive, because every fresh fall in the gold price abroad, of Indian productions, must lower the gold price of silver—that is, provide a fresh bounty on Indian exports, with the result of a further fall of their gold price abroad, by reason of the additional exports under the stimulus of the new bounty.

12. It cannot be admitted that if a country were to change from a silver to a gold standard, or were to demonetise silver in a bi-metallic system, prices in that country would fall by reason of the change. The very reverse has happened in Germany. A currency can affect prices only by its inflation or its depletion; and there is no reason why either the one or the other should accompany a change of the standard of value. Or, if anything, the tendency would be towards inflation and an increase of prices. The reason why prices would not fall is plain. Paper currency (if readily convertible into coin) and a silver token currency (if readily convertible into full legal tender) are just as efficient items as the coins of full legal tender in the mass of a country's currency, which by its exchange against commodities acts upon prices. For, in a properly regulated alteration from a silver to a gold standard, silver would not be altogether

divested of its functions as currency; and there would not be a diminution of the mass of metallic currency (legal tender and subsidiary) which collectively, in the interchange for commodities, acts upon prices. So much of the silver coinage as could be readily exchanged for full legal tender would be retained as subsidiary currency, and the remainder would be withdrawn with the new gold currency. The old amount of metallic currency would not be reduced; nay, by reason of the replacement of a certain number and amount of silver coins by fewer gold coins of equal value, an extra amount of silver coinage would be required to maintain the old numerical proportion of coin to the population.

13. Furthermore, though the alteration of values from a silver to a gold standard would probably be effected in the ratio of 15½ to 1, yet (that object obtained) the new subsidiary silver currency, though of restricted legal tender, might consist of coins containing so much more silver than the superseded currency, as would bring their intrinsic value to a par with that of the new gold coins, according to the market price of silver at the time of changing the standard. With this precaution, and if the new silver coins be freely received in the public treasuries, in payment of the revenue, the limit of legal tender of the subsidiary coins might be enlarged beyond the customary limits, so as to continue a fairly extensive use of silver in the internal transactions of the country.

14. It is through the foreign trade that the currency acts upon prices; and if each country had sufficient of gold currency to bear the impact of that foreign trade, and correct the foreign exchanges, the remainder of its currency might be subsidiary silver currency, constituted in the manner just described. The nations would then have gold as international money, and silver and paper currency for internal trade or domestic transactions; thus supplying a material addition to other most effectual means of economising gold,

which are now diminishing its use in the settlement of international transactions.

15. Hence it appears that with the universal adoption of a gold currency, though gold would come into more extended but moderated use for international transactions, yet it would be less required for domestic trade, while the use of silver would be enlarged. This would be equally the result in bi-metallic countries, from which the relative value of 15½ to 1 had expelled silver coins of full legal tender before the great depreciation of silver.

16. Accordingly, the assumption of M. de Laveleye, that the general adoption of a gold standard would so enhance the value of gold as to cause a serious fall of prices in the countries concerned, and generally, cannot be admitted. It is overlooked that the demonetising of silver does not mean its disuse as currency, but its over-valuation; that is, the raising of its value relatively to gold, thereby enabling it to relieve gold of some of its functions of currency in the internal trade of each country. The total value of the metallic currency in each country would not be reduced, only the numerical proportion of the silver currency to the population would be diminished, and that only in silver-using countries like India, which may not have expelled silver by means of an inconvertible paper currency. There is nothing in these circumstances to warrant the expectation of a considerable enhancement of the value of gold such as could cause a general and serious fall of prices.

17. If these observations be just, it is not necessary to follow M. de Laveleye in his remarks on the gain to the State, in the discharge of its obligations, if it abide, in the bi-metallic system, by the metal which has depreciated; and on the injustice to poor debtors, if their obligations be increased by a change of standard from the metal which has depreciated to that which has appreciated. But from the importance which has been attached to these objections,

they may repay a further examination—though they have been answered in paragraph 8. In India the second objection would be urged more especially on behalf of the numerous peasant proprietors and others who pay the land tax, which has been assessed in silver rupees. If a gold standard be adopted, at a relative valuation of silver to gold of 15½ to 1, the tax-payers will be required to pay a larger amount in gold than the present money's worth, in gold, of their rupee or silver assessment. And this it is alleged would be unjust, until the next revision of the settlements of the land revenue. But for the bulk of the *ryots*, or peasant proprietors, the assessment for each field, though expressed in gold money, would, from the smallness of the amount, continue to be demanded and collected in the over-valued subsidiary silver currency; so that if, on the one hand, the assessment be over-valued in gold money, on the other hand the payment would be made in silver money of corresponding over-valuation. The same remark applies to the assessment payable by larger proprietors; these would receive their rents in over-valued silver money, from their ryots, and they would have no difficulty in converting the subsidiary silver money into gold money; or, failing such conversion, the over-valued silver coins would be freely received by the Government in payment of the revenue. The alleged injustice (like that which, on M. de Laveleye's theory, must have been sustained by peasant proprietors in Belgium, Holland, and Germany, in the instances cited by M. Cornuschi, para. 5*a*) would be imaginary.

18. With regard to State obligations, it is difficult to understand how any benefit to the State can accrue from its obligations, and from the revenue out of which they are discharged, continuing to be expressed in silver money which has depreciated. Private individuals, other than those on fixed incomes, or employed on fixed salaries, may be able to increase their income proportionately to the depreciation of

silver—though this is by no means certain—but the land revenue of a Government is fixed for a term of years, and the revenue from indirect taxes can increase only commensurately with any augmentation of the prosperity of the country, which, with local capital diminished in effectiveness,—and with the importation of fresh capital checked,—by the depreciation of silver, will certainly not advance in proportion to that depreciation. At the same time, the amount payable by the State for its foreign indebtedness, and in salaries to its servants, would increase in the degree of the depreciation of silver money.

19. We may therefore conclude that if a sufficient amount of over-valued silver currency, freely receivable in Government treasuries in payment of revenue, be provided, there would be no breach of faith, nor any disadvantage to the State, in altering its standard from silver to gold at a relative value, whether 15½ to 1, or other, which shall fully correct the effects of the late depreciation of silver. This conclusion becomes overwhelming, when it is considered that heavy additional taxation, pressing upon all the springs of industry and commerce, in a poor country, would be the alternative of not so rectifying the standard of value.

20. Not merely the greatest good of the greatest number, but the welfare of the entire population, calls for such an alteration of the standard in a silver-using country the metal of whose currency is mere merchandise, like iron or copper, in the rest of the world, excepting China. Ethical considerations, therefore, do not bar but support the change. But if, on any view of such considerations, English rulers of India abstain from adopting, in the interests of India, a change of standard which Englishmen, not less honest, adopted in the interests of England in a past generation, the expense or loss from the decision should hardly fall upon India.

21. But, says the organ of either the most advanced or

the weakest school of the mono-metallists of Europe, silver is for the East and gold for the West, and so it must continue. This doctrine, seemingly an after-thought, was broached by the 'Economist' after the great depreciation of silver. Its examination, and that of one or two other objections to the adoption of a gold standard for India, will be reserved for the next chapter.

CHAPTER III.

SILVER IS FOR THE EAST, GOLD IS FOR THE WEST.

An impression prevails that there is not enough of gold in the world for all. The idea might accord well with a spirit of money-getting; but such, of course, is not the temper of the nineteenth century. If there be not enough of gold, there must be something wrong with the world's currency; and the currency doctors should see to it, whether their patient is not in a state of feverish excitement, induced by speculation and disordered fancies about much gain, in which bleeding and drastic treatment would do him more good than indulging him with more gold.

2. Be that as it may, on the assumption that there is not enough of gold in the world for all, some of the possessors of a gold standard proclaim that silver is good enough for the East, and that gold must be reserved for the West. The utterances of this doctrine by the 'Economist' are as follows:—

a. 'The East and the West need different currencies, and the reason of the difference is obvious. Exactly the same circumstances which make it desirable for the West to have a principal gold currency, make it desirable that the East should have a silver one. The West is pre-eminently the seat of large commerce with great transactions; the East, of minor commerce with small transactions. Accordingly, the West needs a large unit of reckoning and exchange, the East a small unit.'—*Economist*, September 11, 1875.

Yet Germany and France have smaller units of reckoning, with gold currencies, than India with a silver currency.

b. 'Probably, if there were gold enough for all the world, it would be best that there should be only a single standard of value throughout the world, and that one—gold. But this is impossible. Some have doubted whether there is gold enough even for the nations which now intend to use it; and there certainly is not enough for all the world. Happily, the East has always been a country which had much silver, and for whose purposes silver was quite sufficient.'—*Mr. Bagehot on the Depreciation of Silver*, p. 2.

c. We must remember that silver is practically the main currency of a very large part of the world. The whole of the East uses it, not indeed to the entire exclusion of gold, but still much more than gold. It suits the minuteness of the payments which in Oriental countries, and in all countries in which there is no credit, of necessity make up almost the whole of the daily transactions which carry on common life, and for which the smallest gold coin that can be safely and economically used is very many times too great.'—*Ibid.* p. 28.

Mr. Bagehot was not aware that in the small transactions 'for which the smallest gold coin is very many times too great,' there is a system of credit in India more extensive than anything of the same kind in Europe, and that for large transactions the mechanism of credit in India is so fine, that no other part of the world approaches it. Large sums are lent by native shroffs to one another, on verbal application, through subordinate gomashtahs, or accountants, and without any receipt for the money, or any record of the transaction other than the entries in the books of the lender and the borrower. A banker in one part of India will draw on a banker in another part, without having any money at credit with the latter, on the simple assurance that their names and credit are mutually known to each other, and in the feeling that the courtesy will be reciprocated whenever required.

d. 'The Latin Union was a group of double-standard countries largely using gold, and the question for them is whether they will give up their gold, and become silver countries exclusively—which would happen if they were to abandon the limitation of coinage while silver is as cheap as now—or whether they will demonetise silver and use gold as a standard only. This would be troublesome and costly, but still it could be done. But India has no problem to consider; she is irrevocably committed to a silver currency, and therefore a similar attitude would, in her case, besides being mischievous, have no meaning. The true remedy, as we have often shown, is not to impede silver's going to India, but to permit the laws of trade to diffuse silver through India and through the world.'—*Ibid.* p. 64.

That is, through the world on the other side of nowhere: silver not diffusing itself from India to China, and in but limited amount through the countries around the Red Sea and the Persian Gulf.

e. The closure of the Indian mints against the importers of silver 'would (*ibid.* p. 106) deprive India of the great advantage she will gain, if the present state of things continue, as the *entrepôt* through which silver is introduced into the East. This is always the effect of a lowered value of the currency metals. The first persons who get them from the mines gain much; those who buy them from the mining people gain much too; and so on, till the depreciation is effected. In the case of India the importation of silver will gradually raise silver prices; this will bring imports into India from other countries where they have not risen.'

Which countries? China receives silver from the West, and latterly, in increased quantities, direct from America; she exports silver to India. Should silver prices rise less in China than in India, the net Indian revenue from opium will be reduced, or the competition of indigenous opium in China with Indian opium will be increased, through the increased cost of production in India. Mr. Bagehot borrowed his account of the flow of the precious metals over the world from Professor Cairnes; he should have concluded with the words of the same authority.

'As the final result of the whole movement, we find that while the metallic systems of England and the United States are receiving but small permanent accessions, those of India and China are absorbing enormous supplies. The former countries, though the first recipients of the treasure, yet not requiring it for domestic purposes, are enabled to shift the burden to others whose real wealth they command in exchange; while the latter, requiring what they receive, are compelled to retain it. Having parted with their commodities for the new money, they are unable afterwards to replace them. As their stock of coin increases, their means of well-being decline, and they become the permanent victims of the monetary disturbance.'

Professor Cairnes had a thoughtful concern for the last receivers of the yearly millions sterling of silver; but Mr. Bagehot, in his fear that there was not enough of gold in the world for all, considered 'the de'il might take the hindmost.'

3. The law that the East should confine itself to silver has been set at naught by Japan and the Philippine Isles, which, with a smaller trade than that of India, have adopted the gold standard; and the dictum that silver is suited to countries with a small trade, while gold is the prerogative of countries with a large trade, has been further contravened by the Scandinavian kingdoms which, with severally a smaller trade than that of India, have acquired a gold currency. There is more than enough of large transactions in India, for employing a gold currency sufficient for correcting the foreign exchanges. The doctrine that silver is good enough for the East, while it is demonetised in the West, contradicts the theory of the transmission of the precious metals, an exposition of which, by Professor Senior, has been quoted in a previous chapter. Only under an oppressive fear that there is not enough of gold in the world for all the countries that need a common money in their foreign trade, could Mr. Bagehot have forgotten that theory. He quickly remembered it when the balance of his mind was regained. In combating a proposition for stopping the coinage of silver, which might have proved the precursor of a gold currency in India, he observed: 'The currency of monopoly coins, so introduced, would be a very bad one. There would be one currency fit for foreign payments—the gold—and another not so fit. The monopoly coins would be unexportable, and

so, when any one wanted to make a foreign payment, he would have to get gold, which, as a rule, would make gold at a premium.' Mr. Bagehot was quite right in his remark that a currency of which the coins cannot be exported, in correction of an adverse exchange, is 'a very bad one.' What then can be worse than an Indian silver currency which is constantly receiving accessions, in yearly sums of several millions sterling, in the face of an adverse exchange, and which cannot re-export silver coins in correction of that exchange? This, certainly, is not an automatic currency which in an adverse exchange rejects redundant coin, with the same facility with which in a favourable exchange it opens the mint to supply a deficiency.

4. Assuming that silver is quite good enough for India, which has a respectable position in the trade of the world, it is interesting to know how she will fare with a silver standard which is continually depreciating abroad, and above all in the country to which she is indebted. Mr. Bagehot tells us—

a. 'The effect, therefore, of the fall in the value of silver on the trade of India will be temporary only, but its effect on the financial position of the Indian Government will continue as long as the fall lasts. The Indian revenue is received in silver, and therefore the less far silver goes in buying, the poorer will the Indian Government be. And this is of more importance to the Indian Government than almost any other, because its foreign payments exceed those of most Governments, and those payments are made in gold... The less valuable silver is in comparison with gold, the less effectual for these necessary purposes will the Indian revenues be.'—*Depreciation of Silver*, p. 5.

b. 'For our Government and that of British India, we believe that there is no other policy possible, except to leave the ordinary economical causes to operate, to suffer the present evil (March 4th, 1876) and to await the ultimate cure.'—*Ibid.* p. 13.

c. 'The low rate of exchange encourages exports from and discourages imports into India. By this combination, therefore, exports from India increasing on one hand, and imports into India diminishing on the other hand, before long a large void will be created, which this silver, set free from Germany, will have to fill. The process will take time, but the effect is inevitable. The tendency of this great import of silver into India will of course be to raise prices. . . When this rise of prices has taken place, the encouragement of exports from and discouragement of imports into India will manifestly cease.'

d. But India and Manchester will not then have rest. 'If new silver should still continue to come into the market, the same process must go on. The first step must be incessantly repeated. The value of the rupee must fall as against sterling money; instead of being 1*s.* 9*d.* it may fall to 1*s.* 6*d.* And then, what we have just described as happening will happen again.'—*Ibid.* p. 5.

With an exchange of 1*s.* 8*d.* on fifteen millions sterling of the Secretary of State's bills on India, the loss by exchange will amount to three millions; at an exchange of 1*s.* 6*d.* it would amount to five millions. In 1873-4 the loss amounted to £987,000.

e. 'Addition to the supply of silver in India will raise prices: that is, will necessitate a larger amount of silver currency, and so will increase the demand in the East for silver.'—*Ibid.* pp. 28-9.

f. 'Silver being cheaper here, more of it will be bought and sent to the countries where silver is money. But its value there against commodities will not fall as suddenly as it has here. We see that it would not, if silver had been the only metal used as money in the world. And the countries where it is used are, within their own boundaries, in the same position. The more silver falls in purchasing power, the more of it will be wanted to purchase commodities; and the demand for it, therefore, will increase incessantly where the supply is augmented. The silver prices of commodities will be slowly raised everywhere where silver is money, and a great deal of it will be required in the process, and the course of trade will be changed. The silver countries must find exports to pay for this new article, silver, which is coming in upon them... One of the ultimate effects will be to raise the value of silver in London—in the *entrepôt*—where the market is so sensitive, by distributing it over vast regions where much more will be wanted, if the value falls comparatively but little.

'Thirdly, we must observe that this process is not at all bad for the trade of England. No doubt, the fall in the rate of exchange is a disadvantage to shippers to the countries where money is silver. But then another class of exporters will be benefited, for we import that silver and have to pay for it. The loss on the one hand will be compensated by a gain on the other.'—*Ibid.* p. 74.

These lengthy extracts darken counsel with words. Let us try to gather the comfort which they afford in the disorganisation of the Indian finances by the depreciation of silver.

I. The price of silver may fall so as to bring the exchange down to 1*s.* 6*d.* a rupee, when the loss by exchange on the fifteen millions sterling of Council drafts will amount to five millions, against a corresponding charge of not quite one million sterling in 1873–4.

II. With exchange at 1*s.* 9*d.*, the remitting of fifteen millions sterling for the home expenditure of the Indian Government would have cost about 170 millions of rupees; — with exchange at 1*s.* 6*d.* it would cost 200 millions of rupees. In other words, Indian exports amounting to about 170 millions of rupees, which would provide the remittance at an exchange of 1*s.* 9*d.*, must be increased to 200 millions of rupees if the exchange fall to 1*s.* 6*d.*, as it did in July 1876.

III. The Indian finances would no doubt suffer; but commerce, if left to itself, would work out a new equilibrium or par of exchange, for the regulation of imports and exports, until some fresh fall in the price of silver in London might give a fresh check to imports and a new impetus to exports, until a second and lower equilibrium or par is attained.

IV. British trade would not suffer, only the exports to India of merchandise might decline; exports to India of silver, previously paid for by British exports of merchandise to some other quarter, would increase under the stimulus of a low exchange, which operates as a bounty.

V. The incessant stream of silver to India would raise prices in the country; but it would also raise the price of silver in London.

There are here weighty matters. The probability of at least four millions sterling of additional taxation in a poor country; an increase of its exports, necessarily to the lowering of their gold price abroad; some disorganisation of industry, through the transfer of labour from the pursuits which are least affected by the new export trade, to the production of the articles which provide the new or additional exports; an inflation of prices from the importation of vast supplies of silver, in consequence, not of the increased value abroad of Indian exports, but of the depreciation of the Indian standard of value; and a repetition of these convulsions of trade and industry with each fresh considerable fall of the price of silver. In other words, a depreciated metallic currency, which will be constantly increasing the cost of remitting India's foreign expenditure, raising local prices and the local rate of interest, and steadily reducing the amount of capital for industrial employments, by checking its importation into India and by stimulating its export with that of merchandise or materials of well-being—the latter, in exchange for barren silver; diminished incomes of the people, from the diminution of capital and from the weight of additional taxation.

But all this need not disconcert us; for have we not a clear, lucid, apparently complete exposition of how, through the increase of exports and the reduction of imports, India will be able to pay her enlarged tribute to England, and relieve London at, it is hoped, an improved price, of all the silver which England may buy from America with her exports? And so, with the further comforting assurance (let us hope it is well founded) that British trade will not suffer, and that, with each fresh fall in the price of silver, commerce will work out a fresh equilibrium or par of exchange for regulating imports and exports, we can shut up the volume on the Depreciation of Silver, and dismiss the subject from our minds as a philosophically settled question.

We may indeed awake some day to find that incessant floods of silver poured into India have resulted in a financial cataclysm: because, after a protracted experience of an universal depression of commerce, which is partly owing to an unequal distribution of gold between the East and the West, some think that there is not enough of gold for all the world. But what then? Our duty, clearly, is not to probe difficult questions with the result of having to search out possibly heroic remedies, but to be content with knowing how it will all come about, and to maintain, meanwhile, a calm philosophical spirit and an expectant attitude.

But let us linger awhile over Mr. Bagehot's exposition.

I. British trade will not suffer from the incessant stream of silver from California to India, though the silver will flow to the East, not alone from an increase of Indian exports, but to fill an additional void from the diminution of British imports. It will not suffer, though the usual effect of new discoveries, or of a greatly increased production, of either of the precious metals is to modify the course of trade, and though the stream of Californian silver is controlled by the shrewdest nation in the world, which has already sent an increased volume of the stream direct to China. It will not suffer, though the United States are awakening to the fact that their own fiscal laws crippled and weighted them in the competition with England for the carrying trade of the world. It will not suffer, despite the warnings of a nation conscious of its strength. In an article on 'Commercial Supremacy, its Growth and Decay,' in the New York 'Bankers' Magazine' for August 1877, the following passage occurs: 'Our geographical position favours our control of Eastern commerce; our fertile valleys, broad prairies, inexhaustible mineral deposits, network of railways and rivers, with a free and educated people, ought to make us rich in all the elements of a substantial wealth. The lesson of commercial history, however, warns us that the seeds of decay are ever present, and unless we bestir ourselves, the golden apple will elude our grasp. This is the age of enterprise, and whichever of the two great Anglo-Saxon nations exhibits the most of this characteristic will win in the industrial race.' It will not suffer, though Manchester's important customers in India will be impoverished by the diminution of incomes from the increased taxation, increased rate of interest, and shrunken capital incidental to a great and progressive depreciation of the silver currency. It will not deserve to suffer, though India, denied the privilege, which is conceded to other countries with a smaller commerce, of a common money in the trade with foreign nations, be commercially delivered over to America, 'a permanent victim (to borrow Professor Cairnes' expression) of the monetary disturbance' caused by Californian silver.

II. India will not suffer from the incessant flow of silver from California, though prices will be inflated from a currency unnaturally swollen through the depreciation of the standard of value; though interest will rise, capital will shrink, taxation will increase, net income will diminish, from the same cause; and though the ruin of Germany's trade and industry from the inflation of her currency by the payments of the French indemnity, and by her currency operations, enable India to read her future, should she abide by the silver standard.

III. The price of silver will rise in London, though India with an impoverished income will be less able to pay a better price, and though, as shown in an Appendix, the price of silver in London sympathises with the price there of Indian productions, which price, from the great increase of exports, will fall.

IV. The progressive decline in the exchange will act as a bounty on exports, and India will prosper, though with each fresh fall in the exchange the amount of rupee payment for her foreign indebtedness must increase, and though bounties on export fall, not on the country which receives, but on the country which sends the exports.

V. With these cheerful prospects we may calmly await the play of the exchanges in the free course of a commerce which cannot correct an adverse exchange by the exportation of silver, and complacently regard the happy, contented state of a people, taxed additionally to the amount of some four or five millions sterling, by rulers who have found it the hardest problem in finance to devise a new tax for India.

VI. Let us 'leave the ordinary economical causes to operate; suffer the present evil; and await the ultimate cure;'—or the financial deluge.

VII. With the financial deluge there may be an end of this chapter on the lucid exposition of how, with silver continually depreciating, commerce will ever work out a new equilibrium, but not of how the Indian Government can work out a new equilibrium between an expenditure ever rising, and an income which cannot rise as fast.

The following rough jottings of what has been stated in this chapter seem to represent with a too sad fidelity the fallacies and cold comfort which are to content India in her retention, as money, of a metal which the West refuses to coin any longer into money:—

I. Silver is for the East, gold is for the West, because of—

a. The smallness of transactions in the East.

b. The East has always absorbed silver.

c. Evil will befall the last absorbent.

d. Of course the Government of India must suffer heavily.

II. With each fresh fall of the price of silver, imports of it into India will increase, and imports of Manchester goods and other merchandise will decrease.

III. Incessant streams of silver to the East will raise prices there.

IV. British trade must suffer in various ways.

V. India will be ruined.

VI. But the United States will benefit; and that fine cosmopolitan spirit, which is the true British spirit of the nineteenth century, can only heed this last comforting thought.

CHAPTER IV.

WILL THE PRICE OF SILVER RISE AGAIN?

In July 1876, when the price of silver had fallen to 48*d.* an ounce, Mr. Bagehot observed:—'No competent person can propose a demonetisation of silver in India and a substitution of gold for it, just at a moment when the price of silver has been thrust down by so strong an apprehension caused by such peculiar circumstances.'

That fools may not rush in where angels fear to tread, it will be useful to ascertain what circumstances would be held to justify a proposal for demonetising depreciated silver.

Stability of value has been considered by all writers on the subject an essential requisite or characteristic of money. It will suffice to quote the utterance of an eminent member of the Committee on the Depreciation of Silver—Mr. Fawcett:—'It is of course quite as important that a standard of value should be as invariable as the nature of the case admits. It is obvious that it is impossible to obtain an absolutely invariable standard of value, because the value of every substance which is known to us is liable to variations. Some substances, however, are liable to much greater fluctuations in their value than others; and it is evident that these are quite unfit to fulfil the functions of money: the substance selected to be used as money should be liable to as few and as slight variations in its value as possible. This qualification is possessed in a high degree by the precious metals. If gold and silver were as liable to as great fluctuations in value as wheat and cotton, it is manifest that money would be no uniform standard of value, although a pound sterling might always contain the same quantity of gold.' We have seen in the first chapter, that for above two years silver has fluctuated in price as frequently as wheat. But Mr. Bagehot, in reviewing the report of the American Commission on the Currency, pointed out that the unstable character of silver is of no consequence. 'The gold price of silver is now like the gold price of tin—left practically for the first time in history without artificial regulation, and free from the manipulation of governments. . . . In former times, M. Léon Say justly said, the fluctuations in the relative value of the two metals were few and small, but now they are many and large. Particular causes—especially the demonetisation of silver by Germany, and the supposed likelihood of great supplies from Nevada—are no doubt aggravating the unstability at this moment. But as they did not create the unstability, it will not cease with them. There is no inherent reason why the gold price of silver should be uniform, any more than why the gold price of platinum should be the same. The old notion of extreme steadiness is one generated by the practice of governments, and which has ceased when the practice ceased, and will not revive till it revives.' With this lucid exposition of how it has come about, we must perforce dismiss prejudices against unstable silver, begotten of old notions of political economists; though the unstability of silver is of serious moment to the Indian Government, insomuch that its finance minister may go to bed in the pleasing consciousness of a surplus of half a million, and wake in the morning to a deficit of like amount. Happy the people whose immunity from avoidable taxation is secured by such favourable conditions of prosperous finance!

But if we must accept silver as the only possible and sufficient currency for the East, we may be indulged in a pardonable curiosity to know whether silver, like Lucifer, has fallen never to rise again.

All hope of a rise of the price of silver is centred in its exportation to the East; but we find that its drain to the East after the discovery of America finally resulted in its depreciation in the West. On that occasion the increased production of silver indeed preponderated through the discovery of the silver mines of Potosi; but the subsequent drain to the East after the gold discoveries in California and Australia had also precisely the same issue, namely, a depreciation of silver. In the first period, as pointed out by Adam Smith, the market of Europe became enlarged, the greater part of Europe having much improved since the discovery of America; while new markets for silver opened out in America itself, in all the English colonies (they having been formed after the increase of production), in the greater part of the Spanish and Portuguese colonies, in the East Indies, which continually took off greater and greater quantities, and in China. Still the final result was a depreciation of silver. In the later period it was the production of gold that increased, and the same extent of new markets, as in the earlier period, was not available for absorbing the new gold; but yet in the final result it was silver that depreciated relatively to gold. In his pamphlet on 'The Fall in the Price of Silver,' 1876, Mr. Seyd writes:—'Never in the history of the world has silver been so low.' Those who controvert M. Chevalier's opinion that silver should be demonetised reproach him with inconsistency, because in 1850 he advised that gold should be demonetised, whereas gold has appreciated relatively to silver. But the ground of their reproach vindicates M. Chevalier, for it shows silver to be a hopeless reprobate, going from bad to worse, under circumstances the most favourable for reform. Mr. Bagehot too confirmed this bad character of silver in recommending its continuance as the standard of value in India. He pointed out that from 1848 to 1856, during which a high gold price of silver was promoted by a high price, and latterly by an exceptionally high price, of Indian commodities in Europe, also by the export of money or capital to the East for the mutiny and for railways, the price of silver rose from 59½*d.* to only 61$\frac{5}{16}$*d.* an ounce, 'which is certainly wonderfully little in comparison with what we now see, though the discoveries of gold then were in every way as remarkable—indeed more remarkable—than those of silver now;' whereas between 1867 and 1875 the price of silver fell from 61*d.* to 56⅛*d.* an ounce.

We may conclude then, that if there be any fresh drain of silver to the East, it will issue in a further depreciation of the metal, not in any rise of its price in Europe; unless in sympathy with a rise of gold prices of Asiatic produce, of which rise the increasing exports from the East, in payment of an enlarged tribute, and under the stimulus of the bounty afforded by the low exchange with sterling, forbid the least hope.

Mr. Bagehot devoted a goodly portion of his book to proving or expounding the self-evident proposition, that with silver depreciated in the West, it must flow to the East, where it has a higher conventional value as money. Like everything else in trade, whether commodities or securities, 'gold or silver seeks that country where it is dearest.' His argument that silver would in consequence rise in the West, where it is not wanted, was of the weakest kind, and it is contradicted by facts. The exports from India in 1876–7 reached 61 millions sterling, or an amount greater by five millions, or more, than in any year from 1866–7 to 1874–5 (excepting 1871-2); and yet the price of silver was much lower at the end of 1876-7 than at the end of 1874-5, as the result of a progressive depreciation. Instead of the exports from India raising the price of silver in London, through the exchange on bills in India upon London, that exchange followed and was depressed by the London price of silver. And in London the price of silver was affected by the Secretary of State's bills on India. These bills, while India has a silver currency, act on the London money market like an import of silver from India; that is, the exchange banks in London find conveniently to their hand two competitors, of whom one offers them coined silver rupees in India, and the other silver bullion; and, since the owners of the bullion are not free to take their bullion to other European markets (for all are closed against the coinage of silver), they are committed to a competition with the Council drafts, which, as in a Dutch auction, must send down the price of silver in a progressive depreciation, that will not cease until India alters her standard of value, or until the cost of the production of silver is approached. With India annually flooded in this manner with silver in excess of what is wanted for exports not settled by the Council drafts (and even Mr. Bagehot contended that the flow will be incessant) Indian exports will not influence the price of silver in London any more than the Bank of England can now control the rate of interest under the overpowering competition of the bill brokers and joint stock banks.

Those, then, who look for a rise of the price of silver in London from its export to India will find the warning 'No hope' inscribed for them, over the portals of that trade. And if they turn to Europe they will find every mint closed against the coinage of silver for the public, except in some insolvent countries which will give inconvertible paper in exchange; and even these purchase but timidly, since they have found that their peoples virtually reject the silver by exporting it.

Thus far there is an utter absence of demand, except for flooding the East with silver, which, in the competition to be encountered from the Council drafts, must progressively lower the price. But there has been further progress in absolute demonetisation of silver, consequent, partly, on its supersession by paper currency, in the manner described in a previous chapter. In 1868, omitting the countries which then had a gold currency, there were, in the West, the following with a silver currency, viz.: Germany and the Northern States (these have now a gold standard), and Holland (which has stopped the coinage of silver and adopted a coinage of gold, at the relative value of 1 to 15·525, but without as yet demonetising silver). And there were the following with a double standard, besides countries in Central and South America, viz.: Belgium, France, Switzerland, Italy, Greece (now forming the Latin Union), Spain (which has modelled her currency on that of the Union), the United States, and Russia. Of these, the United States, Spain, and the countries of the Latin Union, except Italy, will, it is probable (as shown in Appendix II.), adopt a single standard of gold; Italy and Austria (which has a silver standard), are hesitating; the former probably on political considerations, in deference to Germany, which Power might be embarrassed by a too early accession of the Latin Union to the gold standard. In Austria, the opinion of commercial men and of financial authorities outside the Government service inclines to a gold standard; while the necessities of Austria make her look both ways, like her double-headed eagle, borrowing, in gold bonds, the money which she can get only on interest, and hankering after the resumption of specie payments in depreciated silver. But how that insolvent Empire will work its uncertain way out of its difficulties, is not material to the present inquiry.

With regard to gold and silver, which as money have a conventional value quite irrespective of the cost of their production,—it is futile to contend, as Mr. Bagehot did, that the relative value of gold and silver will be determined, in the end, by their respective costs of production. The coinage demand which enhances their conventional greatly beyond their intrinsic value is what determines the relation of value between the two metals. Therefore, when all other causes which have temporarily depreciated silver shall have ceased, the cessation of demand in Europe, from the general demonetisation of silver just mentioned, will continue to depress it as an enduring cause of the lasting depreciation of silver.

Among the temporary causes of depreciation, there has been mentioned, *Panic*. The 'Economist' has repeated this ever since the great depreciation of silver began. So long after the depreciation as March 1876, that is, only four months before silver fell to 47 pence an ounce, Mr. Bagehot, in speculating on the causes of depreciation, observed: 'And lastly, the perturbed state of men's minds which is consequent on these events. So large an increase of the supply makes dealers fear a still larger further increase, and therefore they do not wish to buy, and do not care to hold. When markets are in this temper, there are speculations for the fall, and not for the rise, and therefore there is just now a disposition to "bear" silver, and to force its price down. Over and above the proper effect of the causes in operation, there is an additional effect consequent on apprehensive opinion.' This seems to be a mere euphemism for the simple but disagreeable statement of fact, that the demand for silver greatly decreased simultaneously with a sudden and considerable increase of supply in the market. Bullion dealers are keen, hard-headed men of business, and are the very last persons of whom it can be supposed that they could remain under the influence of panic for two or three years. Bullion, while retained, entails a loss of interest; and hence it is quickly got rid of; so that it is not conceivable how it could be sold any sooner under the influence of panic. If there is no prospect of selling it at a profit over the price asked by the vendors, it will not be bought. In this case the sellers were Germany and the United States, who were in no hurry to sell; the European mints were closed against silver; and the only consumers to whom the bullion dealers could sell it were in the East. The absence of demand from the East, and the cessation of demand in Europe, furnish a rational explanation why bullion dealers bought sparingly, and at low prices, without its being necessary to attribute to them an irrational panic.

Accordingly, the Silver Committee ascribed the fall in the price of silver to four causes, viz.: the sale of demonetised silver by Germany and the Scandinavian kingdoms; an increased production of silver; the closure of European mints against it, and the increase of the Council drafts on India. Now, of these four causes, so to speak, the first two should be transferred rather to a statement of the question, namely, why it is, that the silver demonetised by Germany, and the increased production of Nevada, have sold at a price lower than had obtained in the previous history of the world? The other two causes supply the answer, namely, a cessation of demand in Europe and the East. The first of these causes is permanent; the second is so too, up to 15 millions sterling a year and more, irrespectively of the amount of private indebtedness, in the form of profits, freight, and returns for European capital invested in India, which India has to remit to Europe. Up to the aggregate of these there is a permanent cessation of demand from the East.

Now, with this extensive permanent cessation of demand for silver in Europe and the East, it is quite immaterial whether the stock of Germany's silver which remains to be sold, and the yearly production of Nevada, are large or small. A thing which is not wanted is dear at any price; and with this extensive permanent decrease or cessation of commercial demand for silver for remittance, and of currency demand for coinage, even the offer of smaller supplies in the market would not raise the price of silver. The experience of the past two years confirms this view; the quantities of silver which have been sold would not, in the period down to 1870, have lowered its price at all; whereas, from the permanent cessation of demand there has been a great depreciation in 1876 and 1877.

That silver has been sold at all, is owing to its use in the East as currency. On that account it possesses there a conventional value which, according to the state of the export trade, yields a profit on silver if it be sold in London at a price which gives a relatively lower exchange in rupees than that conventional value as expressed in the Indian or local price of the exports. Hence, if that means of sale of silver were to cease by the closure of the Indian mints against silver coinage, it would not follow that silver would drop to thirty pence an ounce, or to twenty pence; it would simply not be offered for sale, because there would be no buyers, beyond the limited demand for ornaments. The silver mines of Nevada would have to cease their production for awhile; and Germany would have to absorb her surplus silver as best she may. Probably she would then rectify one of the very few mistakes she has made in her currency operations, by putting more silver into her subsidiary coinage, enlarging the limits of legal tender for silver, and increasing the proportion of marks per head of the population—a proportion which, under such conditions, could be greatly augmented. For disposing of its surplus silver, the German currency would in fact be stewed in its own juice, to use a well-known phrase of Prince Bismarck; and a very sensible stew it would make.

The yearly demand on account of the remittance for the home expenses of the Government of India has been stated at 15 millions sterling; but this does not convey an accurate idea of the fact. The amount of rupees for providing that sum in sterling will vary with the rate of exchange; it would be 150 millions of rupees with exchange at two shillings, 180 millions with exchange at 1*s.* 8*d.*, and 200 millions with exchange at 1*s.* 6*d.* We have seen that even if the sum to be provided for the Home Government of India were a fixed amount of 150 millions of rupees, the exports, acted upon by a continually depreciating currency, and their influence counteracted by the competition at home between bullion dealers and the Council drafts, could have no effect in arresting the fall, much less promoting a rise of the price of silver in London. But with an increasing amount of rupees to be provided, at each fresh fall of the London price of silver, for the expenses of the Home Government, the rise of that price through a growth of Indian exports is hopeless.

As therefore our question is, not (as Mr. Bagehot expounded it) how much silver India can absorb at a continually decreasing price, but what demand will raise the gold price of silver so as to correct the Indian exchange, the only answer which can be given is, that there is no currency or coinage demand for silver in Europe, and no commercial demand for it, for remittance to the East, such as can arrest that progressive fall in its price which for above three centuries has attended the drain of silver to the East. The depreciation must proceed at accelerated pace with every addition to the supply of silver, and to the amount of rupees required to meet the requirements in sterling of the Home Government.

Mr. Bagehot, in a preface dated April 1877, to his work on the Depreciation of Silver, stated that 'as yet no one can prove that the permanent value of silver—whether in relation to gold or in relation to commodities at large—will change so much as to render any alterations necessary.' In April 1877 the highest and lowest prices of silver were 55*d.* and 53½*d.* an ounce—the latter giving a relative value of 17·96 to 1. We are not concerned to show that the permanent depreciation has reached 59 pence an ounce, though that price has never been touched since February 1874, and the great depreciation is of somewhat later date. But it is evident, from the preceding observations, that each great drain of silver to the East, after the discovery of America and after the gold discoveries in California and Australia, resulted, by the time that the drain had run its course, in an undoubted depreciation of silver relatively to gold. We are warranted in concluding that at the end of the second drain, or by 1873, the depreciation then reached was permanent. At that time the relative value was below 15½ to 1, which previously had been considered, universally, the real proportion of value between the two metals, when not disturbed by casual influences. We are further warranted, by the cessation of coinage of silver in Europe, and by the cessation of commercial demand for it for the East, for remittances, at any price exceeding 59 pence an ounce (which gives a relative value of 15·98 to 1), in concluding that the depreciation of silver has taken a fresh departure, and that, though it may not be practicable to say how low it will fall, yet this much is certain, that it is now permanently lower than the relative value of 15½ to 1. At the same time, the reasons for apprehending a progressive depreciation are so overwhelming, that it is incumbent on those who resist a change of standard to show that it can and will recover, that it will not fluctuate as frequently as the price of wheat, and that the nations of the West will receive it freely from the East, as international money, should it be sent in correction of an adverse exchange.

This is not a dispute about abstract points—weighty issues depend upon a settlement; and yet it is strange that a practical common-sense decision has been formed and the requisite action taken by all other countries concerned, while the leading financial journal of a nation which prides itself, above other qualities, on its sound practical common-sense, amuses itself with theorising on the subject, indulges in reasoning which darkens counsel, sets at naught sound notions of a standard of value, forgets principles which underlie the transmission of the precious metals from one country to another, and assumes an expectant attitude while a million and a half sterling is annually slipping away from a revenue which can ill afford the loss.

Mr. Fawcett writes:—

'It has thus been shown that a great fall in the price of silver, or a great change in its value when compared with gold, need not necessarily be accompanied by a depreciation in its value estimated by a decline in its purchasing power; and it therefore becomes of great importance to inquire whether the recent rapid fall in the price of silver to 48 pence an ounce has produced a decline in the purchasing power of silver in India, where silver is used as the general standard of value. On this point there seems to be conclusive evidence that up to the present time no such decline in the purchasing power of silver has taken place in India. If such a decline had occurred general prices in that country must have advanced, whereas there seems to be no doubt that during the last three or four years, when silver has been falling in price, general prices have not advanced in India, but, on the contrary, have somewhat fallen.'

Mr. Fawcett himself supplies the explanation, but yet abides by his conclusion that the fall in the gold price of silver is immaterial, because at the time that he wrote its purchasing power had not diminished in India. He explained:—

'It was conclusively established, by the evidence which was given before the Select Committee on Indian Finance which sat in 1871–2–3, that the importation of this great quantity of silver into India had produced a very marked depreciation in its value, which was shown by a general rise in prices. This rise was estimated by many competent authorities to be as much as 30 or 40 per cent. It was also established that this rise in prices was checked so soon as the import of silver began to diminish; and it is only natural to find that as the import of silver has now declined to little more than £3,000,000 a year, the rise in prices which occurred when £15,000,000 of silver were annually imported has not been maintained, but has been succeeded by a slight fall in prices.'

The facts here set forth by Mr. Fawcett are, as regards India, that, owing to the drain of silver to the East, silver became depreciated in India, and reached its maximum depreciation as currency about 1870. Since then the inflated prices of the years down to 1870 have fallen, but, as shown in the Appendix on prices, the depreciation of silver in India as currency is still fully as great as the depreciation of gold in Europe as money. With regard to Europe, Mr. Fawcett states that the gold price of silver has fallen in Europe since 1875, while its value in India has increased in the same time. But he overlooks the fact that down to 1867 or 1870 silver was international money in Europe, and its price was kept up accordingly so long as the prices of Asiatic produce were high in Europe.

Of late silver has been degraded in Europe from international money into mere merchandise; and as the inflated gold prices of articles, including Asiatic products, have been falling in Europe, the price of silver, now mere merchandise in the West, has fallen with them, and in sympathy with the prices of Asiatic products which silver now represents in European markets. If the price of silver has not fallen in Europe to the same extent as that of Asiatic products, it is because these latter do not admit of re-export to India, but must be sold in Europe for what they will fetch, while silver, failing a suitable price in Europe, can be exported to the East. There is no parity in any comparison of the conventional value of silver in India as currency, and its price in Europe in its now degraded position as merchandise, except so far as a relation between the two is established by the circumstance that the gold price of silver falls in Europe together with the gold price of Asiatic products.

It appears from this chapter that—

I. The retention of silver by the East as money is recommended by arguments of a peculiar double-faced character; such, that if they were pressed upon the West for its adoption of a like policy, the West would reject them, as it has unmistakably done by closing its mints against the further coinage of silver, *e.g.*—

a. The price of silver has become unstable as that of wheat; but this is of no consequence, for a standard of value, for the East.

b. The price of silver has greatly fallen, and it must fall, for silver is a hopeless reprobate, going from bad to worse, under circumstances most favourable for reform; and Mr. Bagehot plainly said so, in urging the retention of silver by the East as its standard of value.

c. With each fresh fall of the price of silver, there will be very pretty play, by commerce, with the foreign exchanges, in working out a new equilibrium; the more that silver goes to the East, the greater will be the exports to the West, and the larger will be the amount of the Secretary of State's drafts on India, which are the same as an import of silver rupees into England. Facts show that this increasing import of silver rupees into England, and the increased export of Asiatic products to the West, send down the price of silver in the West; but India must discard this antiquated, inductive method of political economy, and have firm faith that as the West exchanges less and less of its merchandise, for more and more of the merchandise of the East, the price of silver will rise in the West, and the East will drive a most remunerative trade.

II. Every State in Europe has closed its mint against the coinage of silver for the public, so that India cannot correct an adverse exchange by exporting silver to the West. But, no matter; this is mere panic, which has seized the acutest financial abilities in Europe, that is in the world, and which, for three long years, has urged bullion dealers—the shrewdest, keenest, hardest headed calculators in Europe—to sell incontinently the silver which at no time have they ever kept on their hands.

III. The amount of silver which the German Government has sold, added to the amount of silver production in the past four or five years, is not more than the East absorbed in the past, with a high range of price for silver; the only two points of difference, in this respect, between the last four years and the period from 1858 to 1867, are the closure of the mints in the West against the coinage of silver, and the increase of the Indian Secretary of State's Council drafts. These two circumstances have destroyed the demand for silver, which can now be sold only by sending it, at continually diminishing prices, to India, to be coined in the Indian mints.

IV. In other words, silver, which used formerly to be sent to India as money, in settlement of international accounts, is now sent to India as merchandise, in competition with imports of other foreign goods into that country. India's purchasing power being limited, the more this new merchandise, silver, is forced upon her, on payment with her exports, the less of exports she has to exchange against imports of other merchandise, and the less, therefore, does she buy of the latter.

V. Not only are Manchester and British manufacturers injured; India's finances, industry, and trade are disorganised. If India desires to retain the old amount of her imports of manufactures, and so to attain that object of a healthful commerce, viz., the acquisition of the country's material necessaries at the cheapest price, she must provide (against each fresh accession of the silver she does not ask for) a fresh augmentation of the old amount of exports. This she can only do by diverting to the production of the exports which are in foreign demand, some of the industry and capital that are now employed on other productions for which the principal demand is local. It is both possible and probable that the demand for extra exports, through a fall in the exchange and in the price of silver, and through the unchecked floods of silver into India, may increase in two years by 40 millions of rupees. Neither in her home industry, nor in her home markets, nor in her finances, is India equal to the strain by which her exports may advance with those leaps and bounds such as awakened, not many years since, the self-gratulations of England in respect of her own exports, only to leave her commerce exhausted and her industry paralysed at the present time.

VI. Evidently, Mr. Bagehot quite misapprehended the question, when he regarded it simply as an inquiry by what process India and China would be brought to export goods sufficient for paying for all the silver production of the world, which would be sent to them because it cannot be sold elsewhere.

VII. Far weightier issues than this are involved in the inquiry; the facts considered in IV. and V. are of the gravest import, and they are in progress now, and have been in progress for some time; they have but one meaning, and that meaning cannot be explained away by Mr. Fawcett's doubt, whether silver has fallen in value in India. The sooner that facts of grave importance to the prosperity of India and of British manufactures are faced with the courage and common-sense of Englishmen, the better for the British Empire.

CHAPTER V.

INDIA SHOULD HAVE A COMMON MONEY WITH THE WEST.

We have advanced sufficiently far to make it necessary to gather up results. The depreciation of silver has been destroying landmarks and uprooting convictions on questions of political economy which had been regarded as settled long ago; silver has done this mischief at least among its friends, namely, those who oppose its demonetisation. With them we are expected to perceive, by the strong light of the depreciation of silver, that:—

I. Stability of value is not by any means an essential quality in a standard of value. The standard may depreciate abroad relatively with gold, and may depreciate at home relatively to commodities, in the country which it floods, until it has effected a new distribution of what wealth may remain to that country, after the economic disturbances caused by a rise of wages (which, for the working masses, will be disproportioned to the rise of prices); by a rise in the rate of interest (consequent on the diminution of capital, partly through its withdrawal to other countries where antiquated notions about stability of value still prevail); by a diminished production, that is, a diminution of gross earnings, through the restriction of production's motive-power, capital (while population increases and supplies new famine problems of great interest); and by a heavy weight of additional taxation. All this must happen from the instability of the standard of value; but it is of no consequence, for we have a lucid exposition of how commerce, if let alone, will, on each fresh fall in the price of silver, find out a new par of exchange with gold in the direction of vanishing point; we have an excellent new theory that 'the gold price of silver is now like the gold price of tin, left practically, for the first time in history, without artificial regulation, and free from the manipulation of governments;' and we have the priceless consolation that silver is for the East and gold for the West.

II. The silver mines are in the West, but the West won't buy the silver; there it is as tin. But it must be sold; otherwise what are the poor owners of the silver mines to do? And how will it fare with the exports to the United States with which England buys the silver, and in which she hopes she finds a compensation for exports to the East, which, as shown in a clear exposition, must decrease at intervals with each fresh depreciation of silver? Whether Manchester shares this hope and consolation is not clear; of piece goods, the exports to India, Egypt, and China were 2,000 millions of yards in 1876, and to the United States only 55 millions of yards. Be that as it may, the East is the only market for the silver which the West produces but which the West will not buy; and it is clearly shown that the East, so long as silver continues there as money, will absorb any amount of silver which the West may send. True there might, as above stated, be incessant economic disturbance in the East from the floods of silver to be received into the Eastern currencies, without power of re-exportation to the West (where it is as tin) in correction of an adverse exchange, and in the course of the natural process by which (in conformity with the laws for the transmission of the precious metals from one country to another), other countries get rid of any redundance in their metallic currency. But that does not matter; the question, from the standpoint that silver is for the East and gold is for the West, is in advance of those antiquated laws; nor does it concern itself with what may befall the East; its sole concern is whether the East can and must buy the silver, if silver continues there as currency. The reassuring answer is that the East will not be able to help itself, but must buy, and that is enough; though the doctrine of silver for the East and gold for the West is nothing more than an inconvertible international currency forced on the East by the West, which must be worse than inconvertible paper money, in that each country is able to limit for itself the amount of its inconvertible paper, and so keep up its value, while the East will have no power to limit the amount of its international silver money which is inconvertible in the West; *that* must be regulated by the West, which has silver to sell to the East.

III. The depreciation of silver acts at each fresh stage of the depreciation as a bounty upon exports from the silver-using countries; this is the keynote of those lucid expositions of how commerce will adapt itself to each new fall of silver, which are designed to show that the great depreciation of silver is of no consequence. An antiquated political economist, Adam Smith, did indeed tell the world that bounties upon exports are no good; they are paid by the country which exports; they divert labour from profitable to unprofitable channels; they make that country part, at insufficient prices, with materials of well-being, and with the result of increasing at home the price of the articles exported. This is precisely what is alleged of the bounty upon export, which the depreciation of silver provides, according to those lucid (and in this particular correct) expositions of how everything will come about which have reconciled to doing nothing, a nation especially gifted with sound practical common-sense. But as Adam Smith wrote in 1776, and we are in the year 1877, his notions belong to an old world. What could he, poor ignoramus, know of the great strides since of commerce, the great need of gold for the money-market in London, the great need for the West to sell some eight millions sterling a year of new silver to the East, and to throw the cast-off silver currencies of European countries into India and China? True, that France and the countries of the Latin Union closed their mints against the coinage of silver when they saw Germany preparing to threw her snails into her neighbours' gardens; but that is a different matter, and a special concern of the West, with which the East has nothing to do. Has not Professor Jevons told us that 'Asia is the great reservoir and sink of the precious metals. It has saved us from a commercial revolution, and taken off our hands many millions of bullion which would be worse than useless here. . . . In the middle ages it relieved Europe of the excess of Spanish American treasure, just as it now relieves us of the excess of Australian treasure. . . . Raynal affirms that the Spaniards must have abandoned their most productive mines of silver in America, as they had already abandoned many of the less productive ones, if the progress of the depreciation of silver had not been somewhat retarded by the exportation of it to India'? And did not the views of Professor Jevons and of the Spaniards colour the disquisitions of Mr. Bagehot, making him feel (in contradiction to the thoughtful concern of Professor Cairnes for the last absorbents of Professor Jevons' millions of barren silver, which they can export no whither), 'that it does not matter what evil befalls the hindmost'? This is the final form and expression of the latest advanced views in the science of political economy, which in days of now antiquated notions had to do with the material well-being of nations.

Next, as to the facts respecting silver, which has played the mischief with our modern political economists. We find that:—

1. Since the discovery of America silver has gone from bad to worse, notwithstanding the very favourable opportunities it has had of recovering its value relatively to gold.

2. The most competent judges, the countries in America

which have watched its progress from infancy, the countries in Europe best capable of forming an intelligent opinion of its conduct in mature years, from the extensive use of silver in their currencies for centuries, have rejected it, from the inherent tendency of its character to deteriorate, which nothing can correct or reclaim. Even the East, where it was welcomed for centuries, has ceased to demand it; though, from the subjugation of its fairest parts to the West, it is forced to receive it.

3. As a consequence, the value of silver relatively to gold, which for long had remained at a normal proportion of 15½ to 1, has greatly declined, and the price of silver has become variable as that of wheat, with a marked downward tendency, which the new competition between the Council drafts and the bullion dealers in the London silver market will not correct, but aggravate.

4. Silver, in fact, has become mere merchandise in the West, and thus has ceased to be international money between the East and the West. It has thereby become imperfect money, even in the East, where it is degraded to the same level as paper currency, from the impracticability of exporting it in the course of foreign trade. Nay, it has sunk lower than a sound paper currency, of which the test is its ready convertibility at par into the alternative metallic currency or standard of value. The moment this test is applied to silver, by exchanging it with gold, it is found to be below par, with a growing depreciation.

5. In short, silver has ceased to be perfect money—that is, to be in India other than a debased and deteriorating metallic currency.

This last conclusion should have spared us all that discussion in Chapter II. about whether it is just or expedient to alter the standard of value, and especially to change from a metal which is depreciating to one which has appreciated. That becomes an idle question, since silver has ceased to be money, if India is to remain commercially in the comity of nations. She cannot do so without an international money, and with a local money which is depreciated and deteriorating merchandise in the West. But though, in a common-sense view, and at the stage which we have reached, the discussion in Chapter II. is superfluous, yet, for any good to be got from the present inquiry, the discussion could not have been avoided. However abundant the proofs that silver has ceased to be international money, no one who pressed the logical consequences of that fact would be listened to, if he did not first salute the controversialists in the battle of the standards. His incivility would mark his ignorance of what are essential points in the policy of doing nothing.

But having entered on the discussion in the second chapter, and silver, as we have ascertained, having ceased to be money in some of the most important functions of metallic money, we are warranted in now assuming that a change from the single standard of silver in the East is necessary, so as to bring the East into accord with the West.

This accord with the West being the sole necessity and object of the change, so as to prevent India suffering from incessant floods of silver and its progressive depreciation, we are not concerned with the controversy between bi-metallists and gold mono-metallists. We see as a fact, that in Europe, even in countries which are bi-metallic according to law, gold is the efficient currency, and that silver is virtually subsidiary currency; and it is with the facts, not the theories, of metallic currency in the West that the currency of India must be assimilated. At the same time, if it be possible to work out the details of alteration from the silver to the gold standard in India, so that they may fit into the bi-metallic system should it regain ascendency in the West, this might be attempted.

In changing from the silver to a gold standard, a relative value between the two metals must be adopted for translating into expressions in gold value, obligations which are now expressed in silver value. The relative value of 15½ to 1 exists in the currencies of the Latin Union and of Spain; it was adopted for Germany for the transition to a gold standard, because, as stated in the German Coinage Act of 1871, that was 'what is considered the usual ratio between the two metals, viz., 15½ of silver to 1 of gold.' The recent great and sudden depreciation of silver, too, took its departure from substantially this relative value; and in measures for correcting the injurious effects of the depreciation of silver, necessarily this valuation should be restored. To whatever extent a relative value worse than 15½ to 1 may be adopted for effecting the transition, to that extent the measure would be abortive, from its perpetuating the injurious consequences of the depreciation. If, for instance, the transition were to be effected in India at a price, for silver, of 53*d*. per ounce (which gives a relative value of 17·79 to 1), because that may happen to be the price at the time of conversion from a silver to a gold standard, it would for all time continue a very serious and unnecessary additional charge upon the Indian revenues, which would involve a corresponding amount of additional taxation. This extra taxation would only pile up agony for those whom the depreciation of silver had already injured. The Government of India is entitled, fully as much as Germany or Holland, or as England, in the past, to correct a depreciation of the metallic currency which it had no hand in bringing about, and which is yet of recent origin. By converting at a worse rate than 15½ to 1, the Government would fling away an advantage which Parliament, in its responsibility for the administration of India, should have secured for the country when silver began to depreciate.

Silver is unfit to continue the full legal-tender currency in India, and the transition to a gold standard should be effected at the relative value of 15½ to 1. Having arrived thus far, the next step would be to stop the coinage of silver, and to allow the coinage of gold, at the Indian mints, at a relative value with the existing silver currency, of 15½ of silver to 1 of gold. The gold coins, if the Government be so minded, need not, at the outset, be declared legal tender, but they might be freely received by Government, at this valuation, in payment of revenue, in the courts, and on railways. In this there would not be anything heroic; for Holland has done this much without the least injury to herself, or to any one except owners of silver mines. Even were this cautious trespassing on the gold preserves of the West to awaken fear, the Government could go 'back again,' by stopping the coinage of gold and resuming the coinage of silver; for the issued gold coin could be withdrawn without loss, since any and every country in Europe would willingly receive it. This cautious venture, however, though not heroic, would be profitable; it would at least prevent the heavy loss by exchange, which yearly oppresses the Indian finances more and more with its crushing weight.

CHAPTER VI.

PLAN FOR A GOLD CURRENCY FOR INDIA.

By closing the Indian mints against the coinage of silver, and allowing the coinage of gold in those mints, in standard coins exchangeable with the silver rupees in the ratio of 1 of gold to 15½ of silver, India would arrive at this stage, namely, that silver rupees would continue as legal tender, but more of them could not be coined, while the gold coins of which the coinage was permitted would not be legal tender, though exchangeable with silver at the valuation of 1 to 15½. At this valuation, if the exchange were not to be affected by the cessation of silver coinage, gold would not be coined. But, from the closure of the mints against the coinage of silver for the public, the exchange would rise, and when it had risen sufficiently to allow of the importation of gold, gold would be imported and coined, the Government receiving it freely in its treasuries. The importation of gold would be determined not by the price of silver in London, but by the rate of exchange between sterling and rupees, for Council drafts and other bills on India; which rate would rise on the cessation of silver coinage in India. Under such a law, with the smaller demand for remittances between Holland and foreign countries, compared with the similar demand in transactions between India and the West, there was coined in Holland in 1876, for private individuals, above one million sterling of standard gold coins; which evidences that the exchange had been fully corrected in favour of Holland, notwithstanding the depreciation of its silver currency, until the closure of the Netherlands mint against the coinage of silver. A like result would follow in India. The loss by exchange in 1875–6 amounted to £1,429,722; in 1876–7 it was entered in the regular estimate framed in the twelfth month of that year at £2,135,106; and on cessation of borrowing in England, and with a progressive fall of the price of silver which might lower the exchange to 1*s.* 7*d.*, it would amount to 3·95 millions sterling, or with exchange at 1*s.* 6*d.* to 5 millions sterling. Instead of these terrible amounts, the loss would on the cessation of silver coinage, with a consequent rise in the exchange, drop below, and greatly below, a million sterling.

Though, therefore, with silver coins as legal tender, and gold coins as still not legal tender, India will have advanced but a short way towards a gold standard, yet the great drop in the loss by exchange, which must bring happy relief from not unreasonable fears of additional or new taxes, should perhaps encourage a further advance; but there is a lion in the path, and his roaring is thus transmitted by the telephones of M. de Laveleye and Mr. Fawcett:—

a. M. de Laveleye. 'There is not gold enough in the world; and Mr. Goschen ('Bankers' Magazine,' New York, November 1876) strikes in plaintively: "Silver and gold have been in partnership for the purpose of doing the work of the circulation for thousands of years, and I think it is not in the interest of the world that the whole weight of the burden should be borne by gold alone."'

b. Mr. Fawcett. 'But even if a gold currency were not so entirely unsuited to India as it is, the difficulties of changing a currency in such a country would be most formidable. The people themselves, who dislike innovations upon their habits and traditions with an intensity which Europeans can scarcely understand, would strongly resent such a change; and however well-intentioned it might be, they would be sure to conclude that the Government was prompted by some sinister motive to introduce it. Nothing would be more calculated to spread a feeling of insecurity and discontent.'

What a comment on British, compared with Native rule!

Gold is coined freely, and gold coins circulate freely in Native States, and somehow the people like the coinage, with perhaps a regard for faint traditions of the time when, as Adam Smith wrote, gold was so plentiful in India that it circulated with a relative value to silver of 1 to 10 or at most 12, while the ratio in England was 1 to 14 or 15; and on what a lofty moral elevation Mr. Fawcett places the people of India, who would resent the introduction among them of that gold of which some think, on behalf of the Western nations, that they have not enough! Mr. Fawcett continues:—

'But even if there were not these obstacles in the way, it is more than doubtful whether the adoption of a gold currency would avert the inconvenience and loss produced by a fall in the price of silver. It has been already stated that the German Government have purchased 70 millions sterling of gold, in order to effect the change in their currency; but if it has been necessary for Germany to purchase this large quantity of gold, a far greater amount would have to be purchased by India, if silver were demonetised in that country. The purchase of a great amount of gold, and the sale of the large quantity of silver which would be displaced by this gold, would exercise a more powerful influence than is probably exerted by any circumstance now in operation, to depreciate the value of silver compared with gold. A change in the currency of a great and populous country such as India could not be suddenly carried out: many years would be required for its completion, and during the whole of this time, as silver was gradually withdrawn from circulation, India would find herself in this unfortunate position, that the silver which she had to sell was constantly falling in price, and that she had consequently to give more and more silver for the gold she required.'

The objection that there is not enough of gold in the world for all, may be reserved for another chapter; but Mr. Goschen's lament, that it is hard that all the burden should fall on gold, suggests a passing remark of how differently the same thing looks when regarded in different aspects. The bi-metallists protest that silver should not be dethroned or degraded by being demonetised; Mr. Goschen grudges to silver its happy release from toil, and laments that gold should have to bear all the burden. There is a *tertium quid* in which silver may be enthroned as the most general metallic currency in internal trade throughout the world; while gold will, whether silver adherents will it or no, be supreme as the international money of foreign trade.

Putting aside the political objection to a gold currency, which must have been urged when Homer was nodding, Mr. Fawcett's objections may be thus summarised. A very large amount of gold will be required; its purchase and coinage must be spread over many years; each year too the purchase must be effected at a dearer price, through the progressive fall in the price of silver; on the large amount of purchase money interest will be payable until the sale of the silver which will have been withdrawn with the gold; a further loss must be sustained in the sale of that silver, of which the price will have sunk, no one can tell how low, by the time that the coinage operation is completed. The expense will be tremendous. Or, as Mr. Bagehot put it:—

'No one could now propose to the Indian Government the German plan of introducing a gold currency, as a means of relieving itself from financial difficulty, for the cost which it would entail would be enormous. Even with all their resources, they would have great difficulty in getting the immense sum required in gold, and they would hardly be able to sell the silver at any price. The present position of the Indian Exchequer is not good, but it is beyond comparison better than it would be if this expedient were tried.' And again: 'No competent person can propose a demonetisation of silver in India, and a substitution of gold for it, just at a moment when the price of silver has been thrust down by so strong an apprehension caused by such peculiar circumstances. It would be to require the Indian Government to buy the largest amount of gold ever bought in the dearest market for gold, and to dispose of the largest amount of silver in the cheapest market for silver which ever existed. The present financial position of the Indian Government is no doubt impaired by this sudden depreciation of the metal in which it receives its revenue; but the remedy for a minor deficit would bring in, in lieu of it, a deficit of the first magnitude; it would be nothing else but financial ruin.'

If this be so, then, whichever way India turns, she will

encounter financial ruin. Should silver fall in price till the exchange reaches 1s. 6*d.* a rupee (and the exchange did touch that nearly in July 1876), the loss by exchange would amount to five millions sterling, which means financial ruin; a drop of one penny more, or to 1*s.* 5*d.*, and the loss would reach six millions sterling, which, to vary the phrase, would mean a financial cataclysm. What madness, for English statesmen to be guided in their Eastern policy by the protection of British interests, forsooth! It seems high time, if Mr. Bagehot was right, to hand India over to Russia, whose experience in financial ruin may qualify her to help India out of her difficulty.

But this world is governed by a divine Providence, whose beneficent Hand may be traced in the blessings of British rule in India. These will not wither, nor will England's mission to raise India in the scale of well-being, and her people to a purer faith, result (through helplessness or inability to resist a pitiless fate) in a grinding taxation which will leave life without hope or wish for anything but the grave. We learn better things from our Christian faith; and the economists, and those who would do nothing, must be wrong.

Mr. Fawcett, for instance, is certainly wrong in supposing that, because the declaration of a resolve to adopt a gold currency for India would send down the price of silver, India would have to pay dearly for the gold which she would require to buy. Precisely the reverse would happen. As pointed out in the opening paragraph of this chapter, the exchange of the rupee with sterling would rise on the cessation of silver coinage and the declaration of a gold standard; and the importation of gold into India would be determined by the rate of that exchange, not by the diminished price of silver.

On grounds which are set forth in an appendix, on the currencies of various countries, the amount of British Indian silver coin circulating in India may be estimated (over-estimated) at 160 millions sterling. The population of India is estimated at 190 millions under British administration, and 50 millions in Native States. Of the latter, 20 millions may be reckoned as using the coins of the Indian Government; so that the provision of subsidiary silver coinage may be reckoned for 210 millions. In the United Kingdom the proportion of silver coin is nearly ten shillings per head of the population. At that rate a subsidiary silver currency in India would absorb 105 out of the estimated 160 millions sterling of existing silver currency. This would leave 55 millions for withdrawal by substitution of a gold currency. Now the loss in selling these 55 millions would be but a small fraction of the capitalised value of the loss by exchange which the finances of India must meet, to the yearly amount of five or six millions sterling and more, if silver be not demonetised.

By stewing the Indian currency in its own juice, this loss could be very much reduced; that is, by adding a portion of the withdrawn silver to the weight of the present rupee, in a new subsidiary coinage, and by withdrawing a portion of the surplus 55 millions of silver with paper currency instead of with gold.

In altering to a gold standard it is necessary to fix the relative value between the new gold currency and the full legal-tender coins of the old silver currency which have to be withdrawn with the gold coins. This, as already suggested, should for India be 15½ to 1. But it is not necessary to observe either that or a more favourable ratio of silver to gold for the subsidiary silver coinage of the new currency. One of Germany's mistakes was in regulating the intrinsic contents of the silver mark and the gold crown, in the ratio of only 13·95 of silver to 1 of gold. Had the proportion been on the other side of 15½ to 1, namely, at (say) 17 to 1, the difficulty of disposing of the withdrawn silver and of retaining the new gold coins would have been much less than it has proved.

Here the bi-metallists would strike in, with noisy persistency, that the existing silver currency, if it must be superseded by gold, should be simply degraded into a subsidiary currency, without adding to or taking from the weight of the rupee, so that its intrinsic contents may remain adjusted to the intrinsic contents of the new gold coin in the ratio of 15½ to 1: thereby facilitating transition to bi-metallism when the nations shall declare for universal bi-metallism.

Inasmuch, however, as we have no certainty that the millennium is at hand, it will be well that India should boldly adopt the inconsistency of adding to the weight of her full legal-tender silver rupee in the act of demonetising it. The doing so would not hinder any transition afterwards to universal bi-metallism. When that happy time arrives, mint machinery will have been carried to high perfection; and it will be easy to restore the ratio of 15½ to 1, by recoining the comparatively small stock of gold rupees, for putting more gold into them, without recoining the subsidiary coins of the new currency. For an analogous difficulty, the Magna Charta of bi-metallism, the French law of 1803, provides that 'if imperious circumstances compel a change of this proportion (15½ to 1) it is the gold coins alone which shall be re-minted:' implying, not, as some have misread the passage, that silver was intended from the outset as the basis of the French legal-tender currency, but that, as common sense suggests, the expense of re-coinage should be incurred for the numerically smaller or gold currency.

If, with a ratio of 15½ to 1 for the transition from silver to gold rupees, 10 per cent. were to be added to the weight of the silver rupees, the ratio of the subsidiary silver coin to the gold coin of the new currency would be 17 to 1, representing a price, for silver, of slightly more than 55*d.* an ounce.

With the silver coin thus valued in the currency, there would be no temptation for foreigners to import spurious silver coin of full weight and standard purity, under the additional difficulty of a restricted legal tender for silver coins, seeing that the very high seignorage, or difference, which the depreciation of silver has created between the low market price of silver in 1875 to 1877, and the ratio of 15½ to 1, in the enormous 5 franc, full-tender silver currency has produced no such danger in France and the other countries of the Latin Union.

If India had carried on a state of barter, and were now being for the first time provided with a metallic currency, the under-valuation of silver rupees in the manner suggested would prevent their importation; but India being possessed of the coin, the valuation would be an advantage—1st, from its disgusting the manufacturers of full-weight spurious coin; 2ndly, by its permitting an extensive circulation of the subsidiary silver coins concurrently with the gold coins, though with a restricted legal tender. In short, the two main reasons for keeping the amount of a subsidiary silver currency within very narrow limits would not apply; and the Government of India could both safely pass the ordinary limits in their issue of the new subsidiary silver rupees, and in the amount of their limitation as legal tender, and provide, as the best practical and sufficient limitation, that the silver coins should be received without limit in the Government treasuries, in payment of Government demands.

Considering, on the one hand, the smallness of the mass of transactions in India, together with the smallness of the items respectively due from the individual payers of land revenue which make up the aggregate demand from each village, also the innumerable little rills which flow into the other streams of revenue and taxation—and on the other hand the small sums disbursed monthly by Government to numerous troops, police, peons, and petty officials, and by every class for domestic or business expenses, also the more frequent disbursements to labourers,—the circulation of silver coin in India, even as restricted tender, with a gold currency, must far exceed European experience of the circulation of a subsidiary currency. It is not unreasonable to expect that, with a subsidiary silver currency having 10 per cent. more silver than the existing rupees, the limit of legal tender may be fixed for it at 100 rupees, and the amount of its probable circulation may be estimated at more than the 105 millions sterling which have been assumed in a previous paragraph.

Under the magical influence of 10 per cent. of extra silver in the rupee, lowering looks of sullen discontent on the introduction of a gold currency into India, the apprehension of which disturbed Mr. Fawcett's judgment, would be transformed into faces beaming with loyalty; and a people proverbial for hoarding, and for turning rupees into ornaments, would be loud in their applause of a Government which was giving them 182 instead of 165 grains of silver in the rupee, and perhaps taking off some taxes besides, through the reduction of loss by exchange. Applying the lesson taught us by the bi-metallists and Mr. Goschen, we see (respecting the worth of Mr. Fawcett's political argument), that much depends on the way in which you look at it: the argument is handy for any purpose in considering measures for India; and even a cautious judgment like Mr. Fawcett's may be misled by it.

Let us take stock of the advantages of adding 10 per cent. to the silver rupee on demonetising it:

1. The political argument.

2. By promoting an enlargement of the limit of legal tender of the subsidiary silver coin, and its extensive circulation, less gold would be required for effecting the currency reform.

3. A market would be found in India, and within the

Indian currency itself, for the surplus silver which may be withdrawn with the gold currency. For instance, if the amount of the new subsidiary silver currency would be 105 millions, and that of the gold currency 55 millions, one-tenth, or 10½ millions, would be added to the weight of the former, out of the 55 millions that would be withdrawn with gold, leaving only 44 millions sterling for sale. Now, the new rupees of the subsidiary silver coinage might be issued as soon as they are coined; they would circulate at par with the old rupees, though containing 10 per cent. more of silver. Accordingly, they would find their way to the melting pot, to the extent of yearly demand for ornaments, and they would also be exported beyond the British Burman and North-Western frontiers and to Arabia and the Persian Gulf in preference to the old rupees. Thus a portion of the new rupees would be withdrawn by the old, and a corresponding portion of the 44 millions remaining on hand, out of the withdrawn 55 millions of silver, could be used up in the re-coinage of another instalment of the old rupees with the heavier new rupees, while the sale of the remainder could be hastened by a heavy duty on the importation of silver, with a provision in the law for dividing between informers and captors, the silver that may be confiscated. India, as Professor Jevons has told us, has been made by other countries the sink of the precious metals, particularly of silver; she would therefore be warranted in demanding, through such a law, that countries which export silver to India should now cease their imports, and not interfere with her while she is correcting the effects upon herself of their depreciation of silver.

4. Comparatively little silver would remain for sale. Mr. Fawcett fears that it could not be sold outside India, because of a considerable fall in the price of silver, through its demonetisation in India. In that case, it must be retained until it can be gradually worked off by the yearly consump-

tion for ornaments, and for renewal of what would still be an extensive silver currency.

5. Doubtless, on the silver, while it remains on hand, there would be a loss of interest: but 1st, this loss would be insignificant on the comparatively small residue remaining on hand, compared with the present loss by exchange, which it should be remembered is a loss of yearly progressive amount; for, if silver be not demonetised in India, the exchange against India and the price of silver must continue to fall, without any limit to the fall this side of the financial ruin of India; 2ndly, a part of the residual silver will have been withdrawn with paper currency, as will be explained in the sequel; and on the portion thus to be withdrawn interest could be reckoned only on the cost of the paper used for the currency notes, not on the nominal value of the silver. This portion of the withdrawn silver would, in fact, be a gain which would set off part of the loss on the remainder of the account.

6. Furthermore, Mr. Fawcett's apprehensions of an excessive fall in the price of silver outside India may not be realised. The solution of the silver difficulty which is here suggested may occur also to other countries from the necessities of their position, with the result of enlarging the limit of restricted legal tender and the circulation of silver coins. In this regard it should be remembered that in bi-metallic countries with a ratio of 15½ to 1, silver has had but a restricted circulation since the rise in its price after 1854. Even England will be forced, by the depreciation of silver, to reconstruct her silver coinage, by putting more silver into the shilling, and, by arrangement, some of the Indian surplus of silver could be absorbed in the re-coinage. On the whole, this demand for silver as the principal metallic currency in the domestic trade of each country will be greater than it has been, with silver expelled, for many years

past, under the Gresham law, or by inconvertible paper, from bi-metallic countries. This increased demand will of course not compensate for the cessation of silver as full legal tender; but, on the other hand, the owners of the silver mines are shrewd enough to be aware of the evils of overproduction.

Hence, it appears on an examination of the alleged difficulties, that—1st, gold for changing from a silver to a gold currency will be obtained by India at a far cheaper rate than she can now get it; 2ndly, the loss from disposing of withdrawn silver will be very much less than is supposed. It would be 10 per cent. on the amount of new subsidiary currency, and perhaps 15 per cent. on the further amount which could be gradually absorbed as ornaments, *plus* the loss, greater or less than 20 per cent., on the sale of the remainder. On the other hand, there would be a set-off to the extent of, 1st, the portion which may be withdrawn with a permanently outstanding paper currency; 2ndly, the net amount that would be saved in diminished loss by exchange during the progress of the currency reform; 3rdly, the capitalised value of that yearly saving from the time of completion of the reform. Inasmuch, however, as the yearly progression of the amount of loss by exchange, if silver be not demonetised, would know no limit this side of the financial ruin of India, calculations of the amount of net gain can only serve to amuse; and the amusement might be deferred till action is taken for putting an end to the loss of about 1½ million sterling a year which is being incurred meanwhile.

This loss by exchange, from the depreciation of silver, is a running sore which must eat into the vitals of Indian finance; but instead of pressing for the application of the obvious remedy, the public journals are urging an imperial guarantee of the Indian debt as the best way of affording relief to India. It would not be difficult to show, apart from the subjects of loss by exchange and of famine expenditure, that England, as a measure of just restitution, ought to lighten the burden of the Indian debt; but, for the reason just stated, it would be folly for the Imperial Exchequer to afford any help till the ever-growing loss by exchange is both checked and almost entirely removed. Unless that be done, the day for restitution to India is past; no one would dream of offering to a drowning man pecuniary amends for a pecuniary wrong.

And in this connection will it be irrelevant to interpolate here a suggestion that the expense of effecting the change from a silver to a gold standard should be kept separate from the consequent saving in loss by exchange, in the sense that the latter would properly accrue to the Indian revenue, while the former is not wholly chargeable to India? The right of coinage is a prerogative of the sovereign; especially is it so in the traditions and feelings of the people of India. This subject of Indian currency reform is therefore one for which the Parliament of England, which gives expression to the will, and shapes the acts of the sovereign, is peculiarly responsible. If the authorities that are more immediately charged with the government of India have not yet seen their way to a reform of the Indian currency, the responsibility of Parliament in the matter is not thereby diminished. Nay, its responsibility has been increased by the deliberate purpose with which the Committee on the Depreciation of Silver was instructed to report simply on the causes of that depreciation, and was not required to report on any remedies. There was in this an abnegation of responsibility which only increases the ultimate responsibility. And if, passing beyond the walls of Parliament, we went into the City, we would find that, brushing away sophistries and theorisings which contradict received doctrines of political economy, the main, if not the sole reason why India has not, long ere this, had a gold currency, is the fear that there is not gold enough for both England and India. This subject is reserved for another chapter; here it suffices to press the conclusion that if England has aggravated the difficulties of changing in India from a silver to a gold standard, by delaying this necessary currency reform, for the execution of which she is peculiarly responsible, the expense ought either to be borne by England or to be shared with India.

Of course, there are not wanting those who declare with loud voice, and unreason, that India is a drag upon England, a drain on her resources. These have not the imagination to realise what would result from England's relinquishment of India. We may be assured that, in that case, India would pass under other rule, whether of France, Germany, or Russia. Whichever of these States might hold India, it would find, as an incident of the acquisition, an increase of its commerce, mercantile marine, and naval power. In other words, India, if held by Germany, France, or Russia, would cause that Power to endanger the naval supremacy, or to approach very near to the naval strength, of England. The heavy loss by exchange, from the depreciation of silver, acts like a customs duty of 10 or 12 per cent. on the import of British goods into India; and this has contributed much to the commercial depression which is now paralysing British manufacturing industry. It should not require any great clearness of perception to realise how much worse would be the effect upon British trade with the East, if Russia held India, and, with it, the means of imposing prohibitory duties in India on English commerce, and of concluding commercial treaties with China adverse to English interests.

It appears that—

I. By closing the Indian mints against silver, the sterling exchange with the rupee would rise, an amount of loss by exchange exceeding one million sterling yearly would be saved, and a further possible loss of two millions more would be prevented. But, as in fairy tales, voices in the air warn the Indian Government not to press towards the golden prize.

a. Bah! you will take away Europe's gold, cries out M. de Laveleye.

b. Poor silver! is the plaintive sigh of the chairman of the Committee on the Depreciation of Silver.

c. A grave political danger! is the deep hoarse warning of the financial Mr. Fawcett.

d. Rash men, beware! shouted Mr. Bagehot; 'the remedy for a minor deficit would bring in, in lieu of it, a deficit of the first magnitude; it would be nothing else but financial ruin.'

II. Financial ruin, if India advances; a financial deluge, if she does nothing; a strange madness among English statesmen, who talk bravely about British interests in this India, which, if voices in the air speak truly, is past helping out of her difficulty except by Russia, who has experience in financial ruin. And the Russian mode of relief might be the wisest, after all! General Gourko gained renown for successful daring, because he advanced, when to do nothing, or to go back, would have been ruin.

III. The perplexity of the wise has sometimes been resolved by the simplicity of a child. In a system of gold currency for India, if 10 per cent. more silver than there is in the existing rupee were to be put into the new subsidiary silver currency, and if the latter were, in consequence, declared to be legal tender up to 100 rupees, would give the following results:—

a. M. de Laveleye would be reassured, because not very much gold would be required by India.

b. Mr. Goschen would be comforted, because silver would be supreme in internal transactions.

c. Mr. Fawcett would be overcome by the political argument, that the millions in British India would bless the British rule when it gives them 10 per cent. more silver in their rupee, with a gold currency to boot, and takes off taxes.

d. The expense of the change would not be alarming; the comparatively little gold that would be required would be bought cheap, that is, at a high sterling exchange with the rupee; and the comparatively little silver to be sold would entail a loss that would be covered, manifold, by the advantages from the change.

e. Furthermore, Parliament, which is responsible for not having some years since corrected the evils, to India, from the depreciation of silver, would share with India the expense of the coinage reform.

CHAPTER VII.

PRACTICABILITY OF SUBSTITUTING A GOLD STANDARD FOR INDIA.

There is not enough of gold in the world. It will simplify an answer to this objection, if we define the only practical meaning which, in the present inquiry, can be attached to the word 'world.' We may include in it the United States, solvent States (if any) in Central and South America, the countries in Europe which are without an inconvertible paper currency, France, Egypt, India, and Australia. The rest are of no account; there is no reason why India should be left out in the cold, and vacant places at the feast of gold be reserved for countries with an inconvertible paper currency, which are not likely to resume specie payments even long after India shall have completed her change from a silver to a gold standard.

2. Accordingly we may pass by, as irrelevant, the following passage, which M. Emile de Laveleye quotes approvingly, in proof of the impossibility of an universal gold standard:—'As was remarked by M. J. Errara (in the *Nord* of April 21, 1876), all the available gold augmented by the entire production of gold for many years to come would not suffice to furnish America, Russia, Austria, and Italy with the metal which those countries would require in order to resume specie payments.' Such being the hopeless indebtedness of these countries (the United States excepted), they may stay out in the cold, while India goes in to the feast of gold: what could these countries do at the feast, but look at the

gold with glistening eyes, without power or right to touch any of it? They had better remain outside.

3. On running over the list of other countries, we find that Australia has enough and an abundance to spare; that the United States will shortly resume specie payments with ease, not interrupting the yearly flow of gold which comes from California to Europe in a not diminishing volume; that England has waxed rich, very rich, but is oppressed with a nightmare, from much surfeiting, in which she feels that she has not enough of gold, and shrieks when any of it goes to the Continent; that the Scandinavian kingdoms have been satisfied; that Germany's need is not so much the getting of gold as the getting rid of silver, the gold which goes to her from England flowing out to Paris, so that the general stock is not reduced; that France—whose peasantry have learnt to invest in the funds instead of hoarding gold, and whose retail dealers and merchants, for years habituated to paper currency, are now becoming habituated to cheques and remitances through branch banks—has an immense hoard of gold, which she will liberate on resuming specie payments: the echo resounding from these facts seems to be gold, too much gold.

4. Too much gold in one part of Europe, an inconvertible paper money in the remaining parts, the silver currency of the East depreciating as mere merchandise in the West, and a common international metallic money a necessity of foreign trade—what wonder if it should appear on inquiry that this disorganisation of the world's currency has much to do with the general depression of trade!

5. M. Chevalier showed that not much gold is consumed in arts and manufactures, and that as civilisation advances, the tawdry display of gold diminishes; and M. Victor Bonnet states that it is well established now that the annual rate of wear and tear of gold coin is $\frac{1}{10000}$ per annum. When the coins lose from wear and tear more than the

prescribed weight they are re-coined. The yearly demand then under these two heads is not much, while the yearly production is 22 millions sterling at the present time, against a not much greater yearly average from 1853 to 1876 of nearly 25 millions. Of late, too, the supply of gold from Africa has markedly increased.

6. Perhaps in the interests of the world's commerce (which has always found springs of its prosperity in the trade between the East and the West) no time, since the gold discoveries of California and Australia, was so favourable as is the present time for the introduction of a gold currency into India. Had it been introduced in 1854, preventing the outflow of silver from the bi-metallic countries of Europe, but not preventing the importation of gold into Europe, the derangement and inflation of prices in the West might have produced all the evils which were apprehended by M. Chevalier. At the present time the depression of commerce is ascribed to too high a range of prices and wages in the West, where the yearly production of gold is accumulating; while the discontinuance of a common money between the East and the West, through the demonetisation of silver in the West, cannot but have an injurious effect on trade with the East.

7. Some write frantically as if gold were the heart's blood of Europe, but a little bleeding, some outflow of the gold which is accumulating in the West, will do Europe good. It need not be feared that the blood-letting would exhaust the patient. Those who cherish such fears complain inconsistently that the production of gold is falling off; the supply from Australia is diminishing. What else can be expected, when prices have risen in Europe, and more attractive industries than mining are prosperous in Australia? When the gold was extracted from auriferous sands, in which nature had done all the work, leaving man simply to wash and carry away the gold, the produce was necessarily large

and its cost small. With quartz-mining the cost of production has increased, and simultaneously prices of commodities have risen in other countries. It is but natural that under these circumstances the exports of gold from Australia should diminish, without warranting any presumption that the mines are becoming exhausted. Should a diminution of gold supply in other countries raise the value of gold by lowering prices, the exports of gold from Australia would again increase. That they are maintained at their present amount, notwithstanding the adverse influences just mentioned, evidences anything but the exhaustion of the mines. In the United States the production is large, and latterly it has been increasing; and the supply from Africa, too, shows a marked and progressive increase.

8. We have seen that the only candidates for a supply out of the world's stock of gold are the United States and India. On the other hand, the countries in Europe are suffering from repletion, and France will liberate a large amount of gold on resuming specie payments; so will Germany when delivered from the throes of her currency reform; for in a country where small money was suited to the immense mass of its small transactions, the displacement of a smaller amount of silver currency by a larger amount of gold currency implies a mistake somewhere. Ten silver marks may serve the need of five persons, where a gold halfcrown, worth ten marks, can be used only by one. The inadequate limit of ten marks per head of the population must be enlarged; in other words, the amount of Germany's gold currency must be reduced.

9. Thus, the supply for the only two new candidates for gold exceeds the demand; and were gold to become slightly insufficient, a decline of prices would create an increased supply; but the general depression of trade points to a redundance, not a deficiency of gold.

10. One great cause of disturbance in the money markets

of Europe was the yearly remittance of immense sums to the East. This occasioned an annual export of gold to the Continent, for the purchase of silver for the East. The currency operations of Germany, and the silent preparations by France for the declaration of a single standard of gold, caused similar disturbance. These necessitated the retention of large working balances in the several banks in Europe; but these causes of disturbance have now nearly ceased. The fifteen millions sterling a year of India Council drafts, the completion wellnigh of Germany's coinage reform, the near approach of France to the consummation of a financial policy which has ably masked from Europe the operations for the reform of her currency, all promise, at no distant period, rest to the money markets of Europe, which the introduction of a gold currency in India would not interrupt.

11. Indeed, the Indian reform could be carried out in a way which would immensely simplify remittances between the East and the West; for Bank of England notes, against which gold is deposited in London, could be declared legal tender in India.

12. It is a favourite argument with the bi-metallists, that because the amount of gold coin existing in 1877 is not greater, or is possibly one-third less than the amount of gold and silver coin which existed in 1848, therefore, considering the great expansion of commerce in the interval, the present stock of gold coin cannot suffice by itself for the world's metallic currency. But in this argument several considerations are overlooked :—

I. As already explained, the demonetisation of silver does not imply its disuse as currency. It would still be employed as subsidiary currency, perhaps on an enlarged scale, and with an enlarged limit, for subsidiary silver coin as legal tender. Coupled with the condition of its receipt to any amount in payment of Government dues, the silver currency, within its own special range, viz., the mass of inland or domestic transactions, would be just as efficient currency as gold.

II. Supposing that there were no paper currency, the amount of a metallic currency with a single gold standard (and with a subsidiary silver currency of the kind described in the preceding section, and in a previous chapter), would, together, form an effective or efficient currency as extensive as, or greater than, the metallic currency which existed in 1848.

III. At the same time, the use of paper money has since 1848 greatly diminished the amount of requirements of a metallic currency. It is fallacious to compare the amount of trade in 1848 with that in 1877, as implying the necessity of a proportionate increase of the metallic currency, because:—

a. The mass of transactions in foreign trade, and the wholesale transactions of internal trade, are settled by means of foreign and inland bills of exchange, cheques, and the clearing-house. In the foreign trade, this form of settlement derived an advantage from the stability of the relative value of the precious metals; but since the depreciation of silver, there has been some derangement. In some branches of England's export trade, notably in the cotton trade, the depreciation of silver makes, sometimes, all the difference between profit and loss.

b. The trade of the two periods which are compared includes in larger measure in 1877, than in 1848, the trade of countries with an inconvertible paper currency.

c. Since 1848 there has grown up a vast amount of international paper money, in the form of stocks of the indebted nations. The export of these securities serves the same purpose as an export of gold; and as they are not imported except when gold, or other equivalent, is available in the purchasing country to pay for them, their efficiency as circulating medium is on the same side as an addition to the metallic currency.

d. There has also grown up, particularly on the Continent and in the United States, a larger amount of paper currency, much of it under circumstances of inconvertibility of notes, which, by expelling gold and silver from circulation, have habituated the people to paper money; so that, when specie payments are resumed, a large amount of metallic money will be found to have been permanently displaced, from the now rooted preference of the people for paper money. In France, which has a stupendous amount of metallic money, this education of the people in the use of paper money has been systematically carried farther than in other countries, by the multiplication of branch banks, the enlarged use of cheques, and extensive facilities which have been afforded for inland remittances.

e. Steamers, railways, and the telegraph too, have economised the use of specie.

f. And the circumstances mentioned in paragraphs 10 and 11 tend in a remarkable degree to diminish the use of metallic money.

g. Hence, a comparison of the trade of 1848 with that of 1877, as indicative of the proportion or of the amount of metallic currency required in the two periods, is unmeaning.

13. The salient facts are:—

I. That if commerce has greatly increased since 1848, so has the use of paper money; and the increase of the latter has been such as to reduce the use of metallic currency in a greater degree than the former could increase it.

a. Because an increase of commerce means an increase of both imports and exports; and therefore, as regards foreign trade, the bills of exchange created by the augmented imports and exports settle the bulk of the transactions, leaving only the balance to be settled by the import or export of gold or silver.

b. And even for settling that balance, a new form of

international paper currency other than bills of exchange has been created on a prodigious scale since 1848, to the displacement of gold and silver in such settlements:—1st, the Council drafts upon India have increased from 3 to 15 millions sterling a year; 2ndly, there has been an enormous growth of national indebtedness, the registered stocks or securities of which are largely employed as remittances, in which form they serve the same purpose as an export or import of gold and silver.

c. Furthermore, in the years from 1852 to 1868, the movement of the precious metals was not alone for the settlement of balances of international indebtedness; there was a special extra movement for the replacement of the silver currencies, first, of the countries of the Latin Union, then of Germany and the Scandinavian kingdoms, by gold; and this movement absorbed, in the West, the bulk of the yearly production of gold, and in the East the bulk of the silver production. But the demand of these countries on the yearly supply of gold is now nearly ended. France, indeed, must soon liberate large amounts of gold, and Germany will be forced to do likewise, on a lesser scale.

d. With regard, again, to the internal trade of each country, the demand for metallic currency has lessened: in England by the growth of deposits and inland bills of exchange, to stupendous amounts; in France from the same causes on a smaller scale, and from a very great extension of the use of notes, cheques, and other forms of paper money; in other countries in Europe, which have mostly inconvertible paper money, and in the United States, from the people having become habituated to paper money by the use of inconvertible notes: and a further diminution of the use of gold, by the substitution for it of silver for internal transactions, is possible in all these countries, especially by recourse to the expedient of a subsidiary paper currency, payable in silver, the notes of which would supersede the use of gold for all retail transactions of internal trade.

II. The special demand for gold by solvent States in Europe, for the change from a silver currency, has hitherto absorbed each year's fresh supply of gold; but that demand has for the most part ceased, and will soon be ended; thenceforward, the demands of those States for replacing the ordinary wear and tear in their gold coinages will be small, and unless India adopts a gold currency, the yearly supply of fresh gold must soon begin to derange prices, in the manner apprehended, in 1848, by M. Chevalier.

III. This shows that universal bi-metallism, though harmless as a chimera, which amuses writers on the currency, would be a grave disaster, were the nations to adopt it. For purposes of international trade, the existing supply of gold is abundant, if not excessive. Were silver to be additionally employed in that trade, thus causing the united mass of yearly supply of gold and silver to act on prices which are now influenced, in the West, by gold alone, the disorganisation of commerce would be complete.

IV. The disuse of silver as international money does not imply its demonetisation in the internal trade of each country. Hence, the adoption of gold as the universal money would not throw an undue burden upon gold; silver would remain enthroned as the money for internal transactions. Moreover, in like manner, as the India Council drafts, with a silver currency in India, have the same effect as the import of 15 millions sterling a year of silver, into London, so, with a gold currency in India, they would operate like an import into the West of 15 millions sterling of gold.

It appears then, on a detailed examination of the facts, that there is enough of gold for all; there is an unequal distribution of it, but the introduction of a gold currency into India would modify that, in the right direction.

CHAPTER VIII.

MEANS TO BE EMPLOYED FOR ESTABLISHING A GOLD CURRENCY IN INDIA.

We may now conclude that there is enough of gold in the world for enabling India to change to a gold standard, without harming any one. More proofs will be adduced in the next chapter; but meanwhile it may be assumed that the City would give leave for the introduction of a gold currency into India.

2. The full operation of a gold standard in India would involve some important changes, viz. :—

I. It would enable the Secretary of State for India gradually to issue, and permanently to keep afloat, some 50 or 60 millions sterling of India Office Treasury bills, corresponding to the exchequer bills of the English Treasury, which, for the purposes of this exposition, may be styled *quasi*-exchequer bills.

II. The issue of these *quasi*-exchequer bills would enable the Secretary of State for India to reduce the interest on all the sterling loans of the Indian Government to 4 per cent. or less, and (with a gold currency in India) to transfer them to the Indian registers for payment of interest in India to holders of the stock in that country. In this manner, stock of these sterling loans, or else securities of rupee loans, now held in Europe, could be transferred from the English to the Indian loan registers, up to the amount of the *quasi*-exchequer bills, so that the amount of the various forms of Indian loans held in England would not be increased.

III. It would be highly conducive to important financial and commercial interests of England and India that, with a gold currency in India, the Bank of England should establish branches or agencies in Calcutta and Bombay, perhaps also in Madras and Rangoon, for facilitating remittances between the two countries, and for cashing its own notes, which, with English sovereigns, might be made legal tender in India.

IV. The Secretary of State for India now issues his Council drafts on India through the Bank of England, generally in monthly instalments, up to the aggregate, in the twelve months, of his requirements for the year, which are usually reckoned, for the future, at 15 millions sterling.

For doubtless good reasons, which would be inapplicable under the new arrangement, the amounts of the monthly drawings are not varied to suit the periods when the demand for bills on India is active or slack; but were the Bank of England to establish branches in Calcutta and Bombay, the Secretary of State could receive credit in the lump, from the Bank, for the amount of his monthly requirement, the Indian Government affording credit to the branch banks at Calcutta and Bombay, in the lump, for the corresponding amount, at an approximate rate of exchange. The Bank of England would then issue its own bills on India, in the place of the Council drafts. As the issues would only respond to the actual demand for bills, the Bank would obtain for them better rates, on the average for the year, than are obtained on the Council drafts. In consideration of the large balance which the Secretary of State for India keeps at the Bank of England, the approximate rates of exchange charged monthly by the Bank for its monthly credits to the India Office could be adjusted, at the end of the year, to the average rate.

V. From Bank of England notes being made legal tender in India, they would accumulate in the Indian treasuries; on the Government of India presenting these notes at the local branches of the Bank of England for cancellation, corresponding amounts would be placed to the credit of the Secretary of State in London.

VI. Merchants would perhaps be allowed a similar advantage, on their presenting Bank of England notes to the local branches, which might find this mode of settlement better than the discharge of the notes in cash. In that case Bank of England notes would command a small premium in India, such as would gain them a preference over sovereigns in remittances from England to India. Independently, too, of this circumstance, Bank of England notes would be sent to India in the place of sovereigns, that is to say, some millions sterling of notes would be sent to India, and to a great extent would remain outstanding, against gold deposited in the Bank of England, which would never be required out of the country for cashing those notes. In times of crisis, the Bank of England might safely be allowed to issue notes uncovered by bullion, up to the amount of the notes held in treasuries and banks in India.

3. The command which the Bank of England would acquire over remittances between the West and the East would be helpful both to the Government and to commerce, in extraordinary emergencies; to Government, which on such occasions could be emergently assisted by the Bank with funds; to commerce, which, through the Bank of England, and in no other way, could obtain help from the reserve balances of the Secretary of State and of the Government in India. Exceptional drains of gold from England to India would on such occasions be averted, or be very much restrained. The currency system of England would be strengthened.

4. The expectation that the Secretary of State for India would be able to issue gradually, and to keep outstanding, *quasi*-exchequer bills to the amount of some sixty millions sterling is not visionary. In years long past, as shown in a paper in the appendix, on the currencies of various countries,

large amounts of exchequer bills were outstanding, the real magnitude of which should be estimated by the proportion which they bore to the comparatively small deposits and floating capital of those days. Down to 1844 the Bank of England kept in these exchequer bills a part of its reserve against the outstanding circulation of notes. This practice ceased under the Bank Act of 1844. About the same time railway debentures came to be preferred to exchequer bills for temporary investments. From these two circumstances, exchequer bills sold less readily than before, and, in consequence, got into disfavour also with the English Treasury, which for a long period steadily observed the policy of reducing their amount. But in the thirty years and more which have elapsed since the banks ceased to invest in exchequer bills, deposits have enormously increased, to amounts which the mind can express arithmetically, but cannot adequately realise. The banks have been forced, in consequence, failing any safer temporary investments, to deposit with bill brokers, and to hold, in discounts to stock brokers, very large balances, with the result of weakening and often paralysing the control of the Bank of England over the rate of interest. There is room, therefore—unfortunately, too much room—for the issue of exchequer bills to the amount of even twice 60 millions; the doing so by the English Chancellor of the Exchequer and the Indian Secretary of State would be an unmixed good to the country. The perception of this fact, of the control over the money market which these bills would help in restoring to the Bank of England, and of the considerable advantages which the Bank would derive from a closer connection with India, and from the command of remittance operations with that country, would enlist the active co-operation of the Bank in placing the exchequer bills favourably on the market. Nor, in consideration of the great good from thus bracing up the system of currency and credit in England, which will be noticed at length in a later chapter, would the English Treasury hesitate to receive the *quasi*-exchequer bills of the Secretary of State for India in payment of revenue.

5. Hence, by an arrangement with the Imperial Government, the *quasi*-exchequer bills of the Secretary of State for India might be received in the United Kingdom in payment of revenue; and in order that his hand may not be forced, he might be empowered to raise, at any time, on the issue of stock, a sum equal to his yearly requirements. The accumulation of notes of the Bank of England in Indian treasuries would also strengthen his position; for, as already stated, the cancellation of the notes held there would instantaneously place him in funds for discharging his exchequer bills should cash be demanded. So great, however, is the need for this form of investment for the large balances of bankers in London, including the Bank of England, that the bulk of these short-dated bills would be renewed. The short periods for which the bills run are their special recommendation or merit; because the renewal at brief intervals affords the opportunity of adjusting the rate of interest to the current rate of the market, which makes the bills saleable readily at par. This being all that the investors want, the bulk of the bills would be renewed.

6. If, on the declaration of gold as the standard and as legal tender in India, the Secretary of State for India were to cease his drafts upon India, for four years, and were to raise the 15 millions sterling a year for the disbursements of the Home Treasury by means of *quasi*-exchequer bills—the further coinage of silver in India being at the same time stopped, and interest on sterling loans being made payable in India—we should have the following results:—

I. The trade remittances to India would be made—

a. By the transfer of securities of the Indian Government from England to India, both the sterling and rupee loans.

b. By the remittance to India of gold bullion, sovereigns, and notes of the Bank of England.

To the trade generally, and to other than the Bank of England, there would, indeed, be available a third form of remittance, viz., the bills which the Bank of England would sell upon its branches in Calcutta and Bombay; but as the branches would have to be placed in funds by one or other of the modes *a* and *b*, practically those two would be the only real modes of remittance. So long as the first form of remittance would be available, the bank would avoid the second mode. In other words, the issue of the *quasi*-exchequer bills of the Indian Secretary of State, up to 15 millions a year, would cause the transfer of a corresponding amount of Indian securities from the English to the Indian registers.

II. During the five years of cessation of the Secretary of State's drafts on India, to the amount of 15 millions sterling, equal to at least 165 millions of rupees a year, the latter amount would accumulate in Indian treasuries, where it would be available—1st, for the comparatively small amount of yearly borrowing for Public Works Extraordinary; 2ndly, for discharge of rupee loans.

III. This discharge of 15 millions sterling a year of rupee loans would be necessary or expedient for various reasons:

a. To help the Bank of England in making the remittances of securities from England to India, for Indian trade (I. *a*), because the securities would be sent to India only to the extent that they could realise a fair price in India; and therefore, unless a void in the Indian market for these securities be created by discharging 15 millions sterling a year of rupee loans, transfers to that yearly amount, from the English to the Indian registers, would be impracticable.

b. The 5½ per cent. rupee loan, amounting to 10⅓ millions

sterling, must be discharged on 1st May 1879; it is of especial importance that this loan should be converted into four per cents. at par. Were it to be converted at $4\frac{1}{2}$ or 5 per cent., a proportionately higher price would have to be paid for the purchase of the East Indian railway. By discharging 15 millions sterling of 4 per cent. rupee paper in 1878, the conversion of the $5\frac{1}{2}$ per cents. into fours in 1879 would be assured, if indeed a lesser rate than 4 per cent. would not be obtainable. Nearly 43 millions sterling of 4 per cent. rupee loans can be paid off by Government, at its option, on three months' notice.

c. India 5 per cent. stock, to the amount of $17\frac{1}{5}$ millions sterling, is redeemable after 5th July 1880, upon one year's notice. The transfer, by that time, of nearly 40 millions sterling of Indian securities, from the English to the Indian registers, would create, in the London market for such securities, a great void, such as would enable the Secretary of State for India to convert the 5 per cent. stock at a better rate than 4 per cent.; for it should be remembered that the *quasi*-exchequer bills of the Secretary of State would be held by a different class of investors from those who invest in colonial and foreign stocks.

7. Thus far, the declaration of gold as legal tender in India, and the closure of the Indian mints against the coinage of silver for the public, would secure the following advantages:—

I. An actual saving of above one million sterling a year in loss by exchange, and the further prevention of loss from a great but indefinite growth of the charge.

II. The conversion of large amounts of $5\frac{1}{2}$ and 5 per cent. loans into 4 per cents. at par, or at a more favourable rate.

III. The discharge of some 40 millions sterling of 4 per cent. rupee loans in India, by raising that amount in London on *quasi*-exchequer bills at much less than 4 per cent. and by raising it in such a way as not to increase the amount of Indian securities held in England.

IV. Facilities for buying the East Indian Railway by the issue of 4 per cent. stock at a more favourable rate than could be otherwise possible.

V. The transfer of the stock of the India sterling loans from the English to the Indian registers, as a first and important step towards the gradual purchase back, by India, of her securities which are held abroad.

VI. The introduction of a system by which India would borrow yearly, for its requirements for public works extraordinary, in the cheapest, that is, the London market; at the same time that, by absolute cessation of borrowing in India, her people would be forced to buy back from London the securities upon which her Government will have borrowed at cheap rates abroad.

VII. A general reduction of the rate of interest in India; which means increased facility for cheaper production.

VIII. An invigoration, or bracing up of the system of credit and currency in England, through the command over remittances between England and India, and the greater command over the London money market, which the Bank of England would gain from the measures which have been discussed.

8. The measures for introducing a gold currency into India might be somewhat as follows:—

I. Gold coins of an intrinsic value in the proportion of one to 15½ silver rupees of the present currency, to be struck, for the present, for Government only; to be declared legal tender, at that valuation; and to be issued in permanent withdrawal of rupees of the old currency.

II. The coinage of silver for the public and for the paper currency office to cease, and a duty of 20 per cent. to be levied on the importation of silver, under penalty of confiscation in any attempt to evade the duty, the confiscated treasure being divided between the informers and the captors.

III. A new subsidiary silver currency to be coined, the rupees of which shall contain ten per cent. more silver than the existing rupees. The new silver rupees shall circulate at par with the existing rupees as legal tender, for any amount, until the withdrawal of the old rupees, after which they shall be legal tender for not more than one hundred rupees.

IV. The Paper Currency Office shall receive from the public gold bullion, English sovereigns, and Bank of England notes, at the relative value, between silver and gold, of 15½ to 1, in exchange for silver rupees or for currency notes of the existing system, which are payable in silver.

V. The Paper Currency Office shall (in exchange for silver rupees, or for its notes payable in silver) issue notes payable in gold coins of the new Indian currency, or in English sovereigns or Bank of England notes; and gold notes thus redeemed shall not be reissued.

VI. All silver rupees, and currency notes of the existing system, which may be received at the currency office in exchange for gold notes shall be permanently withdrawn. The silver rupees (including silver, from the coin reserve, equal to the currency notes withdrawn) being re-coined into rupees of the new subsidiary currency.

VII. Sovereigns and notes of the Bank of England shall be received at all Government treasuries, in payment of Government demands or as railway traffic receipts, and in exchange for silver rupees, or for notes payable in silver. But as a rule they shall not be reissued by the Government except in permanent withdrawal of silver rupees, or of currency notes with their equivalent reserve in silver coin of the old currency.

VIII. Sovereigns and notes of the Bank of England shall also be received in courts of law, and on all the guaranteed and State railways, and shall be paid into Government treasuries.

IX. On completion of the change to a gold standard, sovereigns and notes of the Bank of England shall be legal tender in all transactions.

9. This sketch provides that the notes of the Bank of England, imported into India, must go into Government treasuries, the Mint, or the Paper Currency Office, to be issued thence, not to the importers (who will receive other full value), but at the discretion of Government, in permanent withdrawal of the old silver currency. Profiting by the warning in the example of the German Government, the object of this is to ensure that the new gold coins, including sovereigns, shall be issued only in withdrawal of the old silver currency.

10. This precaution would be very necessary, because, simultaneously with the declaration of gold as legal tender, the Council drafts on India would be discontinued, exchange on India would rise to more than 1*s.* 10½*d.* per rupee, and even to 2*s.* In consequence, gold would be imported into India, to the amount of the discontinued Council drafts: that is, to the extent of 15 millions sterling a year, less any extra amount of private bills on India which may be offered in the market.

11. Assuming that the currency operation or coinage reform extends over four years, the importation of 60 millions sterling in that period, as an addition to the present metallic currency of India, might inflate prices and disorganise trade. These evils, and the embarrassment experienced by the German Government, would be avoided by the precaution of withdrawing an equivalent of silver coin for every gold coin that may be issued. The high exchange in favour of India, which would rule during the operation, would prevent the exportation of the issued gold coins.

12. No doubt, the measures for promoting the remittance of Indian securities from England to India would prevent the importation of anything like 15 millions sterling a year of gold coin and bullion; but the precaution suggested would not the less be sound and necessary; for the need of yearly remittance to India exceeds 15 millions, and the excess, amounting perhaps to four or five millions, would be remitted in gold, or in notes of the Bank of England.

13. But, at this rate, the completion of the change to a gold standard, by the demonetisation and withdrawal of the existing silver currency, would be a very long process. Hence it would be expedient to borrow in gold a certain amount yearly for the purpose of withdrawing the old silver coinage. The yearly borrowing would include about three millions sterling for public works extraordinary. On the surface it would seem that the amount of gold obtained for the public works extraordinary expenditure in India could not be issued in withdrawal of the existing silver currency; it could, nevertheless, be issued, in the first instance, in exchange for silver rupees, and the withdrawn rupees, after adding 10 per cent. to them in a re-coinage, could be reissued as part of the new subsidiary currency, which, until withdrawal of the old silver currency, would circulate at par with the latter, as full legal tender. In this way, the coinage reform could be completed in about five or six years.

14. Until the conversion of the 5½ and 5 per cents. into fours, the extra borrowing, for obtaining a special supply of gold, for withdrawal of the silver currency, could either be deferred, or be effected through *quasi*-exchequer bills, so as not to interfere with the conversion into 4 per cents.

15. It has been shown how greatly the demand for gold for remittances to the East would be reduced by giving the Bank of England a control over them, and by the other measures which have been suggested. Large amounts of

gold must also be liberated, at no distant period, by France and Germany: indeed, the demand for India would unlock the hoards of the Bank of France; accordingly, there is no reason to apprehend that European markets would be disturbed or distressed by the measures for introducing a gold currency into India.

16. Perhaps all fear of disturbing the money market would be removed if the Secretary of State for India were to entrust the details of the measure for changing to a gold standard in India to the Banks of England and France, the Messrs. Rothschild, and Baring Brothers; paying them a commission which might increase inversely with the amount of gold employed in completing the operation, besides a commission, say a yearly rate, for five years after the demonetisation of the old currency, on the amount of silver that may be permanently withdrawn with paper, in a manner to be presently explained. This form of payment might not admit of very nice adjustment; but the high character of all the parties, and a high sense among those benefited, of the importance of the service, would certainly not hinder a liberal settlement, perfectly satisfactory to the financial ability of those whose wise arrangements may give to the East the inestimable advantage of a common money in the trade with the West.

17. It may be reiterated that, in this regard, the effect of the several measures which have been discussed in reducing the bulk of the remittances between England and India, to simple adjustments in the books of the Bank of England and of its Indian Branches, should not be overlooked.

18. Thus, on the one hand, India would make a large temporary demand on the gold supply of the world, with the view of remaining commercially in the comity of nations; but she would on the other hand abundantly requite the service by converting a large part, perhaps eventually the bulk of the international settlements through England, into a

mere book adjustment, which means that a large amount of notes of the Bank of England would be permanently outstanding in, or in transit to India, without the gold against which they were issued ever leaving the issue department. England has taught India to pay handsomely for every service rendered to her, and even in this her extremity India would not forget the lesson. The West would find the parting, out of its money bags, with some sixty millions sterling of gold, for a gold currency in India, not the least profitable of its investments in its trade with the East.

19. The throes of the City, on account of the exportation to India of fifteen millions sterling a year of gold money, would be assuaged when notes of the Bank of England are included in the export;—and there would be a happy relief—that exquisite pleasure of intense pain steadily and rapidly subsiding and ceasing—as the City awoke to the fact that the surplus gold of France, an increased supply from specie-paying United States, a slackened or discontinued demand from Germany and France on Australia's gold supply (and not diminishing hoards of the Bank of England) were furnishing the gold that was streaming to the East. O happy City! who would not envy your impassioned soul the joy of such grief as disturbs the possessor of untold wealth—idle for lack of use—which after all remains undiminished by an imaginary loss!

20. The Indian mints would be unequal to the re-coinage of 100 millions sterling of silver rupees in five years; but their power can be increased, and it would not be absolutely necessary to demonetise the existing currency at the end of the fifth year. That period would be required for drawing a sufficient amount of gold to India by cessation of the Council drafts on India. After five years the drafts could be resumed, and the gold portion of the currency would adjust itself, by influx or efflux, to the requirements of the country, while the silver of the old currency could continue to circu-

late as full legal tender, at par with the heavier new coinage, the restriction of whose legal tender would have to be deferred. The lighter rupees, by consigning the heavier to the melting pot, would thus steadily hasten their own destruction. As, however, it is not desirable that the Indian metallic currency should remain in a state of transition a day longer than the Government can avoid, special measures, beyond the utmost increase of the powers of the Calcutta and Bombay mints, would be required. Perhaps a part of the re-coinage should be executed in England, the overland troop transports being utilised for the carriage of the silver, and another part might be obtained by leasing the mints of native states, and improving them, should that appear a preferable alternative to the temporary constitution of a third, and even a fourth mint. The extra expense of the special arrangements would be eventually recovered in the saving of permanent mint expenditure; for with a gold currency, including the circulation of sovereigns as legal tender, India could spare one of the two existing mints.

21. As stated in a former chapter, the silver currency in India may be reckoned at 160 millions sterling, of which 105 millions would be required as subsidiary silver currency, even in the small proportion of ten shillings per head of the population, which obtains in England. This, probably, is an under-estimate of the amount of subsidiary silver currency that would be needed; but it may stand as a set-off to any possible under-estimate of the amount which is outstanding of the existing silver currency. Accordingly, there would remain for withdrawal 55 millions sterling of silver. But some abatements must be made from this, to arrive at the net amount which would have to be sold, viz. :—

I. The 105 millions of new subsidiary coinage would contain 10 per cent. more silver than the existing rupees, and so would absorb 10½ millions of the surplus silver.

II. An issue of 55 millions sterling of gold coins would

withdraw, in tale of silver coins, ten times the number of the gold coins, and it is not an unreasonable conjecture that at least 20 millions sterling extra, of new silver coinage, would be required. In other words, at the end of the five years which are assumed as the period for completing the coinage reform, the new gold and silver coinage together might exceed the withdrawn coinage of the old currency by 20 millions sterling of new subsidiary silver currency.

III. Hence, out of a total of 160 millions sterling of existing silver currency, there would be reissued, as subsidiary silver currency, $105 + 20 = 125$ millions, containing extra silver to the amount of 10 per cent. or 12·5 millions, thus raising the aggregate to 137·5 millions, and leaving for sale 43 millions worth.

22. If a loss of even 20 per cent. were to be sustained on the sale of 43 millions worth of silver, the amount would be covered by the five years' accumulation of the savings and advantages stated in para. 7; not to mention the greater loss by exchange from a growth of the depreciation of silver, which the alteration to a gold standard would prevent.

23. Furthermore, it would be a part of the measures for the introduction of a gold currency into India, that a duty of 20 per cent., or other higher prohibitory duty, should be imposed on the importation of silver; and, with this precaution, a yearly sale of 3 to 5 millions sterling of silver rupees, with an allowance of 15 per cent. in favour of the buyers, would be practicable.

24. A part of the 43 millions, sufficient to cover a considerable portion of the loss on the final account, could also be withdrawn with paper money. The sale of the surplus silver, in India, would be gradual; while it remains on the hands of Government there would be a loss of interest; to

prevent this, and on important administrative considerations, the idle money might be utilised.

25. In the Deccan, in the Bombay Presidency, the indebtedness of the Government ryots has become so serious that it may be necessary to reduce the assessment of the land revenue. The peasant proprietors in the Punjab, and in many places the cultivators in the North-Western Provinces, are in similar indebtedness. In fact, the dependence of the cultivating classes generally on the village banker is proverbial; it caused the Santhal rebellion; and its removal by any means which would turn the Indian peasantry from being borrowers into depositors in Government savings banks would unite the governed to their rulers in bonds close, profitable, and agreeable, which would obliterate the feeling of subjection to a foreign rule.

26. England's own experience, the important part which the country banks of a past generation played in the development, and which their successors have continued in the improvement, of British agriculture, show the unavoidable dependence of the cultivating classes upon capital, for the yearly expenses of cultivation. In India, through the astuteness of the village banker, and partly through the improvidence of the cultivator, this limited dependence has grown in many parts of the country, as above stated, into deep indebtedness. In England, the high character of the bankers, and a wealthy landed proprietary, have averted a similar result. In India, if a like happy condition, as in England, is to be attained, the Government, which is the real landlord, by combining the duties of landlord and the functions of banker, must lift the ryot in the scale of wellbeing, help him to pay his debts, thereby enable him to save, and confirm his attachment to British rule by making him a creditor of the British Government, as a depositor in its savings banks. Should that Government ever advance beyond

its frontier to encounter a foreign power, perhaps its rear could not be better secured than by an army of creditors. All-pervading finance improves even strategy.

27. Hence, simultaneously with the declaration of a gold standard for India, a new class of district currency notes, payable in silver, might be issued, to be legal tender in the district and at the office of issue at the chief seat of the local Government in whose province the district is situate. The notes would be issued, not against silver, but to ryots or peasant proprietors, on the security of their estates, (1) for a temporary object, viz., the discharge of their debts; (2) as a permanent arrangement, viz., for their yearly expenses of cultivation. The convertibility of the extra issue of notes for the discharge of debts would be secured by the reissue, to the extent demanded, of the withdrawn silver which may be available for sale. The interest, perhaps 6 per cent. per annum, on the amount advanced to the ryots, would set off a considerable part of the expense of the coinage operation.

28. These measures of relief would of course be put in hand, not simultaneously throughout all districts, but only in so many districts at a time as could be served with the available amount of silver reserve. The other districts would be taken up in their turn. Though the metallic currency might be inflated for a time, and in some measure, by this procedure, the usual effects of such inflation would be neutralised or mitigated by countervailing influences; for the measure suggested would also reduce the rate of interest, and liberate village bankers' capital for other uses, thus cheapening production.

29. The convertibility of the ordinary issue of notes for expenses of cultivation would be secured by a comparatively small reserve of coin, the very purpose of their issue (namely, the expenses of cultivation)—their being received yearly in payment of revenue,—and their being made legal tender in the district—would keep the bulk of the notes outstanding

till the end of the season, when they would return in payment of the revenue.

30. During the five years of progress of the coinage reform the ryots would become educated in the use of paper money, and familiarised with notes which had rescued them from the village bankers, and unfailingly helped to cultivate their fields. At the end of the period a large amount of the notes would be permanently outstanding; and a proportion of the silver currency could be withdrawn from circulation. The silver thus withdrawn with paper would set off loss from the sale of other silver.

31. Any great progress of savings banks in the country is checked by the indebtedness of ryots who have nothing to put by, and by the ability of lenders to obtain from the ryots more than the savings-bank rate of interest. With the extinction of the ryot's indebtedness, by means of paper which he had found more serviceable than gold, he would trust the issuers of the paper, and would leave his savings with them on interest, instead of hoarding gold which yields no interest; that is to say, a further amount of silver, to the extent of the deposits, would be virtually withdrawn with paper.

32. The village banker's occupation would be gone, but not his capital—that would flow into other channels, adding to production or distribution, and cheapening its cost. The ryots' deposits in savings banks, should they reach a large amount and become progressive, would reduce India's borrowings in the London money market.

33. The extension of the paper currency through advances to peasant proprietors and to the cultivating classes is not necessary for the introduction of a gold currency; but it fits into the plan of coinage reform, from the promise it affords of the permanent withdrawal of a considerable part of the old silver currency with paper, and from the means it would provide for employing, for urgent administrative and

fiscal needs, a large part of the yearly 15 millions sterling which would be set free by the cessation of Council drafts. Throughout India, except in the Lower Provinces of Bengal, the district organisation is adapted to the systematic issue and recovery of advances from agriculturists; and even in Bengal the measure is not impracticable.

34. The liberation of the capital of the village bankers for other uses is one of the principal means of developing the resources of India. At the risk of some repetition, this subject will be considered in a subsequent chapter.

35. It is not necessary to discuss measures by which the paper currency of India could be increased even without altering or extending the present organisation of the department of paper currency. No doubt, those who may be entrusted with the execution of the details for the introduction of a gold currency into India would be fully empowered to work their will in promoting the more general convertibility of currency notes, without sparing the present amount of invested reserve of the Paper Currency Department.

CHAPTER IX.

THE DELICATE MECHANISM OF ENGLAND'S CURRENCY AND CREDIT.

There is enough of gold in the world, and England has the first choice of the world's yearly supply. The Californian and Australian mines never omit this homage to their king Crœsus, who, following Oriental custom, lightly touches the offering, which is then passed to other countries. 'Gold, gold, nothing but gold!' but from choice, not necessity, surfeited England uses little of it. Addressing the Committee of Inquiry into the Commercial Distress in 1857, Mr. Slater (of the firm of Morrison, Dillon, and Co., whose transactions are among the largest of the metropolis) observed:—

'To prove how little of real money, that is, of Bank of England notes and gold mohurs, enter into the operations of trade, it may be interesting as well as conclusive, on that point, to refer to the analysis of a continuous course of commercial transactions, extending over several millions yearly, and which may be considered as a fair example of the general trade of the country. The proportions of receipts and payments are reduced to the scale of £1,000,000 only during the year 1856, and they are as under, viz.:—*Receipts*: £900,938 of bankers' drafts, mercantile bills of exchange, country bankers' notes, cheques; Bank of England notes, £68,554; gold, £28,089; silver and copper and post-office money orders, £2,409. *Payments*: £966,346 of bankers' drafts, &c.; £22,743 Bank of England notes; £9,427 gold; and of silver and copper £1,484.'

Later, in a similar analysis by Sir John Lubbock in 1865, we find the proportion still smaller, namely, out of 23 millions sterling of transactions 'in the last few days of 1864,' bank notes, £1,137,000; coin, £139,000.

Yet we read (Mr. Bagehot's 'Lombard Street,' pages 311–12) :—'This is the first and the plainest way in which the German Government could take, and did take, money from this country, and in which it might have broken the Bank of England if it liked.' And so in the vanity with which we regard our commerce (that advances 'with leaps and bounds') and Lombard Street as 'by far the greatest combination of economical power and economical delicacy that the world has ever seen,' we were content in 1873 to be indebted to the forbearance of Germany for the solvency of the Bank of England.

Somehow, our absurdly poor plodding stupid fathers, who slowly crept along in a way which must put their sons to shame, managed at least to preserve their country's financial independence. Francis, in his history of the Bank of England, tells us how a plan to break the Bank failed, though it had been carefully organised by French instigation, in days before the theory of a sound paper currency on a metallic basis, which is our pride. May we, to that pride, add a feeling of calm satisfaction (deepening into a profound self-complacency, as the prospect of war for British interests becomes clearer), that the deposits in the Bank of England on foreign account, and by foreign banks which have offices in London, have greatly increased of late years.

We have become the creditors of powerful indebted nations, on a scale which goads them with heavy taxation to pay us mere interest on their debt; and at the same time we have framed, in Lombard Street, a mechanism of credit of 'wondrous potency,' through which some of those nations can break the Bank of England. The situation is a very pretty one.

Across the Channel we have a neighbour perhaps superior to ourselves in financial ability and skill, the same who, in a generation not long past away, tried to break the Bank of England. Of that country we know that it has more gold and silver than England and Germany together, and that its peasantry have subscribed to their national loans, sums many thousand times more than the corresponding classes in the rest of Europe could muster for investment. Of that country we read that it has experienced less of general commercial depression than the rest of the world; while, respecting it, we know that the manifestation of its wondrous recuperative power was coincident with the recall of its capital from foreign investments; and of that country we were told by Mr. Bagehot in 1873, that 'nothing but their immense misfortunes, nothing but a vast loan on their own securities, could have extracted the hoards of France from the custody of the French people. *The offer of no other securities would have tempted them, for they had confidence in no other securities.*' France has been simply national, not cosmopolitan; and has kept her capital at home to invigorate domestic industry, instead of sending it on a beneficent mission to countries which (raising up a barrier of protective duties) set about seeing whether they cannot dispense with foreign manufactures, particularly with those of the 'perfidious' creditor who advanced to them loans which the creditor paid in goods (at the same time raising the price of the goods), and now receives interest which is furnished by heavy taxation.

But let us examine a little closer this fine mechanism of England's currency and credit, which is so liable to snap under the unfriendly touch of a foreign hand. The repeated investigations of the causes of the more recent commercial crises have established as the safest policy, on such occasions, that the Bank of England should begin sufficiently early to raise the rate of interest, but (this precaution taken) should, during the crises, lend its reserve freely, on good securities.

'We lent it [said Mr. Harman on behalf of the Bank of England, in 1825] by every possible means, and in modes we had never adopted before; we took in stock on security, we purchased exchequer bills; we made advances on exchequer bills; we not only discounted outright, but we made advances on the deposit of bills of exchange to an immense amount;—in short, we helped by every possible means consistent with the safety of the Bank, and we were not on some occasions over-nice.'

The reserve of the Bank of England which has to be so freely lent in a panic is the reserve against its deposits, which include the balances kept in the Bank by bankers, bill brokers, stockbrokers, and merchants. The balances held for bankers are simply the uninvested portion of the assets which those banks possess against their liabilities. The deposits with the various banks in the United Kingdom, all whose reserves are concentrated in London, and of which the uninvested portion is concentrated in the Bank of England, amounted to 616 millions sterling in 1872, with 152 millions more for foreign and colonial banks, having offices in London—total, 768 millions (Mr. Palgrave, 'Statistical Journal' for December 1873). In a time of panic these banks are not able to call in all the invested part of their reserve; to do so summarily would only increase the panic, and aggravate the crisis: and so, having strengthened their reserves at the Bank of England, during the premonitory symptoms of a crisis, they are at such a time peculiarly dependent on those reserves. In a still greater degree is the Bank of England dependent on its reserve at such a time; for the other assets against its deposits are Government securities (which, in a panic, are unsaleable on any scale that could afford relief) and discounted bills—which latter, under the necessity for lending freely in a panic, cannot be reduced. Thus the pressure for meeting the liabilities both of the banks throughout the country, and of the Bank of England itself (to the extent that those liabilities are demanded, and are not met by realising any part of invested reserves), falls on the reserve of notes and of coin and bullion in the Banking Department of the Bank of England.

The tension under these circumstances, in a crisis, of the currency and credit system of England, is thus described by Mr. Bagehot:—

'On the surface there seems a great inconsistency in all this. First, you establish in some bank or banks a certain reserve; you make of it or them a kind of ultimate treasury, where the last shilling of the country is deposited and kept. And then you go on to say that this final treasury is also to be the last lending house; that out of it, unbounded, or at any rate immense advances are to be made when no one else lends. This seems like saying, first, that the reserve should be kept, and then that it should not be kept.'

The sovereign remedy is to increase the minimum coin and bullion reserve, and to begin raising the rate of interest, long before the country is hurt, when gold is being exported. Between this uneasiness when gold is exported (with the frantic efforts to prevent the export from a country which has a permanent general balance against all other countries) and the mercantile theory of wealth (which found no practical expression save in a desire and effort to prevent an export of gold), there does not appear to be any material difference —as to the ultimate object—of the two systems. The mercantile system has long been recognised as vicious; is it too soon to inquire whether the existing system of credit and currency of the United Kingdom also is not unsound?

Of the efficacy of the expedient of raising the rate of interest, to prevent an export of gold, we shall presently speak. Respecting an increase of the coin and bullion reserve in the Banking Department of the Bank of England, Mr. Bagehot observed:—

'I should say that at the present time the mind of the monetary world would become feverish and fearful if the reserve in the Banking department of the Bank of England went below £10,000,000. Estimated by the idea of old times, by the idea of ten years ago, that sum, I know, sounds extremely large. My own nerves were educated to smaller figures, because I was trained in times when the demands on us were less, when neither was so much reserve wanted, nor did the public expect so much. But I judge from such observations as I can make of the present state of men's minds, that in fact, and whether justifiably or not, the important and intelligent part of the public which watches the Bank reserve becomes anxious and dissatisfied, if that reserve falls below £10,000,000. That sum, therefore, I call the apprehension "minimum" for the present times... Then, I should say, putting the foregoing reasoning into figures, that the Bank ought never to keep less than £11,000,000 or £11,500,000; since experience shows that a million, or a million and a half, may be taken from us at any time, I should regard this as the practical minimum at which, roughly of course, the Bank should aim, and which it should try never to be below. And in order not to be below £11,500,000, the Bank must begin to take precautions when the reserve is between £14,000,000 and £15,000,000; for experience shows that between two and three millions may probably enough be withdrawn from the Bank store before the right rate of interest is found which will attract money from abroad, and before that rate has had time to attract it. When the reserve is between 14 and 15 millions, and when it begins to be diminished by foreign demand, the Bank of England should, I think, begin to act, and to raise the rate of interest.'

Thus, with a facility which is not unusual in dealing with millions of money not your own, the minimum is raised in a few seconds from an 'apprehension' minimum of £10,000,000 (which, even ten years ago, would have sounded 'extremely large') to a practical minimum of fifteen millions. In 1840, Lord Overstone, then Mr. Loyd, in his evidence before the Committee on Banks of Issue, observed:—

'The main advantage of the paper currency is the economy arising from accomplishing the purposes of money with a less waste of capital than is contained in the precious metals; the larger the reserve of bullion, the less of that economical advantage you obtain; and I confess I cannot look upon the suggestion of working upon a larger amount of reserve of bullion than we have hitherto acted upon, instead of enforcing the true principles of currency, as anything less than a partial surrender of economy, the main advantage of paper circulation, without any really more effectual protection from that which is its main evil, namely, the danger of non-convertibility.'

It may be said that things have immensely changed, and credit and deposits are on a much larger scale now than in

1840. But Lord Overstone, the Gamaliel at whose feet had sat the author of the Bank Act of 1844, added:

> 'Banking in all its forms is dependent on credit; and the due regulation of the money of the country is the proper means of placing credit, and all transactions that spring out of credit, under due control, and confining them within their legitimate limits.'

Instead of increasing the banking reserve, Lord Overstone would have placed 'credit, and all transactions that spring out of credit, under due control, and confined them within their legitimate limits.' This is what should now be done. It is absurd to be content with maintaining the metallic basis, and the convertibility of the note in the Issue Department, if, through an imperfect regulation and control of credit, the Bank of England can be broken in its Banking Department, with assets more than sufficient to cover its liabilities.

In 1840, Lord Overstone thought that credit would be completely restrained by regulating the currency on a metallic basis. Events have falsified the expectation—credit has become an influence of wondrous potency; and the infant whom Lord Overstone saw in the cradle has become a giant, whose little finger can overturn the Bank of England.

For that Bank has only one means of preventing an undue drain of gold, viz., by increasing the rate of interest. On the advice of Mr. Goschen, the Bank since 1860 has raised the rate by steps of one per cent. at a time, whenever it was desired to affect the foreign exchanges. But it has come about that 'You may call spirits from the vasty deep; but will they come?' If the Bank cannot get bills to discount at its ordinary rate, will any bills be brought under the influence of the advanced rate? The 'Economist' wrote on 14th July 1877: 'It is also understood that, while the advertised minimum of the Bank of England's rate of interest, over a considerable period, represented with substantial accuracy the general rate of interest in London, on the best commercial securities, there have been—more particularly during the last three or four years—weeks, and months, when the market rate was considerably below the Bank of England minimum; and when therefore, for all practical purposes, as regards the discount business of the Bank, its rate might as well have stood at 3 or 4, as at 2 per cent.' On the occurrence of an export of gold, the Bank has more than once raised its rate of interest, but with no effect, owing to the lower market rate established by the joint-stock and private banks and the bill brokers. The deposits held by the banks and brokers being manifold greater than the deposits in the Bank of England, it has lost that control over the rate of interest through which alone a sufficient banking reserve can be maintained. Hence the credit and currency system of England is in a state of tension, in which it may snap under a pressure ridiculously small for the vast wealth, and the large excess of her assets, or moveable or fluctuating capital, over her liabilities of the same kind; and this state of things exists by the side of the solid position of the Bank of France.

This risk, for England, of disturbance of an even course of prosperity such as France enjoys, is not caused by a scarcity of gold, or by England's inability to get the gold; nor is it explained by the state of her commerce and productive industry, though that should awaken the anxious concern of her statesmen. Thus:—

I. The general depression of commerce is ascribed to an absence of demand arising from present high prices; as if they were the principal or real, as well as the proximate causes. Hence there is an endeavour to reduce the cost of production, by a decrease of wages. No doubt all wages which became inflated during commercial excitement, in the period of enormous and continued international borrowings, must be reduced; but high prices cannot be the cause of an universal depression, because the exchange of commodities would still proceed on the old level, though at a higher universal elevation of prices. But the assumption that high prices are the real cause of the depression may carry the conflict between labour and capital to an extreme, in the direction of reversing—that is, of reducing the workman's share of, that re-distribution of wealth in favour of the working classes which, as Professor Cairnes has shown us, was one of the earliest and most promising results of the gold discoveries. In the United Kingdom, this extreme reduction of wages would mean a putting back in the scale of living some millions of workmen, and four or five-fold more millions of human beings—diminished motives, means, and opportunities for education which prevents that larger half of ills that poverty brings on itself, and which is even more indispensable than long hours to the efficiency of labour; a fall in prices that would, in the home market for production, countervail much of the decrease in wages; a lasting breach between labour and capital, as the outcome of the policy of peace at any price, which heralded and promoted the vast international borrowings that (instead of opening) are closing the world's markets through a consequent heavy taxation which has diminished the world's income or purchasing power, and has raised a barrier of protective duties against England in almost every country.

II. Rightly interpreted, the universal commercial depression perhaps means diminished purchasing power in the world, from the outrageous lending of English capital (more particularly) to foreign countries; a consequent liability of the foreign countries to pay interest, and to buy back their securities, when their currencies became depreciated: a further consequent current into the creditor countries, of imports already paid for, which prevents an outflow thence to the indebted nations, of the yearly production of gold which comes in the first instance to their creditors:—a necessary accumulation, accordingly, of the new gold in the creditor countries—the more so, as inconvertible paper prevails in most of the indebted countries; a consequent depression of prices in the borrowing, and of their elevation in the lending countries, which accounts for the universal stagnation of trade.

III. If this be a correct exposition of the facts, the evident preparation in France for a change to a gold standard, and the execution of the similar currency reform in Germany, have mitigated the general depression of trade, by absorbing the new gold for which there was no other outlet.

IV. The prospects of England's manufacturing industry are chequered. Things look very bad in the coal and iron industries; but yet, with the considerable fall in the price of coal and iron on the Continent and in America, the markets for those products will probably improve. But in other industries generally, there is slackened demand; and if labour must contribute to the cheapening of the cost of production, the contribution should be primarily in the form of more efficient labour, and only secondarily in that of reduced wages. In this regard, as an indispensable means of making labour efficient, there should be a resolute suppression of drunkenness, through an exertion of patriotism which (uniting all political parties in the effort) shall beat down the opposition of the licensed victuallers.

V. Over the prospects of British agriculture, which is now hard-pressed by foreign competition, there is gloom that can be dispelled only by measures of reform, conceived in a spirit of true conservatism, with a strict and wise regard for the rights of property; but also with the courage of our convictions. The competition of foreign agriculture threatens to upset the received doctrine that 'rent is not an element of the price of agricultural produce (or, in other words, that corn and food would not be necessarily cheaper if every farmer's rent in England were remitted for a term of years).' The immense importations of corn into England from Oregon are from lands which do not pay rent, and are made at an expense for transport which is less than the rate of rent in England.

Heretofore, British wheat had withstood this competition, through its superior yield in England, namely, 30 bushels an acre, against 12 bushels or less in the United States, Hungary, and Russia; but of late years the exports from these countries have been sent forward under the double pressure of their increased indebtedness (which lowers prices in the exporting country), and of a depreciated currency (which lowers the selling price of the exports in the creditor or importing country). In this unequal competition, British agriculture must succumb, unless rents be reduced, or, through the free application of capital to the land, its produce be greatly increased. Since 1869, wheat cultivation has seriously declined; and now the fast developing meat trade with North and South America threatens British agriculture in its last stronghold, namely, pasture land. Moreover, it is not enough that British agriculture should barely hold its own; it is essential to the well-being of England, with the increased dependence of her manufactures on an enlarged home market, that her agriculture should be lifted from the negative position of not receding, to one of redoubled prosperity such as may materially increase the purchasing power of the agricultural classes. A great improvement in their scale of living would quicken all the industries in the kingdom; but this result can be brought about only by augmenting the production of the land, through the free application to it of capital and labour—that is, by the same means which would avert an else inevitable fall of rents.

VI. Let us see whether the agricultural interest and industry are fitted, in their present condition, for this self-renovation, without external and legislative measures of reform.

a. 'From such consideration [writes Mr. Fawcett] it inevitably follows that land will not, as a general rule, be property cultivated if, as is the case in our own country, those who rent it seldom possess any security that they will be able to claim compensation for unexhausted improvements. The correctness of this conclusion is repeatedly confirmed by those who are intimately acquainted with agriculture. Lord Leicester, a large landed proprietor and a well-known agriculturist, has lately said, that after having travelled through a considerable portion of England and Scotland, and having carefully observed the farming, he has arrived at a very positive conclusion that the produce of the land might be nearly doubled, if our present system of agriculture were improved by the application of a greater amount of capital to the cultivation of the land. A similar opinion has been expressed by Lord Derby. The correctness of these conclusions receives an important confirmation from the excellent farming which prevails in parts of Lincolnshire, where a system of tenant right is maintained by custom.

b. As to the rural labourer, Mr. Fawcett writes:—'Even those who are most decided in their opinions as to the productiveness of England's industry must feel that the condition of those who are employed in agriculture is most unsatisfactory; for there are few classes of workmen who, in many respects, are so wretched as the English agricultural labourers. They are in many districts so miserably poor, that if they were converted into slaves to-morrow, it would for the interest of their owners to feed them far better than they are fed at the present time. * * A moment's consideration will show that such wages are barely sufficient to supply the first necessaries of life. Meat cannot be tasted more than once a week; and those who have to exist on this scanty fare are more exposed than any others to the inclemency of our trying climate. Such wages will not permit the slightest provision to be made, either for sickness or the feebleness of old age. Throughout large agricultural districts, not a single agricultural labourer will be found who has saved as much as a week's wages. A life of toiling and incessant industry offers no other prospect than a miserable old age; for when these labourers are too old to work, they will either be paupers in a workhouse, or they must come as suppliant mendicants for parish relief.'

If England applied this description to the condition of

the peasants in Bulgaria, Turkey would complain of the application as a foul libel on her humanity—nay, on our common humanity.

c. Thus we see that the land produces barely half of what it should; and the condition of the agricultural classes, generally, is wretched.

'But even the physical suffering which is associated with their poverty, is not the worst feature of their condition; their ignorance is as complete as it is distressing. Improved schools, enormous educational grants, and a general zeal for instructing the poor, have failed to educate the agricultural labourers * * Parents may be accused of neglecting their children's welfare; but how can we expect those who are so miserably poor, and who are ignorant themselves, to sacrifice the two shillings a week that a child of eight or nine years of age may readily earn?'

Property has its duties as well as its rights. Of landed property, its most sacred duty to the country, as well as to God, is to increase the production of the land, and to promote the well-being of those who live on it, and work out the farmers' profits and the landlords' rents. If these duties are neglected, it matters little what other duties are done.

d. But neglect of their duties cannot be imputed to the majority of the landed proprietors of England and Scotland; and if the descriptions in *a* to *c* were read respecting another country, and with a knowledge that the landed proprietors were intelligent and conscientious, the ready exclamation would be that only capital was wanting to raise England's peasantry to the happy condition, now interrupted for awhile, of the Bulgarian peasantry. It will be England's shame, and the precursor of her downfall, if the capital for changing the face of agricultural districts, so freely bestowed on foreign countries, be withheld from her own children.

e. 'In the seventeenth century, a lawyer, a physician, a retired merchant, who had saved some thousands, and who wished to place them safely and profitably, was greatly embarrassed. Three generations earlier, a man who had accumulated wealth in a profession generally purchased real property, or lent his savings on mortgage. But the number of acres in the kingdom had remained the same; and the value of those acres, though it had greatly increased, had by no means increased so fast as the quantity of capital which was seeking for employment.'[1]

It cannot excite wonder, if the exportation abroad of the capital which should have fertilised the fields of once happy England has left British agriculture without a sufficient wages fund for raising the wages of the labourer, and improving both his scale of living and the home market for British manufactures. Look at the future (see Appendix) of the misery caused by national indebtedness and foreign borrowings, also at the humiliating inferiority of England's to the Bulgarian peasantry, and then compare both with the future which fancy can readily portray of what might be, were capital to be freely applied in British agriculture; and a burning desire must stimulate the intelligence, the conscientious regard for duty, and the aroused patriotism (never dull, though at times unheeding) of the landed gentry of Great Britain, to sweep away the finance companies and the ill-controlled credit, which, through a lavish waste of capital on foreign nations, are sowing seeds of national decay.

Thus, whether we consider the condition of British commerce, manufactures, or agriculture, the one cause of decadence in these interests which confronts us, is the too free employment abroad of British capital, because the richest field for its employment at home, viz. British agriculture, is closed to the English investor. Even the savings of the farmers are sent abroad, instead of fertilising their own fields.

This brings us back to the radical evil in the credit and currency system of England; an evil which can be destroyed only by dealing a death-blow to financing.

[1] *Lombard Street*, page 132.

The extent of the evil is thus stated by Mr. Bagehot:—

'English money is borrowable money. Our people are bolder in dealing with their money than any Continental nation, and even if they were not bolder, the mere fact that their money is deposited in a bank makes it far more obtainable. A million in the hands of a single banker is a great power; he can at once lend it where he will, and borrowers can come to him because they know or believe that he has it. But the same sum scattered in tens and fifties, through a whole nation, is no power at all; no one knows where to find it, or whom to ask for it. Concentration of money in banks, though not the sole cause, is the principal cause, which has made the money market of England so exceedingly rich, so much beyond that of other countries. The effect is seen constantly. We are asked to lend, and do lend, vast sums, which it would be impossible to obtain elsewhere. It is sometimes said that any civilised foreign country can borrow in Lombard Street, at a price * * There are very few civilised foreign governments that could not borrow considerable sums of us if they choose * * It is true that English bankers are not themselves very great lenders to foreign states; but they are great lenders to those who lend—they advance on foreign stocks, as the phrase is, with 'a margin'; that is, they find eighty per cent. of the money, and the nominal lender finds the rest. And it is in this way that vast works are achieved with English aid, which, but for that aid, would never have been planned.'

The country banks which receive deposits in the rural districts send to London for investment the portion which they cannot locally employ. Mr. Bagehot thus describes the flow of deposits to London:—

'There are whole districts in England which cannot and do not employ their own money. No purely agricultural county does so. The savings of a county with good land, but no manufactures and no trade, much exceed what can be safely lent in the county. These savings are first lodged in the local banks, are by them sent to London, and are deposited with London bankers or with the bill brokers. The money thus sent up from the accumulating districts is employed in discounting the bills of the industrial district. Deposits are made with the bankers and bill brokers in Lombard Street by the bankers of such counties as Somersetshire and Hampshire, and those bill brokers and bankers employ them in the discount of bills from Yorkshire and Lancashire.'

In this manner the savings of the country are gathered into banks in London, where they are quite handy for borrowers on foreign as well as on domestic account. The joint-stock banks transfer the portion of their shares of these deposits which they cannot employ, to the bill brokers on interest. Thus the deposits of the farmer or the country gentleman, which he had entrusted to a private bank of local repute, and which the banker transferred to a joint-stock bank in London with a paid-up capital, is made over to a bill broker. In this manner deposits exceeding in amount the note circulation of the United Kingdom pass into the keeping of bill brokers; and the Legislature, which regards with jealousy the issue of notes by country banks, is unconcerned about the danger to the system of currency and credit of the United Kingdom, from the combination of the uncontrolled functions of bill broker and banker.

Formerly, the bill broker was a mere commission agent between the drawer of the bill and the bank which discounted it; the bank was constrained, in such a transaction, to satisfy itself of the good character of the bill, while the broker was interested in not presenting bad bills for discount. Since the bill brokers have received deposits on interest, they have attracted large deposits, and have acquired, in consequence, credit, on which, rather than on the goodness of the bills, banks now rely on lending money on the security of the bills, instead of discounting them. Thus, of the two checks by which the character of a bill was tried, one, by the bill broker before the discounting of it, has been discontinued, thereby adding a new element of insecurity. Again, the facility with which the bill broker obtains, on interest, deposits from the public, often without his giving any security, and gets advances from a bank on deposit of unguaranteed bills, encourages him to be not very particular about the character of the bills which he discounts with deposits on which he would lose interest if he did not discount the bills. The sums advanced by banks to bill brokers are the invested part of the banks' reserves, which thus are lodged with those who are not under the same influences as a bank, for the cautious discounting of bills. And lastly, the bill brokers are constrained to undersell the Bank of England in their rate of discount.

Bill brokers are perforce indispensable; but it may be doubted whether the old class of brokers, which was not concerned in discounting bills by means of deposits, was not fully as serviceable for all the legitimate requirements of trade. Anyhow, it is certain that the brokers' employment of deposits in discounting bills has a prejudicial effect on the system of currency and credit in the kingdom, by providing a less secure investment for bankers' balances than is desirable, and by paralysing the control of the Bank of England over the rate of interest. As Mr. Bagehot pointed out, 'under a more natural system, no part of the banking reserve would ever be lodged at the bill brokers.'

Stock brokers happily do not receive deposits; but 'they lend large sums on foreign bonds, or railway shares, or other such securities, and borrow these sums from bankers, depositing the securities with the bankers, and generally, though not always, giving their guarantee.' This is financing, and not brokerage business; stock brokers as such have no occasion to borrow on the securities which, within their legitimate functions, they have simply to transfer from the vendor to the purchaser, on his paying the purchase-money. The gains, with the usual penalty of occasional losses incidental to these borrowings, give an unhealthy stimulus to a class of business which more particularly attracts and encourages traffic in foreign securities.

The noxious result of this departure by stock brokers from their proper functions is to provide a less secure investment for bankers' balances than is desirable, and to draw some of the banks into the business of financing, as distinguished from legitimate banking.

The baneful influence of bill brokers and stock brokers upon the system of currency and credit in the country might be prevented, in a measure, by restricting loans to both, and the flow of deposits to the former. The gradual floating of some 120 millions of exchequer bills of the English Treasury and *quasi*-exchequer bills to be issued by the Secretary of State for India, would withdraw bankers' balances from the brokers; and with the increasing need for a safe investment of this kind, that amount might be enlarged. The Indian Secretary of State's exchequer bills would not increase the amount of Indian debt held in England, for a corresponding amount of sterling loans bearing higher interest could be discharged.

Next: the bill brokers and the joint-stock banks obtain on interest enormous deposits. The rates formerly allowed were so high as three, four, and five per cent.; but since the accumulation of unemployed funds in London, they have been reduced. To a great extent the practice must have ceased. The rates of interest, observed the 'Economist' of August 4, 1877, were 'especially attractive to the classes at the two extremes of the general and mercantile public, namely, the humbler people whose savings are in fifties and hundreds, and the great commercial houses whose occasional surpluses are scores of thousands. For the public safety, the allowance of interest by banks and brokers, on deposits withdrawable under one month's notice, might cease; and if the land laws be revised, so as to make verification of titles easy, and the transfer of title cheap and expeditious, a new class of banks would spring up, which, by profitable advances on land, could outbid the joint-stock banks and bill brokers, in the allowance of interest to depositors. The overshadowing influence of the present holders of the mass of deposits in the country would be destroyed; and the Bank of England would resume its former control over the rate of interest. The action of credit, through the deposits with bill brokers and with joint-stock banks, on the banking reserve of the Bank of England, would cease; for the new class of banks that would lend on mortgages of land would not be affected by the commercial crises which gather force from the weakening or distribution of what to a great extent is personal credit.

With such a revision of the land laws as might freely attract capital to land, the yield of land would be nearly doubled; that is to say, the country would pay for some ten million quarters of wheat less to foreign countries. At 45*s*. a quarter, this would reduce by above twenty millions the casual indebtedness which now causes a drain of gold. Similarly, with a prosperous agriculture, the home market for manufactures would be enlarged; that is to say, the charges for interest and for depreciation of stock and plant, which now heavily weight the costs of production, would be paid, perhaps entirely, from the extra profit on the home trade; and England would then be enabled to export to foreign countries at a reduction upon present prices, even though wages and raw materials were not cheapened.

These two influences in lessening the foreign drain would be supplemented by the settlement of a great mass of the transactions between India and the West, through mere transfers in the accounts of the Bank of England, as explained in a previous chapter.

The continuous drain of gold from London to the country might also be corrected by a re-coinage of the English silver currency, and an enlargement of the limits of legal tender for silver. If 20 per cent. more silver be put into the shilling, the limit could be safely enlarged. A subsidiary paper currency, of which the notes (£1 to £3) might be payable in silver, should also be issued. The silver shilling might be legal tender up to one hundred shillings; the subsidiary paper currency payable in silver could be legal tender up to one hundred pounds. It was stated in evidence before the Select Committee on Banks of Issue in 1875, that sovereigns and half-sovereigns (more especially the latter) are largely employed in periodical settlements of wages, but that they quickly return from circulation, being soon replaced by silver. It cannot be doubted that a silver currency of legal tender up to one hundred shillings, sustaining a subsidiary paper currency of legal tender up to one hundred pounds, would effectually stop the autumnal drain of gold. The considerations which restrict the amount of legal tender of a subsidiary metallic currency have not the same force in limiting the legal tender of a subsidiary paper currency payable in silver; hence the larger limit of one hundred pounds which is suggested for the latter.

It will be said that gold coins displaced by the enlarged silver currency here suggested would be exported, and that thereby the stock of gold in the country would be diminished. But no harm would arise. For any purposes which gold serves in a crisis, the gold coins in circulation, in *strata* of society where silver would displace gold, might just as well not be there. The gold thus circulating among the people would certainly not be returned to the Bank in a time of crisis; while the action of a panic (through the deposits) upon the gold reserve is too intense to be affected by any amounts of gold which, under present circumstances, could by special efforts be collected out of the amount in retail circulation.

Thus, we see that if the City, instead of shrieking when gold temporarily leaves a country to which all other countries are indebted, would resolutely set about a reform of the English system of credit and currency, it would shake off an oppressive nightmare.

At the same time, the reform would secure other vital

interests. Unless the produce of the land be nearly doubled by a free application of capital, the wages fund for improving the condition of agricultural labourers cannot be increased, and the growing foreign competition would necessitate a fall of rents. During the transition the relations between landlords and tenants would be strained, and Mr. Arch might find an accession of followers among the farmers. At the same time a diminished market for home manufactures, coinciding with a lessened demand from abroad, would widen the breach between Labour and Capital.

When the agitation for free trade began, masters and workmen in the manufacturing districts were arrayed against landowners and farmers. The consummation of free trade finds England isolated by a barrier of protective duties against her on every side; and at this critical time, when from every feeling of patriotism and humanity, and from a sense of responsibility for the duties of wealth and property, England should present an united front to the world, she is tending to the worst form of disunion—a widening gulf of separation between rich and poor, between capital and labour, masters and workmen, landlords and those who live on their estates.

Inordinate luxury, an infallible sign of a country's approaching decay, appears to be stealing over the nation, though happily its incipient growth can be easily stopped: amongst the rich, a luxury of land, which weakens a sense of the duties of property, by extreme indulgence of the craving for social distinction; among the poor, the luxury of drunkenness, which enervates, excites a craving for short time, deteriorates the quality of labour, and creates a sullen disposition towards capital. Among both, a luxury which by lessening production threatens a growth of pauperism, ignorance, and vice; attests the failure of property in the main duty which is the only charter of its rights that a revolution would respect (because an increase or decline of production means the well-being or wretchedness of those who live on the land); and proclaims that among a people whose energy and enterprise spread British commerce over the world, a proportion of the labouring poor, sufficiently large to procure a reduction of hours of labour, are too enervated and listless to care to raise their scale of well-being by work. In the country, a luxury which, stealing over both rich and poor, will enervate the vigour and destroy the life of the nation.

Sumptuary laws are accepted as a necessity when luxury has begun to eat into the vitals of a nation; and as a drunken Englishman is at the base, while the perfect English gentleman is at the summit of humanity, it is hardly too strong an expression to say that our statesmen and our Parliament will be undutiful to their country if they any longer neglect to grapple effectively with the vice of drunkenness. In a climate like that of England, the moderate use of liquor must perhaps be accepted as a necessity; but, as with sumptuary laws, so in dealing with what, among the poor, generally passes from a necessary to a luxurious indulgence, the object of an excise reform should be, not to prohibit the use of liquor, but to keep it at some distance from, or in some way to make an excessive supply of it difficult of attainment by, those who are prone to turn indulgence into a vice. This has been accomplished among the European soldiers in India with the happiest results.

As to the luxury of land: we borrow the phrase from the advocates of letting things remain as they are, who contend that so long as land is a luxury for which persons are willing to pay a fancy price, it is vain to talk about measures for facilitating the application of capital to land; the buyers at a fancy price must keep out those who could invest only at a remunerative price. Mr. Goschen, however, has taught us that there are two ways of looking at the same thing. In a country with overflowing riches, where the land produces only half of what it could yield under a sufficient application of capital to it, one half of the land is a luxury in which the country indulges, on a scale of extravagance for which it would be difficult to find a parallel. As England cannot claim exemption from the usual fate of spendthrifts, she must be content to abdicate her commercial and political supremacy if she continues this profligate waste of God's gifts: a waste which, to gratify a petty craving for social distinction, keeps myriads who live on the land in a wretched state of existence, and causes the strength, the bone and sinews of the nation to deteriorate, from poor food on scanty wages. For this waste there must be moral retribution; and for a nation, the only moral retribution is in this world, namely, in its decline and fall.

This division of the land into large estates,—with proprietors who have failed in their principal duty, inasmuch as the land produces only half of what it should,—with agricultural labourers who are wretchedly poor, and with farmers who are nowhere, for any interest they have in laying out capital on improvements—is a condition of things which is morally deteriorating to the landowners and to the country. If the landowners who have received their estates from ancestors that have handed down ennobling traditions of many generations, only knew their true interest and that of their country, they would systematically pursue the object of raising, from among their tenantry, farmers into proprietors of land, through the help which banks would afford under a revision of the land laws, and their rural labourers generally so much higher in the scale of education and living, that frugality and intelligence would create gradations even among them. The agricultural interest thus organised, with compact and serried ranks, would lead the public opinion which now it only follows. The respect of the rich for the poor, which these relations would foster, would send upwards a current of healthful manly feeling, instinctive in the mass of the Anglo-Saxon race, which would countervail the enfeebling influence of commerce.

Commerce may bring wealth, but a nation's manly resolute will is derived from its agriculture, from the children of the soil. When the influence of the owners of land predominates, whatever may be its other defects, the spirit of the nation will at least be manly, and daring in deeds of high emprise. Commerce is the handmaid of civilisation; land should remain her master. The associations that arouse patriotism or awaken the martial ardour which has built up the English empire, are connected with land. England's proud boast is of her virgin soil; her resolve is that no nation shall invade her land. Her armies go forth to fight not for merchandise; the thin red line which has carried British armies to distinction and renown followed colours on which were inscribed various counties of rural England, Ireland, or Scotland. The militia is still a rural institution. The traditions of the sacrifices, and of the endurance in long-continued struggles and unequal contests, by which England gained her supremacy among the nations, have been transmitted to us from a time when the resolute will that governed her foreign policy was derived from the land.

We flatter ourselves that we have changed all this for the better. We profess to desire peace for all nations; and, with England's supremacy among them,—that is, with a place accorded to her in the first rank of the special constables who are sworn to prevent breaches of the peace and of international law, by the timely use (not merely by an exhibition) of their batons as special constables,—England's duty it is to preserve order; but, in spite of all this profession of peace, and of the influence which we are supposed to exercise in Europe, somehow nations with prodigious armaments, prodigious debts, prodigious taxes, have multiplied under our policy of peace at any price.

We profess more morality and humanitarianism in our

foreign policy; but somehow, the nations, instead of admiring the spirit of our policy, think that our acts are shifty, not manly and straightforward; that we are not reliable friends; and though not cowardly foes (the courage and might of England have been too clearly established for that, by past governments of landlords), but still, foes of not any account, for we wont fight. And when, to disabuse a mistaken scepticism, we tell the nations that we will fight, we are careful to impress upon them that we will fight not from any generous recognition of our duty to allies, or of our duty, as among the first of the nations, to take an active, effectual part in supporting the side of order, but for 'British interests:' a phrase which smacks of commerce.

The first Napoleon had a political insight at least as keen as Prince Bismarck's, with a military genius at least as great as Von Moltke's, in handling great armies, and more brilliant in the struggles of an unequal contest. Yet England quailed not, felt no sense of inferiority, when that man closed Europe against her. In the present day she is content to acknowledge, once France, next Germany, as the leading power in Europe. In that earlier period the resolute will of the landlords governed the foreign policy of England, which in the present day is shaped by the less healthful instincts of commerce.

The resolute will of England's former statesmen must now be sought in Germany, in France, in the United States, where the influence of land is supreme.

The patriotism, the generosity, the self-sacrifice, the noble instincts which the landed gentry have inherited from ancestors whose deeds are cherished traditions of Englishmen, are not dead. The sense of duty which has ever animated them is still a power that can revolutionise the agricultural districts of England in the spirit of a true conservatism, unlike the revolution that, at no distant time, may otherwise sweep over them. The evil is known, the remedy is apparent; the application is in their hands. A great and rapid improvement of the agricultural districts is required to preserve the strength of the nation, energise its forces, sustain its manufactures, help the reform of its system of currency and commerce, close the widening breach between rich and poor, and unite in the bonds of mutual dependence, all classes in the seagirt isle which may soon need all the strength of her sons. For soon may she have to withstand, as of yore, towering ambitions, and, at the end of the struggle, to compel a general disarmament, and so deliver the nations from a burden that is cruelly bowing down their backs, and oppressing them with a misery worse than the Bulgarian massacres, because it is a misery worse than death.

Our subject was gold: the getting more of it; the loss which the country would sustain, the fearful injury to the commercial and industrial system that would result, from losing any of it; and the solution we arrive at is,—lift up the agricultural poor from their slough of despond, rescue the masses of the English population from the one vice which neutralises their many virtues; and through the beneficial results which will follow, heal the breach that is widening between rich and poor. The disorders in the world of commerce have been caused by the indebtedness of nations, mainly from bloated armaments kept up for the ambition of mighty empires, from much borrowing for rash or dishonest speculations in the haste to get rich, and to rise thereby in the social scale. The spirit of progress—of nations to power, of men towards wealth—broke away from the spirit of religion; but the schemes of the mighty are confounded. The nations most ambitious, and with the largest armies, are seething with discontent; in the country most engaged in getting wealth, productive forces are being paralysed by a growth of drunkenness, which creates a sullen temper towards capital, and by the wretched condition of agricultural districts that would have revived the realities of a once happy England, if there had been directed into them one hundredth part of the fertilising streams of wealth that flowed to foreign countries, under the disastrous effect of the land laws. The result, everywhere, is a growing separation of rich from poor — of capital from labour. The remedy is, to catch the spirit of the teachings of the carpenter's Son; and it is an encouraging circumstance that at the present time, the Church of England, the organisation best fitted for the work, is awakening to the necessity of making the rich and poor bear one another's burdens: the poor, by having charity for the rich; the rich, by having respect for the poor, and lifting them from the mire of ignorance, drunkenness, and vice.

CHAPTER X.

CAUSES OF THE DEPRESSION OF TRADE.

OUR ramble in the last chapter was with a purpose: it brought under survey subjects seemingly apart, but which are intimately connected, namely, the prospects of British manufactures and agriculture, amid a growing separation of rich from poor; and a mechanism of currency and credit in England, so delicate that it may any day snap under the rude touch of a foreign hand. We saw, in a general way, that the causes of the universal depression of trade, which has continued now for above four years, must permanently bear down British industry, unless certain measures be adopted which, additionally, would brace up and strengthen the system of credit and currency in England. It will repay us to investigate the first part of this subject in a little more detail.

2. For a prosperous foreign trade, a country must depend on—

I. NATURAL ADVANTAGES.

(*a*) *Soil.*—The yield of wheat in the United Kingdom is two and a half times that in the United States, Russia, and Hungary; but this arises mainly from expensive farming.

(*b*) *Minerals* (*coal and iron*) *indispensable to manufactures.* The great extension of railways on the Continent and in the United States (mainly with British capital) developed abroad mining industries, and at home improved old mines and opened out new ones. The aggregate result was, *first*, a vast increase of yearly production; *secondly*, a great rise of prices, soon accompanied, through the custom in these industries, by a considerable rise of wages. With the completion of the railways, the extra demand has ceased; but the extra production has not, from the difficulty of closing works on which capital has been sunk, and from a reluctance to disperse skilled labourers. In consequence, the relations between masters and workmen, as determined by wages, are strained, particularly in England; and matters will not right themselves until the fall in the prices of coal and iron shall have destroyed the production on the Continent and in the United States. The present difficulty is nothing more than the competition of British capital, exported abroad through finance companies and stock-brokers, with the British capital invested at home in mining enterprise.

(c) *Labour.*—Skilled labour is an acquired advantage, but we may consider both it and unskilled labour under the present division. When England entered on her career of free-trade, she had a great pull over the numerous Roman Catholic countries on the Continent in her much fewer holidays; but she has surrendered this advantage in her now short hours of labour. Again, she had, and to this day she retains, a superiority in the greater strength, activity, earnestness in work, and endurance of her labourers; but much of these advantages she has surrendered by her acquiescence in a frightful increase of drunkenness. There is a consequent sullenness in the disposition of workmen towards employers, which the latter have begun to withstand in a way that is not for the country's good, viz., by importing foreign labour and exporting British capital, thus burning the candle at both ends. Of like noxious character are the combinations among workmen, for wages irrespective of results or of the quality of labour. Again, though the percentage of rise of wages since 1848, among agricultural labourers, has been great, yet the actual amount of wages compares unfavourably with that in other industries, mainly from the insufficient production obtained from the land, owing to the restricted capital which is laid out on it, the result being a migration from agriculture to other employments, and an increase of permanent pasturage, as when Rome began to decline.

Lastly, while short hours, intemperance, and combinations among workmen for wages irrespective of skill, have been diminishing the efficiency of British labour—on the Continent and in the United States skilled labour is being multiplied through the influence of those railways and canals which British capital has helped to create; for wherever these are in operation, there springs up a local demand for various handicrafts, which creates a local supply.

II. Acquired Advantages.

(a) *A large home market.*—When the home market is large, proportionately to the foreign trade, the profits on the home trade, probably, cover wear and tear and interest on the capital sunk in buildings, machinery, and plant. When this is the case, the manufacturers are able to push their wares in foreign markets. In 1845, the proportion of England's home trade to her foreign was very great; and conversely, on the Continent and in the United States, the proportion of home manufactures to British goods, in their own markets for those goods, was comparatively small. In 1877, the proportions at home and abroad are reversed. England's home market now bears but a small proportion to her foreign, thus throwing on her exports to foreign countries a greater burden in respect of wear and tear, buildings, and plant. Had the production of the land greatly advanced in the interval, in England, even though some way behind the foreign trade, things would have been more favourable to British industry.

(b) *Cheaper raw materials than are available to other countries.*—Until the opening of the Suez Canal, England obtained her raw materials from the East, at a cheaper price than the countries on the Continent. This advantage has been lost.

(c) *Communications, viz., railways and canals.*—In both these respects England had great advantages over other nations when she began that course of free-trade and of international lending, which has resulted in raising up against her a barrier of protective duties in every country on the Continent, except Turkey and Portugal. Since then, to the countries which try to do without her manufactures, England has, in the past eighteen years, lavishly given her capital for the construction of railways and canals; and on Turkey, which has readily received her merchandise, England has bestowed her staunch generous friendship. The result is a greater internal trade in the countries benefited by English capital, which, with an increase of taxation—including increase of customs duties—for paying interest on the sums freely lent for bloated armaments on the Continent, by England, the apostle of peace at any price, has restricted the continental markets for British manufactures.

(b) *Machinery and implements.*—With the extension of railways abroad, through British capital, and the growth of protective duties and of local manufactures, on account of huge borrowings by foreign Governments, the advantage under these heads is not so great to England now as in 1848.

(c) *Capital.*—In this respect, too, England began her career of free-trade under great advantages. Before 1848, and down to 1860 or 1862, British capital was but little employed in industries on the Continent, which compete with British manufactures; and if the foreign countries had been left to improve their means of competition, by acquisitions of capital out of their savings, the competition to this day might have been comparatively unimportant. But British capital was exported to the Continent, mainly through the instrumentality of finance companies;—and the result in the present day is a stagnation of foreign demand for British manufactures.

3. The foregoing statement of facts is, apparently, directed in part against free-trade; but the facts would be misread, were any lesson adverse to free-trade to be drawn from them. The main lesson which they convey is, that England began her career of free-trade with certain advantages, which gave her superior facilities for a profitable foreign trade; and that she surrendered these advantages, one by one, chiefly, nay entirely, by the exportation of British capital through finance companies, and in loans to foreign Governments. Even the combinations among workmen, which led to short hours and a deterioration of the quality of British labour, are attributable to this exportation of British capital, which caused the inflation of prices, and the consequent advance of wages that afterwards augmented the power of trades-unions, when the subsidence of inflated prices brought on the struggle, by workmen, against a consequent reduction of wages.

4. The practical deduction from this lesson is, that British capital should be more freely spent at home, in stimulating British industry, and that the pernicious working of the finance companies should be stopped.

5. But, in order that British capital may be more freely employed at home, it is necessary that the home market for British manufactures should be enlarged, and that facilities should be provided for that investment of capital in the land which, according to the testimony of Lord Leicester and the Earl of Derby, would nearly double its produce. The object is worthy of the patriotism of England's landed gentry, and it cannot be attained, except through their initiation of reforms conceived in a spirit of true conservatism.

6. The objection, that in some parts of England the soil

does not admit of an outlay of capital in large farming, is not of much account;—because those districts are the best for applying the lessons that France, her peasant proprietors, and the solid position of the Bank of France, teach England in respect of the efficiency, and the conservative tendency, of the system of peasant proprietorship for that kind of agriculture in which the land requires minute husbandry, and the steady gradual improvements that are accumulated upon it from the yearly savings of peasant proprietors, such as those who bought back from foreign countries a great part of the War Indemnity Loan.

7. The only effects which we have considered, as yet, of the too free exportation of British capital to foreign countries since 1860, are, *first*, the inflation of production and prices, with their subsequent collapse, and the disorganisation of the relations between masters and workmen; *secondly*, the imposition abroad of protective duties for meeting the charge for interest on foreign loans, and the consequent growth of local manufactures. Outside France, the borrowing by foreign States was accompanied by increased issues of inconvertible paper money, which depreciated the currency. When, to this depreciation of the paper currency, was added the further depreciation of silver, the difficulty of remitting interest to the foreign holders of securities increased, and, with it, increased the disadvantage of holding those securities abroad, and of sending goods to the countries on the Continent whose silver currency was depreciated. Securities were consequently returned to the borrowing countries; that is to say, these countries had to buy back their securities by an increase of exports, which, abroad, sent down the price of those exports, and presented the appearance of a rise in the value of gold.

8. Similar results, though from a different cause, happened in silver-using countries like India, which are solvent; the depreciation of silver, and the consequent fall in the

sterling exchange with the rupee, acted like a bounty on exports, so that increased quantities of Asiatic products were sent to Europe, to the lowering of their gold price abroad. Excepting tea, these products have not a monopoly of the Western markets; they compete there with other Western products, which are used for the same purposes as the Asiatic. It has necessarily resulted that the depreciation of silver has brought down the price of both Western and Eastern productions in respect of those articles in which the two hemispheres compete.

9. But the effect has not stopped there: the Western countries, whose products have depreciated in the London and Paris markets from the competition of Asiatic produce, have thereby lost some of their purchasing power, with the result, necessarily, of reducing their imports of foreign commodities.

10. Apparently, then, the purchase back of their securities by many States in Europe, and the depreciation of silver, have greatly contributed to the stagnation of trade. And the indefinite prolongation of the second cause, while silver may steadily fall every year, would be terrible. It may suit the East foolishly to give a bounty on exports to the West, by retaining as money silver which continues to depreciate; but will it consist with the wisdom of the West to receive the Asiatic products in exchange, not for Western merchandise, but for Californian silver, which will displace the exports of that merchandise? Especially, will the West remain passive under the decadence not merely of its export trade to the East, but partly of the trade among occidental countries themselves? Asiatic exports (continually increasing under the stimulus of the silver bounty)—would gradually expel from European markets, first one, then some other competing Western product, and (with it) the manufacture (British or other) for which that product may have exchanged in those markets. In fact, the depreciation of silver, rela-

tively to gold, means the depreciation in the West of all Asiatic produce,—that is, its competition there, on terms ruinous to all rival Western agricultural produce, and depressing to all Western manufactures for which, practically, that produce used to be exchanged.

The demonetisation of silver would stop this ruinous competition, without raising the value of gold; for the silver rupee Council drafts, which now reduce the price of silver in London, would, with the force of 15 millions sterling, a year, of gold rupee drafts, prevent an enhancement of the value of gold.

The relief to the cotton industry would be instantaneous; and the new competition from Indian wheat, with which the British farmer is threatened, would be averted. A period of respite would be obtained for British trade, during which measures for invigorating the agricultural and manufacturing industries of the kingdom could be considered.

Two papers in the Appendix show the unpromising character of the cotton and agricultural industries. Respecting the latter we give, on p. 143, a table of statistics taken from the 'Chamber of Agriculture Journal.'

The acreage is for the calendar year; the other figures are for the harvest years, from 1st September to 31st August. Thus 1866 represents the harvest year 1866–67. There is some error in the acreage for 1877; the increase in that year over 1876, in Great Britain, having been inconsiderable.

It has been said that, even with its utmost efforts, British agriculture could not provide sufficient wheat for an ever-increasing population, and that, accordingly, what British agriculture cannot supply must be obtained from abroad. But, firstly, it cannot be maintained that, even years back, when British agriculture provided more than 12 million quarters a year of corn, it was unequal, if only there were a free application of capital to the land, to the provision of nearly double the quantity, that is, of the whole yearly requirement. We have the testimony of Earl Derby and Lord Leicester, that the produce of the land can be nearly doubled in the way indicated. Moreover, the figures show that foreign corn does not merely supply what British agriculture cannot provide. The provision by the latter has fallen off by 3 or 3½ million quarters, and the supply from abroad has increased by rather more than that. The British cultivation of wheat has been retrograding; that of oats too, on which Mr. Caird relied for making good the decline in wheat cultivation, has been falling off; and the very greatly increased imports of maize are assailing, with a close competition, all the grains which are used for distillation, or as food for cattle. Lastly, the fast developing trade with North and South America, in meat and cattle, will attack British agriculture in that its last stronghold, which is also the first marked symptom of a decay of the British Empire that, happily, can yet be averted.

The influences adverse to British agriculture arise from the competition, first, of the American farmers, who do not pay rent; second, of indebted nations, like Hungary and Russia, that are forced to export agricultural produce to pay interest on debt: as the debts increase, the force of this influence increases, and how greatly it has augmented of late years, all the world knows; third, the depreciation of silver, which affects principally agricultural countries, and which, in the solvent silver-using countries in the East, acts like a bounty on the export of wheat and of other agricultural produce to the world's market, viz., England. A passive acquiescence in the effect of these tremendous influences will certainly not help to sustain and strengthen British agriculture, which ought to be the best customer of British manufactures. Special measures are necessary. One of the influences can be extirpated by the demonetisation of silver; the other two can be counteracted by investing capital freely in land, for this will have the double effect of withdrawing part of the British capital now floating abroad, and so reducing the indebtedness to England of the competing agricultural countries, and of invigorating British agriculture, even to the doubling, wellnigh, of the production of the land, whereby the English farmer will not succumb on his own soil to foreign agriculture.

WHEAT CROPS OF THE UNITED KINGDOM.

(*Three 000's omitted.*)

	Acres	Yield per Acre	Available Consumption after deducting Seed	Imports of Wheat and Flour during the Harvest Year, less Exports	Total available for Consumption	Average Price of British Wheat for 12 Months, July 1 to June 30
		Bushels	Quarters	Quarters	Quarters	s. d.
1866	3,661	27	11,440	7,600	19,040	58 0
1867	3,640	25	10,390	9,010	19,400	69 3
1868	3,951	34	15,790	7,880	23,670	51 8
1869	3,982	27	12,490	9,580	22,070	45 11
1870	3,773	32	14,100	7,950	22,050	53 5
1871	3,831	27	11,970	9,320	21,290	55 3
Average	3,806	—	12,696	8,557	21,253	—
1872	3,840	23	10,110	11,720	21,830	57 1
1873	3,670	25	10,550	11,230	21,780	61 3
1874	3,833	31	13,700	11,640	25,340	46 4
1875	3,514	23	9,124	13,940	23,064	46 3
1876	3,125	27	9,668	12,150	21,818	55 3
1877	3,821	24	9,035	(13,465)	(22,500)	—
Average	3,550	—	10,364	12,357	22,722	—

The increasing dependence of England on foreign corn must be painful and alarming to every feeling of patriotism; and perhaps, unhappily, one would indulge in truth and sober sadness, more than in fancy, were he to trace the coincidence between the decadence of British agriculture and the decadence, in England's foreign policy, of the undaunted spirit and the resolute will which marked that policy in the days of forefathers whom we are proud of, without emulating; that is, in days when the influence of land on the spirit and in the councils of the country was supreme.

Thus the highest interests of the nation, even its national existence, call for the revision of the land laws, in a spirit of hearty co-operation by landlords, such as shall promote the free application of capital to the land, and enable the landlords to initiate, and steadily pursue, a policy of lifting all classes that are now engaged in agriculture in the scale of well-being. The instincts of a generous patriotism would find in this policy the double reward of not only reviving the manly spirit, the contentment, and the kindly social relations of once happy rural England, but also of restoring the prosperity of British manufactures, and so effectually healing those differences between masters and workmen which, else, may widen into an impassable gulf of separation of rich from poor at a time when England may, any day, have to withstand an irruption of the barbarians.

With the elevation and prosperity of the agricultural classes, and with an enlarged home market for British manufactures, the Bank of England would soon attain to the solid position of the Bank of France.

CHAPTER XI.

INDIA CAN NO LONGER ENDURE A SILVER CURRENCY.

Non possumus—we cannot give the gold, is the thought, if not the reply, of many in England, when a gold currency for India is proposed. *Non possumus*—we cannot afford to remain as we are, is India's reply to those who tell her that she must be content with her silver currency.

The simple fact is, that the revenue of India does not expand so fast or freely as to be able to overtake, or even approach, in its yearly increase, the rate at which the yearly charge for loss by exchange must advance with a progressive depreciation of silver; while again, the yearly borrowing for public works expenditure extraordinary, causes a progressive augmentation of the charge for interest at the rate of above £200,000 a year.

If, for instance, we take the gross revenue, the amount shows but feeble progression since 1869–70, thus—

(Millions sterling.)

1863–4	44·42	1867–8	48·53	1871–2	50·11	1875–6	51·31
1864–5	45.17	1868–9	49·26	1872–3	50·22	1876–7	50·28
1865–6	46·42	1869–70	50·90	1873–4	49·60	1877–8	51·26
1866–7	48·53	1870–1	51·41	1874–5	50·57		

From 1863–4 to 1867–8 the increase of revenue was four millions, or, excluding income tax (which was £830,000 less in 1867–8 than in 1863–4) the increase was nearly five millions; 1877–8 shows an excess of 2¾ millions compared with 1867–8, and of only one-third of a million compared with 1869–70. Since 1870–1 the revenue has been stationary, with a tendency to decline.

Comparing similarly the growth of the charges for interest on debt, loss by exchange, and net military expenditure, we find—

(*Millions sterling.*)

	1863–4	1867–8	1869–70	1870–1	1871–2	1873–4	1875–6	1876–7	1877–8
Interest . . .	4·69	4·91	4·98	5·31	5·47	5·25	5·18	5·41	5·65
Loss by exchange .	·24	·21	·30	·74	·45	·99	1·43	2·14	1·60
	4·93	5·12	5·37	6·05	5·92	6·24	6·61	7·55	7·25
Gain by railway exchange . .	—	—	·25	·30	·26	·33	·36	·42	·35
Net military expenditure . . .	13·50	15·34	15·25	15·12	14·78	14·22	14·26	15·30	15·35

We have seen that the revenue for 1877–8 shows an excess of only one-third million over that of 1869–70, while the items of interest and loss by exchange show an excess of nearly two millions, after deducting gain by railway exchange; the excess of charge has been met by a decrease of ordinary Public Works' expenditure since 1869–70 to the extent of £2,200,000. Henceforth that saving will not be available to meet the progressive charge under these two unsightly heads of interest and loss by exchange. India may indeed gain something by reduction of military expenditure, which has increased through the charges raised against her by the War Office on account of home expenditure for British troops serving in India, for of these charges much seems wrong and apparently illegal. But the two other progressive items would soon exhaust and outstrip any such saving.

The figures respecting interest do not show the really progressive character of that charge. In 1872–3, 16½ millions sterling of 5 per cents. of rupee loans in India were converted, viz., 2¾ millions into 4 per cents. and the remainder into 4½ per cents., from which they will drop after seven years, or in 1879–80, to 4 per cent. The actual saving of interest amounted to £93,698 a year, and the prospective saving will be £67,500. Again, in 1873–4, the capital stock of the East India Company was redeemed under arrangements which caused a saving of £450,000 a year, of which £341,516 accrued in 1874–5, and the remainder in 1875–6. Altogether the saving from these conversions of stock has amounted to £543,698 a year, so that the real increase of fresh charge for interest, since 1869–70, has been ·67 plus ·54, or 1·21 million sterling in eight years, or £150,000 a year. Latterly, however, the charge has increased at the rate of £230,000 a year; for the reason that in the earlier years large surpluses on the ordinary account kept down the borrowing for Public Works extraordinary.

We may take a closer view of the growth of revenue. To this end, it will be expedient to exclude receipts which arise out of expenditure. Such are those under Post-office, Telegraph, and Forests, Interest on Service Funds, and receipts in aid of Superannuation and Retiring allowances; also other miscellaneous items which it is not necessary to recount. The survey, thus, will be confined to the heads of revenue proper, viz., the Land revenue, the Opium revenue, the Income tax, and the indirect taxes under Excise, Customs, Salt, and Stamps. Respecting all of these, except Land revenue, a clearer idea of their growth may be obtained from the net revenue, after deducting charges of collection; but it would mislead to regard the Land revenue otherwise than in its gross amount, because the so-called charges for the collection of Land revenue are really charges for administration; being mostly for the pay and expenses of officers and establishments that are employed, in some parts of India, on magisterial duties, and in the general administration of their districts, while in other parts they are additionally employed in adjudicating civil suits, the bulk of the expense for these services would have to be incurred even were there no Land revenue or Excise or Stamp revenue to collect.

The receipts are as follows :—

(*Millions sterling.*)

	Net Revenue						Gross Land Revenue					
							Ryotwar Territories					
	Land Revenue,—Gross	Opium Revenue	Excise, Customs, Salt, and Stamps	Assessed Taxes	Canal Revenue and State Railways	Total	India and Assam	British Burmah	Madras and Bombay	Total	Under Village or Zemindary Settlements	Total
1862–3	—	—	—	—	—	—	·16	·50	7·56	8·22	11·27	19·49
1863–4	19·9	4·5	10·1	1·1	·2	35·8	·24	·52	7·76	8·52	11·41	19·93
1864–5	19·7	5·0	10·9	1·0	·2	36·8	·19	·56	7·75	8·50	11·20	19·70
1865–6	20·1	6·6	10·7	·6	·3	38·3	·22	·53	7·86	8·61	11·45	20·06
1867–8	20·0	7·0	11·8	·5	·4	39·7	·23	·58	7·86	8·67	11·31	19·98
1868–9	19·9	6·7	11·9	·5	·3	39·3	·31	·57	7·62	8·50	11·37	19·87
1869–70	21·1	6·1	12·0	1·1	·5	40·8	·70	·64	8·05	9·39	11·67	21·06
1870–1	20·6	6·0	12·6	2·0	·5	41·7	·32	·60	7·99	8·91	11·71	20·62
1871–2	20·5	7·6	12·5	·8	·5	41·9	·38	·65	7·84	8·87	11·65	20·52
1872–3	21·3	6·9	12·9	·6	·4	42·1	·39	·66	8·44	9·49	11·86	21·35
1873–4	21·0	6·3	12·9	·0	·5	40·7	·39	·75	8·14	9·28	11·76	21·04
1874–5	21·3	6·2	13·1	·0	·5	41·1	·39	·73	8·33	9·45	11·85	21·30
1875–6	21·5	6·3	13·4	·0	·6	41·8	·41	·82	8·23	9·46	12·04	21·50
1876–7 {Regr. Estimate}	20·0	6·4	13·3	·0	·6	40·3	·41	·78	6·82	8·01	11·99	20·00
1877–8 Estimate	20·9	6·2	13·4	·0	·7	41·2	·40	·79	7·74	8·93	12·01	20·94

The following remarks are suggested by this table.

I. Of the total increase of six millions since 1863–4, the Land revenue furnished only 1½ million, and we shall see presently that there is not much prospect of a material increase for some years. Omitting assessed taxes, the remaining heads increased from 15 millions in 1863–4 to 18·6 millions in 1869–70, 20·2 millions in 1872–3, and 20·3 millions in 1875–6: showing a feeble progression since 1869–70.

II. The net Opium revenue amounted, in the six years from 1863–4 to 1869–70 (omitting 1866–7, a year of eleven months) to 35·9 millions, and in the six years from 1870–1 to 1875–6 to 39·3 millions: giving a yearly average of

5·98 millions in the first period, and of 6·55 millions in the second period. In the four years from 1873-4 to 1876-7, the yearly average was somewhat less, viz., 6·3 millions. Perhaps £500,000 more can be gained by increasing the duty on Malwa opium, and selling more chests of Bengal opium.

III. Under Excise, Customs, Salt and Stamps, the revenue amounted to 10 millions in 1863-4, 12 millions in 1869-70, and 13·4 millions in 1875-6, showing an increase in twelve years of 3·3 millions, or at the rate of £275,000 a year; but the bulk of the increase, namely, 1·9 million, was obtained by 1869-70, at the rate of £316,000 a year, and the subsequent increase up to 1875-6, viz. 1·4 million, was at the rate of only £233,000 a year. The Excise revenue increased from £1,670,000 in 1863-4, by £270,000, or to £1,940,000 in the next four years up to 1867-8; and by £294,000 or to £2,234,000 in the ensuing four years to 1871-2; but this steady progression was not afterwards maintained, the yearly average of the revenue from 1872-3 to 1874-5, in which latter year it amounted to £2,259,000, having been only £2,215,000. The revenue is being made over to the local Governments to improve, on the understanding that one half of any increase may be retained by them.

IV. The Customs revenue gave a yearly average, from 1863-4 to 1867-8, of £2,192,000; it amounted in 1868-9 to £2,517,000; and its yearly average from 1869-70 to 1874-5 was £2,413,000. On the whole it has increased, mainly from the export duty on rice, the trade in which, from British Burmah, steadily increases. If the silver standard be retained for India, the revenue of £800,000 from the import duty on cotton goods will fall off; if a gold currency be introduced, the imports will improve, and with them the revenue; for Manchester would no longer press for the abolition of a duty which really acts as a protective duty in its favour (see Appendix), when once relief, manifold greater than the repeal of the duty on cotton goods, may be afforded by raising the exchange to near two shillings the rupee, by means of a gold currency.

V. The Salt revenue shows a steady progression, mainly from an increase of the salt duties, but latterly from an increase of consumption. The future progress of this revenue is uncertain; if the duties be equalised in the three Presidencies, by raising those in the minor Presidencies and lowering the duty in the Bengal Presidency, consumption may be checked in the former, while it would increase in the latter. If the consumption be checked, the result may be a decrease of revenue. In the Bengal Presidency, the reduction of duty would lower the revenue on the present amount of consumption: it cannot be predicated whether the revenue on the extra consumption would neutralise the loss from the reduction of duty, and give a surplus besides; the result must be awaited. Meanwhile, it can only be said that the prospect of any considerable increase of the salt revenue is not so sure as the certainty of a further and considerable depreciation of silver, with a consequent considerable increase of loss by exchange.

VI. The Stamp revenue has increased partly from a revision of stamp duties, principally from an increase of litigation. It increased by £340,000 in 1864–5 over the amount in 1863–4; and 1870–1 exhibited a further excess over 1864–5, of £557,000, while 1874–5 showed another advance of £243,000. Doubtless, there will be further progress; but half of any increase of the revenue will be retained by the local Governments; and, furthermore, strong opinions respecting this tax on litigation may forbid its employment for counteracting loss from the depreciation of silver, and the growth of charge for interest on account of borrowings for public works' extraordinary expenditure.

VII. The Canal revenue (gross) amounted to £358,000 in 1867–8, and the Land revenue to 20 millions. In 1875–6, the former amounted to £518,000, and the Land revenue to 21½ millions. The total increase was £1,660,000, including £160,000 of Canal revenue. The net revenue from State Railways was £74,800; but it is increasing, and the estimate for 1877–8 amounted to £171,000. Of the increase under Land revenue, much the smaller part can be credited to canals, the greater portion having accrued from lands which are not under the canal systems; and of the increase obtained on such lands, the portion due to rise of prices, to better markets afforded by the State railways, and to increase of population, must be deducted. The augmentation of fresh charge for interest since 1867–8 has amounted to 1¼ million sterling, of which the greater part was for irrigation works and State railways. The real charge for interest on the outlay for these works since 1867–8 exceeds, however, 1¼ million sterling, for a considerable portion of the outlay was provided out of the surplus on the ordinary account, which, but for this application of it, would have been employed in reducing debt. It has been held by some that the way to provide India with more water is to pour out money like water; but the great depreciation of silver will induce caution in making such experiments.

VIII. The increase of Land revenue has occurred principally in the territories under ryotwar settlements, where the revenue improves not alone from a revision of the rates of assessment once in every thirty years (or at shorter intervals of ten or twenty years in districts which are in a backward state), but also from a yearly increase of cultivation. In the provinces in the Bengal Presidency, under village settlements, the bulk of the increase of Land revenue occurs at the distant periodical revisions of settlement for twenty or thirty years, as above explained; in the interval between two settlements there are minor increases, from lapses of tenures of rent-free lands, changes in the course of rivers, and the like; but on the whole these are not of much account.

IX. In the provinces in the Bengal Presidency under village settlements, the revision of settlements was concluded in Oudh about 1874–5, in the Central Provinces a little earlier; in the North-western Provinces it has been nearly finished; in the Punjab the greater portion has been finished, and only poor and generally outlying districts remain for re-settlement. In the territories, collectively, under village settlements, the Land revenue increased from 11·27 millions in 1862–3 to 11·71 millions in 1870–1, or by £440,000; and by 1875–6 it rose to 12·04 millions by a further increase of ·33 million. The total increase from 1862-3 up to 1875–6 was £770,000 upon a revenue in 1862–3 of 11·27 millions; or, excluding the Lower Provinces of Bengal, which are under a permanent settlement, the increase was £735,000 on a revenue in 1862–3 of £7,527,000, or not quite 10 per cent, despite the great increase of prices since 1862–3. Taking the North-western Provinces and the Punjab, which contain the canal systems on which the largest expenditure for public works extraordinary has been incurred, the increase in Land revenue in 1875-6, compared with 1862–3, was £279,000, or, owing to transfers of Canal revenue from the head of Land revenue after 1862–3, we may reckon it at £479,000 or £500,000 upon a Land revenue in 1862–3 of £5,760,000; thus arriving again at an increase of rather less than 10 per cent. As even the whole of this, if credited to a rise of prices and to increase of cultivation since the pre-previous ten to thirty years' settlements, would appear to represent a not over liberal increase, but little margin, out of this augmentation of the Land revenue in the Punjab and the North-western Provinces, appears to be available for a credit to irrigation works.

X. In the territories under ryotwar settlement, the Land

revenue rose from 8·22 millions in 1862–3 to 9·46 millions in 1875-6. Of the increase of 1·24 million, £670,000 occurred in the considerable territories in the Madras and Bombay Presidencies, and all but £69,000 of the remainder in the two provinces of British Burmah and Assam. In Assam the increase amounted to £177,000, of which the greater part, viz. £134,000, occurred from a revision of assessment, and the discovery of concealed cultivation, in 1868–9 and 1869–70. By 1873–4 there was a further increase of £28,000, with another £10,000 in 1874–5, and but little improvement since. In British Burmah, there was steady progression from £495,000 in 1862–3 to £639,000 in 1869–70, and £824,000 in 1875–6, but in 1876–7 the revenue declined to £780,000. The increase has occurred partly from increase of population (for receipts from a capitation tax are included under Land revenue), partly from a revision of assessment, and the remainder from an increase of cultivation and discovery of concealed cultivation in the course of settlements. Perhaps the smallest part of the increase has been from revision of rates of assessment. On the whole, it is unlikely that the future increase of Land revenue in British Burmah and Assam will, for some years, be at the same rate as hitherto, or that it can make any sensible addition to the assets for meeting the growing loss by exchange.

XI. The increase of Land revenue in the Madras and Bombay Presidencies has been as follows:

(*Millions sterling.*)

	1863–4	Yearly Average from 1863–4 to 1868–9	1869–70	Yearly Average from 1870–1 to 1875–6	1875–6	Yearly Average from 1873–4 to 1875–6
Madras Presidency .	4·2	4·2	4·5	4·5	4·5	4·5
Bombay Presidency .	3·3	3·5	3·6	3·6	3·7	3·7

Since 1863–4, the total increase up to 1875–6 amounted

to £700,000 upon a Land revenue of 7½ millions sterling, thus again presenting what would seem to be a recognised conventional rate of 10 per cent., notwithstanding a great increase of prices. From 1863–4 to 1868–9 the Land revenue in the Madras Presidency was stationary; in the following year it increased by £300,000 to an amount at which it has since remained. In the Bombay Presidency, the increase up to 1869–70 was £300,000; in 1872–3 there was a spurt the revenue having amounted to 3·75 millions; but as in the previous year it exhibited the unusually low amount of 3·40 millions, we may reckon its permanent increase to 3·7 millions from 1873–4. There is not much scope for further improvement, for some time.

XII. Thus, we find that in the provinces of the Bengal Presidency which are under village settlements, and in the ryotwar presidencies of Madras and Bombay, the increase of Land revenue since 1863–4 has been small—barely 10 per cent. upon the amount in that year, notwithstanding a rise of prices. The reason of this inadequate increase is that an additional amount has been raised in the form of local cesses upon Land revenue, which are locally appropriated. The theory is that these cesses are a voluntary contribution by the people (over and above what could be taken from them as Land revenue), on the understanding that the money will be spent within their respective districts. The practical effect, however, is that the imperial Land revenue demand is really abated by the sum set apart as local cesses. Should the late inquiry into the condition of the Deccan ryots lead to a reduction of assessment, that reduction would imply that the local cesses, which were imposed for the first time during the period since 1863–4, were the additional feather that broke the camel's back; but the cesses would still remain, and the reduction would fall upon the imperial land revenue. The cesses are subtracted from the resources for meeting obligatory imperial expenditure, in order that they may be devoted to optional local expenditure under public works, and to education of the rural population.

From this survey of the ordinary sources of revenue it appears that—

1. The total gross revenue has shown but feeble progression since 1869–70, when it was 50·90 millions, while in 1875–6 it was only 51·31 millions sterling.

2. Under Land revenue the total increase has been two millions since 1862–3, or 1½ million since 1863–4. The greater part of this occurred in the territories under ryotwar settlement, viz., £1,200,000 since 1862–3, or £940,000 since 1863–4. Nearly the whole of this increase occurred by 1874–5, after which the revenue dropped by £100,000 in the Madras Presidency in 1875–6, while it remained stationary in the Bombay Presidency and in Assam, and gained in British Burmah an increase of £100,000, of which about a third was lost in following years. Beyond a comparatively small rate of yearly increase in British Burmah, there is little expectation of further improvement of the land revenue, for some years, in the territories under ryotwar settlement. And in those under village settlements in the Bengal Presidency, what increase was to be got by a revision of settlements has been nearly all gathered in; the settlements in Oudh and the Central Provinces have been finished, those in the North-western Provinces have been nearly completed, and what remains in the Punjab is the resettlement of some poor or outlying districts, from which no material gain can be expected.

3. Any further increase of the Opium revenue is purely speculative, the sale of a larger number of chests of Bengal opium, and a further increase of the duty on Malwa opium, would probably yield half a million sterling a year; but those who are answerable for managing the Indian finances might reject any irresponsible opinion of this kind.

4. Under the remaining heads, the future progress of the Salt revenue is uncertain; the Customs revenue must decline, without the adoption of a gold currency; the half of any increase of the Stamp revenue will be appropriated by local governments; the portion thereof which consists of taxes on transfers of capital, in various forms, will diminish with the withdrawal of foreign capital from the country under a progressive fall of the exchange; and the tax on litigation cannot be counted upon as a resource for averting financial disorder from the depreciation of silver.

Thus, the old sources of revenue would fail the Government in its extremity. The only other source is an income tax. In the United Kingdom an income tax of fourpence in the pound, or 1⅔ per cent., was reduced to threepence, and then to twopence, or five-sixths per cent., because the higher percentage was too burdensome a rate, as an ordinary rate for a permanent tax. In India, an income tax of 3⅛ per cent. yielded in 1870–1 only two millions sterling. With foreign capital expelled from India by a depreciated and deteriorating silver currency—with an enhanced rate of interest, and with heavier taxation—incomes would diminish, and a rate of 5 per cent. would not yield two and a half millions sterling after three or four years. In England, an income tax of 5 per cent. would be expressed by a rate of twelve pence in the pound—a rate which, if imposed as an ordinary tax, would drive the strongest ministry from office. It has always been the care of Indian statesmen to regulate taxation so as to consolidate British rule in India.

If an income tax could be made to yield sufficient to meet the increased expenditure from an augmentation of salaries, consequent on the depreciation of silver (and there is but scant hope of its doing so), it is as much as could be expected from it.

The Government of India, then, has to reckon, in its ordinary expenditure, first, a charge for interest on the loans for public works extraordinary, &c., which has been growing latterly at the rate of £200,000 a year, but which we may reckon at the yearly rate of £175,000. Every six years would increase the annual charge by one million sterling. In eight years, from 1867–8 to 1875–6, the Canal revenue, apart from any Land revenue due to irrigation, increased by only £160,000. The net revenue from State railways has been increasing at a faster rate, but as yet by much less than the amount of yearly increase of the charge for interest.

To the yearly increase of charge for interest must be added loss by exchange, and a great expenditure for increasing salaries on account of the high prices which a continued depreciation of silver would involve. The last-mentioned cannot be estimated; but, as already remarked, it would not be less—probably it would be more—than the proceeds of any conceivable rate of income tax. With exchange at 1*s.* 8½*d.*, that is, with silver at about 53½*d.*, the loss by exchange to the Indian Government would amount to about 1¾ million sterling; in 1873–4 and 1874–5, it was somewhat below one million. With exchange at 1*s.* 6*d.* (that is, with silver at 47*d.*, which price was touched in 1876) the loss would amount to five millions sterling; and it would increase by one million for every additional fall of one penny in the price of silver.

On the one hand, there would, in four or five years, be an alarming growth of expenditure, which, if it assailed the elastic finances of the British empire, would awaken dread and anxiety. On the other hand, there is an Indian revenue of which the old sources, including the Land revenue, afford but little promise of increase; while the only new tax which the best English financial ability, aided by Indian experience, has been able to devise for India, is an income tax which, if it produced sufficient to pay for the increase of salaries on account of the depreciation of silver, would give as much as could be expected from it, and it could not produce even that except through the imposition of a rate which, if it were imposed in England as an ordinary tax, would overthrow the strongest ministry.

Thus, with a progressive depreciation of silver and a progressive augmentation of the loss by exchange, India's only outlook would be into financial ruin.

All this would be averted by the adoption of a gold standard for India, with a transition to it, from the silver standard, at a valuation of 15½ to 1 of gold.

This view of the Indian finances, and the utter impracticability of counteracting, from the Indian revenues (albeit supplemented by new taxes), the alarming growth of expenditure in loss by exchange through the progressive depreciation of silver, which is inevitable, disposes of an objection to change that has been urged by some. It has been said that everything in India is going on smoothly. Commerce—at least the export trade—is brisk or flourishing; the banks declare good dividends; people on fixed incomes have not suffered, except in any remittances which they make to England; only the Government is at a disadvantage from the exceeding largeness of its home remittances. But surely this cloud, already bigger than a man's hand, is sufficient cause for alarm. A country whose finances are, or will soon be, in disorder, failing the demonetisation of silver, cannot prosper. Production, distribution, exchange, commerce, cannot flourish under the increased taxation in a poor country to which the Government of India will be forced. Famine expenditure may be the apparent cause, but the loss by exchange would be the real cause of additional taxation. Expunge the latter from the Indian finance minister's account of revenue and expenditure, and the surplus would be large enough to provide a considerable yearly instalment towards the redemption of the famine loan after meeting the entire charge for interest. The possible heavy famine taxation next year would be the first movement of the gathering and rising cloud, now but little above the horizon, which must soon darken the sky. Nor would it be the only sign of coming disaster. The rate of interest has risen; this surely is not encouraging to production. For a time, the rise of the rate gave an upward tendency to silver, which has been lost since. And though the bounty on exports is stimulating them, yet it cannot be taken for granted that the stimulus is a healthy one. In 1876, when there were great perturbations in the price of silver, the export trade was much affected by a spirit of gambling or not over safe speculation. There were contracts with banks for the forward delivery of bills, in which one party speculated for a greater and the other for a slighter fall, or for an improvement, in the price of silver; so that the exporters had chequered fortunes, some gaining largely, others losing. For importers there was loss, or but little profit. A repetition of this with each fresh fall, and with fresh perturbations in the price of silver, would not be a healthy, satisfactory state of things, and anyhow the gains would end with the financial deluge.

The great loss by exchange is an unmistakeable fact; impending heavy taxation for famine expenditure may soon be realised; the rate of interest has advanced; in short, the evils predicated from the depreciation of silver are palpable realities, in their first stage. The time for action has surely come; and it would scarcely be a sufficient answer for a Government to say that, though disorder is threatening our finances, yet commerce is getting along tolerably well. Commerce, it is said, will take care of itself, if the Government does not meddle with it. The complement of this theory is, that the Government should look to itself in a time of financial danger; for then only will commerce be able to take care of its own.

CHAPTER XII.

PROVISION OF CAPITAL FOR AGRICULTURE AND INDUSTRY IN INDIA, BY MEANS OF A GOLD CURRENCY.

If, from the demonetisation of silver in the West, its price is hopelessly gone—if, under this malign influence, combined with the operation of the 15 millions sterling of yearly tribute, imports must be restricted, and exports must be sent forward at a diminishing price abroad, for which the only compensation will be the bounty upon exports, involved in the depreciation of silver, it is plain that foreign capital will not flow into India, any more than to a country with an inconvertible and depreciated paper currency. Like cautious generals, capitalists, in advancing, secure their line of retreat; and capital will not flow readily into a country, if it cannot as readily flow out again. With silver falling in price, it must be difficult, if not impossible, for any one not engaged in trade to carry his capital out of India, except at a heavy loss which might absorb the profits of two, three, or more years.

Recognising this difficulty, even in the smaller matter of remitting interest, instead of withdrawing capital, from India, the Government of India favours the policy of not borrowing in England, that is, not importing foreign capital into India. The decision is quite right, if the injurious effects of the depreciation of silver must be accepted as inevitable; but not many years have passed since it was commonly remarked that nothing was wanting to raise India to an unexampled prosperity, but the capital which was then being freely embarked and wasted in unprofitable enterprises on the Continent and in America. A gold currency for India, such as has been suggested in preceding chapters, would assist the flow of capital to India, in a form, —namely, that of Bank of England notes of legal tender in India—which would not endanger the system of credit and currency in England, like the loans to foreign countries.

It is no doubt expedient that, in one sense, India's foreign indebtedness should be diminished; but the reduction should fall, not upon the private capital which is invested in mercantile and industrial enterprise, but upon the India sterling loans in England. For some years those loans must increase; but it is not an unreasonable expectation that by means of a gold currency, and through one of the incidental measures for its introduction, a great part of those sterling loans would be transferred to India.

The first step to this end would be the payment in India of the interest on these loans. This is not practicable with a silver currency; but it would be a natural result of the adoption of a gold currency. The transfer of a large amount of these loans to India would then depend on the cessation of Government borrowing in India, on an improvement of the income of the people, by avoiding heavy taxation, and on the supersession of the functions of the village banker, with the liberation of his capital for other investments.

It has been suggested in a former chapter, that Government should extricate the ryots or cultivators in the greater part of British India from the indebtedness which now crushes them, through the heavy charge of interest, by lending them money in the form of district currency notes, in liquidation of their debts to the bankers and for their yearly expenses of cultivation. The advances would be without risk, for they would be made to the classes who now pay their land revenue with unfailing punctuality, and the advances could, by law, be made recoverable in the same way as land revenue. Even at present, money is advanced to cultivators to assist them in digging wells, and in making agricultural improvements. By means of paper money, freely receivable into the treasuries as Government revenue, and freely circulating in the district, among the cultivators whom the notes will have befriended in a manner beyond their previous experience, the advances could be made on a larger scale, and with the resolute determination to supersede the functions of the village banker, who generally extends his operations over several villages, or through sub-agents over a whole district.

Of the provision of an outlet for the liberated capital of the village bankers we shall presently speak. The effect upon the ryots or cultivators would be that which has been observed in Europe. Mr. Bagehot wrote:—

'A note issue is mainly begun by loans; there are then no deposits to be paid. But the mass of loans in a rural district are of small amount; the bills to be discounted are trifling; the persons borrowing are of small means and only local repute; the value of any property they wish to pledge depends on local changes and local circumstances. . . . The way in which the issue of notes by a banker prepares the way for the deposit of money with him is very plain. When a private person begins to possess a great heap of bank notes, it will soon strike him that he is trusting the banker very much, and that in return he is getting nothing. He runs the risk of loss and robbery just the same as if he were hoarding coin. He would run no more risk by the failure of the bank if he made a deposit there, and he would be free from the risk of keeping the cash. No doubt it takes time before even this simple reasoning is understood by uneducated minds. So strong is the wish of most people to *see* their money, that they for some time continue to hoard bank notes; for a long period a few do so; but in the end common-sense conquers. The circulation of bank notes decreases, and the deposit of money with the banker increases. The credit of the banker having been efficiently advertised by the note, and accepted by the public, he lives on the credit so gained years after the note issue itself has ceased to be very important to him. . . . A system of note issues is therefore the best introduction to a large system of deposit banking.'

And so would it be with the district currency notes payable in silver which have been suggested in a previous chapter, and with the District Savings Banks which Government has established, but of which the progress hitherto has been slow. That progress cannot be other than slow, and the deposits other than small, so long as the masses of the population are indebted to village bankers, or to others, at rates of interest exceeding that which the Government Savings Banks allow; in other words, the millions do not save; and the many thousands who do save are able to lend the money to the indebted classes at high interest. By the Government becoming the sole creditor of these indebted classes, the rate of interest would fall, and greatly augmented deposits would appear in the balances of the District Savings Banks. As pointed out by Mr. Bagehot, the cultivating classes, from being borrowers from the Government, would become lenders to it. This might take time, but not the less surely would it come about in the end. The deposits thus obtained, and savings attracted from the existing lending classes who might find no better investment elsewhere, could be employed in redeeming sterling loans which bear higher interest or the same rate of interest.

The success of any such measure for superseding the functions of the village bankers would depend on the largeness of the issues of notes, and upon their convertibility. If may be said that these two conditions cannot be combined without locking up a large amount of silver, which would make the enterprise too gigantic for a Government that would be in the throes of a currency reform. It is, however, from the nettle danger that we pluck the flower safety. The embarrassing part of the currency reform would be to get rid of the silver without any great sacrifice. This could only be done by selling it gradually, to the extent of the yearly absorption by the demand for ornaments and for hoarding, in India. On the balance in hand, during these gradual sales, there would be a loss of interest. Hence, there would be an especial advantage in holding this silver as a reserve, in the several districts,[1] for maintaining the convertibility of the district notes payable in silver, which will have been issued to ryots under circumstances that would ensure the popularity of the notes. The interest obtained from ryots on the loans to them of district notes, would amply compensate for the interest incurred on the smaller silver reserve that would be kept for maintaining the convertibility of the notes.

Hence, we may assume—first, that the English successors of native Governments who received payments of land revenue in kind, from cultivators, would be quite equal to the extrication of the cultivators from indebtedness to village bankers, by advances (in district paper currency) which would be recoverable as land revenue; and secondly, that, in the manner just explained, deposits large enough to make a sensible impression on the amount of India stock in England would accumulate in a few years.

The village bankers are children of the soil, of a class not given to emigrate; and as they are shrewd, active, enterprising men, we may be sure that their liberated capital would be transferred to other profitable employments, which would increase the productive powers and resources of India. We should thus secure both the reduction of foreign debt and an increased application of capital in India.

It is the Native banker class, great and small, that we must use for the development of the resources of India. The rich Native bankers command resources inferior only to those of Lombard Street; but more than their wealth, they

[1] Perforce, the liberation of ryots from the thraldom of the village bankers would not be attempted simultaneously in all districts; it would be undertaken in a certain number of districts at a time.

prize rank and station, and they desire rank from no ignoble motive or vulgar feeling: their ideas are princely, and a thousand acts of munificence attest their eminent fitness to bear worthily, and to enhance, any honour and dignity which may be conferred on them. The Government can utilise the strong craving, so to speak, among this class, for high rank, in a way that would confer vast benefits on the country.

At present the rewards, distinctions, and honourable career within reach of the Natives of the country are but limited. Some may gain admission into the covenanted civil service; others may be enrolled in the Order of the Star of India; but these rewards or distinctions fail to impress the Oriental imagination. As marking the estimation in which the member of the Order of the Star of India is held by the foreign rulers of India, the honour is prized; but a Native member of the order, when moving in his own circle, or living upon his estate, finds it of little social worth: it does not stir the sympathies, because it does not harmonise with the traditions of the Native population; and it does not awaken in its possessor and in his dependents the unbought loyalty which honours more in accordance with native feeling would evoke.

An order of merit for the landed Native gentry in India might virtually, though not formally, be created by conferring the title of Rajah on wealthy Natives, if they are also landholders who have signalised the management of their estates by care for their tenantry and by acts of judicious liberality aud beneficence.

In England, which has reached the highest state of civilisation, the peerage is recruited from the bar, the banking, and commercial classes; in a word, the efficiency and vigour of the peerage are renewed by the best intellect and life-blood of the nation. India, in a much lower state of development, needs the infusion into the class of her landed gentry of the energy, the activity, the liberal yet judicious use of wealth which distinguish the banking class; and if the Native aristocracy of India are not to become effete, the ranks of the titled territorial gentry must be recruited by the nomination, as rajahs, of rich bankers who, having proved themselves humane and enlightened zemindars, are worthy of honour, and are certain, if thus honoured, to fertilise the agriculture of India from new streams of wealth.

Had this policy been adopted from the outset of the permanent settlement, the difficult subject of the relations of landlords and ryots which every now and again forces itself on public attention in the Lower Provinces of Bengal would not embarrass the Bengal Government. The English landed gentry, whom Lord Cornwallis took as a model for Bengal zemindars, are not constrained by any law into the liberality which they show to their tenantry; and the local Government may do much to infuse a like spirit into the relations between landlords and ryots in Bengal, by conferring the dignity and title of Rajah on any native zemindars who prove by their deeds that they emulate and even surpass the English landed gentry in charity and beneficence.

The formation thus of a titled landed gentry, animated by an enlightened liberality, and worthily spending princely incomes, would set before the zemindars of Bengal examples which they dare not refuse to emulate, lest they force rulers and people to inquire why they should any longer be permitted to possess rights which the new members of their class translate into the humane duties that property owes in virtue of its rights.

In this manner there would be provided for the Lower Provinces of Bengal that relief to the cultivating classes, and those means of ameliorating their condition, which in the rest of India would be supplied by the Government's measures for extricating the ryots from indebtedness to village bankers, and liberating for other more productive uses in agriculture and industry, the large capital of these bankers which is now employed in keeping the cultivating classes in a condition scarcely illumined by a single ray of hope.

The cultivators in India have little to learn from their rulers respecting the best processes of agriculture. Their special disadvantage is their poverty. Transformed into thrifty peasant proprietors, and with the village bankers settling among them as a superior class of landed proprietors, the face of India would be changed, and her contribution to the wealth of the world would be doubled.

But, as we said before, with a continuing silver currency, the only outlook for India would be into the darkness of Erebus, the gloom of despair.

CHAPTER XIII.

SUMMARY.

SILVER has played the mischief with some political economists, confusing their ideas, so that when they tell us that gold is for the West, and that a silver currency is good enough for India, we may believe that it is the very worst for India. Their faith is, gold for themselves and silver for India, while the vindication of the second article of this creed forces them into outrageous heterodoxy, viz.:—

1. That instability of value in the standard of value is of no consequence.

2. That, in order to create an increased balance in favour of India, imports must be restricted, even by recourse to inferior local manufactures.

3. That a bounty upon exports is good for India when it comes in the form of depreciated and ever afresh depreciating silver, though all bounties are paid, with a heavy reckoning, by the country which sends forward exports under that stimulus.

4. That silver is for the East and gold is for the West; though the law which regulates the transmission of the precious metals from one country to another presupposes the use of a common money in the trade between foreign countries. Of late, India's export to Europe of gold has been considerable, her export of silver insignificant.

5. Dear wheat would be good for manufactures, said the 'Economist,' the pronounced organ of free trade, on September 30, 1876, through misapprehending the general depres-

sion of trade, of which the accumulation of gold in the West, with a consequent demonetisation there of silver, is a main cause:—

'Of course, the prospect of another year of cheap food is on the whole a favourable one, in an economic view. . . . That this continued cheapness must also, with other things, be preparing the way for a great revival in trade, is equally certain. On the other side, however, it may be admitted that a stimulus would probably be given to many trades, which would make a conspicuous interruption to the present stagnation by a rise in wheat. The agricultural interest throughout the world has been suffering for two or three years, and this suffering reacts on our exports to many distant countries. A rise in price would benefit that interest, and would probably revive to some extent our own export trade.'

The Corn Law League demanded cheap wheat for increasing the export trade; their organ in the present day longs for dear wheat to bring about that result. Perhaps, however, the closing sentence in this extract simply breathes an aspiration that wheat may be somewhat dear abroad, but cheap at home, for the encouragement of British exports.

Any how, the propounders of these heresies in political economy are thereby disqualified to be heard when they further contend with much sophistry, that silver, which has been demonetised in the West, should not be demonetised in the East. This and the converse, that gold is for the West, may be golden sayings; but a yearly loss by exchange, ranging from one and a half million sterling to five millions, and *ad infinitum*, would be too dear a price for treasuring them.

The price of silver has fallen below all record in history; and the experience of the past three centuries shows that each drain of it to the East only results in its further depreciation in the West. This was the case when silver was common money, with gold, in the West; henceforth this expectation must be surer, now that silver is demonetised in the West. The increase of exports of merchandise from the

East has as yet had no effect in raising the price of silver in London; it has fallen in the face of that export—nor can it be otherwise. Exports from India, in payment of the enlarged tribute to England, or in exchange for imports of depreciated silver, will only lower the price of Asiatic products in Europe, while the price of silver in the West sympathises with the price there of Asiatic products, rising when they rise and declining when they fall.

Even the advocates for the retention of silver as money of full legal tender are prepared to give up their cause as hopeless, should France adopt a single standard of gold. All the known facts during the past three years, respecting the changes in progress in her paper and metallic currencies, show that, with a rare financial ability and skill, France has been silently preparing for the demonetisation of silver. In her wake would follow Spain and the countries of the Latin Union. In the United States, the farthest that the Americans will go in favour of silver will be to retain it as legal tender up to fifty dollars—the limit which in these observations has been suggested for India.

Not only has silver fallen in price, never to rise again; it has become unstable—its fluctuations in the market are as variable as those of wheat, and with a tendency to progressive decline, from the competition in London between bullion dealers, who sell silver, and the Secretary of State for India, who sells silver rupees deliverable in India.

With each fresh fall in price, commerce would indeed work out a fresh equilibrium by increasing exports and reducing imports; a given quantity of imports would exchange for an increased and increasing quantity of exports. Manchester's business may droop, but other British exports would go abroad for purchase of silver, until the Americans dispense with England as their produce broker, and send silver direct to India. Meanwhile, India would buy all the silver which London has to sell: a comforting thought!

With each fresh fall in price, and while commerce might be actively working out a new equilibrium on a lower level, those who administer the finances of India would have an opportunity for the display of the genius which laughs at impossibilities. With exchange at 1*s.* 8½*d.* (that is, with silver at about 53½*d.*) the loss to the Indian Government by exchange would amount to about 1¾ million sterling (in 1873–4–5 it was somewhat below one million). With exchange at 1*s.* 6*d.* (that is, with silver at 47*d.*, a point which was touched in 1876) the loss would amount to five millions sterling, and it would increase by one million for every additional fall of one penny in the price of silver. To meet this there is nothing. The only new tax which has been devised for India since 1859, viz., the income tax, could not, at the highest conceivable rate for its imposition, yield more than sufficient (if sufficient) for meeting the augmented expenditure for increasing salaries on account of the depreciation of silver. The usual heads of revenue give but slender prospect of increase; and the ordinary growth of those revenues would barely suffice for meeting the ordinary growth of expenditure, plus the charge for interest, which progresses at the rate of about £175,000 a year.

Thus a financial deluge would interrupt commerce in its working out of a new equilibrium, through that interesting play of the bounty from depreciated silver, upon exports, which has been offered as a clear and sufficient solution of the silver difficulty.

And England, while bewailing the ruin of her Indian Empire, would have humour enough left to laugh at this abrupt ending of the game of commerce, with its juggling play upon the bounty from depreciated silver, upon which those who talk glibly about the depreciation base the policy of doing nothing; for experience will have taught her that each fresh display of this jugglery had always ended in a reduction of her exports through their displacement by silver.

All this evil is to be encountered, British exports reduced, Manchester's industry paralysed, the material progress of India checked, her financial ruin almost deliberately encompassed, because, in defiance of the laws of political economy, the West would deny to India a common money with foreign countries, in her trade with them. Gold is the only and sovereign common money; sent to India, where it is not money, it fetches its full price, and even commands a premium. Mr. Bagehot told us that silver sent to London is mere merchandise, as tin.

We are not concerned in removing fears of what would happen if all the countries in the world were to adopt a gold currency, though the facts show that nothing but good would happen. The only present candidates for the fresh yearly production of gold are Germany (which has nearly completed her coinage reform), the United States (where the gold premium has nearly disappeared, and where the Gold Ring has been closed), and India.

The adoption of a gold currency by India would not raise the value of gold, because, first, the India Council drafts for the yearly amount of 15 millions sterling worth of silver rupees, which now act on the London market like the import of a corresponding amount of silver, in lowering its price, would, when issued for 15 millions sterling worth of gold rupees, act similarly like an import of gold in preventing an enhancement of its value; because, secondly, silver would still act upon prices as an effective subsidiary currency. By putting more silver into the Indian rupee, so as to bring it nearly to an intrinsic par with gold according to the present value of silver,—by then demonetising it, but receiving it freely in Government treasuries in payment of Government demands,—and by keeping the limit of its legal tender as high as one hundred rupees, silver, for transactions of internal trade, would be as effective a currency as gold, and the action of both together, upon prices, would be the same as the action of silver alone, in the present currency, would have been but for its depreciation. The Land revenue of India would not be affected, as some apprehend; while the purchasing power of the present amount of that revenue would be reduced, if depreciated and depreciating silver were not demonetised. It stands to reason that a gold currency, with a silver currency raised to gold value by its being reduced to a token coinage, and of at least the same amount in the aggregate as the old currency (if not of a larger amount), could not lower prices.

Hence, and for other reasons which have been discussed, the alteration of standard from silver to gold would not injure either debtor or creditor; and the relative value for the transition from silver to gold might be fixed at 15½ to 1, which is the valuation observed by the countries of the Latin Union, Spain, and Germany, and which was the ordinary or normal relative value before the sudden depreciation of silver since 1875. If the Government of India had foreseen the course and permanency of the depreciation of silver when it began, there is no doubt that the evils of it would have been averted by an instant change to a gold standard. But the Government is one of mortals not gifted with prescience; therefore it cannot be held to have acquiesced in and accepted the depreciation which it has hesitated to correct. Accordingly it is free (and in correction of its own shortcomings through want of prescience, it is bound), when at last its eyes are opened, to correct the depreciation retrospectively, by adopting the valuation of 15½ to 1, and not any worse valuation; for the latter would perpetuate more or less of the depreciation, and burden India with a permanent extra taxation on account of the shortsightedness (unavoidable shortsightedness) of its rulers. No one will be injured by the adoption of the relative value of 15½ to 1.

When the alternative is a gold standard or financial ruin,

it is superfluous to discuss nice shades of advantage or disadvantage to debtors and creditors who would be drowned in the financial deluge.

From 1853 to 1876, the solvent countries in the world have absorbed 25 millions sterling a year of gold; and as this amount has been absorbed principally in the West, it is assumed by writers and commercial men that there is nothing to spare, out of the yearly supply of gold, for the countries in the East. In this hasty conclusion the following considerations are overlooked.

a. The 24 millions sterling of yearly fresh supply have been absorbed, not by an ordinary yearly demand which must ever recur, but by an exceptional demand which, once satisfied, will not occur again. France and the countries of the Latin Union, and Germany, and the Scandinavian Kingdoms absorbed the 24 millions a year of gold, not in replacing wear and tear and providing for a gradual increase in previously existing gold currencies, but in replacing the bulk of their silver currencies with a gold currency. This work, once done, is done for ever; thereafter, the yearly requirement of these countries for replacing wear and tear is of no account, for the proportion of yearly wear and tear of gold coins is infinitesimal; nor should any but an inconsiderable rate of yearly increase of gold currency for countries already possessed of it be hastily assumed, because, first, the use of cheques and notes has greatly increased, and must yet extend, beyond the experience from 1853 to 1870; secondly, with gold as universal international money, silver could be enthroned more completely than it now is, as the money for the internal trade of each country, thereby lessening the use of gold in that trade.

b. Owing to the huge growth of national indebtedness, the public securities of the various countries are largely employed for remittances in the course of trade; the export or import of securities has the same effect as an export or import of gold.

c. Of the countries which have an inconvertible paper currency, those which are insolvent are of no account, in the present inquiry; the two solvent countries in this category, viz., France and the United States, will emerge from their state of inconvertibility of notes with a smaller demand for gold than when they suspended specie payments, because, in the interval, their peoples have become habituated to the use of paper money, and France, moreover, has been at especial pains in extending the use of cheques and bills of exchange in internal trade.

d. In the period from 1853 to 1870, there was a drain of silver to the East, from the high price of cotton, and the small amount of the India Council drafts; and the purchase of this silver in European markets, with gold, created special movements of gold in those markets. This drain has revived solely through the depreciation of silver. Were silver to be demonetised, and a gold currency introduced into India, there would be but little demand by India on the yearly supply of gold, after the completion of her coinage reform—by reason, first, of the yearly 15 millions sterling of Council drafts on India; secondly, the purchasing back by India, under the system of a gold currency, of Indian secuities which are now held in Europe; thirdly, the economising of gold through the control which the Bank of England should acquire over the exchanges with the East, by establishing agencies in Calcutta, Bombay, Rangoon.

e. If the considerations *a* to *d* be regarded, it is impossible that 37 millions sterling a year of gold and silver, which is the present production, can be needed for the ordinary currency requirements of the world. Even the 22 millions sterling of gold would be excessive, unless its use as money be extended to the East; for it must not be forgotten that with a gold currency in India, the Indian Council drafts which would be payable in gold rupees would be tantamount to a yearly import into England of 15 millions sterling of gold, so that the effective gold supply would be not 22, but 37 millions sterling a year.

Thus the future ordinary demand will be well within the future yearly supply of gold. As to any present exceptional demands, we find, on taking stock of them, that the unsupplied balance of special requirements of some countries is less than the excess supply of gold which other countries have accumulated, and which they must shortly liberate. The United States cannot require much beyond the hoards already in the country, which the disappearance of the now attenuated gold premium would call forth. Again, India's requirements of gold would be less than the general estimate, if, first, as seems reasonable and prudent, the new subsidiary silver coin be made to contain 10 per cent. more silver than the present rupees, and if the limit of its legal tender be fixed at one hundred rupees; and if, secondly, Bank of England notes be declared legal tender in India. Against these two special requirements of the United States and India, we have to set off the consideration that France, on resuming specie payments, will liberate a large amount of gold, and that Germany, with an excessive metallic currency, must do the same in the end.

Hence, there are abundant grounds for dismissing, as imaginary, the fear that the markets of Europe would be disturbed by the adoption of a gold standard. During the time that Germany was acquiring gold for her coinage of more than 70 millions sterling, France was also accumulating gold for her monetary reform. Yet these two powerful causes did not raise the rate of interest very high or disturb it very violently; the average minimum rate of discount charged by the Bank of England in each month, from 1871 to 1875, was never so high as in 1861, or as in 1866 (a year of financial crisis); in only nine of the sixty months from 1871 to 1875 did the rate exceed 5 per cent. per annum. And, at the present time, when the rate of interest is exceptionally low, it were better surely that the rise (which must follow sooner or later) should be occasioned by measures for giving to India a common money with Europe, which will result in her largely adding to the material riches of the world, than that it should accompany another outburst of the greedy speculations and rash enterprises which issued in a considerable destruction of capital, and the reaction from which is one of the causes of the present stagnation of trade.

Instead of fearing injury from the adoption of a gold currency in India, England should promote the measure, even with substantial help, as one of two effectual means of removing an ever-present danger in the delicate mechanism of her own system of currency and credit.

The grievous burdens under which the United States and some of the fairest regions in Europe are bowed down, are attributable to the fearful growth of national indebtedness; and that has been fostered by an enormous accumulation of deposits in English banks. To one phase of these transactions, viz., the exportation to other countries of the British capital which should have invigorated British agriculture, must also be ascribed the wretched condition of the English agricultural poor. Capital had the excuse that the English land laws prevent the free application of capital to the land, but not the less was the excessive exportation of it to foreign countries a serious injury and a grave social and political danger to England. In the days of our sturdy grandfathers, who refused to take their law from the ruler of the Continent of Europe, Mr. Thornton, the author of the Essay on Paper Credit and Paper Money, wrote:—'A prosperous nation commonly employs its growing wealth, not so much in augmenting the debts due to it from abroad, as in enlarging its capital at home.'

The principal agents for foreign investments of British capital were the joint-stock finance companies and the stock-brokers, and they derived their power of using deposits from the absence of other sufficient means of regular or floating investments of balances by the banks. This power should be much restricted and curtailed by two expedients, viz., first, a revision of the land laws; and secondly, the floating of increasing amounts of *quasi*-exchequer bills to be issued by the Secretary of State for India. The first measure would lead to the formation of land mortgage banks, which could afford to offer to depositors higher rates of interest than are given by bill brokers, and thus would retain at home the bulk of English deposits in safe, remunerative forms of investment; and, in connection with the second measure, would restore to the Bank of England its control over the rate of interest, and would increase both England's independence of foreign markets, through an enlargement of the home market for her manufactures and her command of them with British manufactures, with the result that, as in France, her foreign trade would be less disturbed by crises, and her system of currency and credit would be more stable. But without a gold currency, the floating of the Indian Secretary of State's exchequer bills in England (and, as a counter-poise, the circulation in India, of the notes of the Bank of England) would not be practicable: with it, these measures would strengthen instead of endangering the mechanism of credit and currency in England.

It is not necessary to repeat here the grave political and general considerations which demand a revision of the land laws, such as would facilitate the application of capital to the land, and give stability to England's monetary system. But for those considerations, the laws will not be revised; with such revision, England's currency system would be so effectually secured that, if she had another dependent empire as large as that of India, both might change from a silver to a gold standard, without causing the least monetary disturbance in England.

Even were no substantial advantage to be gained, and were some risk to be incurred by England, during the period of transition in India from a silver to a gold standard, ought not that risk to be encountered for the sake of the millions in India from whose country financial ruin would be averted, and who (the agricultural classes) would be freed from their bondage of indebtedness to village-bankers, by one of the incidental measures of the coinage reform? That measure, by liberating the capital of the village bankers for productive employment in other fields of industry, would have the same effect as the discovery of a gold mine in India; the same effect in enriching, but a more humanising effect in changing the apathy and despair of indebtedness into the hope and self-reliance that accompany thrift; and in elevating the condition of masses of an agricultural population, whose improved means and better scale of living would then return a double blessing to England of the kind nearest to Manchester's heart, namely, an increased demand for British manufactures.

The details of the plan for the introduction of a gold currency into India need not be repeated. But one feature of it deserves marked attention, viz., the means of utilising, and of eventually selling in India, the surplus silver; so that the amount of silver which Germany has yet to sell, the further amount which France may sell, and the future yearly produce of the silver mines, lose their interest for India.

The universal depression of commerce marks, among other things, a depletion, not of England's gold but of England's capital; and, as a consequence, grave social and political danger; a widening gulf between rich and poor; an aristocracy and landed gentry in whom the resolute will of their fathers, ever prompt to act, under the generous, invigorating influence of land, is being enfeebled by the influence of commerce, ever ready with reasons for not acting, unless to gain 5 or 10 per cent. Of this disunion of classes, severance of rich from poor, emasculation of resolute will in England's natural and hereditary leaders, we have, fortunately, but premonitory symptoms. They are sufficiently marked however, to awaken the thoughful concern of statesmen, at a time when England should be preparing to withstand an irruption of the barbarians; and they are traceable to the unsatisfactory condition of the agricultural classes, from the very insufficient application of capital to the land. While these dangers are assailing the heart of the British Empire, financial paralysis is threatening its Asiatic limb. The measures demanded for the respective needs of England and India fit into one another; a common money would bind India closer to England, and help in bracing up the agriculture, manufactures, credit, and currency of England.

APPENDIX I.

PRODUCTION OF GOLD AND SILVER.

MR. W. L. FAWCETT, the author of 'Gold and Debt, a Handbook of Finance,' after consulting various estimates,—perhaps all well-known estimates,—of the yearly production of gold and silver, wrote respecting gold, that the entire gold product of the world was constant at 13 to 14 million dollars (2·6 to 2·8 millions sterling a year), from 1800 to 1825. In that year began a development of the Russian and Siberian mines, and the production rose from one million sterling a year, between 1825 and 1830, to 3¾ millions a year between 1840 and 1850. 'This, together with some revival of the gold product of South America, contributed to increase the total annual gold product of the world to about 6 millions sterling in 1846,' which is the estimate of 'Birkmyre, who made a table of the gold and silver product of all countries in the world, exclusive of China and Japan, with the following results for the year 1846 :—

(*Millions of dollars.*)

	North and South America	Europe, Asia, and Africa	Total	
				£
Gold . .	6·5	22·5	29	5·8
Silver . .	26·	6·	32	6·4

Mr. Newmarch, in his 'History of Prices,' vol. vi., quoted and framed estimates which gave 8 to 10 millions sterling as the yearly production of gold by 1848. The smaller estimate being favourable to the views of the present writer, the larger estimate of 10 millions sterling will be adopted.

2. M. Chevalier estimated the total yearly production of silver in 1848 at 8 millions sterling. M. Léon Faucher estimated in 1851 that the annual production was then nearly $1\frac{1}{2}$ million more than in 1848, thus raising M. Chevalier's estimate to 9·8 millions sterling. M. Herzog, keeping within this sum, began his estimate with 9 millions for 1851. M. Bonnet starts with 8·1 millions for 1852. The silver committee of 1876 adopted M. Bonnet's estimate. All the subsequent increase is from additions to this amount of the increased production since in the United States; the silver production of all other countries having (according to the evidence given to the Committee) been comparatively stationary since 1862.

3. The presence of gold in the gilt silver obtained from Nevada in the United States has thrown uncertainty over the statistics of gold and silver production in those States, for the earlier years since the discovery of the Nevada mines, by causing an understatement of the amount of gold and an overstatement of that of silver production. Imperfect registration, imperfect records, and the exportation of large amounts of gold without their passing through the custom-house, also vitiate the returns of Australian and Californian production from the outset. For the earlier years there was possibly a compensation of errors; overstatements in inaccurate returns being neutralised by the unreported amounts sent away or carried away by miners. The two first-mentioned causes of error have been corrected of late years, but the third source of error, or the unreported export of gold, still continues. A leading Californian paper, quoted by the 'Economist' in the Commercial History and Review of 1876, observed :—

'The yield of the gold mines generally, unlike that of the silver mines, is not published regularly. Many gold mines are worked on a small scale, sometimes by two or three men. Few of them are incorporated in San Francisco; the stock-holders are usually few, and live at the mines; they can get information by letter or orally; and, as the treasure is much more attractive to robbers than silver, the managers try to keep the amount of production and the times of shipment secret.'

4. Sir Hector Hay submitted to the Select Committee on the Depreciation of Silver an estimate of the yearly production of gold and silver which is substantially that published by M. Victor Bonnet, in the 'Journal des Économistes.' For the United States, however, it may be well to abide by official figures which were carefully revised by the Commissioner of Mining Statistics, and which are adopted by the well-informed 'New York Financial Chronicle.' For Australia an estimate may be made as follows, viz. :—

a. Down to 1866, and later, the only mint in Australia was at Sydney in New South Wales. Hence, if the actual production of New South Wales be taken, the net exports from Victoria, down to 1866, may be taken as the production of Victoria.

b. New Zealand, actual production, except for 1852 to 1854, for which years net exports have been taken.

c. Queensland, actual production, or, where not available, net exports, as from New Zealand. Figures down to 1874 have been ascertained on this plan for Australia.

For Russia, the statistics obtained and the estimates framed by the 'Economist,' for other countries, the sums estimated by Sir Hector Hay, though he has not taken note of the increase of production in Africa. The imports into the United Kingdom from West and South Africa amounted to £110,000 in 1862, £96,000 in 1873, and £425,000 in 1876. How much went elsewhere is not known.

5. The figures which may be presented are given in the table on page 184.

6. The following remarks arise on this table :—

I. M. Bonnet's estimate of the yearly gold production does not differ materially from the estimate which has been compiled from the sources already described; and perhaps the chief difference arises from the adoption in the latter estimate, of the 'New York Financial Chronicle's' return of the gold production of the United States, which may be accepted as the best statement that is available.

II. The estimates of silver production for 1875 and 1876 are the amounts for the United States, given by the 'New York Financial and Commercial Chronicle,' *plus* the recognised 7 millions sterling for other countries.

III. For silver, M. Herzog, the delegate from Switzerland to the Latin Mint Conference at Paris, framed an estimate of yearly production down to 1870, which is somewhat higher than that of M. Bonnet, viz., a total production of 74 millions from 1852 to 1859, of 75 millions from 1860 to 1865, and of 71 millions from 1866 to 1870, or in all 220 millions, against M. Bonnet's estimates of 57, 56, and 51 millions for the three periods, or in all 164 millions.

Production of Gold and Silver, and their Distribution.

(*In millions sterling.*)

	Estimate of Gold Production as explained in Paras. 3, 4.				M. Bonnet's Estimate			Exports to the East, M. de Quiteville			Gross Imports into British India			Home Government's Bills on India	Rate of Exchange of the Bills	Price per Ounce of British Standard Silver in London
	United States	Australia	Other Countries	Total	Gold	Silver	Total	Gold	Silver	Total	Gold	Silver	Total		d.	d.
1848	2·	—	8·1	10·1	—	8·7*	—	—	—	—	—	—	—	1·9	—	59½
1849	8·	—	5·1	13·1	—	—	—	—	—	—	—	—	—	2·9	—	59¾
1850	10·	—	4·9	14·9	—	—	—	—	—	—	—	—	—	3·2	—	60 1/16
1851	11·	—	5·	16·	—	—	—	·1	1·7	1·8	1·3	3·7	5·0	2·8	—	61
1852	12·	9·2	5·	26·2	36·5	8·1	44·6	·9	2·6	3·5	1·3	5·5	6·8	3·3	—	60½
	41·	9·2	20·0	70·2	—	—	—	—	—	—	—	—	—	14·1	—	—
1853	13·	13·8	4·3	31·1	31·0	8·1	39·1	·9	5·6	6·5	1·1	3·8	4·9	3·8	24·2	61½
1854	12	11	4·3	27·3	25·4	8·1	33·5	1·2	4·6	5·8	·9	1·1	2·0	3·7	23·4	61½
1855	11·	11·6	4·3	26·9	27·0	8·1	35·1	1·2	7·9	9·1	2·5	8·8	11·3	1·5	23·6	61 5/16
1856	11·	12·6	4·3	27·9	29·5	8·1	37·6	·5	14·1	14·6	2·2	12·2	14·4	2·8	24·1	61 5/16
1857	11·	12·2	5·0	28·2	26·6	8·1	34·7	·5	20·2	20·7	2·8	13·0	15·8	·6	24·4	61¾
1858	10·	11·8	4·9	26·7	24·9	8·1	33·0	·3	5·7	6·0	4·4	8·4	12·8	—	25·8	61 5/16
1859	10	10·9	4·6	25·5	24·9	8·1	33·0	·9	16·4	17·3	4·3	12·1	16·4	—	26·	62 1/16
1860	9·2	10·7	4·4	24·3	23·8	8·2	32·0	2·4	10·8	13·2	4·3	6·4	10·7	—	26·	61 11/16
	87·2	94·6	36·1	217·9	213·1	64·9	278·0	7·9	85·3	93·2	22·5	65·8	88·3	12·4	—	—
1861	8·6	10·1	4·4	23·1	22·8	8·5	31·3	1·4	8·9	10·3	5·2	9·8	15·	1·2	23·9	60 13/16
1862	7·8	9·6	4·4	21·8	21·5	9·0	30·5	3·4	14·6	18·0	6·9	13·6	20·5	6·6	23·9	61 7/16
1863	8·0	8·9	4·4	21·3	21·4	9·8	31·2	8·0	15·1	23·1	8·9	14·0	22·9	9·	23·9	61⅜
1864	9·2	9·3	4·2	22·7	22·6	10·3	32·9	7·0	16·8	23·8	9·9	11·5	21·4	6·8	23·9	61⅜
1865	10·6	9·3	4·5	24·6	24·0	10·4	34·4	4·3	9·8	14·1	6·4	20·2	26·6	7·	23·8	61 1/16
	44·2	47·4	21·9	113·5	112·3	48·0	160·3	24·1	65·2	89·3	37·3	69·1	106·4	30·6	—	—
1866	10·7	9·8	4·7	25·2	24·2	10·1	34·3	2·9	7·1	10·0	4·6	8·7	13·3	5·6	23·1	61⅛
1867	10·3	9·5	4·6	24·4	23·2	10·8	34·0	1·5	2·0	3·5	4·8	7·0	11·8	4·1	23·3	60 9/16
1868	9·6	11·7	4·6	25·9	24·0	10·0	34·0	6·5	3·6	10·1	5·2	10·0	15·2	3·7	23·1	60½
1869	9·9	10·5	5·1	25·5	24·2	9·5	33·7	2·6	6·6	9·2	5·7	8·3	14·0	7·	23·3	60 7/16
	40·5	41·5	19·0	101·0	95·6	40·4	136·0	13·5	19·3	32·8	20·3	34·0	54·3	20·4	—	—
1870	10·0	9·4	5·4	24·8	23·2	10·3	33·5	2·1	2·2	4·3	2·8	2·6	5·4	8·4	22·6	60 9/16
1871	8·7	11·0	6·1	25·8	23·3	12·2	35·5	3·3	3·9	7·2	3·6	8·0	11·6	10·3	23·	60½
1872	7·2	9·0	6·0	22·2	20·3	13·0	33·3	3·4	6·5	9·9	2·6	1·9	4·5	13·9	22·8	60 5/16
1873	7·2	9·0	5·7	21·9	20·7	14·1	34·8	2·9	3·5	6·4	1·6	4·2	5·8	13·3	22·3	59¼
1874	8·4	7·1	5·2	20·7	18·1	14·3	32·4	2·7	7·8	10·5	2·1	6·0	8·1	10·8	22·2	58 5/16
1875	8·4	7·4	5·2	21·0	19·5	14·1	33·6	1·1	4·6	5·7	1·8	3·5	5·3	12·4	21·6	56⅞
	49·9	52·9	33·6	136·4	125·1	78·0	203·1	15·5	28·5	44·0	14·5	26·2	40·7	69·1	—	—
1876	9·4	7·4	5·2	22·0	20·5	14·7	35·2	3·2	11·1	14·3	1·4	10·	11·4	12·7	20·5	52¾

Summary.

	United States	Australia	Other Countries	Total	Gold	Silver	Total	Gold	Silver	Total	Gold	Silver	Total	Home Government's Bills on India	Rate of Exchange of the Bills	Price per Ounce of British Standard Silver in London
1853–1860	87·2	94·6	36·1	217·9	213·1	64·9	278·0	7·9	85·3	93·2	22·5	65·8	88·3	12·4	—	—
1861–1865	44·2	47·4	21·9	113·5	112·3	48·0	160·3	24·1	65·2	89·3	37·3	69·1	106·4	30·6	—	—
Total (13 yrs.)	131·4	142·0	58·0	331·4	325·4	112·9	438·3	32·0	150·5	182·5	59·8	134·9	194·7	43·0	—	—
1866–1869	40·5	41·5	19·0	101·0	95·6	40·4	136·0	13·5	19·3	32·8	20·3	34·0	54·3	20·4	—	—
1870–1875	49·9	52·9	33·6	136·4	125·1	78·0	203·1	15·5	28·5	44·0	14·5	26·2	40·7	69·1	—	—
10 years	90·4	94·4	52·6	237·4	220·7	118·4	339·1	29·0	47·8	76·8	34·8	60·2	95·0	89·5	—	—
Total (23 yrs.)	221·8	236·4	110·6	568·8	546·1	231·3	777·4	61·0	198·3	259·3	94·6	195·1	289·7	132·5	—	—

* Mr. Newmarch.

IV. The summary in the table gives the following results :—

(*Millions sterling.*)

	Total Production			Yearly Average		
	Gold	Silver	Total	Gold	Silver	Total
a. Production from 1853–65 (13 years)	331·4	112·9	444·3	25·5	8·7	34·2
Less exported to the East . . .	32·	150·5	182·5	2·4	11·6	14·
Remained in Western System . . .	299·4	– 37·6	261·8	23·1	–2·9	20·2
Old rate of production	131·3	113·1	244·4	10·1	8·7	18·8
b. Production from 1866–75 (10 years)	237·4	118·4	355·8	23·7	11·8	35·5
Less exported to the East . . .	29·	47·8	76·8	2·9	4·8	7·7
	208·4	70·6	279·0	20·8	7·0	27·8
Old rate of production	101·	87·	188·	10·1	8·7	18·8
c. Total production from 1853–75 (23 years) . . .	568·8	231·3	800·1	24·7	10·	34·7
Exported to the East	61·	198·3	259·3	2·7	8·6	11·3
	507·8	33·0	540·8	22·0	1·4	23·4

V. The following remarks are suggested by the table.

a. Australia is included in the Western system, but the exports thence to China and India are not included in the exports to the East; they exceeded 30 millions sterling in 1853 to 1865, and 20 millions sterling in 1866 to 1875. In all they exceeded fifty millions from 1853 to 1875.

b. Adding those exports, it appears that out of 569 millions sterling of gold produced from 1853 to 1875, 111 millions were exported to the East, and 458 millions were retained in the West, or a sum greater than what the old rate of production of both gold and silver would have amounted to (viz., 432 millions) in that period. The West being thus glutted with gold, it rejected silver in the period from 1853 to 1865; but it was not able to do so entirely in the second period from 1866 to 1875, during which 71 millions of silver accumulated in the West; hence the silver depreciated there, and was demonetised.

c. The production of gold in the 23 years from 1853 amounted to 569 millions; this gives an average of 25 millions, against an estimated production in 1876 of 22 millions. If the exports of gold to the East be deducted, viz. 111 millions in all, the amount which remained in the Western system in the 23 years was 458 millions, which gives a yearly average of 20 millions, so that the supply of gold really continues unabated, if we allow for an exaggeration of the estimates in the earlier years after the gold discoveries.

d. The rate or proportion of wear and tear of gold is an infinitesimal percentage; and the solvent countries in Europe have abundantly stocked their currencies. If Germany is as yet in the throes of her currency reform, so as to be still buying more gold, France, on the other hand, has very much more than she needs, and will liberate a large amount on her resuming specie payments. The United States, too, will shortly resume cash payments. Hence, the time is approaching when the West, which has absorbed 20 millions sterling of new gold, principally in replacing the silver which has been expelled to the East, will require only a small fraction of this continuing yearly supply of 22 millions.

e. It may be thought that as commerce has greatly increased since 1848, so an additional supply of gold, beyond the amount of production in that year, must be required for ordinary use. But the following considerations forbid such an expectation:

1. Self-reliant commerce provides its own medium of exchange in inland and foreign bills which have multiplied to the same extent that commerce has increased.

2. The drain of silver to the East kept a large amount of the precious metals in motion, gold being exported from England for the purchase, from the Continent, of the silver required for the East. This must now cease, with the increase of the Home Government's drafts on India. Instead of 3 millions sterling, as in 1849, the bills now amount to 15 millions; and, in addition, a large amount of bills has been created for remitting to England the returns for capital invested in China and India.

3. The stupendous amount of international borrowings has also created, in the form of stocks, an international paper currency, bearing interest, which is largely employed in settlements of foreign trade.

4. Again, in domestic or home settlements, the occasions for the use of metallic currency have been diminished by the clearing-house system, by the vast development of banking and deposits, with a

consequent multiplication of cheques, and by various forms of remittances. In France, in Germany, in the United States, the number of banks, including branches of the principal or Imperial Bank, has been very greatly increased.

5. There has also been an enormous extension of State paper currency since 1848. In the United States and in France, where specie payments have been suspended, the people have become habituated to the use of paper currency; and, as the usual result in such cases, the public, on the resumption of specie payments, will continue to prefer notes. This was the experience in England on the resumption of specie payments, and it has been the experience in France, where gold issued by the Bank of France has quickly returned to it, the people preferring notes. Italy, again, suspended specie payments some years after 1848; and all her metallic currency has been expelled from circulation.

6. Hence the requirements of a metallic currency are apparently not more in the present day than they were in 1848. But yet we find that in the period from 1853 to 1865 the West retained, out of the total production, a yearly average of 21 millions sterling of gold, against a total supply, in 1848, of both gold and silver, for both East and West, of 19 millions; and in the second period, from 1866 to 1875, it retained a yearly average of 19 millions of gold.

f. It follows that, having regard to *d* and *e*, the West will not be able to absorb any but a small fraction of the future gold supply of 22 millions sterling a year.

g. From 1853 to 1865, the West retained 299 millions sterling of gold; whilst, at the old rate of production, the supply for both West and East would have been 131 millions. The excess of 168 millions of extra gold production was retained, but only by exporting to the East 151 millions of silver, including 38 millions from the old stock of currency in the West. In addition to the 151 millions of silver, 62 millions sterling of gold were exported to the East, from 1853 to 1865. Thus, whereas the total production of gold and silver in that period was 444 millions, while at the old rate it would have been 244 millions, showing an extra production of 200 millions, 213 millions of gold and silver were exported to the East. This export by the West, and receipt by the East, of more than the extra production from 1853 to 1865 implies that silver must have depreciated in the East, during that period, a great deal more than gold depreciated in the West; and this is exactly what occurred.

h. From 1866 to 1875, the West retained 188 millions sterling of gold production, whereas the old rate for both East and West would have amounted to only 101 millions; it also retained 71 millions of silver, which, however, as explained in *b*, it was forced to demonetise. Hence we should find that in this period gold would be depreciated in Europe to a greater extent than silver was depreciated in the East, and that silver would depreciate, relatively to gold, in the West. This, exactly, is what happened. Mr. Fawcett and others concluded that because prices were falling in the East silver was rising in value, and that, this being the case, it could not at the same time be falling in the West. It was overlooked, first, that silver having in a previous period reached an extreme depreciation in the East, to an extent greater than gold has as yet depreciated in the West, perforce the value of silver would continue to rise in the East, until fresh exports of it thither, through its new depreciation in the West, should cause a fresh depreciation of it in the East; secondly, it was overlooked that the local value of silver, as legal tender currency in the East, must always differ from its price in the West. Experience shows that the price of silver in the West sympathises with the price of Asiatic produce in the West, rising when that rises, and depreciating when that falls.

VI. The following questions arise, from the circumstance (see *f*) of the Western drafts on the yearly supply of 22 millions sterling of gold shortly ceasing, and of the yearly production of silver amounting to 15 millions, with silver demonetised in the West.

a. What will the world do, henceforth, with its 22 millions a year of gold, unless some new field of gold currency be occupied? The present universal stagnation of trade gives point to the inquiry.

b. And what will the world do with other 15 millions a year of silver, additional to the 15 millions sterling of the India Council drafts? The falling price of silver emphasises the inquiry.

c. And if the 15 millions a year of silver be not withdrawn from the legal tender currency of the world, but be allowed to keep up the metallic currency at 37 millions sterling, additional to the vast amount of paper money mentioned in *e*, against only 19 millions sterling in 1848, what will be the effect upon prices, and will that effect be beneficial? The universal stagnation of trade, because, with high prices and heavy taxation, consumers reduce their purchases, and because with high wages producers cannot lower prices, seems to answer the inquiry.

7. The following estimates have been made of the stock of the precious metals in the world:—

(In Millions sterling.)

	1848			1875		
	Gold	Silver	Total	Gold	Silver	Total
Mr. Newmarch (including plate and ornaments) .	560	800	1360	—	—	—
Mr. E. Seyd (exclusive of plate and ornaments) .	400	—	—	750	650	1400
M. Victor Bonnet . .	600	1200	1800	1200	1200	2400

It has been contended that if 1,400 or 1,800 millions sterling of gold and silver were required in 1848, 800 or 1,200 millions of gold would not suffice, on the demonetisation of silver. The figures for 1848 appear to be inclusive of plate and ornaments; these do not act upon prices. And the fact remains that silver, except what is circulating as full legal tender in the countries of the Latin Union, in Germany, and in the United States, has been demonetised; yet gold continues depreciated below its value in 1848. Further, it is a mistake to suppose that silver would not be extensively used as subsidiary currency, on its demonetisation.

The facts which appear from this paper are:—

1. That the West, as pointed out by M. Chevalier, shortly after the gold discoveries in California and Australia, was not rich enough to pay for all the new production of gold, as an addition to its metallic currency, and so it exported more than an equal amount of silver to the East. Thereby, the West practically became 'gold-monometallic;' and on 70 millions of silver accumulating in the West from 1866 to 1875, it was demonetised, and in Europe it was depreciated.

2. That the existing yearly production of 22 millions sterling of gold is greatly beyond the capacity of the West to absorb it; by reason of the excessive accumulation of gold in France, of the completion wellnigh of the coinage reform in Germany, and of the approaching resumption of specie payments in the United States.

3. That owing to the enormous increase of paper money of various kinds, the increase of the India Council Drafts from 3 millions to 15 millions, and a yearly production of gold greater, by 3 millions, than the total production of gold and silver in 1848, the supply of gold is ample for any solvent silver coin countries which are in a position to alter their standard. India, apparently, is the only country which answers to this description.

4. That, referring to the enormous increase of paper money, and to the consideration that by far the largest part of the foreign trade of the world is carried on by transactions in paper, the total present production of 37 millions of gold and silver, against 19 millions in 1848, is much in excess of requirements.

5. That for the same reasons, the existing production of gold, which is 3 millions greater than the total production of gold and silver, is fully sufficient, with a subsidiary silver currency, for the world's requirements.

6. That owing to the extra production of gold from 1853 to 1865, having been purchased in the West by the export of a greater amount of silver to the East, silver depreciated relatively to commodities to a greater extent and sooner than gold depreciated in the West; that silver reached its extreme depreciation by 1865, and that hence its rise in value, latterly, in the East has no connection with the fall of its gold price in the West, except to confirm that it is silver which has fallen, not gold which has risen in value in the West, for the price of silver in London sympathises with the price of Asiatic produce in Europe, rising when that rises, and depreciating when that falls.

APPENDIX II.

CURRENCIES OF VARIOUS COUNTRIES.

GENERAL.

'In the early ages of European States silver was the general coin and standard: but as gold came into more general use, gold coins were more extensively introduced, and the value for which they were to pass current, being fixed by the Government of each country, from time to time, a double standard of value was generally introduced.

It is still retained according to law in Belgium, France, Switzerland, Italy, Greece, Spain, Russia, and the United States.

In England the double standard ceased practically in 1717 (when the value of the guinea was fixed at twenty-one shillings) and by law in 1816 (when sovereigns superseded guineas); and in England, as well as in Portugal, Turkey, and Brazil, a single standard of gold prevails.

In Holland, Germany, and the Northern States of Europe, there is a single standard of silver.'—*Royal Commission on International Coinage*, 1868.

LATIN MINT CONVENTION.

2. On December 23, 1865, France, Belgium, Switzerland and Italy entered, for fourteen years, or to 31st December 1879, into a formal convention, known as the Latin Mint Convention or the Latin Union. Greece was admitted into the union on 8th October 1868; but not having any mint, she took no steps to assimilate her coinage with that of the countries forming the union, until February 1876, after the recent depreciation of silver. At the conference of delegates of the union, held at Paris in that month, she obtained assent to a coinage, on her account, at the Paris Mint, of an ordinary contingent of 3·6 millions, and an extraordinary contingent of 8·4 millions of silver five-franc pieces.

3. The Convention of 1865 enacted that the coin of each State should circulate freely in the other three States, as between Government and Government; but although such circulation was not com-

pulsory on private individuals or the public, these last received indiscriminately the gold and silver coin of the four contracting Powers.

4. The standard of purity adopted by the contracting powers for the gold and silver coins of legal tender is nine-tenths fine. For the subsidiary silver coins, viz. two-franc pieces, and the fractions below, which are legal tender to the amount of only 50 francs, it is ·835 fine.

5. The amount of subsidiary silver coinage to be emitted by each country, is calculated at six francs per head of the population; and on this basis (also reckoning the presumed increase of population up to 1879) the total issue during the fourteen years from 1866 to 1879 was fixed at 32 million francs for Belgium, 17 millions for Switzerland, 141 millions for Italy, and 239 millions for France: total, 429 millions.

6. The relative value of the gold and silver coins of full legal tender was fixed at 1 to 15½; at this valuation, silver coins were expelled from circulation until 1873, when a depreciation of silver began, by which silver would have been coined, and the gold coins been exported.

'This state of matters could be attended with no real injury to Italy, whose gold and silver had (1876) long ago disappeared from circulation; but it could not be regarded with indifference in France, Belgium, and Switzerland.'

7. Accordingly, in Belgium, a law was passed in 1873, enabling the Belgian Government to suspend or limit the coinage of silver five-franc pieces. This principle of limitation was subsequently adopted by the other States of the Latin Union; and at the yearly meetings of their respective delegates, which have taken place annually at Paris, since 1874, the limitation of the silver coinage of five-franc pieces was fixed as follows:—

(Millions of francs.)

	Belgium	France	Italy	Switzerland	Greece	Total
1874	12·	60·	40· extraordinary 20·	8·	—	120 20
1875	15·	75·	50·	10·	—	150
1876	10·8	54·	36·	7·2	3·6 extraordinary 8·4	120
1877	5·4	27·	18·	3·6	1·8	55·8

The extraordinary contingent to Italy in 1874 and 1875, and to Greece in 1876, was to enable those States to replace their old silver coinage by five-franc pieces.

8. The declaration signed at the Conference on 3rd February 1876 contains an article by which the contracting Governments engage to communicate to each other all facts that may come to their knowledge regarding false coinage, or tampering with the money of the Union, as well as the measures to be taken in common for its prevention, and for the punishment of the offenders. At the same Conference, a discussion of the question of adopting a gold standard was deferred till the next meeting of the Conference, which it was then intended to hold in January 1877; but

'On the 22nd January 1877, Lord Lyons reported that the Monetary Conference which was to have been held in that month had been postponed to the end of the year, the several powers forming the Latin Union agreeing in the meantime to maintain the existing stipulations respecting the coinage of silver, which, as M. Leon Say explained in a letter, forwarded by Lord Lyons on the 13th of February, restricted the contingent for each nation in 1877 to half the amount allowed in 1876.'

9. Evidences of the intention, more or less clearly declared, of France, Switzerland, and Belgium to adopt a single gold standard, and of the shifting policy of Italy in the matter, will be found in the following notices of the currencies in those countries.

10. SWITZERLAND.

I. 'The principal supply of gold coins comes from France; Switzerland has not, up to the present time (April 19, 1876) coined moneys of gold, but she ought to resolve upon it in the sequel. The metallic circulation of Switzerland ought to be about 300 million francs per annum, of which about 100 millions are in gold, and the remainder in silver currency and bullion. In the Federal Treasury, the proportion of the two kinds of moneys is about three to one on the average.'—*M. Wetti, President of the Confederation.*

II. 'Up to the end of 1872, the circulation of bank notes in Switzerland, whose decentralising system causes the notes of one canton to be undervalued in every other, had never exceeded twenty millions of francs. Since the price of silver sank, in consequence of the existence of a double standard, *gold*, which had been almost exclusively the metal circulated, almost entirely disappeared from the country, and, in its stead, silver 'ecus' came in, the most part of them due to the payment of the French milliards. Now, the public finding the heavy silver circulation a nuisance to which it is not accustomed, the circulation of notes has grown from twenty millions to seventy-two millions of francs in two years.'—*Paris correspondent of the 'Economist.'*

III. 'Since 1873, the Federal Government has persistently striven for the establishment, in due time, of a single gold standard. In 1874, the Government indeed caused seven million silver five-francs (forming the complement of its contingent for that year) to be coined at Brussels, but it did not make use of its right to coin its contingent in 1875, nor does it appear to have the intention of exercising it this year (1876). The President of the

Confederation stated, on April 18, 1876, that the Swiss Government had been anxious to induce the other Governments, members of the Latin Union, to adopt a single instead of the double standard of value now in use; but as they had ascertained beforehand that they would, if it came to a vote, find themselves in a minority, they had not proposed the change. His Excellency added that they would probably make the attempt at a future Conference, and if they could not carry the point, they might find themselves obliged to retire from the Union.'

IV. 'The Swiss banks, though not unprovided with gold, are averse to making use of it in their payments. The banks in Italy and France acting in the same way, the Swiss banks are indisposed to give to those countries what is refused to them, and so contribute to increase the exportation of coin from Switzerland. In point of fact, it may be said that Switzerland is obliged in this matter to follow the example of the neighbouring countries.'

V. 'The Swiss delegates at the Conference of 1876, in their report published in September 1876, considered that the limitation of the coinage of five-franc pieces was the first step towards the demonetisation of silver, and they cited the fact that, in the course of 1875, 12·79 millions sterling, in twenty-franc gold pieces, was coined by the countries of the Latin Union, against only 5·6 millions sterling in silver; as proof that the French, Italian, and Belgian Governments, while refusing to come to a definite decision, are quietly preparing for the adoption of the single gold standard.'

VI. 'Under the Convention of December 1865, there has been issued (12th April 1876) in Switzerland, 8·052 million francs' worth of five-franc pieces, ·900 fine, and 5½ million francs' worth of two-franc, one-franc, and half-franc pieces, ·835 fine; and, according to that Convention, Switzerland is obliged to retire from circulation to the end of 1877, 10·5 million francs' worth of two-franc and one-franc pieces of the old coinage.'

11. ITALY.

I. The Lira Italiana (= one franc) is the unit for all purposes of exchange. Specie payments were suspended on 30th April 1866, on which day, the coin known to exist throughout the then kingdom of Italy was estimated at a value of £36,140,000, viz., 17·22 millions sterling in gold, 3·44 millions in silver five-franc pieces, 13·48 millions in two and one-franc pieces, and the remainder of base metal, copper and bronze. On the same date, the foreign coin circulating in Italy greatly exceeded in value the Italian coin circulating abroad.

II. The old coinage included about 12 millions sterling of money which had been coined in conformity with the French decimal system. All the coinage, after 1860, in the Pontifical States which are now comprised in the kingdom of Italy, was also in conformity with the system of the Union. The remainder of the old coinage has been in course of withdrawal since 1862, and the value of the withdrawals, up to the end of 1875, was 21·74 millions, viz., 1·14 million gold, 19·46 millions silver, and 1·14 million copper.

III. The money in circulation coined according to the present system, both the decimal portion of the old coinage and that coined by the present Government from 1862 to the end of 1875, gives a total of 18·98 millions sterling in gold, 14·44 millions in five-franc silver pieces, 6·24 millions silver tokens, and 3·04 millions copper: total, 42·70 millions sterling.

'There can be no doubt, however, that the greater part of this money has been melted again. It is to be added that, from the effect of the forced currency, the greater part of the Italian coin, both gold and silver, which has ever existed, has emigrated from Italy, and scattered itself principally through the other States of the Latin Union.'

IV. The fact last stated is manifest from the volume of the inconvertible paper currency, which amounted in 1873 to 1,500 million francs, or 60 millions sterling—that is, to treble the amount of the full legal-tender coins in 1866, and to double that of the similar coins, conformable with the new system, which had been coined to the end of 1875. When specie payments were suspended on April 30, 1866, gold commanded a premium of 21 per cent., silver of 15 per cent., and copper of 7½ per cent., with the result that on May 30, 1876, it was officially stated that—

'Italy's gold and silver had long ago disappeared from circulation . . . Even the divisional silver coin, possessing intrinsically nine per cent. less than its nominal value, irresistibly found its way out of the country, when the agio between silver and paper exceeded that rate. Even the copper coin, the intrinsic value of which hardly represents the third part of its nominal value, acquired additional value as compared with the bank notes, and was at one time hoarded to a considerable extent in the Neapolitan Provinces . . . For a long time copper commanded a premium of 3 to 3½ per cent.; while in some of the Italian Provinces it is known to have reached as high a premium as 12 per cent. in relation to bank notes. The small silver coined under the Convention, to the amount of £6,240,000, being the maximum allowed, quickly disappeared.'

V. On October 31, 1876, the gold held in the Treasury and the six banks in the kingdom amounted to 9·49 millions, and the silver coins of full legal tender to 7·78 millions sterling; showing a preponderance of gold.

VI. In 1865, at the Conference which settled the Latin Mint Convention, the delegates from Italy, Belgium, and Switzerland proposed to France to enter as soon as possible upon measures for the adoption of a gold standard. But at the Conference at Paris in 1874, when a cessation of the coinage of silver was proposed—

'The condition of the forced paper currency imposed on Italy the necessity of resisting any proposition tending directly to the adoption of one standard in lieu of the double standard—that is, by demonetising silver or limiting its legal tender, as in the case of the divisional coin; thereby contracting the means of circulation, and rendering more difficult a return to specie payments.'

Since, however, the limitation in 1874 of the coinage of silver five-franc pieces, their coinage for private individuals has been discontinued, and has been reserved for the State and for the National Bank of Italy.

VII. In a memorandum dated 20th December 1876, Mr. Compton, third Secretary to the British Embassy at Rome, reported that—

'It seems more than probable that at the next Conference of the Latin Union, the absolute suspension of the coining of silver (inclusive of that effected for the Governments) will be proposed, Switzerland being the most likely State to make the proposal. To this, perhaps, will be added another, that the legal currency of the coin should be limited, providing for the inevitable result of the withdrawal of all silver money which exceeds the demand. In the event of these proposals the Italian interest would be, not to wish for any *immediate* reforms which would conduce to the single gold standard, nor for delay until after the suppression of the forced currency, but rather for them to be effected simultaneously, and in harmony with the operations leading to this ultimate end.'

VIII. Mr. Compton stated that Italy's objections against any immediate reforms for a single gold standard would be these:—

a. 'The greater part of Italian silver money, not only five-franc pieces, but other smaller coin, has been replaced by paper money, and scattered in the other States of the Union. Therefore, when an immediate limitation of the forced currency of silver and the withdrawal of silver money exceeding the demand are agreed to, it is obvious that the other States of the Union would not wish, by reason of this overflow of Italian money, to be constrained to withdraw a greater quantity than their own, and to see in this way their losses increased.'

b. 'Also Italy could no longer limit herself to the withdrawal of the excess of her silver money, according to the presumable demand in the case of the circulation of coin being again re-established; but she would have to redeem almost all this money, submitting to a much more material loss, while her interest is to put into circulation only a part, when the moment arrived to suppress the forced currency.'

c. 'Nor would a delay in the reforms until after the forced currency is suppressed seem advantageous, as, among the greater dangers which might arise from the renewing of payments in coin, would be the demand of the holders of bank notes for change, when the banks could more easily defend their reserves by paying in silver instead of in gold. To avoid this danger, as well as others which might result from the renewal of coin payments, steps must be taken beforehand for the efficacy of the operations, and an opportune moment must be chosen, instead of having recourse to such artifices as would tend to oppose the change of bank notes. The example of Germany may be brought forward to show how a change in the monetary system may bring about grave results; and these results may be easily avoided, if a country where paper money is in circulation should change its monetary system at the same time as it substitutes coin for the paper.

d. 'Italy's course is to redeem a sufficient quantity of the larger notes, so as entirely to do away with the agio. It will then be the moment to redeem the smaller notes, and also to carry out the monetary reform, because the Italian silver money could then take the place of the paper redeemed, and there would be only that part to be withdrawn which would exceed the wants of the circulation of small coin.

IX. 'This will be the attitude taken by Italy towards its allies, when they are inclined to introduce the reform before the above-mentioned contigencies are carried out; and the Union, as long as it exists, will be forced, however reluctantly, to agree to the wishes of Italy. The Convention of 1865 ceases to have force on the 1st of January 1880, if it should be denounced by any of the States. Therefore they may then injure Italy, by denying all currency to her silver money. But since this money is and will remain in great quantity in their territory until the small paper money is redeemed by her, by acting thus they will do greater injury to themselves.

X. 'The interests of Italy will therefore compel her to support any reform by which the Latin monetary system is based on the single gold standard. But it will be her duty to oppose anything that renders the carrying out of this more burdensome; and at the same time it depends exclusively on the skill of the Government in choosing that moment for the carrying out of those measures which would be most favourable to the interests of Italy.'

XI. In 1873, the loss to the Treasury by the payments abroad, in gold, of the interest on Italian securities held in foreign countries, led the Government to open books for the registration of Italian debt in the principal capitals of Europe, with the object of limiting the gold payments to foreign holders of Italian stock or titles. In September 1876 the Italian Government announced 'that for the payment abroad of the guaranteed interest, and the redemption of the Victor Emmanuel railway bonds of 1863, an affidavit will be required that the bonds are not the property of Italian subjects, and the titles must be presented as for Italian rentes.'

12. BELGIUM.

I. The French system of coinage was introduced about the beginning of the century. In 1850, the gold coinage was demonetised, and silver became the sole legal standard. In 1861, the French system was restored; in 1865, Belgium entered the Latin Union. In September 1873, the coinage of silver was limited by a ministerial order, which was confirmed on 18th December following, by a temporary law that expired on 1st July 1875, when it was renewed and extended to 31st December 1876. On 25th April 1876, a bill was introduced in the Belgian Chamber of Representatives and was eventually passed into law for two years more, whereby the power of limiting the amount of silver to be coined was continued, and the right of coining silver five-franc pieces was reserved to the State. On 6th December 1876, a further law was passed that 'from the 1st January 1877, no more pieces of five-francs shall be coined in silver.'

II. In the discussions which preceded the law of 6th December 1876, the Committee of the Chamber of Deputies desired a nearer approach to a gold standard. M. Malon informed the Secretary of the British Legation, Brussels, that he by no means desires to facilitate the introduction of the single standard of gold into Belgium, as suggested by the Committee, and that

> 'The limitation or suspension of the silver coinage was merely a temporary measure, and was not to be looked upon as evidence of a change of system. The question as to whether such a change were desirable would be decided in 1880, but up to that date no member of the Latin Union could separately adopt a change of the actual monetary *régime*, and M. Malon added that he considered the question of the adoption of the gold standard, raised by the Committee, to be premature.'

III. The restrictions on the coinage of silver which are mentioned in section I. were explained by M. Malon as follows:—

a. When the yearly amount of silver coinage was restricted by the Delegates of the Latin Union, the right of having silver coined was necessarily reserved to the State.

b. The limitation of the amount of silver coinage is designed to restrain speculators. The five-franc pieces are thereby maintained as correct legal money, not viewed suspiciously, nor at present menaced with demonetisation; they continue to be a necessary agency in the currency. In Belgium, more than elsewhere, the absence or scarcity of the money would cause great inconvenience and embarrassment. One needs a piece between the twenty-franc piece and the divisionary currency of two francs and less.

c. It is strictly speaking possible, but very uncertain, that some day or other silver may be demonetised in the countries of the Latin Union; but probably, during the next two years, or to January 1, 1880, when the Convention expires, the Powers of the Union will continue in the expectant attitude which has been maintained by common consent since January 1874.

d. None of the sinister predictions of 1873 respecting the depreciation of silver have been realised as yet; neither in the increased price of everything, nor in the perturbation of the rate of exchange, nor in the rise of the rate of discount. If anything, there has been some complaint as to the fall of certain prices; the exchanges have suffered from fluctuations caused by circumstances foreign to the relative value of the precious metals, but in general the balance of prices has been generally favourable to Belgium, which cannot be said to have been altogether the case in other countries which have long ago or recently adopted the single standard of gold.

IV. The coinage in Belgium has been as follows:—

a. Gold.—From 1865 to 1875 inclusive, 14·52 millions sterling of twenty-franc gold pieces, of which the greater part must have been coined since 1873, for Mr. Seyd states that from 1832 to 1873 the total coinage amounted to 8·77 millions sterling.

b. Silver.—From 1867 to 1872 inclusive, 7·9 millions sterling, and from 1874 to 1876 it will not have amounted to 1·51 million. In 1873, in the eight months up to August 31, which preceded the limitation, from September 4, of the coinage of silver for private individuals, the amount coined was 2·54 millions sterling. Altogether, from 1867 to 1876, the silver coinage was about 13 millions sterling, including a large amount in 1873. Mr. Seyd states that from 1832 to 1873 the total silver coinage amounted to 18 068 millions sterling. On April 18, 1876, M. Malon stated that Belgium had scarcely struck half a milliard worth (20 millions sterling) of silver five-franc pieces, of which the National Bank held on a then recent date 1·22 million sterling. Until the fresh influx of silver in 1873, the silver coins of full legal tender appear to have been exported from Belgium, which would not have to withdraw much silver coin on the adoption of a gold standard.

13. GREECE.

'There is (April 17, 1876) very little coin of any description in Greece; the real currency in the country consisting of notes of the National Bank of Greece, whose value is expressed in new drachmes or francs, of which, according to the last return published by the bank, there are about thirty-two millions of francs' worth now in circulation against a reserve in the bank of fifteen millions of francs in silver coin. These notes are made payable only in Athens, and are inconvertible in the provinces. The Athenian branch of the National Bank has hitherto cashed its notes in either German or Mexican dollars, or in any other silver coins contained in the present Government tariff. According, however, to the new royal decrees, dated March 29 and

April 10, 1876, the notes of the National Bank must be paid in francs on August 1 and 13, 1876, after which period all other silver coins, except national ones and those of the Latin Union, will cease to be a legal tender.'

14. FRANCE.

I. 'By the law of 1803, five grammes of silver, nine-tenths fine, were constituted the monetary unit, retaining the name of a franc; but the provisions of the law as to gold, and also as to copper coins, gave them a legal currency and value, independent of their relation to silver. The result of this legislation was that a double standard was created by law in France. We observe (July 25, 1868) in the recent report of the French commission, on the double standard, that it was stated by the advocates of the single standard that it was the intention of the framers of the law of 1803 to establish a single standard, of which the basis was to be the franc, containing five grammes of silver, nine-tenths fine; and it appears, from the declaration of those by whom the law was introduced, that it was further intended that the quantity of gold in the gold coins should be adjusted from time to time, so as to make silver the sole measure of value.'—*Royal Commission on International Coinage*, 1868.

II. The gold and silver coinages in France have been as follows, according to statistics published in the Report of the Committee on the Depreciation of Silver, and in the 'Economist':—

I. VALUE OF COINAGE.

(*In millions of francs, or 000,000's omitted.*)

	Years	Gold	Silver ·900 fine	Silver ·835 fine	Gold		Silver	
					Net Imports	Net Exports	Net Imports	Net Exports
1795–1802	8	—	106	—	—	—	—	—
1803–14	12	576	948	—	—	—	—	—
1815–47	33	601	2,940	—	—	51	2,051	—
1848–52	5	449	544	—	163	—	606	—
	58	1,626	4,538	—	163	51	2,657	—
1853–64	12	4,784	137	7	3,360	—	—	1,723
1865–70	6	1,355	260	174	1,630	—	562	—
1871–72	2	50	5	46	—	267	117	—
1873–75	3	259	290	2	777	—	735	—
1876	1	177	—	42	505	—	148	—
	24	6,625	692	271	6,272	267	1,562	1,723

II. **BULLION IN BANK OF FRANCE.**

(In millions of francs, or 000,000's omitted.)

	1852	1863	1865	1866	1869	1870	1871	1872	1873	1874	1875	1876 Apl. 25
Gold . .	69	119	238	576	461	429	554	656	611	1,013	1,168	1,379
Silver .	442	72	208	136	798	69	80	134	148	314	504	546
Total .	511	191	446	712	1,259	498	634	790	759	1,327	1,672	1,925
Note circulation .	—	750	850	950	1,375	1,725	2,300	2,625	2,875	2,575	2,400	2,438

III. **MERCHANDISE.**

(In millions sterling.)

	General					Special	
	1841	1860	1865	1869	1874	1875	
Imports . . .	47	106	141	160	177	141	
Exports . . .	40	126	163	160	188	155	

The following remarks are suggested by the table :—

I. The returns of imports and exports of gold and silver are not accurate; but they indicate the set of the trade, whether towards a net import or a net export.

II. Until 1802 there was a single standard of silver; and, notwithstanding the introduction of the double standard in 1803, silver maintained its supremacy in the currency until 1852. The proportion of gold to silver coinage was indeed considerable from 1803 to 1814 (through the exportation, doubtless, of gold from England, during her continental wars and her suspension of cash payments); also from 1848 to 1852, partly, no doubt, from the demonetisation of gold in Holland. In the intervening period from 1815 to 1847, the silver coinage greatly preponderated; and in the course of trade almost all the gold coinage was exported, so that at the date of the gold discoveries in 1848 and 1851 nearly the whole circulation consisted of silver. Hence, in estimating the amount of the metallic circulation in France at the present time, the whole of the gold coinage down to 1847 may be struck out.

III. In 1853 began the drain of silver to the East, principally from the French currency. It continued until about 1865; and it is noteworthy that the gold coinage from 1853 to 1864, when gold was expelling the dearer silver from the French currency, amounted to 4,784 million francs, against a silver coinage of 4,538 millions from 1795 to 1852, during which period, or down to 1847, silver had been excluding or expelling gold.

IV. Mr. James Wilson, in his Minute on a Gold Currency for India, dated December 25, 1859, stated that 'since 1850 a sum equal to 130 millions sterling of gold has been coined at the French mint, and a corresponding amount of silver has been exported. . . . Indeed, it is chiefly the fact that a large portion of the silver coin now in circulation in France has become considerably reduced below its full value by wear that has prevented its being exported.' The total silver coinage of full weight was 186 millions sterling to the end of 1858, 187 millions to the end of 1864, 197 millions to the end of 1870, and 209 millions to the end of 1876.

V. Mr. Wilson's method of measuring the export of silver coin from 1850 by the amount of the new gold coinage since that year, gives a safer result than the inaccurate Customs' returns afford; and in adopting it he must have been guided by a knowledge of the character of the bullion operations from 1850 to 1858. The continuous drain of silver to the East ceased after 1865, and if we take Mr. Wilson's estimate of 1858, viz. 130 millions sterling, as the amount of silver coin exported from the French currency since 1850, to the end of 1870, up to which date the gross silver coinage amounted to 197 millions, the remainder of 67 millions would include the amount of actual circulation in 1870, *plus* (1st) the withdrawals of worn-out coin from 1795 to 1849; and (2nd) the losses from fire, flood, emigration, shipwreck, and in the wars of Napoleon, &c. Similarly deducting Mr. Wilson's 130 millions sterling from the gross silver coinage of 209 millions to the end of 1876, there is a remainder of 79 millions, which would be subject to the considerable abatements just stated.

VI. An outside estimate of the gold coins in circulation or hoarded in France may be ascertained in a different way. Specie payments were suspended in France on August 12, 1870, after which gold was gradually driven from circulation into hoards. In 1869, the note circulation of the Bank of France amounted to 55 millions sterling; in 1873 it reached its highest, and in October of that year it was 118 millions sterling, with a premium on gold of only 3 per thousand. Down to November 1871, the note circulation did not exceed 92 millions sterling; the further extra issue, which raised the amount to 118 millions, was made for facilitating payment of subscriptions, in 1871 to 1873, to the French loans of 1871 and 1872 for the war indemnity to Germany. The extra issue thus was not in displacement of gold coin, but an addition to the inconvertible paper currency; it included, moreover, some 12 to 16 millions sterling of small notes, which probably displaced silver coins. Assuming, nevertheless, that the whole excess of 118 millions sterling, in the amount of notes in October 1873, over the 55 millions in 1869, was that which had driven a corresponding amount of gold coin into hoards, we have 63 millions sterling as the hoarded amount of gold coins. Adding to this the 18 millions sterling in gold in the the Bank of France in 1869, or the 24 millions in 1873, the total gold currency is raised to 87 millions sterling. But though in 1873 business transactions continued to be carried on in notes and silver coin, gold having very rarely appeared in circulation, still some gold must have been circulating, concurrently with the notes; and there must be added the gold coin which was hoarded at the date of the suspension of cash payments. An outside amount for these additions will be obtained, if we assume it as equal to the note circulation before 1870, viz. at 55 millions. This would raise the total gold currency in 1873 to 142 millions; and adding thereto 17 millions for the gold coinage in 1874 to 1876, the gold currency in 1876 becomes 159 millions sterling, of which the Bank of France held 24 millions in 1873, and 55 millions on April 25, 1876, the last mentioned sum including 12 millions sterling in bullion. On the whole, 140 millions sterling would be an excessive estimate of the gold coin in France in 1876.

VII. Mr. Blake, in his work on the production of the precious metals (February 18, 1869), observed :—

'In regard to the metallic circulation of France, there is a wide difference in the estimates. Chevalier estimated it at 100 millions sterling. Roswag, who has examined the subject with great care, estimates that the stock in 1865 did not exceed three milliards of francs (120 millions sterling). Mr. George Walker adds 20 millions to this estimate of Roswag, and considers 140 millions sterling as fairly representing the total circulation of France.'

The total coinage of gold and silver, nine-tenths fine, from 1869 to 1876, amounted to 47 millions sterling. Adding this sum to Mr. Walker's 140 millions, the total becomes 187 millions sterling, against the outside amounts given in sections V. and VI., viz., 140 millions of gold and 79 millions of silver, the latter amount being subject to considerable abatements.

VIII. In December 1873, M. Bonnet stated that the silver coin circulating in France in 1870 amounted to 40 or 48 millions sterling. Adding thereto the total silver coinage, nine-tenths fine, from 1871 to 1876, viz., 14½ millions sterling, the total ranges from 54 to 72 millions. In December 1875, M. Bonnet estimated the metallic currency at 200 millions sterling in gold, and 80 millions in silver: total, 280 millions, or a sum greatly exceeding the metallic currencies of England and Germany, and of the United States before the American civil war. The estimate is manifestly excessive.

IX. The note circulation (section II. of table in para. 14) rose from 750 million francs in 1863 to 1,375 millions in 1869, or by 625 millions, equal to 25 millions sterling, in six years. In 1873 it amounted to 2,875 millions, showing an increase since 1869 of 1,500 millions, or 60 millions sterling. But by September 13, 1877, it had fallen to 2,367 million francs, which gives an excess of 992 millions, or of 40 millions sterling over the circulation of 55 millions sterling in 1869.

X. The numbers, denominations, and value of the notes of the Bank of France, outstanding on various dates, were as follows :—

(In millions of francs.)

Denomination of Notes	Jan. 25, 1872	Jan. 25, 1873	Jan. 25, 1874	Jan. 25 1875	Jan. 27, 1876	Jan. 25, 1877
Francs						
5,000	Thirty-five thousand to thirty thousand francs					
1,000	802	775	719	822	896	1,101
500	212	214	202	216	227	242
200	2	1	1	1	1	1
100	710	806	884	970	1,111	1,189
50	264	307	275	321	179	100
25	261	111	28	5	1	1
20	202	537	628	300	81	26
5	—	107	94	7	2	1
1	—	—	—	—	—	—
Old models	Forty-six to forty-five thousand francs					
	2,454	2,859	2,833	2,641	2,498	2,662
No. of notes	34,145,000	68,030,000	66,757,000	—	20,500,243	17,085,250

Until January 1877, and later, the Bank was concerned in the withdrawal of the small notes, more than with the reduction of the total note circulation. The five-franc and twenty-franc notes were withdrawn in 1873 and 1874, by the issue of silver coins for the former and of gold coins for the latter. The withdrawal of the notes of fifty francs began in 1875; and on March 22, 1877, the Paris correspondent of the 'Economist' wrote that the Bank had ceased to reissue the notes of fifty francs and under. On May 17, 1877, the same writer stated that 'although the Bank of France has withdrawn all its notes of less than 100 francs, and only issues those with great reluctance, the cash reserve shows no signs of diminishing.' Before the suspension of specie payments, the note of smallest denomination was the fifty-franc note; its total withdrawal during the present year, notwithstanding the more extended use of the paper currency, is a significant circumstance. The amount of the circulation in September 1877 scarcely exceeded that in 1871, while the number of notes was perhaps less than that in 1870. Hence, the present state of the currency seems to be that of specie payments and cheques for small transactions, and notes and cheques for large transactions.

XI. To the domestic currency of France, paper and metallic, must be added the five-franc pieces of the other countries of the Latin Union which are circulating in France. A French writer, whom the Committee on the Depreciation of Silver quote as a high authority, states that eight millions sterling have been thus imported into the French currency. The same writer estimates the total silver circulation in France at 88 millions sterling.

XII. The amount of metallic and paper money in France in 1870 and in 1876 may be stated as follows, in millions sterling:—

(Millions sterling.)

	Gold Coin	Silver Coin	Total	Note Circulation	Grand Total	Gold and Silver in Bank of France
In 1870 . .	108	48	156	55 (1869)	211	18
In 1876 (sections V. & VI.)	140	79	219	106	325	86
M. Bonnet .	200	80	280	106	386	86

For the year 1870, the total of gold and silver has been obtained by adding the coinage of 1869 and 1870 to Mr. Walker's continuation, down to 1868, of M. Roswag's estimate for 1865. For silver, M. Bonnet's estimate has been taken, and the difference between that and the total of gold and silver coins has been reckoned as the amount of gold coins in 1870. In judging of the figures, the following considerations must be regarded:—

a. The ordinary effect of a paper currency is to drive an equal amount of metallic currency out of its old channels of circulation, and the ordinary effect of an inconvertible paper money is an exportation of the precious metals. In France, however, during the period of inconvertible paper, there has been a considerable net import of those metals. The result is, that the coins in circulation in 1870 and the additions thereto, except the portions actually circulating, are hoarded.

b. The great mass of the metallic currency accumulated in bygone years, when the dealings in France were essentially of a retail character, and facilities of banking were few. The first considerable substitution of paper for metallic money was consequent on the law of 1857, which required the Bank of France to establish gradually a branch office in each of the eighty-nine departments of France, and later through the revolution in the currency from the drain of silver to the East. Only since 1871, however, have the branch offices been freely established; the number open at the end of 1876 was seventy-six, and fourteen more remained to be opened. Through these branch banks the facilities for remitting money by bills, instead of in the form of specie, have been very greatly increased, while the floating amounts and deposits with these branches have largely promoted the use of cheques. Inconvertible paper also popularised the notes. Thus, in the report of the Bank of France for 1875, it was stated that—

> 'Whilst gold has come to us from abroad, in payment of the balance on international transactions, we have not made a proportionate use of metallic money in our own country. The country has employed by preference the notes of the Bank, which are more convenient, and in which it places unlimited confidence. This is the cause, gentlemen, that both gold and silver increase in our tills.'

Again, the Paris correspondent of the 'Economist' wrote on May 31, 1877:—

> 'The large amount of private deposits at the Bank, which, from 220 millions in May 1873, have now increased to 650 millions, has also added over 400 millions to the reserve, a great part of which has no doubt been cash. The development in the use of cheques for payments, aided by the creation of a bankers' clearing-house since the war, has besides contributed to diminish the proportion of cash employed in trade; but perhaps the chief reason for the increase in the cash reserve is the gradual substitution of a note circulation for a metallic one, by the dying out of the old prejudice against paper money in the rural districts: a prejudice due, no doubt, in a certain measure, to recollections or traditions of the assignats of the first revolution. Until recent years, bank notes were almost unknown, or looked on with suspicion, in country places; and the French peasant or small pro-

prietor only thought his money safe when carefully secreted in the form of silver five-franc pieces or gold. The diffusion of Rente, which commenced under the Empire, first brought money from those hoards. The regularity with which the dividends have been paid during the most disturbed times has won the confidence of the small proprietor; and the establishment of branches of the Bank of France in the most remote departments has helped to popularise bank notes. Referring back to the month of May 1870, just before the war, the cash in the Bank is seen to have amounted to 1,268 millions, and the note circulation to 1,442 millions. At present there is, in round numbers, 1000 millions more cash in the Bank, and 1000 millions more notes in circulation. The total circulation remains the same, but the paper money has taken the place of the coin. If the cash at the Bank has lately increased, without a corresponding increase of the note circulation, the cause is the accumulation of deposits.'

c. It is evident from the preceding considerations, that when France resumes specie payments, the total currency, paper and metallic, will be considerably reduced from its present amount, and that the reduction will fall more especially on the metallic currency, though also partly on bank notes. In other words, there will be liberated a large amount of the hoarded coin in the country and of cash in the Bank. The latter amounted on September 13, 1877, to 88 millions sterling, against 18 millions in 1870.

XIII. Respecting the resumption of specie payments, the Paris correspondent of the 'Economist' wrote on September 13, 1877 :—

'An item in the Bank of France return, which had remained unchanged since October 1876, shows this week a diminution of 28 millions, or from 338 to 310 millions. This reduction is in the Government debt to the Bank (Treasury bonds); and, as will be seen, is of no small importance. An article of M. Leon Say's Budget Law of 1876 declares expressly that the Bank shall resume specie payments when the Government debt shall be reduced to 300 millions, on the 1st January 1878. By the last convention between the State and the Bank, the Government debt was to have been reduced to 600 millions on the 31st December 1875, and sums of 150 millions were to be paid off annually, in each of the years 1876 to 1879, thereby reducing the debt to 300 millions on the 1st January 1878. On the 21st October 1876, the debt had been reduced to 338 millions, and the 38 millions of excess over 300 millions could also have been readily paid early in 1877, for the Treasury balance at the Bank has constantly remained considerably higher than in 1876; and at the present time the remaining 18 millions could be paid from the Treasury balance of 18th September 1877, which amounts to 175 millions against 77 millions in 1876. The Government has evidently preferred to pay interest on those 38 millions since October 1876, in order to protect the cash reserve of the Bank, by leaving that establishment with the option of refusing to pay in coin. A sum of only 10 millions now separates the Bank from the point at which the forced circulation of notes shall cease. The Treasury may still leave that small balance until the end of the year, although the precaution is admitted to be quite unnecessary.'

16. The following facts regarding the silver currency may be noted:—

I. It is seen from the table in para. 14, that though gold preponderates over silver, in the reserves of the Bank of France, and that though the amount of increase in the balance since 1873 has been greater for gold, yet the proportion of increase has been greater with silver.

II. On May 31, 1877, the Paris correspondent of the 'Economist' wrote:—

'The Bank does not make public the proportion of silver to gold of which its reserve consists, but it is generally accepted in well-informed quarters, that the silver represents from 20 to 25 per cent. of the total cash reserve, and at present stands at about 22½ per cent. The proportion of silver is, in fact, much smaller than formerly, before that metal was depreciated, when it formed about one-third of the total stock of specie. It is also generally believed that the Bank does not hold any bar silver, its reserve consisting of coin only.'

III. 'The annual report of the Bank for 1876 states that during that year the Bank paid out 628 millions in gold coin, and 532 millions in silver coin; and encashed foreign specie to the amount of 465 millions in gold and 45 millions in silver. The difference in the proportion of gold to silver from abroad received by the Bank, and in that paid out, shows that the Bank has been endeavouring to reduce the stock of silver coin that it holds, and explains the present smaller proportion of silver.'

IV. On August 16, 1877, the same writer stated:—

'Some complaint had been made of the practice of the Bank of clipping the foreign silver coin not accepted, when presented at its counter, before returning. The Bank now gives notice that it will only receive payments in silver coin on the express condition that it will return clipped all the foreign pieces of which the circulation is not admitted under the monetary convention of 1865.'

V. On February 1, 1877, the same correspondent wrote:—

'Inquiries have been made here from London as to the truth of a telegram received at Bombay, stating that the French Government had sold a large quantity of bar silver for India. Such a statement could only have been made for purposes of speculation, as it is well known that the French Government does not possess any bullion, and that the only silver held by the Bank of France consists of coin, which it would not part with below its nominal value'—

unless (the writer should have added) the Government undertook to make good the loss, as an expense incidental to measures for preparing for the adoption of a single standard of gold.

VI. The British Consul at Cherbourg reported on October 17, 1876, that—

'Judging from an experience of six months, and from the information I have been able to collect from bankers and others likely to be well acquainted with the subject, I should think that the use of Bank of France notes and five-franc silver pieces is diminishing, whilst the use of twenty-franc gold pieces is on the increase. Of small silver there is a sufficient, but by no means excessive supply. The silver of the Latin Union, other than French, is entering more largely into circulation; this consists mostly of one-franc and half-franc pieces. Of these, the greater part are Italian, and next Belgian, which are numerous. Altogether these moneys, as compared with the French silver circulating, do not comprise more than 12 per centum. The British Consul at Marseilles (December 22, 1876) reported, "there is a large quantity of Italian silver currency in circulation in this part of France." The British Consul at Bordeaux wrote (December 28, 1876) "there can be no doubt, however, that in the country districts of France there is a want of silver money. This want is complained of in the Bordeaux district, but not more than in the other parts of the country."'

17. It appears from the preceding, and from para. 15, section X., that a want for silver coin has been created by the withdrawal from circulation of all notes of smaller value than 100 francs (though fifty-franc notes circulated before the suspension of specie payments), and by the closure of the French Mints in 1876, against the coinage of silver, also by the accumulation of silver coin in the Bank of France. This want is being partially met by the influx of foreign silver coins of the Latin Union, but with the net result that still a considerable void has to be filled. Probably it will be filled by a Government paper currency of notes of fifty francs and under, payable in silver coins of a reformed currency based on a single gold standard. The silver thus displaced with paper would be sold in Asia, the sink of the precious metals.

18. The Bank of France having some time since ceased to advance money on silver bullion, and the coinage of silver five-franc pieces having been suspended, the silver which has been accumulating in the Bank is necessarily silver coin. There is doubtless a prevalent feeling in France that silver, owing to its depreciation, will be demonetised, and under that feeling banks, railways, public companies, merchants and others, appear to be parting with their silver reserves to the Bank of France. Whether through a deliberate purpose, or from the force of circumstances—apparently the former—the silver coins of France are being withdrawn from circulation, in preparation for a single standard of gold. The attraction of silver coin to the Bank's reserve, despite the withdrawal from circulation

of notes of 100 francs and under, and the prohibition of further coinage of silver, hardly admits of any other explanation.

19. There is more than one sign of the determination of the French Government to adopt a single standard of gold, and of the co-operation of the Bank of France in the necessary preparatory measures.

I. There are two methods for the transition from a silver to a gold currency, or from a double to a single standard where the coins of both metals are of considerable amount, as in the French currency. One is the method which Germany has adopted, the other is the method (suitable to countries whence gold is liable to be exported) by which recourse is had to an inconvertible paper currency for the period of transition to the new standard, in order that during such period, the principal and subsidiary coins of the new currency may be accumulated. France has adopted the latter method, and the masking of her purpose, for the secrecy favourable to success, has been encompassed through the seemingly needless prolongation of the period of that suspension of cash payments which originated in the financial necessities of the Empire. Since 1874, the notes of the Bank of France have been at par, and even for some time previous the premium on gold was nominal.

II. The French Minister of Finance has described this period of transition as the maintenance by France of an expectant attitude, and in August 1876, when he opposed a proposition to suspend entirely the coinage of silver five-franc pieces (now virtually suspended) and to limit to 100 francs the legal tender of that silver coin, he admitted that if the value of silver compared with gold should fall, the Government might be forced to reconsider the present monetary system. He did not, however, even under that hypothesis, admit that the abandonment of the double standard would be inevitable.

'The value of silver might fall to a certain point, and then remain relatively stationary; it would then be a question for consideration, whether the concurrent circulation of the two metals should not be established on a new basis.'

20. But while these were the Minister's hesitating utterances, the action of the Government and of the Bank of France has been in accordance with the safest measures for the change from a silver to a gold standard (or from a double standard where the second metal is yet of considerable amount), to a single standard in countries from which gold is liable to be exported. Those measures are:—

I. The cessation of further coinage of silver (this was virtually done in 1874, and absolutely in 1876).

II. The issue of notes inconvertible during the period of transition, but payable in gold at the end of that period. (France already possessed an inconvertible paper currency, which by December 1873 was on a par with gold.)

III. The withdrawal of silver coin with paper money, in large transactions, that is, chiefly in the metropolis; and the forcing it into circulation in the interior, for small retail transactions, so that, on the introduction of a gold currency, the silver of the old currency may be in the hands of those engaged in small dealings, who could receive for it, in exchange, the subsidiary silver coins of the new currency without loss, whereby the replacement of the old silver coins by the over-valued new silver coins would not hurt the holders. The steps taken to this end are clearly discernible, viz.:

a. Whereas the smallest denomination of notes, before the suspension of specie payments, was the fifty-franc note, all notes of fifty francs and under have been withdrawn from circulation.

b. Silver coin flows into the Bank from railway and steamboat companies, and those engaged in large enterprises, but it is as steadily returned into circulation in the interior. On April 25, 1876, the Bank of France held, in Paris, 16 millions sterling in silver, to 33 millions in gold, whilst the branch banks held only 5¾ millions sterling in silver to 22 millions in gold. In June 1876, the silver held in the branches in the interior was still less. In that month, M. de Parieu complained in the Senate that 'the Bank had for some time past been paying out at its branches a much more considerable quantity of silver than before; and had ordered its branches to compel certain customers to receive one-third of their payments in silver.' This is confirmed by the Bank's report for 1876, which, as already stated, showed that the Bank and its branches had paid out 532 millions silver to 628 millions gold.

IV. The education of the people in the use of paper money, so that, on the resumption of specie payments, a considerable portion of the paper money might remain permanently outstanding, as a set-off to the loss on the sale of a far greater amount of withdrawn silver coins. (This education has been imparted by the prolongation of the period of inconvertible notes for some years beyond what was necessary for simply resuming specie payments. All this time, the Bank of France has been sedulously employed in popularising its notes and other forms of its paper money. Agencies for the issue and cashing of notes have been multiplied, till now there is a branch bank in nearly each of the ninety departments of France; and in July 1876, it was arranged that these branch banks should issue drafts, payable on demand, on the other branches direct, without the intervention of the central office in Paris, at a charge of only five centimes per 100 francs —with the result that bank notes, on being superseded by this very cheap mode of remittance, would remain permanently outstanding, in local circulation.

V. It follows from the preceding, that the cost of a change to a single gold standard will not be considerable, and that the measures towards that end are advanced so far that the French Government is not likely to retrace its steps.

VI. It may seem to invalidate this conclusion, that the French Government would hardly have ventured, without the express sanction of the Legislature, upon the steady prosecution, for some years, of measures for altering the standard. But, considering the advantages attendant on secrecy, and the authoritative expressions of opinion, in the past, in favour of a single gold standard in France, no enlightened Government could have shrunk from the responsibility. Declarations in favour of a single standard of gold were made by the numerous States represented at Paris at the International Monetary Conference of 1867; by a Commission of Inquiry, instituted in 1868–69, after it had consulted all the Chambers of Commerce, the majority of whom declared for a gold standard; and in 1870, by a majority of the superior Council of Trade and Industry, after a long and profound inquiry; also by leading members of the French Legislature in 1876.

21. France has really changed her standard twice, viz., from 1795 to 1847 or 1852, when gold was gradually expelled from the currency by silver, which was the cheaper metal; and again from 1853 to 1864, when silver was expelled by gold, which by a rapid depreciation became the cheaper metal. Throughout the period from 1795 to 1864, the double standard provided the cheaper metal for home circulation, and the dearer for exportation in the course of foreign trade; and when the relative value of the two metals altered abroad, twice the consequent change of metal for the home currency was, in both cases, from the dearer to the cheaper metal.

22. It is commonly urged against a double standard, that as the cheaper metal expels the dearer, there is injury to creditors who have to receive in the cheaper metal the sums which they lent in the dearer. But the material progress and prosperity of France were

never so marked as during and since the second transition, or that from dear silver to the cheaper gold. Thus :

(*Millions.*)

	1841	1860	1865	1869	1874	1875 Special
	£	£	£	£	£	£
Imports . .	47·476	106·292	141·096	160·348	176·900	141·468
Exports . .	39·678	125·900	163·460	159·744	188·084	154·904

The expansion of the trade and industry of France during this period has been so prodigious as to modify the national character; and, the motive power for this marvellous progress having been supplied by capital and the creditor class, the change to the cheaper metal did not injure creditors. In her foreign trade France benefited, or did not suffer, during the transition, by exporting the dearer metal, and on completion of the change she still benefited by her acquisition of the same metallic currency as that of the principal countries with which she trades. The objection that creditors or debtors suffer from a change of the metallic currency would seem, from this striking example, to be more visionary than practical.

23. Sections I. and III. of the table in para. 14 contain a suggestive lesson for those charged with the administration of Indian finances. They show a steady net importation of the precious metals into France, from 1873, which the mere excess of exports over imports does not explain, seeing that in 1871 and 1872, France raised loans to the amount of 220 millions sterling, for payment of the French indemnity. A great part of these loans was taken up abroad, by syndicates of bankers, who paid their subscriptions by bills on England, Holland, Germany, and other countries, which bills, being transferred to the German Government, were slowly realised, for the power which they gave Germany to control the exchanges during the progress of her coinage reform. For much of the interest on the loans for 220 millions sterling, France was liable in the first instance to foreign holders of the stock, but rapidly the securities were bought back by the investments of her peasant proprietors, and by transfers from foreign stocks, so that the interest became payable in France. At the next stage, foreign stocks held in France were exported, and the large importations of gold and silver set forth in the table in para. 14 were obtained. As stated in the report of the Bank of France for 1876, 'the favourable exchange to France cannot, as formerly,

be attributed to a balance of commercial operations, but must be connected absolutely with the movements in the market for public securities, and in paper negotiable between France and foreign countries.'

24. Thus, in the brief period of six years, a debt of 220 millions sterling, or an amount exceeding the whole metallic currency of France, was paid to the foreign creditor without, in the final result, the exportation of a single coin, and in the same period, indebtedness to foreign nations was extinguished, and there was accumulated a large amount of gold for, evidently, the transition to a single gold standard. All this was effected with paper.

25. AUSTRIA.

I. The coin of legal tender in Austria is the silver florin or gulden, of which, under the Convention with Prussia dated January 24, 1857, which was rescinded on June 13, 1867, three florins were equal to two thalers, and a thaler being reckoned as equal to $6\frac{2}{3}$ shillings, a florin is equal to about two shillings.

II. On June 13, 1867, Austria signed a preliminary treaty with France for assimilating her coinage with that of the Latin Union, on the stipulation, however, that the Union should adopt a single gold standard. Thus, the treaty never took effect.

III. Excepting a brief period from November 1858 to a date in 1859, during which specie payments were resumed, the inconvertible State paper currency of Austria dates from 1848. It amounted in March or April 1877 to $35\frac{1}{2}$ millions sterling against $33\frac{1}{2}$ millions in 1876.[1] There is no immediate prospect of the resumption of specie payments.

IV. Besides the State notes, the National Bank of Austria has issued notes which are inconvertible, and which from May 1873 to October 1874 were issued without limit, but from November 1874 a limit was revived, namely, that all notes in excess of 20 millions sterling should be covered by coin and bullion. The circulation and the reserve have been as follows:—

(*Millions sterling.*)

	Nov. 19, 1873	Nov. 11, 1874	Sept. 5, 1877
	£	£	£
Circulation . .	36·7	31·2	28·2
Coin and Bullion .	14·4	14·3	13·7

[1] *Economist*, August 13, 1876.

The circulation has been reduced without a corresponding diminution of the coin and bullion, so that the uncovered notes are considerably below the limit of 20 millions sterling. The issues, however, are large.

V. The inconvertible State and Bank notes together amount to about 64 millions sterling, with a cash reserve in the Bank of 14 millions sterling, besides any separate reserve of the Government. Accordingly, the British Ambassador at Vienna, writing on June 10, 1876, of the florins as the existing currency, observed—

'But although, nominally, this currency exists, there is none of the silver in circulation, and the large quantities of silver in the country are in the possession of the National Bank and the Government. Every Bank and State note bears on its face the promise to pay its value in silver; but the fulfilment of the promise cannot be demanded so long as the law remains in force for the suspension of cash payments in silver currency.'

VI. The amounts of gold and silver in the National Bank have been as follows:—

(*Millions sterling.*)

	1855	1858	1865	May 31, 1870	1871	1875	May 31, 1877
Gold .	—	·29	·15	·23	4·44	6·79	6·68
Silver .	5·19	10·06	12·	11·28	9·91	6·66	6·98

The Bank has been steadily accumulating gold.

VII. After the considerable depreciation of silver, the Vienna correspondent of the 'Economist' stated in September 1875, 'We hear that Austria has decided upon retaining the silver standard, although experts have counselled the adoption of the gold standard.' The inducement to adopt the silver standard was the small premium which silver commanded against the State notes, but it was correctly observed that—

'The greater expenses incumbent on the introduction of a gold standard will be amply repaid by avoiding the continual losses which the rate of exchange of silver against gold brings with it. The Austrian Government has at present more extra expenses to defray, from a depreciated currency, than the interest of a loan would amount to, with which it could withdraw its 34 millions sterling worth of legal-tender notes. These extra expenses are due to the silver necessary for the payments of the Austrian 'Silberrents,'—for acquisitions out of the country—and for the army. I have heard this calculation confirmed by the Ministry of Finance, which caused a similar computation to be made, and came to a similar conclusion.'

VIII. The considerable depreciation of silver in 1876, with a consequent increase of the premium on gold, supplied another reason for disregarding the supposed advantage of resuming specie payments in silver. In April 1876, a banker in Vienna pointed out that the securities, the interest on which is due in gold,

> 'Stand about 18 or 20 per cent. higher than the securities whose interest is due in silver; and that accordingly the Austrian Ministry should declare itself ready to pay the interest of Austrian *rente* in gold, if 15 per cent. of the capital be paid down by the proprietors of these effects. The titles of all shareholders who agree to these conditions would become newly stamped. As gold stocks are at present quoted 20 per cent. higher than silver stocks, it is to be supposed that most proprietors of *rente* would agree to the Government's proposal. By this means the Government would obtain capital enough to be able to withdraw almost the whole of the State's notes, and return to cash payments.'

IX. Great disadvantages from the continuance of the silver standard have been felt, notwithstanding the expulsion of silver coin from circulation, *e.g.* :—

a. To obtain silver for paying interest on its foreign loans, the Austrian Government has for a long time demanded Customs' duties in silver, and all the tariffs contained in treaties of commerce have been expressed in silver, the silver standard being legal in Austria. With the fall in the price of silver, more of it has to be sent abroad for the payment of interest on gold *rente*, while the amount of Customs' duty remains as before; the result being 'equivalent to a reduction of the duty tariff of 25 per cent. for Austria, whilst for the neighbouring German Empire the duty tariff rises by as much.'[1]

b. The Austrian railways have debentures payable in silver, and before the depreciation of silver they paid interest on the debentures to their creditors in France in francs, and to their creditors in Germany in thalers; in some cases, there is a distinct promise to pay in thalers. But, the coinage of silver five-franc pieces having been stopped in France, that coin in France, and the thaler in Germany, since the declaration there of the gold standard, are equal to gold. Accordingly, they bear the same premium as gold, in exchange with Austrian silver money, so that practically the Austrian railways have now to pay the interest on their debentures in gold, while their tariffs are in silver.

c. The decline in the price of silver depreciated, in foreign markets, all Austrian securities and railway stocks which were held abroad;

[1] *Economist*, July 8, 1876.

immense quantities of these were returned and thrown on the market in 1876. 'More of them were offered for sale on the Bourse of Vienna than there was capital to purchase them with.'[1] In other words, a large amount of capital was withdrawn from Austria.

d. The only compensating circumstance was an increase of exports, which the low rate of exchange stimulated, but this too had of course its drawback.

On the whole, in 1876, the opinion of the leading journals and of bankers and financial authorities in Vienna was pronounced decidedly in favour of a gold standard.

> 'Whilst the leading paper of Austria, the *Neue Freie Presse*, pleads for the adoption of a pure gold standard, the rest of the press is, almost without exception, for retaining the silver standard. The representatives of great institutions of credit, and of larger banks, all side with the introduction of a pure gold standard; and the National Bank prudently changed the greater part of its ready coin and bullion into gold a long time ago.'—*Economist*, April 22, 1876.

X. In January 1876, the Minister of Finance entered into negotiations for an issue of Austrian gold *rente* for 40 millions gulden, the reason assigned for the gold loan being that 'Austria is still subject to foreign money markets, especially the English and German, and she may depend upon obtaining better terms in the way of lower interest, by paying it in gold. It is calculated that Austria will save 300,000 gulden a year on this loan, which is to amount to 49 millions *effective*.' On January 23, 1877, the Vienna correspondent of the 'Economist' wrote:—

> 'Within the last fortnight the Austrian gold rente rose five per cent., whilst paper rente remained stationary, and silver rente improved very little. The extraordinary progress of the gold rente caused the Austrian Minister of Finances to sell the rest of the gold rente, which makes up a total of gold rente of 110 millions.' Again—on March 27, 1877:—'The exceedingly favourable reception given to the Austrian gold rente in foreign countries has encouraged the Hungarian Minister of Finances to issue a Hungarian loan, with a view to put some order into the finances, viz., a Hungarian gold rente to the amount of 76½ million florins at six per cent. interest. This interest is to be paid in gold, and free of taxes.'

XI. The Austrian Minister of Finance declared in one of the meetings of the Reichsrath in February 1876, 'that the gold *rente* emission was in no way to be regarded as a promise of a gold standard.'

[1] *Economist*, April 1, 1876.

XII. But though the double-headed eagle looks both ways, the acts of the Austrian Government have been tending towards the adoption of a gold standard, *e.g.*:

a. The Committee on the Depreciation of Silver reported:—

'The coinage of silver has been almost stopped in Austria. In 1867, thirteen million guldens were coined:—in 1870, fourteen millions; during the whole of the next five years little more than two millions have been coined.'

And since the Committee's report, the coinage of silver on private account has been stopped.

b. An imperial decree, dated March 9, 1870, for the introduction of a new gold coinage, authorised the fabrication of crowns, or eight-florin pieces, equal to 20 francs, in gold, and of half-crowns; and declared that 'until the introduction of the gold standard contemplated in Act XII. of the law of December 24, 1867, the rate at which these gold coins shall be received is left to open agreement.' In 1876, the Austrian Government issued *rente* of which the principal and interest are payable in gold.

c. The Austrian coinage of gold and silver has been as follows, in millions of florins:—

	1873	1874	1875	1876
Silver:				
Austrian currency	8·07	2·62	5·26	7·47
Thalers of the Levante for commercial purposes	—	5·21	6·97	10·64
Gold	0·08	2·31	1·80	4·55

26. SPAIN.

I. Under the Mint Law of October 19, 1868, which came into force on January 1, 1871, the monetary unit is a peseta, an effective coin equal to 100 centimes. Gold coins are struck of the value of 5, 10, 20, 50 and 100 pesetas, and a five-peseta silver coin is also full legal tender under that law. These coins are nine-tenths fine; the smaller silver coins of 2 pesetas, 1 peseta, 20 cents, and 5 cents are ·835 fine. The metallic currency was, in fact, assimilated by the law of October 19, 1868, with that of the Latin Union. Under the previous law the relative value between gold and silver was nearly the same as in the Latin Union, viz., 1 to 15·477, so that, before the late depreciation of silver, it was expelled from the currency.

II. Since that depreciation silver flowed back to Spain, as reported by the Committee on the Depreciation of Silver, but the importations proved embarrassing, and the coinage of silver for the public generally was stopped.

'The Madrid Gazette publishes a royal decree, notifying that the mint there will recommence receiving gold and silver bullion for coining, but from Spanish subjects only; and precautions will be adopted to admit only metal the origin of which shall be satisfactorily proved. In case, however, of an insufficient quantity of gold and silver being furnished by private individuals, the Government will purchase it abroad. The gold will be converted into a new piece of 100 reales, or 25 pesetas, nine-tenths fine, or the exact equivalent of 25 francs, or a fraction over £1. 0*s.* 2*d.* English. The decree does not fix the amount of gold and silver to be thus coined; but the monetary committee admits that the coinage of silver will eventually require to be limited. When, therefore, gold shall be sufficiently abundant for the circulation, a new decree will be published, to restrict the legal tender of silver to a sum of 150 pesetas.'—*Economist*, September 9, 1876.

III. Spain, therefore, has determined to adopt eventually a gold standard, in the belief, doubtless, that France, on whose metallic currency she has modelled her own since 1868, will do so. Spain's demand on the yearly production of silver will accordingly cease. But the time when she will resume specie payments cannot be estimated.

IV. The currency of the Philippine Islands having 'become confused by the promiscuous introduction and circulation of foreign, and especially silver coins,' the Governor-General of the islands published a decree that henceforth the Spanish or the Hispano-Philippine coinage of gold, silver, and copper shall be the only legal tender, and that the Philippine gold dollar shall be the monetary standard.[1]

27. RUSSIA.

I. The Royal Commission of 1868, on International Coinage, included Russia among the countries in which the double standard is still retained according to law. Mr. Seyd, in a paper published by the Select Committee on the Depreciation of Silver, observed :—

'The law of 1810 established the full-valued silver rouble, that of 1817 the gold half-imperial. In 1867, the small silver change was debased in fineness. Both gold and silver full-valued coins have disappeared, through the paper valuation; but the Imperial Bank is said to hold 30 millions sterling of gold. For the present, the metallic valuation is non-effective.'

The fixed rating of $5\frac{3}{20}$ silver roubles for the gold half-imperial gives a relative value of 1 to $15\frac{4}{5}$. At that valuation, had the

[1] *Economist*, July 14, 1877.

metallic currency been effective, gold would have expelled silver when the price of silver exceeded 60 pence per ounce. Nevertheless, Russia is reckoned among the countries with a silver valuation; an imperial decree of 1839, still in force, having established it as the legal and unalterable unit of the money current in the Empire. The exportation of silver is prohibited, whilst that of gold is periodically allowed.

II. The probability of a resumption of specie payments in Russia is too remote to be of any practical account at present, though the inconvenience and the disadvantages of the excessive issues of an inconvertible paper currency are felt to be grievous. On September 8, 1877, the 'Economist' gave the following returns of the note circulation on January 1, and August 15, 1877 :—

	Notes	Gold and Silver	Total of uncovered Notes
	Roubles	Roubles	Roubles
January 1, 1877 . .	735,222,025	180,535,803	554,686,222
August 15, 1877 . .	734,772,025	180,085,803	554,686,222

This account is evidently incorrect. It does not show any change in an interval of $7\frac{1}{2}$ months, during which it is known that there were enormous issues of inconvertible paper. Even the opening amount of 555 millions of uncovered notes is unreliable, the corresponding amounts having been 612 millions in 1857, 568 millions in 1867, and 566 millions in the beginning of 1875. In 1844, after the reform of the paper currency, there were only 170 million roubles of paper in circulation, according to the New York 'Bankers' Magazine,' and 121 million roubles in gold and silver to cover it. But this too must be erroneous, the amount of uncovered notes having amounted, in 1847 to 172 millions, accordingto a return in the 'Economist,' of the debt of Russia, at intervals of ten years from 1817 to 1875. In 1857, two years after the Crimean war, the gross issues of paper money reached 735 millions, or the amount with which Russia, according to the return in the 'Economist' of September 8, 1877, began the present war. The amount in November 1877 must be much larger.

III. While the resumption of specie payments is too remote a contingency to be regarded at present, there are indications that, from the sheer force of circumstances, a gold standard must be eventually adopted by Russia, *e.g.* :—

a. The money coined at the St. Petersburg mint from 1866 to

1875 was 177 million roubles in gold, and 6 million roubles of full legal tender in silver.

b. Interest to Russia's foreign creditors is paid in gold. This pressure is felt not alone by the State, but by Russian commerce. In the first eight months of 1876, the foreign indebtedness of Russia caused a drain of ten millions sterling of gold, from a country which could not pay in exports of merchandise, and whose yearly production of gold is four and half millions.

c. In October 1876,[1] the Russian Imperial Bank was driven to buy gold by the issue of gold assignats.

d. Since January 23, 1877, the Russian Customs' duties have been levied in gold.

e. 'The Landtag of Finland has had presented to it a bill for introducing the gold valuation into that State, from January 1, 1878, apart from any considerations as to what may be the currency of Russia generally. Up to the present, the valuation there has not been paper, as in other parts of Russia, but silver. The gold valuation will be introduced in all official accounts; but up to July 1, 1878, the notes of the Bank of Finland are to be equivalent to the gold currency which shall be coined up to that period. All debts due in the existing Finnish silver marks are to be reckoned in gold at the fixed rate of 15½ to 1. This is fresh proof of the tendency of the gold standard to spread, and to displace the silver currencies of Europe.'—*Economist,* May 26, 1877.

Evidently, theoretical objections of a supposed injustice to creditors from the rectification of the effects of the sudden depreciation of silver are not apprehended from the Landtag of Finland.

IV. The considerations which will probably determine Austria to adopt a gold standard apply even more forcibly in Russia, whose foreign debt is payable in gold.

28. HOLLAND.

I. The money of account is the florin or gulden, between which and the sovereign, the intrinsic par of exchange, at the relative value of 15½ to 1, is 1*s.* 8*d.*, or 1*l.*=12·010 florins. In 1847, Holland 'possessed a double currency, based on a relation of value of 1 to 15·604. On November 26, 1847, almost all the countries in Europe having then had a silver currency, and silver being the currency of Netherlands India, gold was demonetised.' Apparently, however, practical effect to the decision was given later; Mr. Newmarch (History of Prices, vol. vi., page 80), mentioning 'the rejection of gold from the circulation of Holland, in pursuance of the law voted

[1] *Economist,* November 4.

in June 1849, and carried into execution by the Royal Commission, as from the date of June 23, 1850; that is to say, the gold coins of five and ten florins ceased to be a legal tender after June 23, 1850.'

II. The Dutch Minister of Finance had reckoned on an actual gold coin circulation of eight millions sterling, as the amount to be withdrawn, but, as stated by M. Léon Faucher, in a paper in the 'Revue des Deux Mondes' for August 1852, it proved to be 14½ millions sterling. The demonetisation caused an influx of gold coins into France, and reduced the premium on gold in Paris from 9 per mille in July 1850, to par in December 1850. During the greater part of 1851, the quotation of gold at Paris did not even remain at par, but fell to 4 or 5 per mille discount. The total reduction was about 14 per mille, from the exportation of some 14 millions sterling of gold from Holland. Manifestly, undue importance has been ascribed to the sale of a much smaller amount of the silver coins of Germany, in accounting for the considerable depreciation of silver.

III. On October 30, 1872, a Commission was appointed by the King 'to inquire what disadvantages would befall to our country in consequence of the monetary measures lately adopted by other nations, especially Germany, and to propose the remedies which would tend to remove them.' The Commission reported on December 28, 1872, and again on June 26, 1873. They stated:—

a. 'As the adjoining countries are adopting a single gold standard, it will be singularly inconvenient for the people if the opposite standard of silver is any longer adhered to in Holland.

b. To avoid serious difficulties, the further coinage of silver should be stopped.

c. But, so long as the currency of a country consists of gold and silver in *tolerably equal quantities*, it is practically impossible, and would be grossly unjust, for the Government to proclaim a single standard, making one of the metals legal tender and simultaneously demonetising the other. In such a country, the coin deposited in banks will be gold and silver in nearly equal quantities, and it would be unjust for the Government to decree that the banks shall return this money in only one of the metals; for if this metal were to be depreciated, then the banks would gain at the expense of the public: while, if the metal thus made sole legal tender were of higher relative value than the other, then by an equal act of injustice the banks would lose, and their depositors would gain.

d. In course of time Holland will follow the example of her neighbours, and adopt a single gold standard; but to do so at present would be inopportune, and the right thing for Holland, with its large amount of silver money, is the adoption of the double standard.'

IV. The Government adopted the Commissioners' proposals so far as to stop the coinage of silver in May 1873, by a temporary law which expired on May 1, 1874. Thereupon 'the coinage of silver soon recommenced to a large extent; and on December 3, 1874, the coinage of silver was prohibited afresh, for six months, and on June 6, 1875, a law which, by an express provision in it, had to be revised before January 1, 1877, suspended the further coinage of silver. By the same law, the coinage of a gold ten-florin piece was authorised, which resembles very much, 'that which had been demonetised in 1847, only containing 1 per mille less of gold, viz., 6·048 grammes, in order to secure the advantage of making 12 florins almost exactly equal to 25 francs.' The relative value is 1 to 15·625. In December 1876, the provisional law of 1875 was prolonged until December 31, 1877, 'whereby time would be given to the Government to reconsider the whole question of the definitive regulation of the monetary system.'

V. In one of the several bills discussed in the Second Chamber of the States General in 1876, there was a provision, which the Minister of Finance afterwards abandoned, for the adoption of a gold standard. In 1877, a bill for the establishment in Holland of a gold standard was passed by the Lower House, but was rejected by the Upper House, but apparently the main reason for the rejection was a fear that the provisions respecting the withdrawal and sale of the existing silver coinage would disturb the money market. The present state of the law, therefore, is that the public are allowed to coin florins of gold, but are not allowed to coin silver, the privilege of the silver coinage being reserved to the Government.

VI. The Minister of Finance gave reasons for his opinion that the depreciation of silver is permanent; and with regard to the proposition that the Government should be authorised to demonetise silver whenever they might consider it to be necessary, he contended that the proposition was not new, and that 'the most important financial associations of this country, amongst others, the Bank of the Netherlands, had approved it, and had expressed the opinion that it would afford the best means of counteracting the rise in the exchange and the export of gold.'

VII. The Finance Minister estimated 'the silver now in circulation as amounting to 14¾ millions sterling,' or about the same amount as the gold coins which were demonetised in 1850.

VIII. Nothing has been done with regard to Netherlands India; but it was stated by the Finance Minister on November 4, 1876, that 'in preceding years, and for a short time recently, the Dutch East Indies have remitted silver to the mother country.

IX. The gold coined from July 1, 1875, to May 31, 1876 (since when, to October 1876, no coinage had taken place), amounted to 57 million florins. The gross silver coinage from 1840 (the date when the present silver currency was introduced) up to and inclusive of 1873, amounted to 429 million florins; and in 1874, 32 millions more were coined: making a total of 461 millions, of which 293 millions were exported to Netherlands India up to 1875, of which eight or nine millions may have been sent back to Holland.

29. UNITED STATES.

I. The value of the gold, silver, and minor coins struck in the United States' mints is as follows:—

(Millions of dollars.)

	Gold Coin	Silver Coin	Minor Coin	Total	Relative Value of Gold to Silver in the Currency
1792–1829	8·7	25·3	·5	34·5	1 to 15
1830–1849	76·7	50·3	·7	127·7	1 to 16 from 1834
	85·4	75·6	1·2	162·2	
1850–1859	845·7	45·7	1·	392·4	1 to 16, until the Coinage Act of 1873, when the silver dollar was dropped
1860–1869	286·6	14·2	8·2	309·	
1870–1875	183·2	25·8	2·1	211·1	
	469·8	40·	10·3	520·1	
	900·9	161·3	12·5	1,074·7	

Gold and silver were concurrent legal tender to any amount, until the Coinage Act of 1873; except that, in 1853, the half-dollar piece and smaller silver coins were reduced in weight, and degraded to a token currency, which is legal tender for not more than five dollars. This was done to retain the coins in the country, because the full-weight coins of these denominations, through their under-valuation at 16 to 1, were melted and exported to an extent which rendered change money very scarce. By an Act of March 3, 1849, a gold coin of one dollar was authorised of 258 grains weight, 900 fine=23·22 grains fine gold; and from that time until 1873, the gold dollar and the silver dollar of 412½ grains, ·900 fine=373·5 grains fine silver, were legal tender for any amount. Even had the gold and silver dollars been rated at 1 to 15½, the silver dollars would have been expelled from the currency after 1850, when the market price of silver was dearer than the price included in that relative value; but inasmuch as the relative value of the two coins had been as 1 to 16 from 1834, silver was expelled from the currency from an earlier date. The Director of the United States Mint, in his report for 1875–6, wrote:—'The silver dollar certainly could not have been intended as the money in which coin obligations were to be discharged, for the reason that from 1834 to 1873 it had rarely appeared in circulation.'

II. 'With the exception of the Act of April 2, 1792, the various Acts of Congress make no reference to a proportional standard of gold and silver, but simply fix weight, fineness, and legal tender of coins.' Accordingly, when, by a deliberate Act of the Legislature, based on a clear statement of the past and then existing footing of the silver dollar in the currency, and on the report of a select committee, it was decided to discontinue the coinage of the silver dollar, the coinage Act of 1873 simply omitted the silver dollar, while it retained, among the coins of full legal tender, all the existing denominations of gold coins, including the gold dollar piece.

III. As shown in I. the currency of the silver dollar ceased in 1834; and the Director of the United States Mint observed:—

> 'It cannot be ascertained that the silver dollar ever entered to any extent into the fixing of international tariffs, or in United States receipts and payments. The general understanding, at home and abroad, has been that the money of coin payments in the country since 1834 was gold, and that when the word coin was used in connection with the financial transactions of the Government, it meant gold coin.'

IV. In harmony with these facts, it was declared by a decision of the Supreme Court of the United States, in October 1874, that 'the basis of our dollar of account (when not affected by the exceptional condition of legal-tender notes) is the standard gold dollar of 25·8 grains, containing one-tenth alloy.' The same decision confirmed the rating by the Director of the United States Mint, of the gold coins of foreign countries according to their intrinsic par with the gold coins of the United States, as being in accordance with the Act passed on March 3, 1873, that 'the value of the foreign coin as expressed in the money of account of the United States, shall be that of the pure metal of such coin of standard value;' and that this valuation 'is to be applied in all cases where the estimation of the value of foreign moneys is required by law.'

V. In similar accordance with the cessation of the silver dollar from the currency in 1834, was the fact that the first issue of paper money by the Federal Government of the United States, in 1861, was in notes payable in gold, on demand. In like manner, on May 26, 1863, 'the first formal declaration was made by the Secretary of the Treasury, in a letter written by his order, to the President of the Revere Bank, Boston, that the 5-20's would be redeemed in gold.'

VI. The bonds issued under the Funding Acts of July 13, 1870, and January 20, 1871, in withdrawal of those, bearing higher interest, which were issued during the civil war, are indeed declared by the Acts to be payable, principal and interest, in coin; but the interest on all the United States bonds, payable in coin, has been paid in gold, and by the decision of the Supreme Court of the United States in October 1874 (section IV.), the principal too is payable in gold. A letter from the Treasury, in June 1877, also affirmed this explicitly, though on different grounds.

VII. Accordingly, when the 4 per cent. bonds of the funded loans were issued in 1877, the Secretary of the Treasury answered as follows an inquiry whether the principal and interest of the bonds were payable in gold coin:—

'The subject, from its great importance, has demanded and received careful consideration. Under the laws now in force, there is no coin issued or issuable, in which the principal of the four per cent. bonds is redeemable or the interest payable, except the gold coin of the United States, of the standard value fixed by the laws in force on July 14, 1870, when the bonds were authorised. The Government exacts, in exchange for these bonds, payment, at their fall, in such gold coin: and it is not to be anticipated that any future legislation of Congress, or any action of any department of the Government, would sanction or tolerate the redemption of the principal of these bonds, or the payment of the interest thereon, in coin of less value than the coins authorised by law at the time of the issue of the bonds, being the coin exacted by the Government in exchange for the same. The essential element of good faith in preserving the equality in value between the coinage in which the Government receives and that in which it pays these bonds, will be sacredly observed by the Government and the people of the United States, whatever may be the system of coinage which the general policy of the nation may at any time adopt. This principle is impressed upon the text of the law of July 14, 1870, under which the four per centum bonds are issued, and requires, in the opinion of the executive department of the Government, the redemption of these bonds, and the payment of their interest in coin of equal value with that which the Government receives upon their issue.'

VIII. This decision has been stamped as irrevocable by the following engagement in the prospectus dated July 12, 1877, of the 700,000,000 dollars United States Four per cent. Funded Loan.'

'These bonds are issued in accordance with the provisions of an Act of Congress entitled "An Act to authorise the Refunding of the National debt, approved July 14, 1870, amended by an Act approved January 20, 1871," and are redeemable at the pleasure of the United States, after July 1, 1907, in coin of the standard value of the United States on said July 14, 1870 (gold coin), with interest, in such coin, from the day of their date, at the rate of 4 per cent. per annum, payable quarterly, on January 1, April 1, July 1, and October 1 in each year. The principal and interest are exempt from the payment of all taxes or duties of the United States, as well as from taxation in any form, by or under State, Municipal, or Local authority.'

IX. As this last funded loan of 700 million dollars is fully sufficient for redeeming all the outstanding loans raised during the civil war, it matters little whether the Government of the United States is under any express obligation to redeem the civil war loans in gold coin. But as indicative of the good faith of the Government, and of a policy which is unaffected by the strife of parties, it may be mentioned that the declaration of the Secretary of the Treasury on May 26, 1863 (section V.) has been faithfully observed, and the notices calling in portions of the 5–20 bonds contain a clause that 'holders of 5–20 bonds, bearing January and July interest coupons, will be paid the interest from 1st January last to 1st May next, at 6 per cent., or £2. 0*s*. 10*d*. per bond of 500 dollars,' that is, at an exchange between dollar and sterling reckoned at the intrinsic par of the gold sovereign and the gold dollar. As already observed, the interest on all the United States bonds, payable in coin, has been paid in gold.

X. Under the Funding Acts of July 14, 1870, and January 20, 1871, the total of the civil war loans was to be funded in three loans bearing lower interest, as follows:—

a. FIVE PER CENT. 10-YEAR BONDS: ISSUE, 500,000,000 DOLLARS.

Issued	Millions.
February and August 1871	200
February 1873	121½
July 1874, to January 1875	178½
	500

b. FOUR-AND-A-HALF PER CENT. 15-YEAR BONDS: AUTHORISED ISSUE, 300,000,000 DOLLARS.

Issued	Millions
August 1876, to June 1877	200

c. FOUR PER CENT. 30-YEAR BONDS: AUTHORISED ISSUE, 700,000,000 DOLLARS.

Issued	Millions
July 1877	700

The credit of the United States Government having rapidly improved, the $4\frac{1}{2}$ per cent. loan was closed for two-thirds of the authorised issue. It will be observed, that even had the explicit declarations of the Treasury, and of the prospectus of the 4 per cent. funded loan, not emphasised the Government's obligation to redeem the earlier funded loans in gold coin, 380 millions thereof would have been secured in gold by the decision of the Supreme Court of the United States in 1874 (section IV).

XI From the first, the Government of the United States has clearly recognised the necessity and duty of redeeming the United States bonds with gold coin; and in its now fixed determination to do so, it is supported by all intelligent or enlightened opinion in the States, and by the vast interests which are concerned in upholding the gold character of the bonds, that is, in maintaining the favourable estimate of the bonds in the stock exchanges in New York and in the several monetary centres in Europe. In January 1876, the 'New York Financial Chronicle' wrote: 'The whole amount of the United States bonded debt, outstanding December 31, 1875, was 1,725 million dollars. Of these, 399 millions were held by the National Banks on the 31st October, and 85 millions by financial corporations in the city of New York—total, 484 millions. Of the remaining 1,241 millions, 700 to 500 millions are estimated to be held by our own citizens, and the remainder to be held abroad.' Thus the greater part of the stock was held in the States; and not the holders alone, but the still larger numbers interested in the cheap money which is promoted by the favourable price of the Government debt, are concerned in maintaining the gold character of the bonds.

XII. And if it were possible that self-interest could stimulate a Government which has needed no persuasion in its unwavering fixed determination to redeem the United States bonds in gold coin, the figures in section X. supply the motive. With a marvellously improved credit on European exchanges, it cannot be long before those who have administered the finances of the States with singular sagacity and resolution (the latter an inestimably precious quality in finance), will proceed to the conversion of the 5 and $4\frac{1}{2}$ per cents.

into fours. To do so, the former must be redeemed in gold; and by doing so, all further temptation to any party in the States to agitate for the redemption of the bonds in silver will cease.

XIII. Thus it appears that the coin of legal tender in the United States is the gold dollar; that, accordingly, under the general law of the States, the United States bonds, both those which were declared payable in coin and those which have been expressly declared to be payable in gold, are payable in gold; and that redemption of the bonds in gold is necessary for the protection of important interests in the States, and for completing the well-conceived funding operations, by conversion of the five and four-and-a-half per cents. into fours.

XIV. It further appears that the silver dollar had ceased to regulate transactions for fully two generations before it was demonetised in 1873, by omission from the list of coins of full legal tender in the Coinage Act of that year.

30. It is seen from para. 29, section X., that the funding operations began in 1871, but that probably not more than 300 million dollars were funded by June 1873. The changes in the debt of the United States since 1873 have been as follows:—

(*In millions of dollars.*)

	June 30, 1873	June 30, 1874	June 30, 1876	June 30, 1877
Fives	415	510	712	703
$4\frac{1}{2}$ per cent. . . .	—	—	—	140
	415	510	712	843
Sixes	1,281	1,214	985	855
Total funded . . .	1,696	1,724	1,697	1,698
Unfunded . . .	452	420	402	362
	2,148	2,144	2,099	2,060

I. It appears that 426 millions of six per cents. have been reduced, and that the amount of fives and four-and-a-half per cents. has been increased by 428 millions, the odd two millions, with the yearly surplus of income over expenditure, having been applied, doubtless, to the reduction of unfunded debt and to the increase of the gold reserve. The preceding account, however, is not quite accurate; for it is seen from para. 29, section X., that 200 millions of $4\frac{1}{2}$ per cents. were issued up to June 30, 1877; the amount of sixes outstanding on that date was probably 783 millions: for the extinction of which the new funded 4 per cent. loan of 700 million dollars was issued in July 1877.

II. The 500 millions of 5 per cent. funded loans have still some four to eight years to run; and the 200 millions of 4½ per cents. have fourteen years to run. It will be shown presently, that a small reduction of the funded debt will suffice for bringing the greenback currency to par, and resuming specie payments; the money for effecting this reduction can be borrowed without any eventual increase of the total charge for interest, by converting the fives and four-and-a-half per cents into fours. On August 17, 1877, the Secretary of the Treasury, in mentioning that the funding operations since March 1, 1877, had saved 3½ million dollars in interest, annually, added: 'this, however, was a mere beginning, and he felt confident that if there were no adverse legislation, the entire debt would be converted into four per cent. bonds.'

31. The premium on gold has declined up to 1874, since 1868, in which year the highest was 50, and the lowest 32⅛; in 1874, the corresponding figures were 14⅜ and 9; in 1875, they were 17 and 12½; in 1876, the highest was 14⅞ and the lowest 7⅛ on 31st December. On April 30, 1877, the Gold Room in New York was closed; and in the circular of Messrs. McCulloch and Co., dated New York, September 6, 1877, the following passage occurs:—

'The rates for sterling bills have been somewhat firmer, owing to a demand for the purpose of returning exchange borrowed about 60 days ago. Rates have advanced slightly, in consequence; and, in sympathy, the price of gold rose to-day from 103¼ to 103⅜. The gold premium, however, is predominantly weak, owing to the growing feeling in favour of the feasibility of accomplishing resumption under the existing law, and also to a feeling that, the premium having already fallen so low, Congress will be disposed to allow the experiment to be fairly tried.' On August 17, 1877, Mr. Sherman, the Secretary of the Treasury, observed, 'specie payments meant the equalisation of paper with coin, which could and ought to be secured under the Resumption Act.'

32. There are two kinds of notes, viz., those of the United States, or greenbacks, and those of the National Banks. The greenbacks are legal tender in all transactions among the public, and in the payment of dues to or by the Government, with the following exceptions, viz.:—

1. Customs import duties, and interest on the public debt (payable in gold coin).

2. Debts in existence at the time of the passing of the Act of 1862, which suspended specie payments, if such obligations have not,

since been expressly or constructively renewed in currency: and in the Pacific States of the Union, specie payments were never suspended. The notes of the National Banks in the several States of the Union are legal tender to Government (except for Customs' duties), but not between individuals. They are convertible in legal-tender notes or green backs.

33. The laws relating to the paper currency, which are material to the present subject, are as follows:—

1. *Joint Resolution of January* 17, 1863, and subsequent Acts, authorised the Secretary of the Treasury to issue, within prescribed limits, greenbacks 'of such denominations, not less than one dollar, as he may prescribe.'

2. *Act March* 3, 1863, authorised, 'in lieu of postage and revenue stamps for fractional currency, and of fractional notes, commonly called postage currency,' the issue of 'fractional notes of like amounts, which in the aggregate shall not exceed fifty millions of dollars,' and which shall be received in payment of any dues to the United States less than five dollars, shall be exchanged at the several treasuries of the United States for greenbacks, in sums of not less than three dollars, and shall be redeemed on presentation at the treasury of the United States, in such sums and under such regulations as the Secretary of the Treasury shall prescribe.

3. *Act March* 3, 1863, also empowered the Secretary of the Treasury to receive deposits of gold coin and bullion, and to issue certificates of the deposits, and certificates representing coin in the treasury, the latter certificates to be issued only in payment of interest on the public debt, and to an amount not exceeding (with the first-mentioned certificates of deposit) twenty per cent. of the amount of coin and bullion in the treasury. The bullion and coin received for certificates of deposit are to be reserved for the payment of the certificates.

4. *Specie Resumption Act of January* 14, 1875, authorises, and as regards resumption of specie payments, directs the Secretary of the Treasury,—

a. To coin silver coins of ten, twenty-five, or fifty cents of standard value for redeeming an equal amount of fractional currency of similar denominations, until the whole amount of such fractional currency outstanding shall be redeemed.

b. To reduce the circulation of greenbacks by 80 per cent. of the amount of every increase of the circulation of notes of National banks beyond the aggregate limit, viz., 354 million dollars, which was prescribed by law before the passing of the Specie Resumption Act; provided that only the excess over 300 millions of dollars of greenbacks outstanding shall be so redeemed.

c. On and after January 1, 1879, to redeem in coin the United States legal-tender notes then outstanding.

d. To enable the Secretary of the Treasury to prepare and provide for the redemption in this Act authorised or required, he is authorised to use any unappropriated surplus revenue in the treasury, and to issue, sell, or dispose of, at not less than par, in coin, any of the kinds of bonds described in the Funding Act of July 14, 1870.

5. *Joint Resolution, July* 13, 1876, empowers the Secretary of the Treasury—

a. To acquire ten millions of dollars of legal-tender notes in exchange for an equal amount of silver coin which may be at any time in the treasury, and to reserve the legal-tender notes as a special fund for the retirement and destruction of a like sum of fractional currency.

b. To manufacture and issue subsidiary silver coin to an extent which (with the amount of outstanding subsidiary silver coin authorised by law to be issued in redemption of the fractional currency, and with the amount of fractional currency outstanding) shall in the aggregate not exceed 50 millions of dollars.

The Joint Resolution declared further,

c. That the trade dollar shall not hereafter be a legal tender, and the Secretary of the Treasury is authorised to limit from time to time the coinage thereof to such an amount as he may deem sufficient to meet the export demand for the same.

34. **The note circulation in the United States has been as follows:**

(In millions of dollars.)

	States Notes (July 1 each Year)			Bank Notes (Jan. 1 each Year)			Grand Total
	Greenbacks or Legal Tender	Fractional Currency	Total	National Bank	State Banks	Total	
1861	—	—	—	—	202	202	202
1862	150	—	150	—	184	184	334
1865	433	25	458	67	—	67	525
1869	356	32	388	294	4	298	686
1873	356	45	401	336	1	337	738
1874	382	46	428	350 } July 1	—	350	778
1876	370	34	404	331 } July 1	—	331	735
1877 Aug. 31	358	20 (July 31)	378	315	—	315	693

The following remarks are suggested by the table :—

I. Since 1874, the total paper currency had been reduced, on August 31, 1877, by 85 millions of dollars, including a reduction of 26 millions of fractional currency.

II. Under the legislation of 1862 and 1863, the maximum limit for the issue of greenbacks was 450 millions, afterwards reduced to 400 million dollars—exclusive of fractional currency. By 1868, the greenbacks were reduced to 356 millions, when further reduction was suspended, and, by a compromise with the inflationists, the limit was raised in June 1874, to 382 million dollars, the amount then in circulation.

III. National bank notes are payable in legal-tender notes; so that, on return to specie payments, any amount of bullion and coin reserve which would secure the convertibility of the greenbacks would provide also for the convertibility of the national bank notes. In this view the 14 million dollars of greenbacks (included in the 358 millions outstanding on August 31) which were deposited in the treasury to retire national bank notes, should be deducted from the total circulation, which, accordingly, may be stated at 679 millions on August 31.

IV. The amount of coin (including that in the treasury and banks), which was in circulation in 1860, in the United States, excluding California, has been variously estimated at—

275 millions, by the Director of the Mint in 1861 (but apparently inclusive of some 40 millions for California).

210 millions, by Secretary Chase, in his annual report for 1862.

200 millions, by the New York 'Financial Chronicle,' in its annual Financial Review in January 1876.

Adding to the smallest of these sums the circulation of the State banks in 1861, viz., 202 millions, the total becomes 402 millions, against 679 millions (section III.) on August 31, 1877, including 20 millions of fractional currency which are redeemable in silver tokens. The legal-tender money in 1861 was 200 millions; in August 1877, it amounted to 358 millions, exclusive of 315 millions of national bank notes which are legal tender against Government, except for Customs' duties.

V. Besides this considerable increase of legal-tender and bank notes, there has been a great augmentation of cheques and other banking expedients for economising the use of money. In 1861 there were about 1,600 local banks with 800 million dollars of capital and liabilities; in 1874 the corresponding figures were 1,980 banks and 2,908 million dollars. In 1876 there were 2,089 national banks and nearly 4,000 States banks and private bankers. The deposits in the banks of the New York Clearing House amounted to 106 million dollars in 1860, and to 255 millions in 1876.

VI. There has been a similar expansion, through the Funding Loans, of the means of settling foreign debts without the export of gold. The subscriptions to the last 4 per cent. loan are to be paid in gold coin, owing to which stipulation the loan will for the most part be taken up abroad, causing an importation or preventing an exportation of gold, with the result, in either case, of increasing the amount of gold in the country; and this effect will last for longer than the time required to extinguish the present small premium on gold.

VII. Notwithstanding the figures in IV., and the considerations in V. and VI., there is a feeling in financial circles in the United States, that the greenbacks should not be reduced below 300 million dollars before the resumption of specie payments on January 1, 1879, lest this contraction of the legal-tender reserve in which the national bank notes are payable should make money scarce; though every fresh reduction of the amount of greenbacks must bring them nearer to par, and so facilitate the issue of gold even before the formal resumption of specie payments. If, to-morrow, with the gold pounds of the new funded loan, the amount of greenbacks were to be reduced from 358 to 258 millions of dollars, the currency would not be diminished one whit; the notes being brought to par, the gold coin employed for the withdrawal of the 100 millions of dollars would circulate in the country with full security against export, except in the usual course of trade, while the gold reserves of the treasury, the banks, and private individuals would also be fearlessly unlocked.

VIII. Only four millions sterling of fractional currency remained for withdrawal on July 31, 1877.

35. The resumption of specie payments before January 1, 1879, and that without making demands on the fresh yearly production of gold, may be considered certain; and the result would place the United States on the same vantage ground with England as to metallic currency, through the attainment of, practically, a single standard of gold, or of the metal which has appreciated relatively to silver. In view of the facts, that gold has been, practically, the sole standard in the United States since 1834—that the obligations of the Government are payable in gold—that the success of the funding operations, which must be continued till the conversion of all the funded loans into

four per cents., depends upon adherence to gold payments—that the premium on gold is nearly extinguished—and that the resumption of specie payments can now require but little effort—on all these considerations, it seems idle to discuss the pros and cons of the question which has agitated parties in the States, whether silver should not be remonetised by restoration of the double standard. A practical people like the Americans will accept the logic of facts as unanswerable.

36. Secretary Sherman has given no faltering expression to the view which he has long entertained that gold should be the principal, and silver the subsidiary coin in the American currency. The 'Economist' of July 7, 1877, quoted from him the following remarks:—

'The silver question gives me no uneasiness. There are two extremes of opinion upon it. One extreme opinion would force everybody to take silver in payment of all debts, public or private. The other opinion would entirely demonetise silver. It is an old dispute that has periodically risen for more than two thousand years, and has always been adjusted by the Government issuing both metals as coin, and maintaining their equal value as a fixed rate by limiting the amount it issues. The metal more valuable in the market than its legal ratio can be issued without limit. The metal less valuable in the market than its legal ratio must be limited in its issue, leaving the absolute need of it to fix the amount. The way for us is to issue silver coin whenever demanded (the old silver dollar as well as the smaller silver coin) in exchange for paper money, either for fractional currency or United States notes, and retire them. The silver dollar ought to be received by the Government, and made a legal tender, precisely as the paper dollar now is. In this way, perhaps fifty millions of silver dollars will supersede fifty millions of paper dollars. Some say more, some say less, but let that be determined by the popular demand. . . . We cannot afford to deny ourselves the great convenience of an ample silver currency, kept equal to gold by confining its issue by the Government to the actual demand for it.'

In this passage the Secretary of the Treasury states that silver coin, which is to be made legal tender at the existing relative value of 15½ to 1 of gold, will be issued by the Government, on the demand, not of those who may bring silver bullion to the mint, but of those who may bring paper dollars to be exchanged for silver coins. In other words, the coinage of silver will be closed to importers or bringers of silver bullion; and the Government will coin only so much silver as may suffice for the public demand, which will be measured, first, by the applications for silver coin in exchange for paper dollars; and, second, by the unlimited acceptance of the silver dollars at Government Treasuries, in satisfaction of Government demands, for which they will be freely tendered to Government whenever, through an over issue of the silver coins, they circulate at a discount. Mr. Sherman estimates that the country may absorb at par about 50 million dollars of this subsidiary silver currency.

37. If these views be adopted by Congress, as is probable, the currency of the United States will consist of the following, viz.:—

1. Legal Tender.

a. Gold coins, without limit of the coinage.

b. Silver dollars, to an amount limited by Government, the coinage of silver being closed to the public.

c. United States notes, payable on demand in gold or silver coins.

2. Limited Legal Tender.

d. Silver and copper tokens, as legal tender for fractions of a dollar, and perhaps the limit of legal tender of the silver dollar will be enlarged.

e. Notes of national banks, as legal tender in satisfaction of Government demands, but not in transactions between individuals.

Before the suspension of specie payments, the legal tender consisted entirely of gold and silver dollars, and of multiples of the former. There were no United States notes; while the notes of the several States banks (not being legal tender, and superseded in 1863 by national bank notes, circulated within narrow local limits, outside which they were at a discount. In a currency constituted like that above described, among a people who have been familiarised with the use of paper money, by seventeen years' use of inconvertible notes, and for whom cheques and banking facilities have been multiplied (para. 34, section V.), the notes in circulation must greatly preponderate over the metallic currency. In 1861, the coin in circulation was estimated at 200 to 275 million dollars, and the notes amounted to 200 millions—the proportion being about half of each. A proportion of one-third metal and two-thirds paper is more probable in future.

38. On January 22, 1876, the New York 'Financial and Commercial Chronicle' stated that the exports, less imports, of gold coin from 1859 to 1875 amounted to 484 million dollars; and as the total gold coinage during that period was somewhat over 470 millions, the amount subtracted from the gold coin previously in circulation was small. The same journal, on January 13, 1877, gave the net export of gold coin and bullion from 1860 to 1876 as 702 million dollars, against a total gold production in the United States of 767 millions. The editor's investigation on January 22, 1876, of the amount of metallic currency in the country at the end of 1875 was summed up as follows:—

'The result of the foregoing is that there is in the country, in 1876, at least as much gold and silver as there was in 1860. This certainly is contrary to the general impression, and is at variance with any conclusion which one would draw from the present *visible* supply. It is possible that gold left the country through the South during the war. Whether there was any such movement, or what was its extent if there was, we have no means of knowing. Our opinion, for evident reasons, would be against any considerable change having resulted in that way. We have been informed by two Southern gentlemen of large experience, within a very short time, who claim to speak from their own knowledge, citing several instances, that even now there is much gold hoarded in the South. Of course we can easily understand that this should be so in Texas. There must be, at present, compared with 1860, an increased supply in California, and also throughout all the mining region.'

In 1876, the gold production in the United States amounted to 46·85 million dollars, against 42 millions in 1875, while the net export of gold coin and bullion was 30 millions less than in 1875. The New York journal, summing up its review of the production and movement of gold and silver in the United States in 1876, stated:—'Our production of the precious metals during 1876, over and above the amount exported and manufactured, is about 40 millions of dollars,' thus confirming the conclusion of the previous year, that there has not been any diminution, in the country, of the amount of gold and silver which was in it in 1860, while, as we have seen, paper dollars will form a larger proportion of the currency, after resumption of specie payments, than in the past.

39. The legislation in 1876, for promoting a silver coinage in the States, kept within the bounds which the present Secretary of the Treasury is willing to recognise—namely, a silver coinage of limited amount. This limit was fixed at 50 millions of dollars, by the law of July 24, 1876. The Bland Silver Bill of December 1876, which proposed to make the old silver dollar 'a legal tender for all debts, public and private, except where the payment of gold coin is required by law,' was indeed passed by the United States House of Representatives by a large majority; but it was rejected by the Senate, and the infelicitous recommendations of the American Silver Commission, of whom the majority advised resumption of the double standard, and the minority advised an International Conference for fixing a relative value for gold and silver throughout the world, proved abortive.

40. Public feeling on the subject is, of course, still unsettled. Messrs. McCulloch and Co., in their circular dated June 13, 1877, wrote:—

'At the same time the financial prospect is beclouded by a renewal of agitation on the silver question. So rapidly has the feeling spread throughout the West in favour of remonetising the silver dollar, and making silver an unlimited legal tender, that it is very generally conceded that at the next session of Congress something will have to be done to conciliate this sentiment. At the East, where opinion is generally opposed to the reintroduction of silver, this much is commonly acknowledged. The only question is, whether the silver party will be able to carry their extreme demand that silver shall be made a legal tender for unrestricted amounts, or they may find it necessary to compromise upon a recoinage of the 412½ grains silver dollar, and the extension of the amount to which silver shall be a lawful tender, to, say, twenty-five or fifty dollars. The Secretary of the Treasury has just declared himself in favour of the latter policy; and the President acknowledges to having changed his views materially in the direction of the silver party, but has not distinctly indicated to what extent he would go.'

41. Meanwhile, the facts remain—

a. That the two considerations which gained advocates for the double standard, among others than the silver mining interest, have lost their force, the Americans having found that specie payments can be resumed without effort by January 1, 1879 (or sooner, in Secretary Sherman's opinion), and that the interest on their civil war debt can be reduced to four per cent. per annum, by which reduction they will gain more than if the principal of the old debt had continued at the old rate of interest from its being redeemable in silver.

b. That all the considerations which are determining France in her preparations for a single standard of gold apply with greater force to the United States, by reason of the considerable foreign indebtedness of those States; at the same time, America is more favourably circumstanced than France for resuming specie payments in gold, inasmuch as the silver currency of the United States was long since exported, while France will have to dispose of a large amount of silver coin on its being demonetised.

c. That with gold valuations, with a public debt redeemable in gold, with gold already accumulated in the treasury and the banks, and with a trade for which the final settlements are made through gold coin countries, gold is already in possession, and silver, with its value depreciated relatively to gold, has to dislodge it from that position.

d. That if the West is noisy, the South and East are influential, and in accord with a well-judging public opinion.

e. That all the acts of the Government of the United States hitherto have tended towards the recognition of a gold standard, with silver as a subsidiary currency.

42 GERMANY.

I. The silver coinage which is in course of withdrawal, on account of the coinage reform in Germany, was regulated in conformity with the German Mint Convention of 1857, from which Austria withdrew in June 1867. Under that Convention 2 Prussian thalers were equal to 3 Austrian and 3½ South German gulden.

II. In June 1870, immediately before the outbreak of the Franco-German war, Prussia convened a monetary conference of the German States, to consider the expediency of changing, even gradually, to a single gold standard, which a short time previous had been recommended for France by the High Council of Commerce in Paris. The primary object, however, with Prussia, was to replace the diverse coins of the several States in Germany by an uniform currency. Without a change of standard, the expense of withdrawing the old coinage and issuing new would have been great. When the change to a gold standard was finally determined upon in 1871, it was expected that the profit from reissue, as tokens, of a great part of the withdrawn silver coinage, would cover the expense of the new coinage and the loss from selling the remaining silver which might be withdrawn from circulation. The French indemnity also supplied the means of carrying out a coinage reform; and a single gold standard was chosen in accordance with European opinion, as expressed in the Monetary Conferences of 1867 and 1870.

III. The contraction of the paper currency, by the withdrawal of all notes of lower denominations than 100 marks, was another object of the currency reform. In the statement of objects and reasons of the first Coinage Bill, the following passage occurs:—'The inconvenience of the silver coin led of necessity to a very considerable circulation of paper means of payment, which in ordinary times are willingly taken as a welcome facility, but, in critical times of awakening mistrust, contain the germs of serious dangers.'

43. The laws for the reform of the coinage are those of—

a. December 4, 1871, which prohibited the further coinage of full-weight silver coins; decreed the coinage of gold coins of the new standard, and directed that, until the passing of a further law for the withdrawal of the large silver coins, they were to continue as legal tender, but that 'all payments which, by existing law, are made in silver money of the several German States, may be effected in the Imperial gold coins, reckoned at the ten-mark piece for the value of 3⅓ thalers, the twenty-mark piece for the value of

$6\frac{2}{3}$ thalers' (and so forth, for the gulden currency of South Germany). This valuation (the preamble of the Act stated) was 'as near as possible to what is considered the usual ratio between the two metals, viz., $15\frac{1}{2}$ of silver to one of gold.' The Act also empowered the Chancellor of the Empire to ordain the withdrawal of the existing silver coins of the States of the Confederation, and to take the necessary means for that purpose from the Imperial Treasury.

b. The Coinage Act of July 9, 1873, among other provisions, directed that the silver coins of the new currency should contain silver one-tenth less than nominally equivalent silver coins of the old currency. Thus, there are 1,395 marks of fine gold in a German pfund ($=\frac{1}{2}$ kilog.). In the relative value of $15\frac{1}{2}$ to 1, one pfund of fine silver should have been coined into ninety marks, or $\frac{1395}{15\frac{1}{2}}$; but the law directed that the pfund of fine silver should be coined into 100 marks, giving a relative value of gold to silver of 1 to 13·95. The same regulations of 1873 decreed that 'no one is compelled to accept more than twenty marks of the new coinage in silver, nor more than one mark in nickel or copper, in payment. Imperial and Federal treasuries, however, will take in payment any amount of silver coin.'

c. The Hamburg, Bremen, and South German currencies having been withdrawn in the interval, the Federal Council decreed in September 1875, that the gold standard should 'come into force on January 1, 1876,' from which date gold valuations have prevailed in the German empire in all contracts, obligations, &c.

d. The greater part of the two-thaler pieces of Prussia having next been withdrawn, a law of January 6, 1876, gave power to the German Government to fix the dates from which the one and two-thaler pieces might be degraded to tokens. The two-thaler pieces and one-third thaler pieces were demonetised in November 1876, but the one-thaler piece and the one-sixth thaler piece, which constitute the bulk of the thaler currency, have not yet been demonetised.

44. The gross coinage of the German States, under the old law, to the end of 1873, after deducting withdrawals by the mints, amounted to gold, £26,547,216; silver of full legal tender, £85,848,088; small silver coins, £4,093,119; and copper coins, £4,641,141. The gold coin had been virtually expelled from circulation during the long period that silver was sole legal tender. There was actually presented for withdrawal, up to September 30, 1875, £4,932,556 worth of the gold coins; the remainder is considered to have been

melted down or exported, or to have disappeared in other ways. The gold coins current in the States were withdrawn by the end of 1873 or the beginning of 1874, and they ceased to be legal tender from April 1, 1874, and to be exchangeable at the Government treasuries from June 30, 1874.

45. The gross coinage of the old silver and copper currencies, less withdrawals at the mints, up to December 31, 1871, and the subsequent withdrawals in furtherance of the coinage reform, are as follows:—

(*In millions of marks.*)

	Thaler Currency	Gulden Currency	Hanse Towns and other	Total	Copper Coins	Grand Total
Gross coinage, less withdrawals at the mints, to Dec. 31, 1871 . . .	1,534·9	236·4	27·4	1,798·7	11·	1,809·7
Less $\frac{1}{4}$ . . .	383·7	59·1	6·9	449·7	2·7	452·4
	1,151·2	177·3	20·5	1,349·0	8·3	1,357·3
Withdrawn:						
To Sept. 30, 1875 .	153·2	129·0	13·2	295·4	Possibly included in Hanse Towns	295·4
To March 31, 1876 .	244·8	180·4	14·3	439·5		439·5
To Sept. 30, 1876 .	388·7	195·6	14·3	598·6		598·6
To Feb. 28, 1877 .	520·2	195·6	14·3	730·2	3·1	733·3
Remaining on:						
Sept. 30, 1875 . .	998·0	48·3	7·3	1,053·6	—	1,061·9
March 31, 1876 .	906·4	−3·1	6·2	909·5	—	617·8
Sept. 30, 1876 . .	762·5	−18·3	6·2	750·4	—	758·7
Feb. 28, 1877 . .	631·0	−18·3	6·2	618·8	5·2	624·0

46. The following remarks are suggested by this table.

I. The abatement of one-fourth from the gross coinage is that which was estimated by the German Government in May 1874, in a paper which, to the net result of 1,357 million marks, or 67½ millions sterling, 'added the Austrian thalers and florins at that time (1871) circulating in Germany. The Austrian florins have, as is well known, since then disappeared from Germany, but Austrian thalers to the amount of 20 or 30 millions (3 to 4½ millions sterling) may perhaps still be in Germany.'

II. In the Blue Book on the Depreciation of Silver the following estimates occur of the amount of silver coinage of the old currency which was probably in existence in December 1871, viz.

a. Mr. Giffen (March 30, 1876): 'The best authorities seem to lean to an amount between 50 and 60 millions sterling (I should say 57 millions) as the circulation of silver alone, out of the 90 millions sterling. The authorities lean to thirty per cent. as the proportion which was melted down and exported, when the price of silver was high.'

b. Mr. Pietsch (April 6, 1876): '39 millions sterling, against an actual withdrawal, to February 28, 1877, of 36 millions sterling.'

c. Mr. Seyd (May 1, 1876): '60 millions sterling of full-value silver coinage, and 16 millions of subsidiary silver coins (besides foreign coins).'

d. A German Expert (in a memorandum, in April 1876, communicated by Lord Odo Russell, who described him as a gentleman who is well acquainted with the subject): 'It may fairly be calculated that at the commencement of the reform of the coinage, there were in circulation silver coins of the value of at least 900 millions of marks (45 millions sterling).'

III. The German Government's estimate of the silver coin in circulation in December 1871, was the highest; but for the gulden currency, and that of the Hanse towns, &c., which may be considered to have been wholly withdrawn, that estimate has been exceeded by the actual withdrawals.

47. The details of withdrawals of the thaler currency are as follows:—

(Millions of marks.)

	One Thaler pieces	Two Thaler pieces	Fractional Currency (Legal Tender)	Total
Gross coinage, less withdrawals at the mints, to Dec. 31, 1871 . . .	1,103·45	195·	188·97	1,487·42
Less ¼	275·86	48·75	47·24	371·85
	827·59	146·25	141·73	1,115·57
Withdrawn:				
To March 31, 1876 . .	85·82	109·	50·	244·82 [1]
To Feb. 28, 1877 . .	316·76	153·50	50· (say)	520·26 [2]
Remaining on:				
March 31, 1876 . . .	741·77	37·25	91·73	870·75
Feb. 28, 1877 . . .	510·83	−7·25	91·73 (say)	595·31

The following remarks are added.

I. Deducting one-third, instead of the German Government's one-fourth, Herr Soetbeer ('Economist,' June 3, 1876) estimated the outstanding thaler currency of December 31, 1871, at 989 million marks. The German expert, whose memorandum was communicated by Lord Odo Russell, estimated the amount at 900 millions at least.

[1] Blue Book, 1876. [2] *Economist*, March 31 and April 7, 1877.

The withdrawals of two-thaler pieces have exceeded even the higher estimate of the German Government.

II. In September 1875, Herr Soetbeer and other German authorities estimated the total silver coinage then outstanding at 38 millions sterling, viz., 30 millions in one-thaler pieces and 6 millions in two-thaler pieces.[1] And a member of the Reichstag (a banker) reckoned the total amount of thalers outstanding, including the sums held by banks and in treasuries, at 34 millions sterling. On September 30, 1875, the thalers withdrawn amounted to 153 million marks; on March 31, 1876, to 245 millions, and on February 28, 1877, to 520 millions; giving 367 millions of marks, or 18 millions sterling, as the withdrawals from September 1875 to February 1877. On the basis of the estimates in September 1875, there should have been only 16 or 18 millions sterling outstanding on February 28, 1877. Yet, in June following, the well-informed Vienna correspondent of the 'Economist,' and in July the editor of that journal, wrote as follows :—

a. 'There were, and there are still (June 5, 1877) more silver thalers in circulation than the Government cared to believe at the time. The recollection of the examination of all the banks and public pay offices which, on September 30, 1875, announced the existence of but 30 million thalers is striking at this moment. Camphausen, the Minister for the Board of Finance, declared at the time, that under such conditions the Currency Act could be put into execution with the greatest ease possible. However, although the Bundesrath was authorised in January 1876, to degrade the silver thalers to imperial silver coins, still, this part of the law has not yet been carried out. . . . Still the circulation of old silver thalers is at present valued at 500 to 600 million marks. A great part of them stream into the Reichsbank, as the other note banks are trying to refuse them. We have no figures to give us a precise idea of the amount of silver and gold in the tills of the bank, because the latter makes a secret of the proportion. We must therefore trust to private information. On the introduction of the Coinage Act of 1871, but very little gold was to be found in the Prussian bank's tills. After the introduction of the new Currency Act, the newly-coined gold, little by little, replaced the silver; still, I am informed by a friend from Berlin, that the greater half of the Imperial Bank's coin and bullion consists of silver to the amount of about 300 million marks. This large proportion of silver makes the Bank feel every demand on its stock of coin and bullion in quite an extraordinary manner, most likely, because its stock of gold is too small for its requirements.'—*Economist*, June 9, 1877.

b. 'Official reports state that the amount of old silver withdrawn from circulation at the end of May 1877 was 798 million marks (say 40 millions sterling) of which 404 millions (say 20 millions sterling) were taken for recoinage, as shown by the Mint returns for the beginning of last month.

---

[1] *Economist*, December 11 and 25, 1875.

Of the difference (about 20 millions sterling, nominal—although it is difficult to be exact, because of the wear of the old coins and the low intrinsic value of the new silver currency)—15 millions have been sold, and 5 millions remain for sale. But the sum which has yet to be sold will be further augmented by an unknown quantity, viz., the quantity of old thaler coins which are yet to be withdrawn. . . . The great final step in the German coinage reform will not have been taken until the 1-thaler pieces are demonetised or debased to the rank of token coins. We see estimates—there have all along been estimates which have varied much, because the guiding facts have been so few—that the quantity of silver which the German Government will have henceforward to sell will reach 25 millions sterling,—and that the four years which have elapsed since such sales began will stretch into another four years, and perhaps eight years more, before the demonetised silver currency is altogether cleared out of Germany. It is clear the silver crisis is not yet done with.'—*Economist*, July 14 and August 25, 1877.

And yet Mr. Pietsch, who claimed to speak with knowledge and apparent authority, correcting a higher German estimate of 20 to 22 millions, stated in July 1876 that the silver remaining to be sold amounted to only 13 millions sterling.

48. It appears from paras. 45 and 47, that up to February 28, 1877, the withdrawals of gulden, two-thaler pieces, and Hamburg and other currency except thalers, were as follows:—

(*In millions of marks.*)

	Gulden	2 Thaler Pieces	Hamburg and other	Total	1 Thaler	Fractional Thalers	Total
Gross coinage in Dec. 1871, outstanding .	236	195	27	458	1,103	189	1,750
Withdrawn, to Feb. 28, 1877 . .	196	154	14	364	317	50	731
Percentage of gross coinage withdrawn.	83	79	52	79	28·7	26·5	41·7

Of the gulden currency 83 per cent., and of two-thaler pieces 79 per cent. have been withdrawn; while of the total thaler currency of full value, only 38 per cent. has been withdrawn, the withdrawals of one-thalers and of fractional thalers having amounted to only 28 per cent. of the gross coinage estimated to be outstanding in December 1871. In the Blue Book of 1877, relating to silver, it is stated that of the thaler coinage, two-thaler pieces were first withdrawn, as being the largest and most available for melting. For the same reason they must have been preferred for export, during the drain of silver to the East, and whenever the exchange was unfavourable to Germany. Hence, since 79 per cent. of the gross coinage of two-thaler pieces was withdrawn up to February 28, 1877, the proportion of the ultimate withdrawals of one-thaler pieces and of fractional thalers must be greater. Reckoning it at a not much higher proportion, viz., at 83 per cent., the same as in the gulden currency, the amount of ultimate withdrawals becomes 1,027 millions, of which 367 millions were withdrawn up to February 28, 1877, leaving 660 millions of marks, or 33 millions sterling, as outstanding on that date. This accords, in a measure, with the estimates quoted in para. 47, section II., that 25 to 30 millions sterling of silver currency remained for withdrawal at the end of May 1877. Inasmuch, however, as the 300 million marks (15 millions sterling) of silver in the Imperial Bank, in May 1877 (para. 47, section II. *a.*) must be reckoned with the coin which remains for withdrawal, and as large amounts of thalers are still in circulation, the outstanding silver coinage probably exceeds 30 millions sterling, exclusive of 3 millions sterling of Austrian thalers which are redeemable by the German Empire. The British Secretary of Legation at Stuttgart wrote on September 25, 1876: 'Thalers are used very extensively in the ordinary daily transactions of the public, in place of the bank notes of small amount withdrawn from circulation.'

49. Including silver token coinage, the total withdrawal of silver currency, to the end of June 1877, was £40,941,000; and if 34 millions be added for further withdrawals, the gross total becomes 75 millions. Up to August 31, 1877, there had been coined 20 millions sterling of silver; and to the end of May 1877, 15 millions worth had been sold ('Economist,' August 25, 1877), giving a total of 35 millions: so that some 40 millions sterling of silver remain for disposal, unless the limit fixed by law for the silver token coinage be raised from 10 to 15 marks per head of the population. Lord Odo Russell wrote on November 1, 1876—

'So strong is the feeling in the Reichsrath against the measure, that the Imperial Government have decided not to bring before it the resolution passed by the Bundesrath, to increase the coinage of silver from 10 marks to 15 marks per head of the population—an operation which would have absorbed silver to the amount of about 250 millions of marks.'

50. The increase of the rate per head from 10 to 15 marks is opposed on the consideration that during 'extraordinary disturbances and revulsions, with general distrust,' all the overvalued silver coinage not necessary for daily clearings would flow into the public treasuries,

where it would accumulate. The 'Frankfort Mercur' of January 1877, controverting this argument of Professor Soetbeer, observed:—

'In France, and still more so in Great Britain, the gold standard has long since become, so to say, flesh and blood. But with us in Germany, our ideas and customs, especially those of that most tenacious of all other classes of people, the peasants, cling so closely to silver money, and will, as may be expected, continue to do so for a long time to come, that every thoughtful policy must take these considerations to heart. The peasant prefers silver, not for payments but for hoarding. No argument would make him believe that he would do better to make use of the more valuable gold for such purposes. Besides this, the peasant keeps, as a rule, large amounts of cash on hand, and according to his old acquired custom, generally in silver. It is therefore not at all to be wondered at, if now in Germany—although there are still about 600 millions of silver thalers in circulation—here and there a want of two and five-mark pieces already makes itself felt. There is even now in Bavaria—although it has already more than its due proportion—has in fact 15 marks per head,—there is a demand for two and five-mark pieces. In North Germany analogous phenomena will ensue, just as the silver thalers are more and more withdrawn from circulation.'

51. On September 1, 1877, the new money coined in Germany amounted to—

	Marks
Gold coins	1,514,818,780
Silver „	409,349,190
Nickel „	35,160,344
Copper „	9,595,930

The gold alone amounts to 75 millions sterling, or to more than the highest estimate of the gold and silver coins of the old currency which were outstanding in December 1871; and the gold and silver coins amount to 96 millions sterling, against 86 millions of gross gold and silver coinage of the old currency, less withdrawals at the mint, to the end of 1871. On the surface the coinage reform must have been completed, and silver been demonetised ere this; but we know that the greater part of the mass of the thaler currency, viz., the one-thaler pieces and the fractional thalers of full value, has not yet been withdrawn. The usual explanation is, that a great part of the gold coins has been exported; but perhaps it is more correct to say that a considerable part of the small note circulation in Germany was really withdrawn with gold.

52. No doubt large amounts of gold coin have been exported, but principally in 1876 and 1877. The coinage of gold began in 1872, and on November 11, 1873, it amounted to 48 millions sterling, after which there was a cessation from the coinage of gold pieces; for, on April 24, 1875, the gold coinage amounted to only 57 millions sterling.

In the interval from 1872 to January 1875, when the gold valuation was introduced throughout the empire, the German Government controlled the foreign exchanges, by means of the commercial bills in which a part of the war indemnity was paid; and it also issued gold coins sparingly to the public, the bulk of the issues having been to bankers, on an understanding that they should hold it in their reserves as far as possible. On the whole, the arrangements were fairly successful; and as the German Government recovered a portion of the exported gold coins, through its control over the foreign exchanges, the net export to December 31, 1875, may be reckoned at 5 millions sterling as an outside estimate. The estimates of German authorities were successively reduced, with better knowledge, and with experience of the returns in the course of exchange and through the German Government's purchases of gold abroad, from 500 million marks in November 1874, to 300 or 400 million marks in July 1875, to 200 millions in September, and to 30 millions in December 1875; the last-mentioned amount being the estimate of the Minister of Finance. Hence, it is mainly from the German Government having issued gold coin in withdrawal of small notes, instead of issuing it principally in withdrawal of silver coins, that the excess of gold coinage has arisen. While only 40 millions sterling of old silver currency were withdrawn to May 31, 1877, 75 millions sterling of gold coins and 20 millions worth of new silver coins were issued up to August 31, 1877.

53. The facts relating to the note circulation in Germany are as follows:—

I. The old paper currency consisted of notes issued by the Governments of the several German States, and of notes issued by banks. The States' notes have been replaced by Imperial tender notes (Reichskassenchieme) of 5 marks, 20 marks, and 50 marks, in the proportion of one-third for each denomination, and within a limit of 3 marks per head of the population. For bank notes the reform consisted in the withdrawal of notes of smaller denominations than 100 marks, and in altered conditions for the issue of notes not covered by coin and bullion.

II. The States' notes amounted to 184,390,800 marks (£9,219,540). The permanent limit of Imperial tender notes in replacement of these is 120 million marks (6 millions sterling); but a temporary excess issue of 54,919,841 marks, to be withdrawn by-and-by, was allowed, to facilitate the withdrawal of the States' notes.

III. With regard to the notes issued by banks: under the old law certain proportions of the note circulation had to be covered by coin and bullion; under the new law of January 30, 1875, the portion not covered by coin and bullion is in two divisions of taxed and untaxed. The untaxed amount of bank note circulation, not covered by coin and bullion, is limited to 385 million marks, equal to 19·25 millions sterling. For any issue in excess of the 385 millions the banks pay a tax of 5 per cent. a year.

IV. On July 1, 1874, out of 393 million thaler notes in circulation, 178 millions were in notes of less than 100 marks worth, and of these only 78 millions worth of notes of 20 to 25 thalers (60 to 75 marks) could be replaced by notes of 100 marks. But the remaining 100 million thalers (15 millions sterling) could not be replaced by notes under the new law, which prohibits the issue of bank notes for less than 100 marks. According to this estimate, 15 millions sterling worth of notes had to be withdrawn by paying out gold or silver coin, as the case might be.

V. The German Bank Act, which reformed the circulation of bank notes, is dated January 30, 1875. According to an official return published in the 'Economist' of April 17, 1875, the notes of banks in circulation on January 31, 1875, were as follows:—

	Thalers	£
Thaler and gulden notes:		
Under 100 marks	169,178,852	25,376,828
100 marks and above	220,231,443	33,034,716
	389,410,995	58,411,544
	Marks	
Marks, notes of 100 marks and upwards .	79,623,600	3,981,180
		62,392,794

VI. The bank note circulation on various dates from July 1870 was as follows:—

(Millions of marks.)

	July 1870	March 1872	End of 1872	End of 1873	End of 1874	End of 1875	June 30, 1876
Covered by bullion .	374	672	840	926	985	680	769·4
Uncovered notes .	421	354	502	426	340	374	250·8
Total circulation.	795	1,026	1,342	1,352	1,325	1,054	1,020·2

The circulation increased after the Franco-German war; and its subsequent progress was not checked up to 1874; after that, under the restrictive measures for introducing the new German Bank Act from January 1, 1876, the circulation steadily fell from 62·39 millions sterling on January 31, 1875, to 51 millions on June 30, 1876, or by 11·4 millions. A main object of the reform was to contract the circulation by withdrawing all the small notes of under 100 marks. These amounted to 25·376 millions sterling on January 31, 1875, and they were reduced afterwards to the following sums:—

(*In millions sterling.*)

	At end of		
	Sept. 1875	October 1875	June 1876
Notes of:			
50 marks and under . . .	3·644	2·784	·042
Between 50 and 100 marks . .	1·850	1·167	·053
	5·494	3·951	·095

And since June 30, 1876, the small notes have been entirely withdrawn. Had they been withdrawn with coin, the total note circulation would have been reduced by 25 millions sterling below the amount on January 31, 1875. But the actual reduction on June 30, 1876, below the total note circulation on December 31, 1874, was only 305 million marks, or 15 millions sterling, which sum was reduced by paying out silver. This is precisely the amount which it was estimated (section IV.) would have to be withdrawn from the note circulation of July 31, 1874, with gold or silver coin, as the case might be.

VII. The German banks, from the outset of the coinage reform, retained the new gold as much as possible, giving out silver in preference, with the result that the Vienna correspondent of the 'Economist,' August 28, 1875, wrote—

'The truth is, however, that men of business, and above all bank establishments, do all they can to keep the gold in their hands, and to make silver circulate—a very natural state of things, when one considers the low price of silver. It is for this reason that more silver circulates in the hands of the population than has ever been there before. On the other side, the fact is ascertained that the banks have very few silver thalers indeed in their possession. Thus, an official paper mentions that, a short time ago, one of the German governments required one million of silver thalers at a very short notice, and could not get them from any or even all the German banks, the Prussian bank being able to offer but 50,000 thalers.'

In other words, the banks had paid out all their silver in withdrawing notes of small denominations. It is not surprising, therefore, to find the Secretary of the British Legation at Stuttgart writing on September 25, 1876, that 'thalers are used very extensively in the ordinary daily transactions of the public, in place of the bank notes of small amount withdrawn from circulation.'

VIII. The objection to small notes is that, ordinarily, they remain permanently outstanding, to the displacement of coin which is exported; so that when a panic, or other exceptional cause, creates a run on banks by the holders of small notes, there is no available specie reserve for cashing them; what reserve there may be, having been retained practically for cashing the notes of larger denominations, in the assurance that ordinarily the small notes remain permanently outstanding. Hence, the sudden demand upon the German banks for the withdrawal, with coin, of fifteen millions sterling of small notes for which they did not ordinarily provide specie, must have forced them to create other paper obligations for replacing an equal amount of specie in their reserve for their other liabilities in respect of notes of larger denominations, and of deposits. It is probable that the German Government accommodated the banks by a transfer of part of its store of new gold currency to the reserves of the banks, on low interest, and on an understanding that the gold coins would be sparingly issued. But, in whatever form the paper obligations of the banks, for replenishing their specie reserves, may have been created, the obligations must have been eventually discharged in gold. Thus, in the final result, the small notes were withdrawn with gold, though, at the same time, an equal amount of the old silver currency was thrown back into circulation among the public.

54. The metallic and paper currencies in 1871, and the old currency remaining for withdrawal in 1877, with the new coinage, and the amount of note circulation in 1877, are shown in table on page 251.

I. The paper currency shows an increase of only 6 millions sterling, and the metallic currency an increase of 29 millions. As, however, 15 millions sterling of small notes were withdrawn, the real increase of paper currency is 21 millions, while, by a corresponding abatement, the real increase of metallic currency for transactions not formerly served by small notes is 14 millions. The total increase of notes and metallic currency is 35 millions, which nearly corresponds to the 33 millions sterling of thalers still outstanding. The figures show that a considerable amount of the new gold coins has been exported.

II. The low estimates which prevailed in the middle or autumn of 1876, respecting the thaler currency outstanding, added to the actual withdrawals at the dates of the estimates, gave 62 millions sterling as the probable amount of full-weight metallic currency in circulation in 1870. This amount being 24 millions sterling less than the figure deduced from the withdrawals and amended estimates, in 1877, the excess of the new circulation over that of 1870, on the basis of the 1876 estimates, would be 57 millions—or an increase so manifestly improbable, as to show that the amounts of old silver currency outstanding were under estimated in 1876.

	Circulation in 1870 and 1871	Circulation in 1877		Maximum presented by Law
		New Coinage and New Paper Currency	Preceding, with Thaler Currency outstanding	
	£	£	£	£ Original estimate
Full value coins:				
Gold . . .	4,932,556	75,740,939	—	60,000,000
Silver withdrawn .	40,941,000	—	—	—
„ to be withdrawn	34,000,000	—	34,000,000	—
	79,873,556	75,740,939	109,740,939	60,000,000
Subsidiary coins:				By Law
Silver . . .	3,069,837	20,467,459	—	21,000,000
Copper and nickel .	3,480,856	2,237,813	—	5,250,000
	6,550,693	22,705,272	22,705,272	26,250,000
	86,434,249	98,446,211	132,446,211	86,250,000
Note circulation:				
States notes . .	9,219,540	6,000,000	—	6,000,000
Imperial tender notes, special or temporary . .	—	2,750,000	—	—
Bank notes, viz.: uncovered by bullion.	21,050,000	11,134,450	—	11,134,450[1]
	30,269,540	19,884,450	—	17,134,450
Ditto, covered by bullion . . .	18,700,000	35,491,550	—	35,491,550
	48,969,540	55,376,000	55,376,000	52,626,000
Grand total . .	135,403,789	153,822,211	187,822,211	138,876,000
Total, excluding notes covered by bullion .	116,703,789	118,330,661	154,330,661	103,384,450

[1] Actual on July 31, 1877.

55. The currency in the two periods may be compared in aggregates, as follows :—

(*In millions sterling.*)

	In 1870 and 1871	In 1876	Increase	Maximum per Programme of 1873, or by Law
Metallic currency:				
Full weight	79·87	109·74	29·87	60·
Subsidiary	6·55	22·70	16·15	26·25
	86·42	132·44	46·02	86·25
Paper currency:				
Covered by coin and bullion .	18·70	35·49	16·79	35·49
Other notes	30·27	19·88	–10·39	17·13
	48·97	55·37	6·40	18·36
Grand total, excluding covered notes	116·69	152·32	35·63	104·61
Metallic currency, less coin and bullion reserve	67·72	96·95	29·23	50·76

III. The futility of prescribing a bullion and coin reserve against notes, for banks which can have no other or separate coin reserve for deposits, is manifest from the table—which shows the large increase in notes covered by coin and bullion of 17 millions beyond the amount of 19 millions sterling in 1871.

IV. An increase of deposits implies an increased use of cheques; and there has been a great extension of banking facilities—'the German Imperial Bank continues to institute branch offices all over the country.'[1] On the whole, the impression left by the table is that the total currency of Germany, paper and metallic, is much in excess of requirements. In other words, as the paper money is not in excess, because, if it were, it would be returned to the banks, the excess is in the metallic portion—which in the preceding table consists of (1) the reserves of gold and silver in the banks and treasuries, (2) the amount in actual circulation, (3) any error in the estimates. Under the third head, the amount of error is the unknown amount of gold coin which has been exported, for the amount of silver outstanding is apparently not over-estimated. Hence, the portion of total excess which cannot be accounted for by exports of gold coin must be withdrawn silver which the treasuries—(and reserve silver which the

[1] *Economist*, July 14, 1877.

banks)—cannot dispose of, and gold coin which is being accumulated for the withdrawal of thalers still outstanding.

56. The coinage of gold began in 1872, and was continued till November 1873, when it amounted, on November 11, to £48,772,309. The German Government then announced that, throughout 1874, it would coin silver and copper almost exclusively; but by February 25, 1875, only £3,472,242 of silver had been coined. Since then the progress of the gold and silver coinage has been as follows:—

(In millions sterling.)[1]

	Coined			Withdrawals of Silver
	Gold	Silver		
				£
April 24, 1875 . .	58·84	4·29	1874	7 447
October 23, 1875 .	59·88	6·97	1875	10·878
July 1, 1876 . .	70·36	12·72	1876, first half .	6·670
October 28, 1876 .	71·47	16·96	1876, second half .	8·651
December 2, 1876 .	71·53	17·84	1877, first half .	7·295
May 19, 1877 . .	71·85	20·13		
September 15, 1877 .	75·74	20·46		40·941

The German Government has fabricated 76 millions sterling of gold coins and 20 millions sterling of silver coins—total 96 millions—in the course of operations for withdrawing 80 millions sterling of gold and silver coins of full weight, and 7 millions sterling of silver tokens—total 87 millions; and yet it is so embarrassed in the operation of withdrawing the lesser with the greater, that about 33 millions sterling of thalers are still outstanding. The inadequate results of vast preparations imply a defect in the plan of operations.

57. The chief errors were the issue of gold coins before a sufficient amount had been accumulated for the simultaneous demonetisation of silver; their issue otherwise than in withdrawal of silver coins; and the withdrawal of the small notes virtually with gold. The last error is continued in the refusal of the Reichstag to enlarge the limit of 10 marks per head of the population, for the subsidiary silver currency.

58. The first error, or the issue of gold coins in instalments, would have resulted in failure but for the financial ability and sagacity with which the foreign exchanges were controlled—by means of the bills received from France for the war indemnity. The bills were employed,

[1] *Economist*, August 25, 1877.

not alone, as is commonly thought, for withdrawing gold from London, but more frequently for checking a drain of gold from Germany, in the face of a falling silver market. The exchange between the gold sovereign and the silver currency of Germany was affected by both the commercial demand and the price of silver. As affected by the latter, the variable price, or the amount of silver money payable for sovereigns, became larger as the price of silver fell, whilst the object of the German Government was to maintain rates yielding smaller amounts of silver for sovereigns. In this object that Government succeeded. In 1870 and 1871, before the coinage operations began, when the price of silver ranged generally above 60½ pence an ounce, the rates of exchange were not quite so favourable to Germany as those which, under the influence exercised by the German Government, were maintained in the subsequent years down to December 1874, in which month the price of silver was 57⅞*d.* an ounce.

59. In yet another respect, the German Government has fairly succeeded; one object of the currency reform was to reduce the circulation of bank notes, which had risen from 795 million marks in July 1870, to 1,352 millions in 1873; by June 30, 1876, they were reduced to 1,020 millions, and on July 31, 1877, to 892 millions.

60. Of the alternative methods (for countries whose gold is liable to be exported) of changing to a new standard of value, France has adopted the safe one of accumulating, first, the full amount of gold coin which is required for demonetising silver. Germany, in the hope of reducing expense, and avoiding a charge for interest, adopted the other method of gradual issues of gold coin before the demonetisation of the silver coins. If there has been failure, in any degree, it must be ascribed to disadvantages inherent in the latter method, which even the great financial ability that has guided the operations of the German Government could not countervail.

61. SCANDINAVIAN KINGDOMS.

Silver ceased to be legal tender in Sweden and Denmark, from May 1, 1873, under a Convention concluded on May 27, 1873. The relative value of gold to silver, for the conversion to the gold standard, was taken at 1 to 15·675. By the end of 1876, the whole of the silver withdrawn in Denmark, and the greater part of that withdrawn in Sweden, had been sold. Norway acceded to the Convention by a Treaty dated October 16, 1875, after having, by a Law of June 4, 1873, enacted that gold should be substituted for silver as the sole standard of the currency. About 1½ million sterling of silver was sold from 1872 to 1876; but the old coinage still in circulation is allowed to have currency till the end of the year 1881, except the pieces representing 12 and 3 skillings (silver), which must be withdrawn by 1884. The extensive use of paper money, and the small amount of coin in circulation, have facilitated the change to a gold standard in Norway. The principal reason, with the three kingdoms, for the change of standard, was their foreign trade with gold coin countries.

62. EAST INDIES.

I. Regulation XXXV. of 1793 recited that, 'under the Native administration, and until the year 1766, the gold mohur was not considered as a legal tender of payment in any public or private transaction. The sicca rupee was the established silver coin of the country, and the rupee in which the public revenues were payable. In the year 1766, the value of the gold coin with respect to the silver was first fixed, and the gold coin declared a legal tender of payment. The intrinsic worth of this coin was estimated to be equal to the nominal value of it (viz., 16 sicca rupees) or as nearly so as was deemed necessary to render it current at the prescribed rate.' With the same object of promoting its circulation, Regulation XXXV. of 1793 altered the relative value of the gold and silver coin to 1 of gold to 14·861 of silver. Regulation XIV. of 1818 altered the relative value afresh, fixing it at 1 to 15. Gold was not demonetised until Act XVIII. of 1835 declared 'that no gold coin shall henceforth be a legal tender of payment in any of the territories of the East India Company.'

II. Regulation I. of 1793 embodies the permanent settlement of the land revenue in the Lower Provinces of Bengal, and Regulation XXXV. of 1793, as above stated, made the gold mohur legal tender, concurrently with the silver sicca rupee, at a relative value of 1 of gold to 14·861 of silver.

III. The coinage from 1835–6 to 1854–5 exceeded the net import of silver into British India, from foreign countries beyond sea (*plus* the re-coinage of old rupees), by 14 millions sterling. This sum represents ornaments and the coinage of Native States melted and tendered to British mints as bullion. In turn, the mints of Native States coin the melted rupees of British mints. This source of supply of silver to the mints of Native States, which are all in the interior of the country, being cheaper than direct importations from abroad, and the trade of the Native States with countries abroad being carried on through British Indian seaports, by British subjects.

IV. The existing silver coinage of Government rupees was established by Act XVII. of 1835, in supersession of previous currencies. And its gross amount, as distinguished from former coinages, has been as follows, from 1835 to 1876 :—

(*In millions sterling.*)

	Net Imports of Silver by Sea, from Foreign Countries	Old Rupees coined into existing Rupees	Total	Total Coinage of existing Rupees and Fractions	Years	Export of Silver by Sea to Foreign Countries
1835–6 to 1844–5	20·535	11·919	32·454	35·966	10	4·488
1845–6 to 1854–5	15·327	6·786	22·113	32·544	10	11·454
	35·862	18·705	54·567	68·510	20	15·942
1855–6 to 1865–6	118·871	2·338	121·209	105·382	11	11·127
1866–7 to 1869–70	28·478	·235	28·713	22·112	4	5·422
1870–1 to 1875–6	16·808	·179	16·987	17·207	6	9·393
1876–7	7·199	—	7·199	6·329	1	2·794
	207·218	21·457	228·675	219·540	42	44·678

V. The amounts entered in the column of 'old rupees coined into existing rupees' include rupees of the British Government withdrawn from circulation, and the coinage of former Native dynasties withdrawn from circulation in territories acquired by lapse of heirs, annexation, and conquest. Therefore, the entry in the above-mentioned column overstates the amount of British Indian rupees withdrawn at the mints, by the amount of withdrawals, by the British Government, of the coins of Native dynasties current in newly acquired British territories.

VI. Of the existing coinage of Government rupees, which was introduced from 1835, perhaps little was worn out, down to 1854–5, though this cannot be affirmed with certainty. The British Indian rupees re-coined from 1835–6 to 1854–5, were of the coinages that were superseded before 1835, or by the Coinage Act of 1835. Several of those coinages were recalled by proclamation, and the chief of them, the sicca rupee, was recalled by proclamation in 1836, whereby, after the interval fixed for their payment into Government treasuries, they were degraded to bullion. Hence, it may be safely assumed that but little of those old coinages is outstanding in the shape of coin, while the little that may be so outstanding would, with insignificant exceptions, not be received into Government treasuries, or British mints, except as bullion. Accordingly, in estimating the amount of silver coins in circulation, the old coinages may be disregarded.

VII. It will be useful, however, to see what proportion of the old coinages was withdrawn after the introduction of the existing coinage in 1835. The silver coinage in the several mints in the Bengal Presidency, and in the Madras mint, was as follows, down to 1833-4:—

Bengal Presidency, from 1801-2 to 1832-3 .	48,580,927
Madras Mint, from 1820-1 to 1833-4 . .	7,467,196
	56,048,123

Information regarding the amounts of coinage of the Madras mint for earlier years, and of the Bombay mint, is not at hand. The coinage of the Madras mint from 1820-1 to 1833-4 was at the rate of half a million sterling a year; that of the Bombay mint, in a period of five years, from 1832 to 1836, was somewhat less. The coinage of the mints in the three Presidencies, from 1801-2 to 1833-4, probably exceeded 70 millions sterling. On the other hand, the amount of the old silver coinages withdrawn at the British mints from 1835-6 to 1854-5 was less, for the reasons stated in V. and VI. than the 18,705 millions sterling shown in section III.; and the abatements indicated in V. and VI. must be considerable, especially for the period from 1845-6 to 1854-5, which included the annexation of the Punjab—partially in 1845-6, and the remainder in 1868-9. Probably not one-fifth of the old silver currencies was presented at the Government treasuries for withdrawal, or at the British mints for re-coinage, from 1835 to 1854.

VIII. The exports of silver are principally to Mauritius and (occasionally by the Government) to England; and, together with the bulk of the remainder, they are principally in rupees. For the present inquiry, nearly the whole of the exports may be regarded as exports of rupees. In that case, the gross imports of silver (i.e. the net imports in section II., plus the exports) and the re-coinage of old rupees, formed the amount of bullion available for coinage, which has to be set against the actual coinage. Reckoned in this manner, the amount available, from 1835-6 to 1854-5, was 70½ millions sterling, while the actual coinage was 54⅓ millions, leaving an excess of only 16 millions for absorption, in twenty years, in the coinages of Native States and for ornaments. As this period included the Afghan,

Gwalior, Sindh, and Sikh wars, during which the mints of Native States, including some not directly concerned in those wars, must have been very active, there is a fair presumption that a considerable part of the British Indian rupees was melted during that period.

IX. From 1855–6 to 1869–70, a period of fifteen years, the gross imports of silver amounted to 164 millions sterling, and the re-coinage of Government rupees to three millions, giving a total of 167 millions, against an actual coinage, in that period, of 127 millions. The remaining 40 millions in that period of fifteen years, which includes the absorption of vast amounts of silver by the cotton districts in Berar and Gujerat, and by the opium districts in Central India, represents very inadequately what must have been the amounts absorbed in that period by coinage in Native mints, by conversion into ornaments, and by hoarding, consequent on the enrichment of cultivators by the cotton and opium trades. At the same time, a coinage of 127 millions in fifteen years, or at the rate of eight millions sterling a year, was in manifest excess of permanent purely currency requirements; and putting the two facts together, a considerable part of the coinage must have been melted for ornaments, and in the Native mints.

X. In the 42 years from 1835–6 to 1876–7, the gross imports of silver amounted to 252 millions, and the re-coinage to 21 millions, giving a total of 273 millions sterling. The silver coinage during that period amounted to 220 millions, leaving a remainder of 53 millions as the amount which may have been absorbed for ornaments and in Native mints. This is at the rate of $1\frac{1}{4}$ millions a year. Some writers have estimated the yearly consumption of silver in India, for coining in Native States, and for ornaments, as high as 6 millions sterling. Assuming it at two millions sterling a year, or 84 millions in 42 years, of which only 53 millions have been provided from the gross importations of silver into British India, the remaining 31 millions sterling was provided from the melting of existing and former coinages of Government rupees. We may assume that only 10 millions sterling of the Government coinage of 220 millions since 1835 has disappeared in this way. Some may consider this an under-estimate; but, on the other hand, the returns of imports and exports of silver cannot be accepted as accurate.

XI. The exports of silver to foreign countries beyond sea amounted from 1835–6 to 1876–7, to 45 millions sterling; but additional large amounts were also carried beyond India in other ways, viz.:—

a. For disbursements to troops, in the first and second Afghan wars, in the three expeditions to China, and in the expedition to Persia. The first and third of these would have been very imperfectly included in trade returns.

b. Losses and meltings during the mutiny.

c. Yearly remittances to Mecca by Mahomedans in India; the pilgrims to Mecca carry additional sums, and these, for the 42 years, together with the rupees, intact or melted, which emigrant coolies carry with them to British and French colonies, must form a very considerable amount.

d. On the N.W. frontier of the Punjab, the imports of merchandise from abroad exceed the exports by £100,000 to £200,000 a year, or more; and if, before the annexation of the Punjab, the imports thence exceeded the exports thereto, from British territories, that circumstance must have caused a further export of rupees. There is a large absorption also by Ava and China, through British Burmah.

e. It may not be unreasonable to assume a diminution of the silver currency, since 1835, by 30 millions sterling, from the circumstances described in *a* to *d*, and of 20 millions from exports by sea to foreign countries, making a total export of 50 millions.

XII. The gross silver coinage from 1835–6 to 1876–7 amounts to 220 millions sterling; the abatements under sections X. and XI. amount to 60 millions, which would leave 160 millions sterling as the existing silver currency.

XIII. It has been said that India is insufficiently supplied with coin. Had it been so, the net importations of nearly 120 millions, and the coinage of 105 millions sterling of silver from 1855–6 to 1865–6, would not have sensibly affected prices. But they raised prices enormously.

63. The Government paper currency of British India was introduced on March 1, 1862, and the circulation on January 1 of each year was as follows:—

(*Millions sterling*).

	1863	1865	1867	1872	1873	1876	1877 Jan. 31
Notes in circulation .	4·52	7·48	9·96	10·87	12·87	11·22	12·43
Invested in Government securities .	·68	3·04	3·64	3·29	5·69	5·69	5·99
Coin and bullion reserve . . .	3·84	4·44	6·32	7·58	7·18	5·53	6·44

The limit prescribed for the invested reserve of the Paper Currency Department is six millions sterling; that limit has been reached.

64. Consequent on the considerable fall in the exchange of the rupee with sterling, through the depreciation of silver, the Committee of the Bengal Chamber of Commerce urged the Government of India to close the mints to the public for the coinage of silver, and to retain that coinage in the Government's hands, in order that a discreet limitation of the yearly amount of silver coinage might prevent the country from being swamped by silver sent in by foreign nations. The Government of India refused compliance with the recommendation, for the following reasons:—

I. The recent change in the value of silver, measured in gold, may be due to changes in the value of one metal or the other, or both. It cannot be assumed, without decisive proof, that the divergence of the two metals is due wholly, or even chiefly, to the fall in the value of silver. The prices of commodities, and of the precious metals, in London and in India, attest a considerable rise in the value of gold since March 1873, and especially since December 1875, and a corresponding fall in the value of silver no greater than in that of other commodities, the latter circumstance showing that the value of silver, measured in other commodities than gold, has not fallen.

II. The divergence in the values of the two metals is owing (1) and principally to the change to a gold standard in Germany, the Netherlands, and the Scandinavian Kingdoms, and to the limitation of the coinage of silver in the countries of the Latin Mint Convention to small amounts, whereby the customary alternative or compensatory standard of silver has ceased; (2) the increased production of silver in the United States; (3) a decreased demand for silver in India. The first-mentioned cause was calculated to raise the value of gold no less than to lower the value of silver; and excessive importance is not, *per se*, attached to the increased production of silver in the United States.

III. The fear of an excessive importation of silver into India was unfounded.

'When India is in a normal condition, i.e. when there is no abnormal demand for any of her staples, and she is not borrowing large sums abroad—the amount of treasure required to settle her accounts with the world is not considerable; and of the treasure received, a substantial proportion has always been gold. The large imports of treasure into India, since 1850, are due to abnormal circumstances, as follows:—

1. The Crimean War transferred to India large demands for produce, theretofore obtained from Russia.

2. The American Civil War exaggerated, temporarily, the value of Indian cotton.
3. Great sums of money have been borrowed for the suppression of the mutiny, the construction of railroads, and the Bengal Famine.

It would be altogether misleading to treat the great imports of treasure in the last 25 years as normal, or to expect that they will or can continue. There is, therefore, no reason to expect that silver will be poured into India, although, of course, if it falls in value, a greater weight of it must come to represent the same value.'

IV. The Government of India summed up as follows:—

a. The divergence of the values of gold and silver does not necessarily imply a diminution of the value of silver; there are strong reasons for believing that gold may have increased, as that silver has decreased, in value; and this consideration must have an important bearing on the action of Government in reference to the present disorder.

b. Although it is most desirable in the interests of trade, that the standard of value in England should be the same as the standard of value in the chief countries with which India interchanges commodities, yet trade will not be permanently injured by a fall in the value of the rupee, measured in gold, provided only that a fresh stable equilibrium of the precious metals be attained.

c. Up to the present moment (September 22, 1876), there is no sufficient ground for interfering with the standard of value.

65. UNITED KINGDOM.

In the time of William I., the pound, in tale, of silver coins (20 shillings) was equal to the pound weight of standard silver. In the reign of Queen Elizabeth the same pound of silver, $\frac{37}{40}$ fine, was coined into 60 shillings, and she altered it to 62 shillings, which gave a price of silver of 5*s.* 2*d.* an ounce. In 1717, the guinea was ordered to pass for 21 shillings. This, with 62 full-weight shillings to the pound, gave a relative value of about 1 to $15\frac{1}{5}$, and at that valuation gold and silver concurrently circulated for a time, but with a steady expulsion of silver, until, in 1774, the limit of legal tender for silver was reduced to £25. In 1797 cash payments were suspended; in 1816 and 1817, notes were so popular that the country banks found it difficult to dispose of their coin. Sir Robert Peel's Currency Bill of 1819 provided for the gradual resumption of cash payments, through the exchange of bank notes for ingots or bars of gold at an initial price of £4. 1*s.* per ounce, which, in nearing the period for resumption, was reduced by the Act, after an interval, to £3. 19*s.* 6*d.*, and then to £3. 17*s.* 10½*d.* In 1821, specie payments were resumed; but five years previously it had been ordered that the pound of silver should be coined into 66 instead of 62 shillings; and that silver should cease to be legal tender for more than 40 shillings.

66. Thus England entered the state of suspension of cash-payments in 1797 with a restricted double standard, but with gold as the virtual currency of the country, and she emerged from it with a single gold standard. Similarly, the United States and France suspended specie payments when gold was the current money in all transactions, while by law there was nominally a double standard. In France there are signs, amounting almost to proof, that, like England, she will resume specie payments with a single standard of gold.

67. The amount of gold coin in circulation in the United Kingdom may serve to indicate whether it is not probable that Germany and France will eventually liberate much of the gold coin which they have accumulated. From 1790 to 1815 the total coinage of gold in the United Kingdom amounted to £22,642,561; the greater part of which must have been exported: that of silver amounted to £1,640. The present metallic currency of the United Kingdom may be reckoned as dating from 1816, and it has amounted to the following sums:—

	£		£
1816 to 1829	44,238,502	1849 to 1857	52,787,683
1830 to 1848	48,243,259	1858 to 1876	93,823,237
	92,481,761		146,610,920

I. By the English Coinage Act, sovereigns which have lost more than ·616 per cent. in weight cease to be legal tender; and Mr. Jevons, in a paper read before the Statistical Society in November 1868, wrote—

'It is easily calculated that just about eighteen years' wear or 0·43 grains a year, will reduce a sovereign below its point of legal currency. Of course, it is not meant that every sovereign will be light after eighteen years' wear; for some are coined heavier than others, or undergo less wear from accidental circumstances. But these will be balanced by others coined lighter, or subject to more severe wear. . . . My results are strongly corroborated by experiments made at the Mint in the year 1833, by weighing parcels of 300 sovereigns coined in each of the years 1817, 1821, 1825, and 1829. The annual average wear was ·047 grains per annum.'

Afterwards more exactly stated by Mr. Jevons at ·043 grains, out of a sovereign's full weight of 123·274 grains. For half-sovereigns, which offer more than three-quarters of the surface of sovereigns, the average annual wear was greater, or ·069 grains, from their being much more actively used in circulation.

II. Hence, it may be assumed, on the safe average of eighteen years' wear and tear for reducing a sovereign below the point of legal currency, that the gold coinage of only the last nineteen years, from 1858 to 1876, amounting to 94 millions sterling, represents the outside limit of legal tender gold money. The greater part of the gold coinage, down to the end of the year 1857, must have been rejected from circulation as no longer current money of legal tender.

III. Mr. Jevons indeed estimated, in 1868, on actual testing of coins in circulation, and from communications from bankers in all parts of the country, that 'it is very probable that one in three sovereigns is light.' But this high proportion is due not merely to the number of light sovereigns, but to the exportation of full-weight sovereigns; the newest sovereigns being preferred for export. Allowing, then, an export of one-third of the new sovereigns coined from 1858 to 1876, to balance the light sovereigns of older date which may be circulating to the extent of one-third of the total gold currency in the country, that circulation might be assumed, for 1876, at 94 millions sterling; but as an outside estimate.

IV. For the amounts reckoned as the gross coinage include a re-coinage of light sovereigns—that is, they include a great deal of what contributed in 1868 to Mr. Jevons' proportion of one-third light sovereigns in the total gold circulation. Information respecting the actual withdrawal of light gold coin since 1868 is not at hand, but the amount must be large, for, in 1876, the light gold coin withdrawn from circulation, and recoined, amounted to £638,575; and the Deputy-Master of the Mint, in his report for 1875, wrote: 'Rather more than one-third of the gold bullion imported for coinage between November and January last, viz., £2,129,881, consisted of light gold coin withdrawn from circulation and sent in for re-coinage.'

V. There have been various estimates, as follows, of the gold currency in the United Kingdom:—viz.:

Lord Liverpool: 30 millions sterling in 1792.

1844. 'Very competent authorities, as stated by Mr. Newmarch in his 'History of Prices,' considered that the 12 millions sterling of light sovereigns withdrawn from circulation in 1840 to 1844 was equal to one-third of the total circulation, thus making it 36 millions.

Mr. NEWMARCH: 48 millions, for 1844; because, on an average of four years, from 1838 to 1841 (during which period the public avoided as much as possible tendering light sovereigns at the Bank), the proportion of light sovereigns tendered averaged only 25 per cent., which, for the 12 millions sterling of light sovereigns withdrawn from 1840 to 1844, gave 48 millions as the total circulation.

Mr. WEGUELIN, Governor of the Bank of England: 50 millions sterling in 1857.

Col. J. T. SMITH (March 1868) 'was informed at the Bank of England that they calculated the amount of gold in circulation at about 105 millions sterling,' which assumes a jump of 55 millions sterling in eleven years.

Mr. JEVONS: In 1868, 80 millions.

Mr. HANKEY: In 1873, 100 millions.

Mr. SEYD: On May 1, 1876, 130 millions, including the stock of gold in the Bank of England, which (gold coin and bullion) amounted, at the time, to 25 millions.

68. In France, during the period of inconvertible paper since 1870, the people have come to prefer notes to coin; and in the past two or three years the Bank of France has afforded facilities for cashing notes to a greater extent than in England. Hence, if 100 millions sterling be a fair estimate of the gold coin circulating in the United Kingdom, France on resuming specie payments will liberate a very large amount of gold.

69. In November 1868, Mr. Jevons estimated the silver coin in circulation at 14 millions sterling; from 1868 to 1876, the gross silver coinage amounted to £5,460,442; and the silver coins withdrawn amounted £1,332,430. Perhaps another million sterling might be abated for the silver coin exported to the Colonies, which in only five of the years, namely, from 1872 to 1876, amounted to £650,025. Professor Jevons' estimate for 1868 would be raised, therefore, for 1876, to an outside amount of about 18 millions sterling. Mr. Seyd (May 1, 1876) considered that 15 millions sterling would be a full estimate.

70. The total silver coinage from 1816 to 1876 amounted to 25 millions sterling, of which nine millions sterling were coined from 1816 to 1829: and another considerable amount was exported to the Colonies. The preceding estimates of 15 to 18 millions sterling as the amount of silver currency in the United Kingdom imply that a great

portion of the nine millions sterling, coined from 1816 to 1829, which would now be from 60 to 47 years old, must be in circulation; and that, apart from exports, there need not be any abatement for losses of small coin.

71. The population of the United Kingdom is estimated for 1876 at 33 millions. An estimated silver currency of 15 millions sterling gives nine shillings per head of population, against five shillings per head for Germany.

72. The paper currency of the United Kingdom is maintained through the Department of Issue in the Bank of England, and by certain banks which have powers of issue of notes, limited to the amount of their issue in 1844 and 1845, which they cannot exceed unless they add to their till, and retain in it, an amount of gold equal to the extra issue. The gold thus nominally retained as a reserve for the notes of these Banks of Issue, other than the Bank of England, is equally liable, however, to meet payments of deposits.

73. Before the suspension of specie payments, the note circulation of the Bank of England amounted to 11 millions sterling. From 1799 to 1808 it ranged from 15 to 18 millions; from 1809 to 1818, from 23 to 28 millions. From this latter amount it fell rapidly, through the measures ordered in 1819 for the resumption of specie payments; for from 1819 to 1828 it ranged at 21 millions, and from 1829 to 1833 at 20 millions.

74. There are no authentic returns of the actual circulation of the country banks down to 1832; but it must have been reduced about that time, from the cessation of the issue of £1 and £2 notes. The note circulation in the United Kingdom since 1833 has been as follows:—

I. *(Millions sterling.)*

In December:—	1833	1836	1839	1841	1843	1844
England and Wales:						
Bank of England	17·4	16·9	15·8	16·3	18·8	21·
Private and Joint-stock Banks	9·8	11·3	10·7	8·9	7 6	7·5
	27·2	28·2	26·5	25·2	26·4	28·5
Scotland	3·2	3·2	3 4	3·4	3·2	3·5
Ireland	5·5	5·4	5·9	5·9	5·9	6·8
	35·9	36·8	35·8	34·5	35·5	38·8
Bullion in Bank of England	10·1	4·2	4·1	5·0	12·09	14·4

II. YEARLY AVERAGE CIRCULATION.

(*Millions sterling.*)

	1844	1849	1853	1865	1866	1871	1874	1875	1876
England and Wales:									
Bank of England, London	13·7	12·5	14·8	13·4	14·7	15·1	16·1	16·9	—
" Branches	6·5	5·9	7·8	7·7	8·5	9·3	10·1	10·4	—
	20·2	18·4	22·6	21·1	23·2	24·4	26·2	27·3	27·7
Private and Joint-stock Banks . . .	8·2	6·2	6·8	5·8	5·1	5·1	5·0	—	4·6
	28·4	24·6	29·4	26·9	28·3	29·5	31·2	—	32·3
Scotland	3·0	3·1	3·8	4·4	4·4	5·2	5·9	—	7·
Ireland	5·9	4·3	5·7	6·0	5·9	7·5	6·8	—	8·1
	37·3	32·0	38·9	37·3	38·6	42·2	43·9	—	47·4
Issue not secured by Gold.									
Bank of England . . .	14·	14·	14·	14·65	15·	15·	15·	—	15·
Country Banks in England and Wales . . .	8·7	8·2	8·1	7·4	7·3	6·7	6·6	—	—
Total of country issues in England and Wales .	14·7	12·1	14·6	13·5	13·6	14·4	15·1	—	—

75. The following remarks are suggested by this table—

I. If the use of paper money, or promissory notes payable to bearer on demand, issued under securities which keep the paper at par, be an improvement on the exclusive use of gold and silver, the march of improvement has sadly halted in England, while the progress of the note circulation in Scotland and Ireland has been good.

II. After the resumption of specie payments, the note circulation of the Bank of England ranged at 21 or 20 millions from 1821 to 1833. The amount of notes of private and joint-stock banks during that period is not known, but it was greater than their circulation of 10 millions in 1833. Reckoning it at 12 or 13 millions, we find that the note circulation in England and Wales was the same (32 millions) in 1876 as it was fifty-five years since in 1820; nay, England retrograded from 1833 to 1843, when the circulation was below 28 millions, about which amount it fluctuated until 1866. An increase of four millions, or one-seventh, has been gained since, against an advance during the same period of nearly five millions, or one-half in Scotland and Ireland.

III. In the last thirty-three out of the fifty-five years of torpor in England, in which time the note circulation increased there by only four millions, or by 14 per cent., the increase in Scotland and Ireland was six millions upon nine millions, or 66 per cent., the proportion of increase in Scotland being 133 per cent.

IV. The principal increase has occurred in the ten years since 1866, to the amount of four millions sterling, or the first-mentioned 14 per cent. in England and Wales; and of nearly five millions sterling or 47 per cent. in Scotland and Ireland, the proportion in Scotland being 59 per cent. The theory is maintained that in Scotland and Ireland, the increase beyond the authorised issue is covered by an increase of coin and bullion, but this, of course, is a fiction, the increase of deposits having a commensurate lien with the notes upon the increase of coin. In England the note circulation has been restricted by the Bank Act of 1844.

V. England may be right, and Scotland, Ireland, France, Germany, &c., which keep their notes at par—while the circulation of the notes expands, without the hard and fast rule in England—may be wrong; but the facts remain that (*a*) nowhere is there such shrieking as in London when gold is exported; and (*b*) nowhere, outside England, is there any complaint, as in the City, that in the year 1877, which abounds with evidences of the vastly augmented production of gold and silver since 1849, business is carried on with a dangerously insufficient amount of gold, in the country to which the bulk of the produce of the mines is sent, and to which all the surplus wealth of the world flows for investment. The rule for limiting the note circulation in England is made up of gold, silver, and a theory. Of gold and silver there is more than enough, as England's share of the world's production, and the world's supply: but still the cry resounds that the theory is all right, and that yet the business of the country is carried on with a dangerously small amount of gold, by a people remarkably prudent, practical, and cautious. Among the ills to which flesh is heir, and to which the peoples who depend upon their governments are heirs, not the least terrible and baneful is theory, the last infirmity of conscientious rulers.

VI. No doubt the increase of notes has been checked by the very great increase of deposits all over the country. As observed by the 'Economist' (August 4, 1877),—

'The economy in the note circulation is intelligible, and has been rendered possible by the vast increase in the practice of keeping banking accounts by all classes of traders, down to the smallest; and by the extension of the system of the clearing-house to most of the large towns. A balance at credit of a banking account has happily superseded the coin and notes hid away in the shop or dwelling-house.'

The fact of a considerable displacement of coin and notes by cheques being recognised, it remains for the currency school to obtain an Act of Parliament requiring bankers to keep, in addition to their customary reserves, gold equal to the excess of their deposits over a certain average amount. Unfortunately, however, for this logical extension of the currency doctrine, to cover the apology that the note circulation in England would have been considerably larger, but for an increase of deposits, there is the fact that in Scotland and Ireland the great proportionate increase of notes has accompanied a considerable increase of deposits.

VII. Half of the increased circulation of Bank of England notes has been gained from the private and joint stock banks, which show a corresponding reduction, and the bulk of the gross increase has occurred in the provincial circulation of the Bank of England. The growth of this country circulation is imperfectly shown by the amount of increase of notes of the branch banks; a portion of the three millions of increased issues of the head-quarter office, since 1844, being also for the country circulation; for a great number of banks which issue Bank of England notes are far away from branches of the Bank of England, and even many of those which are near the branches get their notes from the head office.

76. For a proper view of the state of the circulation of notes of the Bank of England it is necessary to combine the accounts of the Issue Department and the Banking account. The statistics are as follows—

(In Millions sterling.)

	1793 Feb. 28	1823 Feb. 28	1828 Feb. 28	1844 Sept. 7	1847 Feb. 27	1856 Feb. 23	1866 Feb. 28	1867 Feb. 27	1873 Feb. 26	1875 Feb. 24	1877 Feb. 10	1877 Sept. 12
LIABILITIES (except Proprietors' Capital and Rest).												
Total Issue . . .	—	—	—	28·3	25·3	24·4	28·1	33·4	39·3	35·2	40·6	38·6
Notes in Banking Reserve . . .	—	—	—	8·2	6·0	5·9	8·7	11·0	14·8	9·8	12·8	10·9
Notes with public .	11·9	18·4	22·0	20·1	19·3	18·5	19·4	22·4	24·5	25·4	27·8	27·7
7-day Bills . . .					·8	·7	·4	·4	·4	·3	·3	·4
Deposits . . .	5·3	7·2	9·2	12·3	15·3	18·9	18·2	24·6	32·6	24·2	29·1	27·2
Total . .	17·2	25·6	31·2	32·4	35·4	38·1	38·0	47·4	57·5	49·9	57·2	55·3

	1793 Feb. 28	1823 Feb. 28	1828 Feb. 28	1844 Sept. 7	1847 Feb 27	1856 Feb. 23	1863 Feb. 28	1867 Feb. 27	1873 Feb. 26	1875 Feb. 24	1877 Feb. 10	1877 Sept. 12
ASSETS (excepting Government debt to Bank).												
Government Securities:												
Issue . . .	9·5 (Issue and Banking)	13·7 (Issue and Banking)	19·8 (Issue and Banking)	3·0	3·0	3 5	4·0[1]	4 0[1]	4·0[1]	4 0[1]	4·0[1]	4·0[1]
Banking . . .				14·6	12·0	11·9	9·9	13·1	13 4	13·6	16·0	14·2
Other Securities . .	6·5	4·6	3 8	7 8	15·8	19·2	18·8	18 0	21·9	18·2	17·8	19·9
	16·0	18 3	23·6	25·4	30·8	34·6	32·7	35 1	39·3	35·8	37·3	38 1
Coin and Bullion: Issue	—	—	—	12·7	11·3	9·9	13·1	18 4	24 3	20·2	25·6	23·6
" " Banking	—	—	—	·8	·7	·7	·9	1·0	·9	·9	·7	·9
Total . .	4·0	10·4	10·3	13·5	12 0	10·6	14·0	19·4	25·2	21·1	26·3	24·3
Total assets .	20 0	28·7	33 9	38·9	42·8	45·2	46·7	54·5	64·5	56·9	64·1	62·4
Notes not covered by gold	—	—	—	14·	14·	14·5	15·	15·	15·	15·	15·	15·
Proprietors' capital .	—	—	—	14·5	14·5	14 5	14 5	14·5	14·5	14·5	14·5	14·5
Rest	2·8	3·1	2·8	3·2	3·9	3 5	3·8	3 5	3·0	3·4	3·3	3 7
Government debt .	—	—	—	11·0	11·0	11·0	11 0	11·0	11·0	11·0	11·0	11·0
DETAIL OF DEPOSITS.												
Public . . .	—	—	—	3·6	5·9	4·1	5·5	6·7	14 6	6·7	5 6	4·5
London bankers . .	—	—	—	1·0	1 3	4 6	4·5	6·2	7·6	17·5 (London bankers and Private)	23·5	22·7
Private . . .	—	—	—	7 7	8·1	10·2	8·2	11·7	10·4			
	—	—	—	12·3	15 3	18·9	18·2	24·6	32·6	24·2	29 1	27·2

77. The following remarks are suggested by this table.

I. In the period of nearly 25 years during which the people were educated in the use of paper currency, by the suspension of specie payments, the note circulation increased by 6½ millions sterling,[2] and the deposits by two millions. By 1844, the notes with the public had increased by two and the deposits by five millions. In the next thirty-one years, to September 12, 1877, the notes increased from 19 to 28 millions, or by less than 50 per cent, and the deposits from 12 to 27 millions, or by 125 per cent. The proportion of increase of deposits other than those of the Government is still greater.

II. The notes with the public, the deposits, the coin and bullion reserve for meeting them, and the other assets, were as follows, on the undermentioned dates:—

[1] 3·98 is the figure throughout.

[2] The increase was really greater, for the one-pound notes, which took the place of coin, should be deducted from the circulation of 1793.

(Millions sterling.)

	1844 Sept. 7	1847 Feb. 27	1866 Feb 28	1867 Feb. 27	1873 Feb. 26	1877 Feb. 10	1877 Sept. 12
I. Notes with the public . . .	19·3	19·3	19·4	22·4	24·5	27·8	27·7
Deposits, other than Government .	8·7	9·4	12·7	17·9	18·	23·5	22·7
	28·0	28·7	32·1	40·3	42·5	51·3	50·4
II. Deposits, public	3·6	5·9	5·5	6·7	14·6	5·6	4·5
	31·6	34·6	37·6	47·0	57·1	56·9	54·9
III. Coin and bullion in Issue and Banking Departments . . .	13·5	12·0	14·0	19·4	25·2	26·3	24·3
Excess of I. over III. . . .	14·5	16 7	18·1	20·9	17·3	25·0	26·1

The whole of the coin and bullion in the Issue Department being reckoned as an asset against the joint liabilities of that Department and of the Bank, the Banking reserve of notes is not reckoned in addition. The practical conclusions from the table are as follows :—

a. If all the private depositors in 1844 had conspired in a run upon the Bank, there could still have been left 4·8 millions sterling in gold to meet 19⅓ millions of notes with the public. A similar combination on September 12, 1877, would have left 1·6 millions sterling for meeting 27·7 millions in notes, despite the metallic basis provided for the note circulation by the Act of 1844. Manifestly the convertibility of the note is secured by other influences than the operation of that Act.

b. It may be said that the Bank would meet a run upon its deposits by contracting its discounts; but this would not increase the gold available, in the preceding account, for paying the deposits: it would only reduce the amount of notes that would remain in circulation, against the residue of gold stated in *a*, after completion of the repayment of the deposits with gold—and if a portion of the notes against which 15 millions sterling are invested were thus returned, the diminution of notes would break the Issue Department, as effectually as the Banking Department would be broken. The Bank has but small faith in this means of meeting a run on the deposits; for we find as follows :—

	1844 Sept. 7	1847 Feb. 27	1867 Feb. 27	1877 Sept. 12
Deposits, other than Government.	8·7	9·4	17·9	22·7
Government securities, Banking .	14·6	12·0	13·1	14·2
Other securities	7·8	15·8	18·	19·9
Notes in Banking reserve . .	8·2	6·0	11·	10·9
	30·6	33·8	42·1	45·0
Government securities, Issue Dep.	3·0	3·0	3·98	3·98
Deposits, Public	3·6	5·9	6·7	4·5

Of the increase of 13 millions sterling in private deposits since February 1877, one million has been eased off by a diminution of public deposits; and of the remaining twelve millions eleven have been met by an increase of four millions in discounts, two millions in Government securities, and five millions of notes in the Banking reserve, this last showing the Bank's main dependence upon gold. If the increase since 1867 be regarded, the result is slightly modified. Of the five millions of increase in private deposits, two millions are set off by a decrease in public deposits, and the remaining three millions are counterbalanced by an increase of one million in Government securities, and of only two millions in discounts. Out of a total increase of five millions in deposits, the Bank could employ only two millions in discounts.

c. The Bank's manifest want, with the great increase of its deposits, is an augmentation of investments, realisable at short dates, which would supplement the discounts, in which the Bank is now undersold by the City banks and bill brokers, with their enormously increased deposits. The introduction of a gold currency in India (accompanied by a declaration of Bank of England notes as legal tender in India) and the issue in London, by the Secretary of State for India, of short-date bills similar to the exchequer bills, or the recent Treasury bills of the Imperial Government, would provide such an investment. Were these bills to attract, additionally, the City banks and bill brokers, so much more of discount would flow back to the Bank of England, which would regain its control over the exchanges.

III. Down to 1864, the notes with the public fluctuated about the point of 20 millions sterling, being generally near to, but below that amount. In 1865 they ranged above or below 25 and 26 millions; but after the crisis in 1866 they fell to 22 millions in December.

Thereafter, the circulation slightly improved, till June 1870, near to or somewhat above 23 millions. From July 1870, or coincidently with the outbreak of the Franco-German war, the circulation advanced to 24 millions; in July 1871, to 25 millions; in July 1872, to 26 millions; in July 1875, to 27, and in July 1876 to 28 millions. In July 1877 it was 28¾ millions. Since December 1866, the circulation with the public has steadily advanced from 22 to 28 millions sterling. Down to 1866, there were indeed fluctuations between the last permanent advance attained and the next permanent advance; but these were caused by the notes in the balances of the City banks. Since the transfer of those balances to the Bank of England in 1867, the progress in the circulation of notes has been steady. The weekly returns of the Bank, from 1857 to 1876, show furthermore that, with rare and unimportant exceptions, the greater part or the whole of each casual decrease of notes with the public was compensated by a corresponding increase of the notes in the Banking reserve. The coin and bullion in the Issue Department were not affected on such occasions.

IV. It further illustrates the permanency of the circulation of notes among the public, outside the circle of bankers, that the increase of nearly eight millions sterling, since 1849, in the notes with the public, has occurred wholly in the notes of £100 and under, and chiefly in those of £5 and £10. Up to 1871, the notes of £200 and upwards had been stationary, since 1860 (through the operation of the Clearing House), at an amount less by about one million sterling than that in 1849.

V. It follows from III. and IV. that the drain upon the bullion in the Issue Department has not come from the return of notes by the public, other than bankers; and that the fluctuations in the gross circulation have mainly affected the Banking reserve. Hence the currency school did but half its work in providing a reserve of bullion against notes with the public, without also providing against the baneful and overshadowing influence of deposits.

VI. There are two other reassuring facts:—

a. The bankers' balances in the Bank of England have never fallen below five millions since 1865, and probably they will not fall again below six millions; the minimum, taken at intervals, being on an ascending scale. Moreover, since 1868, bankers' balances have varied inversely with the other private deposits; while these latter, since 1867 (excepting a brief period of depression in 1870), have ranged not lower than 17 millions sterling, which was nearly their amount in 1867.

b. From 1860 to 1866, the bullion in the Bank of England was under 16 millions; in 1867 it was 18 millions; on January 1, 1868, it was nearly 21 millions: but thereafter, to January 1, 1870, it was 18 millions. The bulk of the investments, abroad, of British capital, in foreign loans and in railways (which are not an unmixed good to England), occurred during this period; reducing the amount due to England in the settlement of international transactions, and promoting extreme demands for the exportation of gold. Since 1873 these investments have been much reduced; and a yearly increasing amount of imports is obtained as returns for British capital invested abroad. The drain of silver to the East, during the cotton famine, also caused large exportations of gold to the Continent for buying the silver; this pressure on the bullion reserves has ceased, and the bullion balance is greater than that which, in the earlier years, met heavy exportations of gold such as are not likely to recur.

78. The following statistics, by Mr. Palgrave, published in the report of the Select Committee on Banks of Issue in 1875, dispel a prevalent impression that the metallic currency of the world must expand in proportion to its trade.

(*In Millions sterling.*)

	Exports of British Produce, and Imports	Amount of Clearing	Note circulation in United Kingdom	Proportion, taking 1844=100		
				Exports and Imports	Clearing	Note circulation
1844	144	1,500 (say)	37·38	100	100	100
1868	473	3,466	39·75	328	231	103
1869	484	3,602	39·85	336	240	107
1870	502	3,904	40·	347	260	107
1871	551	4,777	42·	382	318	112
1872	610	5,903	43·6	423	394	117
1873	625	6,161	43·37	434	411	116
1874	607	5,916	43·91	421	394	117

The amount of clearing, but not that of the note circulation, has been commensurate with the increase of trade; and we have seen that the metallic currency of the United Kingdom but slightly more than doubled from 1844 to 1874, while the foreign trade quadrupled in that period. The bulk of the increase of trade occurred by 1869, with a smaller proportionate increase of clearing; but whereas the trade in 1874 exceeded that in 1869 by 123 millions, or by 25 per cent., the excess of clearing was 2,314 millions, or 64 per cent. upon

T

the amount in 1869. In other words, there was a gradual transfer of business from first-class merchants to others of smaller means, but more numerous, who from greater competition obtain a smaller rate of profit.

79. In the three kingdoms the circulation of half-sovereigns has increased for the payment of wages, owing to the expansion of various industries, a rise in wages, and the substitution, in some industries, of payments of workmen individually, instead of, as formerly, in gangs; but the half sovereigns quickly return to the local banks, and in the agricultural counties in Ireland bank notes are preferred to gold. In both Scotland and Ireland, where the bulk of the issues of one-pound notes is not covered by gold, their use enables the banks to cash notes of an office of issue at any branch at which they may be presented. The notes of larger denominations are exchanged, not into coin, but into £1 notes, whence the need for exchanging them into anything further is not felt.

80. In Ireland, all the notes are payable at all the branches, and are exchangeable everywhere at all the banks. In Scotland, by agreement among the banks, exchanges of notes are held in every town where two or more of the banks have branches; in every instance, once a week, on Saturday; at the larger towns twice a week, and at Edinburgh and Glasgow three times a week. The rules of the exchange provide that no bank shall issue another bank's notes; that the settlement of the Glasgow and County exchanges shall be made by draft, on demand, on Edinburgh, and that the general balances of the whole exchanges and clearing shall be settled at Edinburgh, by draft on London, at five to eight days' date. This last provision restrains each bank from excessive issues. The notes that are exchanged among the different branches of banks in provincial towns do not necessarily go near the head office, and they may remain for years circulating in the country: yet forgeries are infrequent. The Scotch banks do not pay forged notes.[1]

81. In England the facilities for cashing notes in the country are as follows:—

I. *Bank of England*. The flow of gold is outwards from the Bank of England to its branches; hence, under law, the notes of the branches are payable in London, as well as at the respective offices of issue, but those of the head office are payable only in London, and not at the branches. 'The Bank could never accept a legal liability to pay at any branch its notes issued at other branches; that would be

[1] *Banks of Issue*, 1875.

quite impossible. As a rule, however, the public are accommodated with any moderate amount of coin that they require,' in exchange for notes issued from other offices of the Bank of England. But the applicants have to be properly introduced, 'because the notes which they offered might be stolen or improperly obtained.' The notes issued by different branches circulate generally all over the country.

'The Bank of England notes circulate all over the world, and I (Mr. Palgrave) think it extremely likely that, at some period of the year, even a larger amount than three millions sterling may be circulating abroad.'—*Ibid.*

II. *Country Banks.* As a rule, the circulation of a country bank keeps within its district; but in that district it is readily exchanged for coin by any shopkeeper or trader, while the country bank is able, through its notes, to cash freely notes of the Bank of England of any branch, or of other country banks; and also cheques drawn upon other banks, provided the banker knew the person, and felt that the payment was safe.[1]

82. Until 1797, the minimum value of a note of the Bank of England was £5; in that year £2 and £1 notes were allowed, until the Act 7 Geo IV. cap. vi. 1826, when the further issue of notes under £5 was forbidden; and after April 5, 1829, the uttering in England of notes under £5, which had been made or issued in Scotland or Ireland, was prohibited, under penalties, by 9 Geo. IV. cap. 65.[1] When £1 notes of the Bank of England were withdrawn in 1821, they amounted to £6,700,000, exclusive of the £1 notes of country banks.

83. The circulation of exchequer bills must have been considerable in the early part of the century. From 1809 to 1823 the Bank of England held, generally, 18 to 20 millions sterling of these bills. By 1848 the demand for them fell off, from the multiplication of railway debentures; but still, in 1850, the bills outstanding amounted to 17¾ millions sterling. In 1858 they were increased to 21 millions, from which amount they were reduced in 1860 to 13 millions, in 1865 and 1866 to 10½ and 8½ millions, by the cancellation of 4 millions, and the issue instead of terminable annuities; and from 1867 to 1875 they declined yearly from 5·887 millions in the former to 4·479 millions in the latter year.

84. Exchequer bills were issued to run for a year. In March 1877, the Chancellor of the Exchequer issued a new class of Treasury bills, for £2,200,000, payable in three months, or in six months, at the

[1] *Banks of Issue*, 1875.

option of the person tendering. The bills being made, thus, as like bankers' or mercantile bills as possible, it is expected that since private individuals can borrow, on short-dated bills, at 1 to 2 per cent., the Government should no longer pay 2 to 3½ per cent., as on exchequer bills.

85. Summing up this account of the currencies of various countries we find that—

I. Until the drain of silver to the East, since 1854, the only gold coin countries worth mention were, the United Kingdom, Portugal, Turkey, and Brazil. Practically, too, the United States became a gold coin country in 1834.

II. The remaining countries in Europe had a silver standard, or a bi-metallic standard, in which, owing to the relative value of silver to gold, and the low price of silver, that metal had expelled gold from the currencies of those countries.

III. When the drain of silver to the East raised its price in Europe, gold replaced silver in the currencies of the bi-metallic countries, which afterwards formed themselves into the Latin Union.

IV. Later, when the drain of silver to the East abated, and the price of silver began to fall, Germany and the Scandinavian Kingdoms, whose principal transactions were with countries where gold was practically the current coin, became apprehensive that they would suffer in the foreign exchanges, from the depreciation of silver. Urged by these fears, and other considerations, they have altered from a silver to a gold standard.

V. Under similar apprehension of commercial inconvenience, while surrounding countries were altering to a gold standard, a very competent monetary commission of inquiry in Holland reported that Holland must eventually adopt a gold standard; but that this final change should be preceded by a period of transition during which a double standard should be declared, and the coinage of silver should be stopped. The recommendation has been carried out so far that the coinage of silver has been stopped; and the coinage of gold has been permitted at a fixed valuation with the silver coins, though it has not yet been declared legal tender.

VI. The countries of the Latin Union, from similar apprehensions of the depreciation of silver, and from fear of their being flooded with demonetised silver from Germany and the Scandinavian Kingdoms, have closed their mints against the coinage by the public of silver coins of full legal tender. Spain, which has modelled her currency on that of the Latin Union (without, however, joining the Union), has done the same. So has Austria; and the silver coin country of Russia coins but little silver, evidently small change, while her coinage of gold is comparatively very large. The coinage of silver, except as small money, has ceased in Europe.

VII. The countries in Europe, which are universally filled with apprehension of injury to their finance and commerce, from the great depreciation of silver, have not, by closing their mints against silver, committed themselves to the adoption of a single gold standard. With the help of the best financial abilities in Europe, and after much deliberation with competent advisers, they have decided that it is wise to stop the coinage of silver, while allowing the coinage of gold. The Government of India shrinks from this conclusion, because it cannot see its way to allowing the coinage of gold, and so it allows the continued coinage of silver. A very large amount of loss by exchange evinces the earnestness of its conviction that nothing is certain.

VIII. A hope, born of despair, is entertained that some countries with inconvertible paper money will resume specie payments in silver, and that the countries of the Latin Union will yet attest their faith in bi-metallism by letting silver expel gold from their currencies. Regarding these countries it appears that—

a. The United States will resume specie payments on January 1, 1879. The premium on gold has already fallen so low that the funding of a portion of the greenbacks would bring them to par. The operations with their Funded Loan have resulted in the conversion of nearly all the civil war loans regarding which there could be any contention that they should be redeemed in silver, notwithstanding the pledge, implied in several ways, that they should be redeemed in gold; and redemption of the Funded Loan in gold is so indispensable to the success of the funding operations, that a distinct and irrevocable pledge has been given for such redemption of the latest and largest issue of the Funded Loan. A decision of the Supreme Court of the United States has also made a large class of obligations repayable in gold. The Government of the United States has never swerved from its conviction, manifested in 1861 and 1863, that the greenbacks of the loans should be redeemed in gold. The Secretary of the Treasury favours the rational scheme of having gold as full legal tender, with silver as legal tender up to fifty dollars, while the large amount of United States bonds which are held within the States, and the large amount of interest on loans, and of returns for foreign capital invested in the country, which has to be paid abroad in gold, enlist powerful and important interests on the side of a single standard of gold.

When an answer to the question has been thus largely anticipated by facts, there can be no doubt of what the final decision of so practical a people as the Americans will be.

b. In the countries of the Latin Union, Switzerland has in a marked manner decided in favour of gold. In France, the Finance Minister is reserved about the ultimate decision, which, he says, must rest with the members of the Union on the approach of the termination of the present convention on December 31, 1879. Meanwhile, there are unmistakable evidences that France is preparing for a gold standard. Silver is being withdrawn from circulation among the classes who, on the declaration of a gold standard, would require its exchange for gold; and it is being driven into circulation among classes whose small transactions would reconcile them to the acceptance of a subsidiary silver coinage, of the same value as gold, in withdrawal by the Government of silver coins of full legal tender. With this view, the silver which flows into Paris from the railways, and great industrial enterprises, is returned by the Bank to its branches, which force it into circulation in the interior. Meanwhile, the Bank must be selling some of the silver; for the result of all this activity in its circulation is an increasing scarcity of silver. Other signs show that the withdrawal of the silver currency is being carried out with great ability. The paper currency is excessive, yet the Bank of France is popularising it, and new forms of paper money, by every means in its power. It has increased the number of its branches; it promotes remittances from one part of the country to another at a ridiculously small charge; it has converted the French retail dealers from being keepers of gold into keepers of passbooks and users of cheques. The obvious result is that the paper money, both notes and cheques, thus established among the people on a scale unparalleled before 1870, must permanently displace a large part of the enormous metallic currency of France; and, inasmuch as the surplus metallic currency will have been inexpensively withdrawn with paper, there can be little doubt that in deciding whether the surplus should be expelled in the form of silver, or in that of gold (the latter necessitating an immense re-coinage for many years)—the decision will be given against silver.

c. Of the remaining principal countries of the Union, Belgium professes to maintain an expectant attitude, but is steadily coining gold, and has discontinued coining silver. Italy has declared in favour of a gold standard, but wishes to defer its adoption; a decision convenient and helpful to her German ally. Spain has no wish but to follow the Latin Union. A conference of the countries of the Union, to consider the subject, will be held in December 1877.

d. In Austria, the bankers and like financial authorities, the railway interests, and other classes, favour the adoption of a gold standard, from considerations similar to those which have forced Austria to stop the coinage of silver, to accumulate gold in her national bank, and to borrow money abroad in gold *rente.* But the other head of the eagle looks away in the direction of resuming specie payments in silver, as an easy means of paying debts.

e. The solvent dependencies of two insolvent countries, viz., the Philippine Islands and Finland, have adopted a gold standard.

f. It appears that the nations which are strong, or of resolute will, have adopted or are sure to adopt a gold standard: those which are weak or irresolute are halting, though they must perceive that, in the end, irresolution will go with the stream, or be carried away by it.

g. We close the account without finding any country in Europe at all likely to re-establish a silver currency.

IX. With regard to the relative value between silver and gold, it appears that the countries of the Latin Union and Germany have adopted the valuation of 1 to 15½; Holland, 1 to 15·625; the Scandinavian kingdoms, 1 to 15·675. In British India the relative value was established at 1 to 15, in the year of the permanent settlement.

X. In England, which has long had a single standard of gold, there is stillness or calm, enlivened by profit from the depreciation of silver; but the currency and credit of the United Kingdom are in a state of extreme tension, which causes shrieking in the City when gold temporarily leaves a country that has a permanent international balance in her favour. Everywhere else in the civilised world the currency is in an unsatisfactory condition, being unnaturally swollen, as in Germany, from some mistakes in the execution of her coinage reform, including the principal error of withdrawing small notes with gold, instead of with silver thalers which it is now difficult to sell; on which account Germany has not yet completed her coinage operations, though she has coined 76 millions sterling of gold and 20 millions sterling of silver, total 96 millions, for withdrawing 86 millions of the extant coinage of the old currencies of gold and silver. In France we have 219 millions sterling of gold and silver, or (according to M. Victor Bonnet) 280 millions, with 106 millions sterling of notes, total 325 or 386 millions in 1876, against 156 millions of gold and silver, and 55 millions of notes, total 211 millions, in 1870, before the Franco-German war. Of the excess of 114 to 175 millions, only 51 millions are accounted for by an increase of the note circulation. The huge remainder of excess is in the metallic currency, notwithstanding an extensive permanent displacement of metallic by paper currency and paper money. And yet, this seemingly inflated currency has not caused any derangement of prices like that which resulted from a similar inflation of the currency in Germany. The anomaly is not explicable, except on the assumption that the French Government has been long engaged in preparing for the demonetisation of silver. Evidently, both Germany and France will, in the end, liberate large amounts of gold. In Italy, Austria, and the United States, the paper currency is swollen greatly beyond normal requirements. The consequent expulsion of the precious metals from the currencies of those countries, with a consequent cessation of demand for gold and silver (except latterly in the United States for measures preparatory to a resumption of specie payments), has interrupted the ordinary work of commerce in distributing the precious metals. Added to these are the cessation of demand from the East for silver, the increase of the Council drafts on India to 15 millions sterling, the closure of the European mints against silver, and the unabated production of the precious metals. All these circumstances have caused a block of the precious metals in the West, outside the insolvent countries, of inconvertible paper, and a depreciation of silver: two results which go far to explain the general depression of trade.

XI. In France, neither in the first stage of her currency revolution, when gold expelled the greater part of the silver currency, and now in the second stage when she is preparing to demonetise silver, there have been no commercial or financial convulsions, the ruin of neither debtor nor creditor, from the alteration of standard from bimetallic to gold; for her, the period has been one of unexampled material progress and prosperity. The changes that are rung (against any alteration of standard) on the injury to debtors or creditors, may be very interesting speculations in the abstract; but as moral objections to a change they are of no value. The course of morals is in the region of facts; and the example of France shows that in that region these objections are unmeaning. In Germany the difficulties which have been experienced are attributable to mistakes of the Government, not to a change of standard.

XII. In the United Kingdom it appears that neither the metallic currency nor the paper currency has increased at all in proportion to the marvellous increase of the foreign trade. The progress of clearing-house transactions, however, has kept pace with that increase; thus evidencing that the requirements of commerce are provided for, by means of paper resting on a comparatively very small amount of whatever metallic money may be common money among the nations. The clearing-house transactions have indeed grown in a greater proportion than the foreign trade, which indicates an unwelcome increase of small firms that engage in an injurious competition with the first-class merchants who acquired for British commerce its once unsullied reputation for integrity and fair dealing. On examining the system of currency and credit in England, we find that the Bank of England has now a larger store of coin and bullion than in the days when that reserve sustained the drain of bullion to the Continent for buying silver for the East, and for the large investments in foreign loans and industrial enterprises; yet never, as in the present day, have such strong fears been expressed of the extreme tension of the system of credit and currency. The notes in circulation with the public awaken no alarm; they are permanently outstanding; or if they return to the Bank, it is only to its Banking Department: they cause no drain from the Issue Department. The well-grounded fears are entirely caused by the action of the deposits on the banking reserve, and through it on the Issue Department; and the insecurity, from the action of the deposits, is owing to the overshadowing, baneful influence of the overgrown deposits with the joint-stock banks and bill brokers, which have paralysed the control by the Bank of England of the rate of interest. The floating and progressive growth of exchequer bills to be issued by the Secretary of State for India, concurrently with the adoption of a gold currency in India, and the declaration of Bank of England notes as legal tender in India, would be one efficacious means of bringing back the current of discounts to the Bank of England. The exchequer bills of the Imperial Government do not appear to have exceeded 21 millions sterling for many years before their systematic reduction by the Treasury.

XIII. In the East Indies, gold was legal tender in India at a relative value of 1 to 16 from 1766, and of 1 to 15 from 1793, until it was demonetised by Act XVIII. of 1835. From the small proportion of actual withdrawals of silver coins of the old currencies which have been withdrawn by proclamation, it appears that there is a large destruction of it, by consignment to the melting-pot for ornaments, and for recoinage in the mints of Native States, also by export in the course of seaborne trade, and inland trade beyond British frontiers; likewise for yearly remittances by Mahomedans to Mecca, and in yearly exportations by pilgrims to Mecca, and by emigrants. While, at this distant time, all the old coinages may be regarded as having become extinct, in any form and weight in which they could be presented as legal tender, and while the coinage of existing Government rupees, since their introduction in 1835, has amounted to 220 millions sterling, it would appear that from the operation of the foregoing circumstances,—of the numerous wars, beyond British India, in which Indian troops were employed—and of the mutiny, during which there were large losses, meltings, and burials of rupees in what are still concealed treasure,—the present amount of silver currency, if reckoned at 160 millions sterling, will be greatly over-estimated. Such an estimate allows for the operation of all these causes of diminution, destruction, and waste, in 42 years, an average of only 1½ millions sterling a year.

XIV. The limit of legal tender for subsidiary silver currency is, in Germany 20 shillings, in England and France 40 shillings, in the United States 5 dollars, but with a probability that it will be raised to 25 or 50 dollars (100 or 200 shillings). The proportion of silver coin per head of the population is 6 francs, or nearly 5 shillings, in the countries of the Latin Union, 10 shillings in Germany, 9 shillings in England. The German Government prudently wishes to raise the rate to 15 shillings per head. The German Parliament refuses assent; a re-coinage, with the object of putting more silver into the German mark, might remove objections which would then be unreasonable.

APPENDIX III.

NATIONAL INDEBTEDNESS AND MERCANTILE CREDIT.

The growth of national indebtedness, its effect on the fiscal systems of the borrowing countries, the expenditure on railways, the growth of joint-stock enterprise and of deposits, commercial failures, and financial collapses will be noticed in this Appendix.

2. *RAILWAYS.*

I. The open lines of railway in all the world were :—

	Miles		Miles	
In 1840	4,838	In 1860	60,468	The figures from 1860 are for the United States and Europe
„ 1845	10,500	„ 1865	78,087	
„ 1850	24,310	„ 1870	115,740	
„ 1855	41,470	„ 1873	141,613	
—	—	„ 1876	158,883	

The cost per mile of railways in the United States is estimated at £8,800 per mile, but the latest statistics give an average cost of £12,000 a mile. In Europe, generally, it must have been higher, from the purchase of land, and from the construction of a great extent of the Continental lines after the rise in the price of iron. In the United Kingdom, the cost exceeds £37,000 a mile. Taking the average at £15,000 a mile, the expenditure increased from 365 millions sterling in 1850 to 900 millions in 1860, and to 2,100 millions in 1873. The 'Pall Mall Gazette' of June 30, 1876, observed that the greater part of the railway construction in the five years from 1869 to 1873 occurred in the first three years. 'As in 1847, this undue haste in extending railways produced the panic of 1873, from the effects of which we are now suffering.'

II. In the United Kingdom the number of miles of railway open was in—

	Miles	Capital paid up (Millions sterling)	Increase
1850	6,500	not known	—
1860	10,433	348·13	—
1866	13,354	481·87	133·74
1870	15,537	529·91	48·04
1876	16,872	658·21	128·30

III. In the ten years from 1866 to 1875, Europe added to its railways a total of 42,000 miles, against 25,000 miles in the previous ten years. The addition in the five years after 1870 was 24,000 miles, of which the greater part occurred up to 1873. The amount expended in France up to 1865, was 261 millions sterling.

IV. In the United States, the number of miles of railway open has been as follows :—

	Miles		Miles
On July 1, 1848	5,599	In 1870	52,898
„ December 31, 1860	25,037	„ 1871	60,568
„ June 30, 1865	33,908	„ 1873	70,784
„ June 30, 1866	35,085	„ 1875	74,614
—	—	„ 1876	77,470

For 42,255 miles of railway open on January 1, 1869, the cost was estimated at 360 millions sterling, at £8,800 a mile. For 73,508 miles in operation in 1876, the stocks and bonds amounted to 4,609 millions of dollars, or 894 millions sterling, or slightly more than £12,000 a mile. Many defaults of railways, and sales under foreclosures occurred after the panic of 1873. In January 1876, the New York 'Financial Chronicle' stated that 'the whole amount of railroad bonds on which any default was made in the payment of interest accruing between the panic of September 1873 and January 1, 1876, foot up a sum total of 789 million dollars (157 millions sterling), issued by 197 different companies.' On March 17, 1877, the 'Economist,' reviewing a table of the American railroads which, in the year 1876 alone, have either been sold under foreclosure, or have been marked for probable foreclosure, from default in the payment of interest, observed :—'The list, though incomplete, shows that about one-fifth of the railway mileage of the United States, and a similar proportion of the total capital invested in railways, have, during the past year, become subject to a forced reorganisation, the result of which has yet to be ascertained.' This was exclusive of the defaults from September 1873 to January 1, 1876. Russia, which has dabbled in State railways and guaranteed railways, is in not much better plight.

3. *DEPOSITS AND DISCOUNTS.*

UNITED KINGDOM.

I. In a paper published in the 'Journal of the Statistical Society' for June 1876, Mr. R. Baxter stated that the deposits in the whole kingdom were estimated not to exceed

(*Millions sterling.*)

	In 1844	In 1856	In 1866	In 1874
Deposts . . .	70	100	350	800 (including 95 millions of capital of the Banks)
Exports & Imports	134	312	490	685

So that the deposits, from being one-third of the exports and imports in 1856, had come to exceed the latter in 1874. In that year they were tenfold the amount of deposits in 1844, and sevenfold the amount in 1856.

II. In the same journal for March 1876, Mr. Dun gave a somewhat different account of the capital and liabilities of the private and joint-stock banks in the United Kingdom, including the Bank of England: viz., in 1850 (Mr. Newmarch) 260 millions; in 1871 (Mr. Palgrave) 612 millions; in 1873 (Mr. Moxon) 732 millions; in 1874 (Mr. Dun) 782 millions. This latter account accords better with the magnitude of the home trade and the foreign trade. The growth of deposits indicates a proportionate growth in the number and amount of cheques, which must greatly exceed the whole of the metallic currency and note circulation of the United Kingdom.

III. The estimated bills under discount in Great Britain amounted in 1850 to 100 millions (Mr. Newmarch), and in 1874 (Mr. Dun) to 260 millions. Mr. Palgrave ('Statistical Society's Journal,' December

1873) estimated the amount of both inland and foreign bills in circulation in the United Kingdom, at probably 300 to 350 millions. 'Mr. Newmarch's estimate in 1851 was that the corresponding amounts then were from 180 to 200 millions.'

IV. The facilities for deposits and discounts have multiplied as follows:—

a. The number of joint-stock and private banks (including the Bank of England) in England and Wales was 386 in 1860; 370 in 1865; 366 in 1870; and 369 in 1875.

b. The number of branch offices was

IN ENGLAND AND WALES: 962 in 1851; 1,651 in 1870; 1,885 in 1875.

IN SCOTLAND: 382 in 1845; 480 in 1855; 654 in 1865; 884 in 1875.

IN IRELAND: 170 in 1851; 365 in 1872; 404 in 1875.

The proportion to inhabitants is now one bank office to 13,000 inhabitants in England and Ireland, and one to 4,000 inhabitants in Scotland.

4. FRANCE.

In the Bank of France, the deposits, other than those of the Treasury, amounted to 7½ millions sterling in 1862, and to 16¾ millions in 1876. The total deposits in the six principal financial houses in Paris 'amounted in round numbers to 619 millions of francs on December 31, 1876, and 571 millions at the end of 1875, against which the banks held an aggregate cash reserve in their tills, or at the Bank of France, of about 78 millions in each year.' These are small sums, compared with the immense amounts of deposits in the United Kingdom, where there are neither the same facilities, nor the same general desire, for the investment of small sums in the public funds; but they serve to underrate the growth of banking and financing in France of late years.

5. UNITED STATES.

The capital and liabilities of the banks in the United States amounted to 800 million dollars in 1850, 2,720 millions in 1871, 2,800 in 1873, and 2,909 millions in 1874, showing an advance from 160 to 582 millions sterling. In 1858 the deposits in the New York Clearing-House banks amounted to 103 million dollars; in 1876 to 255 millions.

6. *FAILURES.*

1 UNITED KINGDOM.

From 1856 to 1868, 7,056 joint-stock companies were formed with a capital of 893 millions sterling. Of these, only 2,918, or 41 per cent., remained in existence at the close of 1868.

Of 240 companies formed with a nominal capital of 400 millions sterling, 87, with a capital of 160 millions, were wound up; two obtained Acts of Parliament; 29, with a capital of 60 millions sterling, filed no returns; and 122, with a nominal capital of 180 millions sterling, were supposed to be in existence in 1868; but, of those 180 millions scarcely ten per cent could be estimated as the amount of paid-up capital.

II. UNITED STATES.

From the 'New York Bankers' Magazine,' for November 1876, it appears that the mercantile failures have been as follows :—

	1857 to 1862	1863 to 1872	1873 to 1876
No. of failures	25,391	16,427	27,845
Amount (millions sterling) .	152	88	155

Commenting on these failures, Messrs. Dun, Barlow, and Co., in a passage quoted in the magazine, observed :—

'It is significant that the gloom which pervades the commercial horizon of the rest of the world has not only been more disastrous and destructive of confidence abroad, than in this country, but that the signs of vitality, and of a return of healthy trade, seem far more distant than here. Excepting France and Belgium, in almost every other commercial country, the failures have been quite as numerous in proportion to the number engaged in business, as in the United States. But in addition to this, the daily reports indicate an extent of liabilities far exceeding in magnitude those in this country. So that an expansion in permanent expenditure in this country, far exceeding the bounds of prudence, an enormous debt, a disorganised currency, a recklessness in trade, and an extravagance in living, have not prevented our commercial fabric from sustaining itself with far less signs of distress than appear in other countries that are free from these hurtful disabilities.'

III. GERMANY.

From a statement in the 'Economist's Commercial History and Review,' for 1876, it appears that in Prussia the numbers of joint-stock companies which came into existence, and their capital, were as follows :—

	Before 1800	1801 to 1850	1851 to 1870	Total	1871 to 1873	1874
No. of societies . . .	5	148	334	487	797	19
Nominal capital (millions sterling)	·7	36	128	165	175	21

In the three years from 1871 to 1873 more capital was proposed to be raised than in all the preceding seventy years. The new German joint-stock law came into operation on June 11, 1870.

IV. AUSTRIA.

'From January 1, 1873, till December 31, 1876, in Vienna alone, 135 joint-stock companies resolved to liquidate, viz. 59 in 1873, 36 in 1874, 18 in 1875, and 22 in 1876. Railway companies are not included in these figures. Most of these undertakings perished at the commencement of their career, 73 in the first and second years, and 43 in the third and fourth years of their existence. Of the gross total of 135 companies, 85 have completed their liquidation, repaying 120 million guldens out of a paid-up capital of 263 millions. The 50 liquidations still proceeding had repaid 18 out of 107 million guldens of capital, and it was expected that they would repay 25 millions more. Therefore 207 millions, or almost 56 per cent. of the whole capital, may be considered as utterly lost.

'The consequence of the crisis may also be seen from the yearly sales of landed property, viz. :—

	1871	1872	1873	1874	1875
Number of estates sold .	154,531	758,427	163,815	167,938	158,425
Million gulden . .	51	131	212	88	71

In 1870 the value of estates sold was only 38 million guldens: in 1876 it was 45 millions.'—*Economist*, February 3, 1877.

7. *NATIONAL DEBTS.*

I. Mr. R. Dudley Baxter, in a paper read before the Statistical Society in January 1874, and the 'Westminster Review' for January 1876, gave the following statements of foreign loans and national debts :—

(*Millions sterling.*)

	1819–1820	1848	1870	1873	1875
'Westminster Review' Continent of Europe	570	747	2,165	—	2,773
United States	26	48	765	—	775
Latin America	3	60			
British India	29	50	105	—	131
Asia	—	—			
British Colonies	—	6	36	—	49
Australasia	—	—			
Africa	—	—	40	—	75
	58	164	946	—	1,030
	628	911	3,111	—	3,803
Great Britain	902	820	800	—	775
	1,530	1,731	3,911	—	4,578
'Mr. Baxter'.	—	1,700	—	4,680	—

Adding to the 'Westminster Reviewer's' figures the capital of railway companies in India, interest on which is guaranteed by the Indian Government, his total would substantially agree with Mr. Baxter's. Mr. Seyd's total is 4,400 millions; but he reckoned for British India 106 millions instead of 221 millions, including the capital of guaranteed railway companies.

II. At the rates given by Mr. Baxter, the yearly amount of interest on this debt was as follows:—

	1 United Kingdom	2 Denmark, Sweden, Holland, Belgium, Germany	3 India, Canada, Australasia	4 France, United States, and other countries with moderate Interest	5 High Interest	6 Excessive Interest	Total
Rate of Interest	per cent. 3	per cent. 4	per cent. 4	per cent. 5 to 6½	per cent. 6½ to 10	per cent. 14 to 66	
				(*Millions sterling.*)			
1848	24·6	6·7	2·3	18	13·5	23·7	88·8
1873	23·5	11·1	7·7	97·9	87·4	89·5	317·1

The average rate of interest for the countries in columns 2 to 6 was seven per cent. in 1848, and 7·7 per cent. in 1873; but the amount of interest payable by the countries which borrow at high or excessive interest was 55 per cent. of the total interest in 1873, against 42 per cent. in 1848.

III. Excluding England, which has been reducing debt, the total amount of debts of the rest of the world was 911 millions in 1848; 1,231 millions in 1858; 2,431 millions in 1867; and 3,803 millions in 1875; the last-mentioned amount exceeding that in 1848 by 2,892 millions, and that in 1858, by 2,572 millions. Had this lending and borrowing, of which the amount since 1848 exceeds the amount of gold and silver coin in the world, been conducted in metallic money, the markets of the world would have been convulsed. The consideration was paid, chiefly, in various forms of mercantile credit, and was availed of, to a great extent, in the shape of railway materials, ships, steamers, armaments, munitions of war, works for bridges and canals, &c.

IV. Mr. Baxter states that the total loans from 1848 to 1860 averaged—

	Millions	
20 millions a year since 1848 to 1854 . .	120	
50 " " from 1855 to 1860 . .	300	
		420
to which, on the authority of the Statistical Abstract of the principal foreign countries dated 1875, there may be added: from 1861 to 1867, at 157 millions a year		1,100
		1,520

Leaving 1,460 millions sterling, or a yearly average of 243 millions, as the borrowing from 1868 to 1873, against a yearly average of 32 millions from 1848 to 1860.

V. The interest on the debt, in 1873, of other countries than Great Britain amounted to 266 millions, or a sum eight-fold the yearly average borrowing from 1848 to 1860, and one and three-fifths times (169 per cent.) the yearly borrowing from 1861 to 1867. Hence, when borrowings ceased, commerce was affected, the imports from the borrowing countries (up to the amount of the interest) reaching the lending countries as payments of interest, and no longer in exchange for exports from the latter.

VI. Since 1873 there has been a collapse of the credit of impecunious nations. 'Herapath's Journal,' quoting the Brussels 'Moniteur des Intérêts Matériels,' gives the following statement of sums asked for, for various purposes, throughout the more civilised portions of the globe, viz.:—

(Millions sterling.)

	1870	1871	1872	1873	1874	1875	Total for five years from 1871
States and towns .	—	468	219	173½	63½	18¾	942¾
Financial companies . .	—	160	78¼	70	12	17½	863¾
Industrial companies . .	—		208	193	93	31¾	
	228½	628	505½	436½	168½	68	1,806½
						In 1870	228½
							2,035

For the six years, the aggregate of 2,035 millions gives a yearly average of 340 millions; but the greater part (1,570½ millions) was asked for in the three years 1871 to 1873, or the years of inflated prices.

VII. Another account in the 'Investors' Manual' gives the following statement of new capital created and issued in each year:—

(Millions sterling.)

	1867	1868	1869	1870	1871	1872	1873	1874	1875	1876
New capital created and issued:										
In England . .	33	29	24	39	57	81	80	82	45	42
In England and other countries . . .	11	45	68	53	153	230	75	32	17	1
	44	74	92	92	210	311	155	114	62	43
Actual money calls:										
In England . .	21	20	22	34	38	57	58	66	41	42
In England and other countries . . .	10	29	38	46	121	163	76	44	20	1
	31	49	60	80	159	220	134	110	61	43

The total of new capital created and issued in the ten years from 1867 to 1876 was 1,197 millions, of which more than half, or 676 millions, were created in the three years 1871 to 1873, or the years of inflated prices.

VIII. In the absence of countervailing influences, prices are raised in a country which largely borrows abroad, so long as the borrowing continues; and they fall in that country, on cessation of the borrowing, when interest has to be remitted to the creditor country. During the continuous and immense borrowings, down to 1873, the remittance of the heavy amounts of interest was neutralised, and the borrowings enhanced the prices of commodities. With the collapse of credit in 1873, prices of commodities (now largely exported in payment of interest) inevitably fell.

IX. Estimating the returns from foreign indebtedness at an average rate of interest of 7 per cent. (section II.), we have the following increase of yearly payments of interest on the amount of indebtedness of other countries than Great Britain:—

(Millions sterling.)

-	Amount in 1858	Increase over 1858 in 1867	Increase over 1867 in 1873	Total
Principal amount . .	1,231	1,200	1,372	3,803
Interest at 7 per cent. .	86	84	96	266

How much of this debt is held in England is not known. It is hardly conceivable that only one-fourth is so held; but Mr. Seyd, who reckons the national debts, other than those of England, at 3,615 millions, distributes this amount as follows:—

	Millions sterling
1. Nations which hold their own debts, viz., France, 750; Germany, 165; Holland, Belgium, and Denmark, 130	1,045
2. Nations that partly hold their own debts, while the remainder is held abroad, the portion held at home being	570
	1,615
3. Remainder held abroad	2,000
	3,615

Considering that the country which has the largest commerce and most wealth must have the greatest share in loans to countries which have foreign creditors, it is difficult to understand how England, as stated by Mr. Seyd, holds only 800 millions out of 2,000 millions of debt. France has been enabled to hold her own enormous debt only by selling the foreign securities which she had previously held.

8. The debt and revenue of the undermentioned countries have been—

(*In millions.*)

	1860	1863	1864	1865	1869	1873	1874	1875
UNITED STATES:	$	$	$	$	$	$	$	$
Debt . . .	68	1,734	2,683	2,783	2,481	2,259	2,232	2,180
Revenue . .	41	261	329	558	411	289	288	297
UNITED STATES (dollar at four shillings):	£	£	£	£	£	£	£	£
Debt . . .	14	347	537	557	496	451	446	436
Revenue . .	8	52	66	111	82	58	58	59
RUSSIA:								
Debt . . .	256	—	—	—	302[1]	—	—	445
Revenue . .	55	55	63	60	72	74	77	79
FRANCE:								
Debt . . .	386	467	473	488	515	—	—	938
Revenue, ordinary	74	73	71	72	73	—	94	100
Departmental .	5	10	10	10	12	—	—	—
Extraordinary .	1	8	7	5	1	—	—	—
TOTAL FOR FRANCE, RUSSIA, & UNITED STATES:								
Debt . . .	656	—	—	—	1,313	—	—	1,819
Revenue, ordinary	137	180	200	243	227	—	229	238
UNITED KINGDOM:								
Debt . . .	826	825	821	816	805	786	779	775
Revenue . .	69	70	70	70	73	77	77	74
„ Local taxation (England and Wales) .	—	—	—	17	17	20	—	—

9. The following remarks are suggested by this table ;—

I. For Russia the amount of revenue in 1863 has been assumed as the amount for 1860. For France, the revenue from 1873 to 1875 consists of the actual indirect and the estimated direct revenue: the latter does not vary much from year to year.

II. England, which can bear more taxation than other countries, has reduced her debt by 50 millions, and has increased her taxation by only 5 millions—an increase which becomes nominal, if the receipts from telegraphs and certain other items of departmental receipts be excluded. The revenue, that is, mainly, the taxation, in the other three States rose from 137 millions in 1860 to 238 millions in 1875, that is, from double the English revenue in 1860 to more than treble the aug-

[1] 1867.

mented amount of that revenue in 1875. If the Russian debt up to 1877 inclusive be reckoned, the total taxation for the three States must be double the amount in 1860. In that interval of seventeen years the population of France has declined, and emigration to the United States has been checked, there being now also a returning tide to the old countries. In Russia the population is sparse.

III. Fifty millions, or one-half of the increased taxation of 101 millions since 1860, was for meeting the increased charge for interest on debt, which rose in the three States from 31 millions in 1860 to 82 millions in 1875.

IV. In the United States, the interest on debt amounted to 19·8 millions sterling in 1876–7 against ·8 million in 1860; the receipts from customs' duties amounted to 25·4 millions in 1876–7 against 9·8 millions in 1861–2; so that the considerable increase of protective duties in the United States was, in one view, forced on the Federal Government by the increase of debt; the excise revenue, the great financial resource in England and Russia, having been locally appropriated by the several States.

V. In Russia, the ordinary receipts have amounted to—

(Millions sterling.)

	1863	1870	1871	1872	1873	1874	1875	1876
Alcoholic liquors .	14·9	22·5	24·	23·8	24·7	27·6	27·1	26·4
Customs' revenue .	4·4	5·7	6·5	7·4	7·4	7·8	8·6	8·3
	19·3	28·2	30·5	31·2	32·1	35·4	35·7	34·7
Other receipts	26·3	37·9	39·4	40·8	41·9	41·3	43·6	38·8
	45·6	66·1	69·9	72·0	74·0	76·7	79·3	73·5

Interest on debt amounted in 1863 to 7·9 millions sterling, and in 1875 to 14·8 millions. The improved receipts from alcoholic liquors have met the increased charge for interest, and a part of the increased military expenditure. But even this financial position has been altered for the worse, by the war with Turkey. In May 1877,[1] Russia borrowed 3 millions sterling from a syndicate of bankers on the Continent. In the following month [2] a 5 per cent. foreign loan of 15 millions sterling was announced, and an internal 5 per cent. loan of

[1] *Economist*, May 26. [2] *Economist*, June 16, 1877.

200 million roubles (since issued) was under consideration. Describing the financial position of Russia, the 'Economist' on July 28, 1877, wrote:

'The interest, which is the only point worth considering, amounted in 1876 to 10½ millions sterling for the national debt, and 4½ millions for the Railway Debt, or 15 millions in all. To this must be added 1¾ million for loans of 15 millions sterling, and 20 millions nominal, sanctioned since the war, at 5 per cent., making the total charge for debt 17¼ millions, or nearly one quarter of the revenue.'

On September 15, 1877, the same journal recapitulated—

'For some years past, the exchanges remained steady at or about 33*d.* per rouble (the conventional English equivalent being 3*s.* 2*d.* per rouble), at the present moment it is scarcely above 24*d.*, and this decline has taken place almost wholly within the past year. . . . The Strousberg collapse of 1875 was followed by an extreme crisis in the banking system of the country, facilities which had been given to trade were suddenly withdrawn; and it was remarked at the time, figuratively of course, "another year without crops, and nearly everybody in South Russia will be bankrupt." A shock of this description could not fail to have a disastrous influence upon the aggregate trade of the country. The trade demand for money being thus contracted, the paper currency of Russia began to depreciate. The imposition of customs' duties on imports, in gold instead of paper money, has further restricted imported trade. And while the demand for rouble notes for business purposes was thus diminished, there has been no diminution in the quantity emitted by the Imperial Bank; on the contrary, there has been a quiet emission of rouble notes, which appear under the accounts of the bank as *billets de crédit émis pour compte des succursales*, and which amounts to 160,350,000 roubles (20 millions sterling) against which figures a counter-entry of 105,647,396 roubles, as "current expenses on account of the Treasury." Last year the Government invited subscriptions to 100 million roubles of 5 per cent. notes. This year the Government has endeavoured to raise 200 million roubles as an Oriental loan, which, it is affirmed, has been partially successful, and which is not yet fully paid up. Meanwhile, these *billets de crédit* have been emitted, as above described.'

Of the paper currency, about 20 millions sterling of the issue outstanding was in excess, the paper having been much below par,[1] and the subsequent excess issue in 1877 has amounted to 20 millions sterling. Of foreign loans there were issued, in May and June 1877, 18 millions sterling; and of internal loans, in 1876 and 1877, 15 millions sterling. Even if there were to be no further borrowing, the interest on these loans, and on the sum required for withdrawing inordinately excessive issues of paper roubles, must raise the charge for interest by more than 3 millions sterling beyond the amount in 1875. A thumping income tax,—and drinking, with the revenue

[1] *Economist*, July 28, 1877.

therefrom,—are the sovereign remedies for financial disorder, as now conventionally recognised. In Russia, the excise revenue has begun to decline; and the burdens of the peasantry do not admit of increase. Among the upper strata, the extreme depression of trade does not promise much for an income tax, and although the Russian nobility, as large landed proprietors, are willing to bear additional burdens, yet the amount recoverable from them as income tax must bear a small proportion to the increase of charge for interest. On the other hand, if, as is probable, much of the Russian export trade, now checked by the war, will be permanently superseded by that of the United States, the receipts from railways must decline.

VI. In France, the indirect taxes have been as follows:—

(*Millions of francs.*)

	1862	1863	1873	1874	1875	1876
Registration and stamps	359	395	561	582	607	624
Customs	419	455	229	202	243	262
Salt, maritime and inland	40	31	36	28	35	37
Wines and spirits	201	196	329	348	386	400
Tobacco	224	215	291	299	312	322
	884	897	885	877	976	1,021
Native sugar	48	45	103	106	117	123
Post office	63	66	110	113	119	114
Railway duty	—	—	70	85	79	81
	995	1,008	1,168	1,181	1,291	1,339
Other receipts	—	—	78	102	144	143
	1,354	1,403	1,807	1,865	2,042	2,106

The revenue for 1863 did not differ materially from that for 1870. According to the old form of stating the accounts, the charge under public debt, in 1860, viz., 22·4 millions sterling, included about 3 millions for the redemption of debt which was not so applied. Excluding this item, the interest on debt amounted to 19·4 millions sterling in 1861, to 19·9 millions in 1863, to 20 millions in 1867, to 22 millions in 1870, and in 1875 to 47 millions, showing an increase of about 28 millions sterling since 1860, and of 25 millions since the war. Towards this, wines and spirits have contributed only about one-third, and the remainder has been obtained from other indirect taxes, which, as the population has not increased, and as the people do not feel the weight of the additional taxation, denotes a general increase of income and wages throughout the country. The Paris correspondent of the 'Economist' (March 31, 1877) wrote:

> 'The receipts in 1869, deduction being made for the territory ceded to Germany, amounted to a total sum of 1,777 millions of francs; the estimates for 1877 were voted at a sum of 2,737 millions; the increase, in round numbers, is 959 millions of francs, or more than 38 millions of pounds sterling; and this enormous augmentation in the burden of taxation is borne without any apparent effort, and without impairing the prosperity of the country, or checking the accumulation of wealth. In fine, without the people appearing any the worse for it.'

The figures in this extract differ from those in the table, which for 1875 and 1876 are taken from the 'Economist' dated January 27, 1877, and for earlier years from previous issues of that journal and from publications of the Board of Trade. The amount of excise duty mentioned by the Paris correspondent of the 'Economist' includes the duties on matches, chicory, &c. The main fact is, that owing to the division of land among small proprietors, and to the great number of small shopkeepers, a recourse to an income tax has been considered inexpedient; and France has had to provide the enormously increased charge for interest on debt by means of indirect taxes; on which account, unless the French nation drink themselves into free-traders, they may not see their way to a very great reduction of customs' duties.

VII. France, moreover, is not yet out of the wood. In March 1872[1] an account was opened

> 'For the reconstitution of the war material lost or destroyed during the war, reconstruction of fortifications, and other extraordinary expenses arising out of the invasion. In March 1872, its limits were fixed at 535 millions of francs;'

but by subsequent additions it had, on December 31, 1875,

> 'Reached a sum of 915 millions; and as the resources realised or disposable for that account then amounted to a like sum, the Government resolved to close it at that sum, and reopen a second chapter of it. . . . The resources for the second chapter of the liquidation fund were to be obtained by the issue of long-dated Treasury bills falling due from the year 1880, and to be successively redeemed by the annuity of 150 millions a year now paid to the Bank of France. The new liquidation account amounted on December 8, 1876, to 385 millions, and a further sum of 400 millions would be required for the same service, making a total for the two chapters of 1,699 millions. That

[1] *Economist*, May 26, 1877.

it will stop at that sum is scarcely probable, for this system of disguising the war expenditure by discharging a part of it on future years is too convenient to be readily abandoned.'

Will the expenditure of a new war with Germany be met with the same apparent facility as the interest charge for the last war?

VIII. In England the revenue has been as follows :—

(*Millions sterling.*)

Year ended March 31	Excise	Customs' Revenue from Spirits	Other Customs' Revenue	Stamps	Assessed Taxes	Total	Other Revenue	Grand Total
1858	17·8	2·2	21·2	7·4	11·6	60·2	7·8	68·
1860	20·4	2·5	21·9	8·0	9·6	62·4	8·8	71·2
1863	17 2	2·7	21·3	9·0	10·5	60·7	9·9	70·6
1865	19·5	3·3	19·2	9·5	7·9	59·4	10·9	70·3
1868	20·2	4·3	18·4	9·5	6·2	58·6	11·3	69·6
1871	22·8	4·4	15 8	9·0	6·3	58·3	11·6	69·9
1873	25·9	4·9	16·1	9·9	7·5	63·3	13·3	76·6
1874	27·1	5·3	15·0	10·5	5·6	63·5	13·8	77·3
1875	27·3	5·7	13·6	10·5	4·3	61·4	13 5	74·9
1876	27·6	6·1	14·1	11·0	4·1	62·9	14·2	77·1
1877	27·7	5·8	14·0	10·9	5·3	63 7	14 9	78 6

a. The customs' revenue from foreign spirits, and the excise revenue, in 1876–7, amounted to 33·5 millions, against 20 millions in 1857–8, showing an increase of 13½ millions. The income tax was imposed by Sir R. Peel for extinguishing deficit, and for a revision of the customs' duties. Assessed taxes, and the customs' revenue other than that from spirits, amounted in 1857–8 to 33·8 millions, and in 1876–7 to 19·3 millions, showing a reduction of 14·3 millions, of which 13½ millions have been provided by the customs' revenue from spirits, and the excise revenue;—but at what cost?

b. In France, with a population of 36 millions, the revenue from wine, beer, and spirits amounts to 16 millions sterling, or two-fifths the interest on debt; in the United Kingdom, for a population of 33 millions, it amounts to 33½ millions excluding, or to 35¼ millions including wines; that is, to one-fourth more than the interest on debt. In France, a great part of her enormous debt is held by peasant proprietors; in Great Britain (from other causes than drunkenness) 'many of the best cultivated districts [observes Mr. Fawcett] will have to be travelled through for many miles, before a single rural labourer can be found who has saved sufficient to make the smallest provision for old age or sickness.' Nor have the working classes generally improved in habits of thrift commensurately with their improved means, as evidenced by the increased expenditure on drink. The population of the United Kingdom has doubled since 1845, and there has been a great increase of wages since that year, with a diminished cost of food and clothing—yet, in 1876, the deposits in the savings banks under the post-office amounted to only 27 millions, and in those under trustees to 43 millions, total only 70 millions, against 30¾ millions in 1845, and 35 millions in 1857. The excess of accumulated saving in the later over the earlier year is only 35 millions; while the excess of only one year's revenue from spirits, in 1876, over the amount in 1858 is 13½ millions, which represents only a part of the increased expenditure on spirits. Moreover, the bulk of the increase in the savings banks under trustees, viz., to 43 millions, occurred up to 1861, when the deposits amounted to 42½ millions, against 43¼ millions in 1876–7. Now, 1861 was prior to the considerable rise in wages, and to the great expansion of the excise revenue after 1865. Hence, it appears that the growth of population and the rise in wages have augmented the excise revenue, but that means of considerably improving the condition of the labouring classes have been wasted. In India, in caring for the European soldiers who are drawn from those working classes of the British population, the best results have followed from making it difficult for them to obtain more than their regulated allowance of liquor.

IX. The productive indirect taxes are those on necessaries of life, and on stimulants which are in general consumption. Among the latter is the revenue from spirits, which, where the revenue is large, implies an enormous waste of money of which a portion is arrested and diverted to the State. This revenue flourishes in the creditor country far more than among the indebted nations, which are struggling under greatly augmented taxes that press upon the springs of industry and check production of the exports wherewith the indebted nations have to pay their foreign debts. Were those nations to consume liquor on the scale of the British consumption, repudiation of debt would naturally follow. Let us hope that their excise revenue will not increase much more; but whether it does or not, the prospect of extended markets for British manufactures among nations whose means of purchase are reduced by heavy taxation, seems unpromising.

X. The debt which is pulling down Russia was incurred chiefly, and that in France and the United States was incurred entirely, for military, naval, and other expenditure which has not added an iota to the productive powers or resources of the States. Even the railway expenditure of Russia was for the most part bestowed on poorly paying military lines of railway. A similar remark applies to the bulk of the borrowings of the indebted nations since 1848, which have raised the public debt, or that of the Governments of the borrowing countries in the world, by 2,800 millions sterling. Interest on debt for unproductive expenditure of non-repudiating States can be met in no other way than by an increase of taxation; and when that taxation cannot be made productive through the vices or weaknesses of the indebted nations, it must fall with injurious effect on the land, and on the various industries of the people.

The additional taxation has supervened, too, on an unhealthy commercial condition in which prices and wages have been raised by the extra temporary expenditure during years of vast borrowings, and a higher scale of living has been induced by increased wages, among those to whom reduction of wages must now mean, not loss of the means of earning, but surrender of a customary scale of living.

In this regard, Germany falls into the same category with the indebted nations, by reason of the excessive casual expenditure which followed on receipt of the war indemnity, and of the enterprises which were stimulated by the temporary investments of the indemnity money. The effect upon Germany's material condition, of the receipt of the 200 millions sterling paid by France, is the same as if the money had been borrowed; if there is this difference on the one hand, that the money has not caused any increase of taxation, there is the consideration, on the other hand, that the scale of expenditure which it induced was disproportioned to the actual supply of labour (both of captains of industry and of the working masses), and to the previous scale of Germany's commerce and trade.

XI. Outside the public debt which we have been considering, there has indeed been incurred a large amount of other debt in the form of capital subscribed for commercial lines of railway, for canals, and for joint-stock companies. These, no doubt, have invigorated and organised the industry, and have developed resources of the borrowing countries, thus enabling them to bear, better than they could otherwise have done, the heavy weight of additional taxation which has accompanied the growth of public debt. But these invigorating influences have been neutralised, in a measure, by gigantic financial and mercantile failures, and collapses of joint-stock companies and of railway and other industrial enterprises.

XII. The outcome of all this is primarily, diminished means of purchase from foreign nations, and consequently a stagnation of trade which has lasted for four years, and which is not relieved by any decided signs of revival. The 'Economist's' Commercial History and Review for 1875 and 1876, and other notices in that and other journals, give the following account of the existing state of trade and industry:—

GENERAL.

a. '1875 has been, almost without exception, a bad year in every trade, and for every interest, not only in this country, but all over Europe and North and South America. This pressure has now been two years and a half in operation, reckoning from the American Railway Panic of September 1873; and it cannot yet be said that there are any clear signs of a better state of things.'

b. 1876. 'The year 1876 has in all respects corresponded in character and results, to our forecast, at the close of last year's review. It has been a third year in the cycle of reaction and readjustment, and, until quite the close of it, has been marked by dull and limited trade, restricted confidence, the rigorous application of reduction and economies, lessened wages, and the failures of numberless commercial and manufacturing concerns, unable by the capital, credit, and skill at their command, to bear the pressure of adverse times. This description applies with even more force to North America, Germany, Austria, Russia, and Belgium, than to this country. In France the dulness has been somewhat less severe, but still marked and wide-spread.'

c. 1877. The commercial depression has continued through 1877, and the public journals speculate on the causes of it.

UNITED STATES.

a. 1876. 'The very slow recovery of North America from the commercial distress which began with the railway panic of September 1873, is among the most important and instructive facts of the time. In spite of protection, all the protected industries remain in collapse; and in spite of inconvertible paper money and unlimited land, the working classes are worse off in the United States than in any other part of the world. . . . Emigration to the United States and Canada is almost stopped, and steamers from New York bring to Liverpool, weekly, hundreds of artisans in search of work in the old country. . . .

b. 'The case of New York, where the value of personal property has diminished in amount about 38 per cent., and that of real estate by nearly as much, since 1873, is only a typical one, and no doubt there has been a similar, though it may be a less heavy decline, throughout the whole country. The crisis, therefore, has not nearly arrested its progress; it has also caused an enormous, and as the figures show a continuous loss of wealth. The country is poorer than it was, and it has therefore been compelled to restrict its expenditure, and to buy less than it formerly did of foreign commodities. Looking at it in this light, the excess of exports over imports, upon which there has, in America, been some self-congratulation, becomes an evidence not of increased prosperity but of diminished wealth, and a less degree of well-being among the mass of the people. . . . The state of Pennsylvania in 1870 had a population of 3½ millions; at the present time it is scarcely so much as the population of London (3¼ millions); yet, I believe, there are more persons, able and willing to work, out of employment in this State than there are in all England. . . . The only immigrants to the United States now required are agricultural labourers, and persons who can buy land and settle on it.

c. 'The leading result of this table of failures is the rapid increase of the insolvencies in each year, since 1873. In New England the increase in 1876 over 1873 was nearly three-fold; in the Middle States double; and in the Southern States 50 per cent. Another leading result is, that in each year the insolvencies embrace a smaller and poorer class of traders.'

d. The circular dated January 17, 1877, of M'Culloch and Co., of New York, describes as follows the prostration of that leading centre of American trade:—

'There is a degree of torpor apparent in all interests, that is somewhat discouraging as respects the prospects of the opening season. Several causes seem to conduce to this state of things. The influences surrounding the political situation are unhealthy. *Then, the presentation of the annual statements of States, Corporations, and financial institutions, has not produced favourable impression.* An unwelcome picture of excessive debt, oppressive taxation, bad debts, heavy losses, and light profits is presented; and the effect for the time being is anything but encouraging. *Then, the severity of taxation is being very keenly felt.* The reduction of these burdens has been nominal, compared with the diminished ability of the people to bear them; and the pressure now begins to tell with great effect upon business. The tax receipts of this city, which are collectable at this season, are not equal to 30 per cent. of the usual amount, *simply because the people cannot pay them*; and yet there is some twelve million dollars of arrears of previous years.

1877. *e.* 'Here is a population of nearly or quite 45 millions, possessing a soil and climate varied and desirable in the highest degree, ample water communication in all directions, and a great network of railroads begging for freight: nevertheless, probably one-third of the people are without adequate remunerative employment, and many who would gladly have work to do have none at all; railroads are going into receiverships, and their employés are deserting their work to engage in unprecedented acts of violence, while, what transportation there is to be done is thus interrupted. On one hand, capital needing investment is so plethoric in abundance that it takes many millions of bonds at a rate of interest contrary to all the past; on the other hand, both skilled and unskilled labour want employment and wait for it. What is the thing that keeps apart the capital and the industry which ought to come together?'

GERMANY AND AUSTRIA.

1875. 'The commercial crisis in Prussia appears by no means to have come to a close. Not many days ago a private deputation of large employers of labour waited on the Minister of Commerce to represent the alarming condition of the artisan class of the capital. Three of the chief manufactories, which averaged in their employment, not long since, 2,000 hands each, can barely now find work for a third as many, and it was stated that in the city there are at present no fewer than 23,000 artisans or skilled labourers, *wholly without anything to do*, and every prospect of the number of those turned adrift for the want of orders increasing. Under these circumstances it was urged that Government should take such measures as the budget allows for promoting a demand for labour.'

1876. After a table of the companies started in 1871–2, and of the prices of their shares on December 31, 1872, and December 31, 1875:

'At the end of 1875, the market prices showed a loss of fully one-third, say 54 millions sterling, on the par amount of the 170 millions involved in the 432 companies; and the probability is that the large part of the residue of 116 millions must be regarded as a dormant and contingent asset yielding no present revenue to the holders. Now, 170 millions sterling is equal to nearly six years' public revenue (30 millions) of Prussia, and 116 millions are equal to nearly four years' revenue. Prussia is a country of small fortunes and small incomes; and it is not easy to exaggerate the disturbance of trade, and the curtailment of expenditure, inflicted by so large and sudden a diminution of the dividend-bearing character of a total sum representing a very large proportion of the savings of the country.

February 3, 1877. 'The organs of the democratic party in Germany demand the immediate construction of public works as a remedy for the depression of every branch of business. These organs protest against the neglect of this part of the Government's duty.'

February 28, 1877. 'In the Prussian Landtag, the Government has been advised to undertake a great number of public works, with a view of alleviating the general distress. The Secretary of the Board of Trade was reproached with having made but little use of the credit granted by the Reichsrath, and he defended himself by stating that the Government had just commenced the construction of several railway lines that would demand a capital of over 100 million marks.'

March 24, 1877. 'The Prussian Government has published a report on the present condition of general distress, in which it is stated that for railway works done 70 million marks have been expended during the past year, and that further works will be given over to public competition.'

March 17, 1877. 'It is a surprising fact that the immense depression of business has not decreased the import of articles for food and luxuries; on the contrary, they are rather increased.'

August 11, 1877. 'The iron and coal industries in Germany are, according to the *Frankfurter Zeitung*, going from bad to worse. Forced sales are every day on the increase.'—*New York Financial Chronicle.*

January 30, 1877. (Austria). 'In the five years from 1871 to 1875 there were sold 803,136 estates of the annual value of 2,135 million gulden. These figures prove what an enormous influence the crisis has had also upon landed property; and (February 20, 1877) efforts are being made in Vienna to relieve the general distress. The municipality of the town has chosen a committee which has already proposed the construction of some public works as a remedy. A deputation of some members of the Reichsrath of the Landtag of Lower Austria, and a number of mayors of neighbouring towns has been received by the Minister of the interior. They all demand State help in relieving the universal distress. The Minister answered that parishes and provinces are the first that must help; but that the Government is certainly disposed to do all it can; as, for instance, to grant to the parishes loans without interest, if they but consent to redeem them. He advised them to send in their projects for such a purpose.'

GERMANY.

An Article in the *Revue des Deux Mondes* on the commercial crisis in Germany thus sums up:—'With regard to the operative classes, their condition was not much improved, though in many cases their wages were doubled, and their hours of labour reduced by one-half. Extravagance and indolence united to rob the labourer of his earnings. The deposits in the savings banks did not increase; the house of the mechanic and the labourer was no better furnished; and his family were no better lodged and no happier; so that when the day of panic and cessation of work arrived, the mechanic, after all his increase of wages, found himself as poor as before, but more discontented than ever, and more ready to believe in the magical power of strikes, revolutions, and political or financial chimeras. . . . There remains nothing of the increased earnings of the workman, nor of the immense sums expended upon ill-advised railroad schemes, upon houses badly built, upon colonies without colonists, and upon workshops which have remained empty; so that, after all, Germany has been unquestionably weakened and impoverished.'—*Bankers' Magazine*, January 1877.

BELGIUM.

August 1877. 'It is estimated that in this country the mercantile capital engaged in industrial pursuits has undergone a shrinkage of from twelve to twenty-five per cent. during the last year and a half. The vast losses which have thus been brought upon our people have been the subject of considerable remark. The *Economiste Français* of May 26 has an interesting article showing how a similar shrinkage has been going on in Belgium, between the years 1874 and 1876, in the value of government and municipal bonds, shares in banks and finance companies, in railways and other industrial enterprise, and in foreign bonds and shares, which represent somewhat more than one-fifth of the whole. In 1874 the values amounted to 177 millions sterling; in 1876 to 154 millions, showing a depreciation of thirteen per cent., and the country is poorer to that extent. What has become of the 23 millions sterling of capital which has thus disappeared, and how long Belgium will have to wait before this vast sum of latent capital can once more be recovered and realised, are questions which, in the present depressed condition of the bourses of Europe, it is quite impossible to solve with any approximation to accuracy.'—*New York Bankers' Magazine*.

SWITZERLAND.

The railway crisis in Switzerland is now (February 13, 1877) spreading to industry also. Thus, the watch industry of Geneva is in a very depressed condition. In Montroux and Geneva 26 hotels and pensions are said to have failed, and the Federal Government is obliged to construct more public roads to find work for the needy.'

FRANCE.

'The absence of demand at remunerative prices for nearly all kinds of manufactures, but especially for iron, coal, and hardware, has now lasted for four years in this country (England), the United States, Germany, Austria, Hungary, Italy, and, during the last year and a half, in France. Since July 1876, the depression has been deepened and complicated by political apprehensions, arising out of the dispute in the South East of Europe. . . . Since the summer of 1873, there has been a notorious diminution of the means of consumers—that is, of the cash demand for commodities of all kinds, but especially coal, iron, and hardware. This has been most marked in Germany and France.'—*Economist*, May 5, 1877.

'In the discussion of the Conseil Supérieur du Commerce et de l'Industrie, last month, it was stated that some of the largest and most important iron and steel works in France have been five and seven years without paying a farthing of interest or dividend to shareholders; and Mons. Tezenas de Moncel adds: "At the present moment the shares of metallurgical establishments are in such discredit on the Lyons Exchange that if these great iron and steel works, or blast furnaces, which employ millions of workpeople, were to cease work, and be obliged to borrow capital, they would find it difficult to get what they want."'—*Economist*, June 2, 1877.

RUSSIA.

An empire in which discontent is smouldering among the working classes and the peasantry; a people freed from serfdom yet demoralised from the despair engendered by heavy taxation, born of the deep indebtedness of the Empire. There is a deficiency of floating capital in the country, and owing to the great depreciation of the currency, none is imported. And even what floating capital there is cannot find full employment.

'The rate of interest on current accounts, allowed by the State institutions of credit, which was 4 per cent. up to the Crimean war, was subsequently reduced to 3 per cent. in consequence of the superabundance of capital then lying unemployed within the country. This rate was continued by the State Bank, which absorbed the various credit institutions, from 1860 until 1875, in April of which year it was reduced to 2 per cent. But a week or two ago the State Bank intimated, by means of circulars to the private banks, who had a credit of about 46 millions at the Imperial institution, that it would no longer allow any interest whatever on current accounts. Afterwards the State Bank agreed to allow 1 per cent. to the private banks on their current accounts, but with the stipulation that the latter should reduce the rates they allow on the sums deposited with them by the public, by 1 per cent. By these means it is hoped to check the accumulation in the banks of unemployed capital. It seems from this, that means for the employment of capital are extremely limited.'—*Economist*, May 12, 1877.

This is stated of an extensive empire, traversed by railways and capable of great development. Apparently, burdensome taxation, by crippling the means of consumers, lessens demand, and the need of capital to meet it.

'The country, though it has considerable natural riches, besides such resources as spring from the introduction of an immense system of banks and railways, has for the time exhausted its credit abroad, and the immediate limits of the taxation of its population appear to have been nearly reached. Apart from the annual produce of the soil, Russia has at the moment few resources beyond what can be forced from her people by such devices as issuing paper currency.'—*Economist*, September 15, 1877.

UNITED KINGDOM.

Though England has not borrowed, but on the contrary has reduced her debt, yet, as the principal offender, she could not escape the general depression which has overtaken the rest of the world; for, unless she had lent, the indebted nations could not have borrowed the stupendous amounts, which, though easily enough expressed in figures, the mind cannot adequately grasp. The 'Pall Mall Gazette' wrote of the year 1876 as follows:—

'The three years of distress, 1874 to 1876, have cured effectually the undue conversion of floating into fixed capital. They have purged away most of the abuses and excesses of credit, *but they have not yet brought down the cost of production* to a point which tempts capital, by reason of cheapness, to rely upon the prompt and effectual response of consumption. Still, rapid progress is being made in that direction. The losses of manufacturers, merchants, dealers, and tradespeople have become so general, and the lessened dividends upon all capital invested in joint-stock companies have so seriously impaired large classes of incomes, that the process of correction is now at work with accelerated force. During 1876, all attempts of trade unions to resist reduction of wages have been more or less defeated, and the decrease of employment has enabled the masters to get rid of the less efficient hands, and thus amend, somewhat, the circumstances of production. Emigration to the United States and Canada is almost stopped, and steamers from New York bring back to Liverpool, weekly, hundreds of artisans in search of work in the old country. Moreover, in particular industries, the competition of Belgium and Germany has become active in some trades in this country hitherto wholly native. Added to all these correcting influences, there is the effect of sharp necessity, all over the commercial world, compelling retrenchment, contrivance, and extra work. We see already the effects of these causes in the fall of the rate of discount in this and other countries, a fall so far due, less to surplus income than to lessened trade; but still, a significant fact, as indicating that we have already reached the first positive stage towards the cheapness of commodities, namely, the cheapness of borrowed money.

5. 'In this country (England) there is the largest number of such solid

fortunes; in declining progression, they exist in the following countries;—Holland, France, Germany, Austria, Italy, Russia, Spain. In America, New England States present the same phenomena as does this country, but upon a scale comparatively small. The creation and increase of these solid fortunes is one of the most beneficent results of civilisation and law. Among ourselves, at this moment, it is the expenditure of the opulent class, which, in spite of the distress among manufacturers and merchants, keeps in profitable employment the large industries devoted in supplying the wants of the wealthy and well-to-do. But for this, a collapse of manufacturing enterprise would mean, as it did mean in former periods, a collapse of nearly all the trades and employments of the country. We have therefore assured to us, by reason of these accumulations of capital, a home and foreign trade of no small magnitude, but a trade which, from its nature, varies little in character or extent—a trade of the same nature as that of Holland, a country almost wholly dependent on the expenditure yielded by capital invested in securities.'—*Ibid.*

XIII. Let us take special note of the facts which are so well stated in these two extracts from the 'Pall Mall Gazette.'

1. There has been universal commercial distress for the past three years, but the following faint streaks of silver lining in the cloud are visible, viz.:—

2. Failures, losses, and a shrinking of credit, have been effectually correcting the undue conversion of floating into fixed capital.

3. But they have not yet brought down the cost of production. Still, rapid progress is being made in that direction by a reduction of wages.

4. From this diminished income of the working classes look away towards the colossal fortunes which have been accumulated, and the owners of which are only waiting a diminished cost of production to embark on a fresh career, financial and commercial, which, after the usual cycles of unhealthy excitement, temporarily increased wages, failures, and intelligent speculations on the causes of general commercial distress, shall bring the world back to the present result.

5. In the meanwhile, the fortunes which have been accumulated are doing good service; for the expenditure of their owners keeps in employment the large industries that are devoted to the supply of their wants.

6. For we have assured to us by these accumulations of capital a trade like that of Holland, a country almost wholly dependent on the expenditure yielded by capital invested in securities.

XIV. In short, the cold comfort afforded in these facts is that England is commercially approaching the condition of a nation retired from business; politically she has, perhaps, already retired from the working world, which is busy in act and deed. But what shall the next stage be?

Will England, if content merely to live upon her savings, be able to retain within her islands the strength and manhood, the bone and sinews of the nation, by which she protects the accumulated fruits of her labour? And in the facts which have been passed in review, is there assurance that the savings, however securely protected, will not be reduced by the diminished income of the debtors in whose securities the savings are invested?

XV. The subjects which have been discussed are—

1. The growth of Public Debt, or of the indebtedness of States. This means—the might and the rivalry of colossal Empires, and their imitation by second-rate Powers; a civil war in America, of gigantic proportions, like everything else in that country; and a nation which desired nothing better than to lend to these States, and that they should take out the loans in goods.

2. The growth of joint-stock companies, and of banking, railway and industrial enterprise—which means, the marvels of science in its application to industrial arts, to locomotion, to communication with the ends of the earth—the triumphs of the railway, the telegraph, and steam; the organisation of the world's industry through the wondrous power of ubiquitous finance; the concentration of the world's products in the world's market; and the world's bankers fast lapsing into citizens of the world, till awakened into patriotism (not a whit too soon) by the exhibition of armaments which have brought the world into their debt, but with a dangerous increase of strength, though insufficient, as yet (let us hope), to plunder the Bank and find a new way to pay old debts.

3. Increase of taxation, and of the excise revenue; collapse of credit; stagnation of trade; disorganised relations between labour and capital.

4. These facts mean pressure on the springs of industry of the working millions, of whom one portion, raised during the past fifteen years, by education and the high wages which they have enjoyed, to a higher, and now accustomed scale of living, find it hard to descend from that scale to the lower wages which are considered necessary for prosperous trade; while another part, which wasted high wages in drink, infuses sullenness into the relations between capital and labour. On the continent and in America, men willing to work cannot get work; on the Continent, in the midst of abundant food, public works on a large scale are undertaken as a measure of industrial famine

relief; and in America, 'an unwelcome picture of excessive debt, oppressive taxation, bad debts, heavy losses, and light profits is presented; the *severity* of taxation is being very keenly felt; and seventy per cent. of the taxes is not realised, *simply because the people cannot pay them.*'

XVI. The general commercial depression is explained by the euphemism of the undue conversion of floating into fixed capital. The facts are, that since 1848 the indebted nations have borrowed enormous amounts from, principally, two or three countries which had both money to lend and goods to export; that, on the one hand, the borrowing was in great part for unprofitable expenditure which could not last for ever; and, on the other hand, the provision of a considerable part of the loans in the form of goods created an increase of production which, though originating in a temporary cause, has thus far resulted in continuous over-production, from the necessity of keeping in work the additional mills, mines, and machinery which were provided for the special increase of demand. The special demand having ceased, it is hoped that, by cheapening the prices of goods, an additional ordinary demand may be created, with the virtual result of meeting part of the interest on the loans borrowed since 1848, by a reduction of wages of the working classes in the creditor countries. The expectation is not unreasonable, but this final stage of the distribution of the wealth acquired in the past thirty years, which this reduction of wages would involve, is disorganising the relations of capital and labour; and, supposing the reduction to be completed, will an increase of the ordinary demand commensurate with the past special demand which has ceased, be much nearer practical attainment? The producers may offer at cheaper rates, but will the consumers, with incomes diminished by heavy taxation, imperial, local, and municipal, be able to buy much more than they now do, especially as the trade, henceforth, will to a great extent be conducted, not as between countries which have goods to interchange, each giving to the other that which it produces cheaply, and so buying the exchanged article at a cheap rate, but as between a debtor country which sells its goods at a disadvantageous rate in payment of interest, and which therefore cannot afford to buy as freely from the creditor country, goods for which its own products are not given in exchange?

XVII. The situation is a dead-lock. Production has outstripped the ordinary demand abroad; under ordinary circumstances, a reduction of price would raise the demand to the amount of existing production;

but the diminished incomes of peoples that are staggering under heavy loads of taxation induced by the indebtedness of nations, states, and municipalities, cloud the prospects of escape, in this way, from the commercial depression which for long has prevailed throughout the world. Meanwhile, capital or labour must suffer.

XVIII. The outcome, then, in less than one generation, of the manifestations of power and might of colossal empires; of a mental activity which, proud of its achievements, is even more astonished at them; of an enterprise which has covered the ocean with steamers, the West with railways, joined the West to the East by the Suez Canal, and by the telegraph has put a girdle round the earth; the outcome of all this ambition, energy, and mental power,—which have produced triumphs of civilisation,—and of a money-seeking and money-getting which have multiplied manifold the wealth of the world, is a wail of distress from suffering myriads, that they cannot get work in a world in which labour was constituted the inheritance of man. Herod, clad in his royal robes, and vain and proud like the civilisation of the nineteenth century, was shortly eaten up by worms: is that civilisation, amid all its triumphs, rotten at the core?

The fabric of enormous wealth, which is chiefly owned by the creditor countries of England and Holland, is comprised mainly of debts which the indebted nations may soon be unable to pay; and its base rests upon millions of labouring poor among whom the agriculturists have no hope,—the artisans—many of them—are ceasing to have work; and the rest include numbers who maintain the prosperity of the finances through the excise revenue. If humility be the royal road to knowledge, perhaps these results of the civilisation of the nineteenth century only herald some greater achievements yet, of its intellectual pride.

Debtor and creditor nations alike shut their eyes to these evils. Already is Russia engaged in a war which must add many millions to her debt, other millions to her taxation, and almost unbearable burdens to those which now oppress her working classes; and already, leaders of English thought, fascinated with the grandeur of colossal fortunes, are looking forward to a fresh career of commercial progress, and of accumulations of still vaster fortunes, which are to be brought about by a reduction of wages.

That reduction is inevitable; but the fall may be broken and arrested. It will perhaps be found on reflection that a strong curb should be put on the too facile disposition to lend to foreigners, and that the destruction which swept over England in the commercial crisis of 1866, and over the Continent in the crisis of 1873, is distinctly attributable to the growth of joint-stock companies under the law of limited liability. The expansion of credit, through these companies, has worked mischief which is ascribed to an insufficient supply of gold. Without them the enormous loans which have been spent on bloated armaments, and in other unprofitable ways, could not have been obtained, and the heavy butcher's bill which has startled and horrified Europe in the present war in Eastern Europe might not have occurred.

XIX. One of the besetting difficulties of commerce is the over-production induced by excessive competition. The abolition of the law of limited liability for new banks and joint-stock companies, and the prohibition of payment by deposit banks of interest on floating accounts, would apply a check not more effectual than wholesome. Accompanied by facilities for investments in land, the yearly savings of the people, now sent abroad, to invigorate foreign competition, would be applied in the improvement of the land, to the doubling of its produce, the increase of agricultural labourers' wages, and such a growth of the home trade as would not only compensate for feeble progress of the foreign trade, but would restore its vitality; for the certainty of a home market for covering the expenses of a total manufacture is an effectual help in selling cheaply abroad.

XX. The vast amount of deposits, and not the moderate amount of gold in the country, constitutes the real danger to the metallic basis of the currency of the United Kingdom. With trade and finance constituted in the way just described, the danger would be mitigated.

Under the influence of the measures suggested, England would also gradually recede from the unsatisfactory position in which she now stands, in the double relation of banker and merchant, to the rest of the world. The relations are conflicting in cases where, as banker, England has lent money to foreign States for non-productive expenditure. In such cases, the interest paid to England as banker is so much subtracted from the amount of goods which would have been purchased from England as merchant. In other words, English producers now suffer, though English investors may grow rich. The foreign trade would not be so frequently convulsed, if the land laws be revised, and the law of limited liability be repealed, to the extent above indicated.

There are two schools of finance:—one would cut down expenditure, leaving the revenue to grow, and reducing debt, or repealing inexpedient taxes, as the revenue increased; the other would pursue what is termed an enlightened and liberal policy in expenditure, for the development of the country's resources, and would raise the income to the level of the enlarged expenditure by fresh taxation, if necessary. Manchester has supported the former school at home, the latter abroad. The first-mentioned school was encouraged by Manchester's policy of peace at any price to reduce expenditure until England lost her former preponderating influence of material and visible power in the councils of Europe. With that power unimpaired she could long since have prevented or reduced the bloated armaments that are crushing Europe with a grinding debt and taxation, from which England is now suffering in her trade and industry, and may yet suffer in her political position,—which God forbid. Through the diminished influence of England on the Continent, a policy of peace at any price has led to fearful wars, and created for England a grave political danger. Wherever the other school of finance, led away by the seductive applause of a liberal and enlightened policy of Government expenditure for developing a country's resources, has entered on a course of large borrowing, we find that public works extraordinary have produced financial disorder, as in Canada, Egypt, Australia. Both schools of finance might derive profitable lessons from this chapter on national indebtedness.

APPENDIX IV.

PRICES.

GOLD which has fallen in value cannot also have risen in value; but the latter having been affirmed in the United States, the facts relating to the depreciation of gold must be stated.

2. High prices, induced by an addition to the metallic currency, or by the greater rapidity of its circulation, denote a depreciation of the precious metals; but the same may not be affirmed of the inflated prices which prevail in periods of excitement and speculation.

3. A certain amount of credit, which we may call normal credit, rests upon gold or silver, namely, the credit of those who can discharge their obligations, as they fall due, in a form convertible into legal tender which rests upon gold or silver. Obligations secured by Government stock, or other substantial security which is readily convertible into an amount of legal tender equal to the value of the obligations, would also come within this category. Prices which result from the action of this credit may be regarded as metallic prices.

4. But in periods of speculation and excitement various forms of paper money are created, which further multiply credit. The purchases made from this credit are additional to those which were possible with only the normal amount of credit; and the demand created by the extra purchases causes additional production, with its attendant multiplication of credit. So long as the excitement and speculation continue, prices rise, or remain at an inflated level, stimulating production. When the collapse comes, the credit which had set the additional purchases and new industry in motion, collapses; prices, which had risen with the expansion of credit, fall with its contraction; and they fall the more surely from the over-production which continues after the crisis, through the difficulty of disengaging the fixed capital which had been sunk for increasing production during the period of excitement.

5. A similar enhancement of prices, not induced by an increased production of the precious metals, might be predicated from a long course of borrowing, by the nations of the world, on a scale which dwarfs the productions of the gold-fields in California and Australia—and which developed or created vast industries, but which yet involved, not so much a transfer of gold and silver, as a transfer of credit, from the lender to the borrower. And a similar decline of prices (as on the contraction of credit after a financial or a commercial crisis), might be expected from the sudden arrest of the borrowing, and of the demand upon the various industries for production, distribution, and supply, which the several thousand millions sterling of borrowing had employed for many years. More especially would this depression continue, from the diminished means of purchase of the nations, now burdened with heavy taxation on account of their indebtedness.

6. The value of the precious metals is measured by the prices of the articles which they buy; but the variations in these prices depend upon accidents which affect (1) the metals, or (2) the articles, or (3) the expansion or contraction of credit. Only where the variation arises from the first cause are we warranted in speaking of an appreciation or depreciation of the precious metals, at least so far as any safe practical inference can be drawn from the use of the terms.

The inflation of prices by excessive credit, and their undue depression by a rigid contraction of credit after a crisis, are well recognised. Thus—

a. Mr. Patterson, writing on the rate of interest during commercial and monetary crises,[1] observed—

'I have not at hand any commercial price list relating to the crisis of 1866; but during the shorter and less severe crisis of 1857 (when the Bank rate was raised from 5½ to 10 per cent. in a month), the fall of prices in the markets is shown in the following extract from the "Commercial Daily List" of November 1857, which gives the prices of the undermentioned articles *before* and *during* that crisis.

	Before	During		Before	During
	s. per cwt.	s. per cwt.		s. per cwt.	s. per cwt.
Tallow . .	60	50	Turmeric . .	60	30
Sugar . .	55	35	Shellac . .	120	80
Saltpetre . .	65	45	Jute . .	28	20
Linseed oil .	40	32	Hemp . .	36	30
Tin . . .	135	122			

[1] *Statistical Journal*, September 1871.

By the depreciation or appreciation of gold must be understood the change produced in its value by an increase or diminution of its yearly supply for the world. The violent change of prices in a mercantile crisis, as in the preceding table, is attributable not to any circumstances of the gold supply, but to the contraction of credit.

b. Professor Cairnes wrote in 1858—

'But what renders the present time peculiarly important as a point of comparison with former periods, is its being in immediate sequence to a severe commercial crisis. The effect of the crisis of last winter has been effectually to eliminate one great disturbing element from those causes to which a rise of price might be attributed, the element of credit. Trade is now suffering depression in almost all its branches, and prices, after a period of undue inflation, have, through an ordeal of bankruptcy, been brought to the test of real value. In the fluctuations of commerce we have reached the lowest point of the wave. Whatever, therefore, be the range of prices at the present time, we may at least be sure that no commercial convulsion is likely to lower it.'

c. In the same sense wrote Professor Jevons, in May 1869—

'The present year is especially suitable for a retrospective inquiry, because we have just passed through nearly three years of commercial prostration, during which the use of credit has been undoubtedly reduced to its minimum, and prices have suffered a corresponding depression. Taken in connection with the similar depression which followed the collapse of 1857, this gives ample means of judging whether a real rise of prices has been established, because it assures us that any rise of prices which may be detected is not due to a temporary cause, such as the inflation of prices by credit.'

7. Hence, in comparing prices at moderate intervals, the suitable periods for comparison are the first or second year after each crisis, such as the crisis of 1847, that of 1857, that of 1866, and the crisis of 1873 on the Continent and in America. The standard years for comparison would be 1849, 1858, 1867, and a period after 1873. In the commercial history and review of the 'Economist,' the average of the prices in the six years from 1845 to 1850 is taken as the standard, and the prices of subsequent years are estimated by the proportion which they bear to that standard. But in this way the subsequent increases of price, if regarded as measuring the depreciation of gold, are overstated in the table; because, as pointed out by Mr. Newmarch, or the writer of the earliest of the reviews, 1846–50

'Was a period of small demand, and great stagnation, in consequence of the pressure of the railway calls; it included the Irish famine, the commercial panic of 1847, the French revolution of February 1848, and the year of war which followed it all over Europe. Hence the prices of 1845–50, when reduced to an average, present a low datum line, and convey a false impression of the changes in subsequent years.'

8. Our immediate inquiry is, whether the depreciation of gold from the gold discoveries in California and Australia is still going on, or whether it has been arrested, and the current has turned, so that prices are now lower than those metallic prices which measured the fall in the value of gold before the inflation that culminated in the prices and the crisis of 1873. In any useful investigation of this point, the course of depreciation since 1848 cannot be disregarded; but it will save an elaborate array of statistics to state the conclusions formed respecting the greater part of the period by authorities of repute.

I. M. Lavasseur, quoted by Professor Cairnes. Summarising conclusions from the official statistics of French prices, including all commodities produced or consumed in France from 1847 to 1856, inclusive, M. Lavasseur observed :—

'But passing by these considerations, the important facts remain that French prices, comprehending those of all articles produced or consumed in France, have, after making liberal allowance for the effects of war, scarcity, and undue speculation, undergone since 1847 a marked rise, and that the rise has taken place (so far as the classification has been carried), in the manner according to which, supposing it to have proceeded from an increase of money, it might be expected to take place:'

Namely, to the greatest extent in natural products, and in a less degree in manufactured products.

II. Professor Cairnes, on a review of tables constructed by him, containing altogether about one hundred commodities, observed :—

'Out of the whole number of commodities, only six have fallen (1858) since the epoch of 1849–51; the remainder have all risen, and the greater number in a very marked manner. In this progress of prices, the advance has, on the whole, taken place in the order in which, as I have endeavoured to show, prices may be expected to advance under an increase of the precious metals. Thus, he will find Victorian prices to have advanced in the proportion of about 200 per cent., or rather more. He will find the movement in English and American prices, on the whole, greater than in the prices of Continental Europe; while these latter show a greater advance than prices in Asia. This local divergence of prices will be very remarkable if we take some leading commodities of British and American produce, and contrast them with some of the leading products of Asia. Thus, if we take provisions and butchers' meat, the metals, agricultural produce, raw cotton, and tobacco, and compare these with some principal Asiatic products, as cotton, silk, coffee, tea, sugar, rice, and spices, we shall find that while the prices of the former articles have risen from 15 to 45 per cent., as compared with their prices in 1849-51, the prices of the latter have in no case risen more than 15 per cent., and have in several cases probably fallen, in one important article, rice, by so much as 11 per cent. The only important Asiatic products in which a marked rise has taken place are saltpetre and indigo, and in both these cases the rise is owing to causes of an exceptional nature.... It will be seen, too, that on the whole, the other doctrines of the paper are pretty well borne out. Thus the advance in raw materials is much greater than in manufactured articles, while amongst raw materials the advance is more marked in animal than in vegetable products; such articles, e.g., as leather, tallow, provisions, and butchers' meat showing a very remarkable rise.

'In the fluctuations of commerce we have reached (1858) the lowest point of the wave; whatever, therefore, be the range of prices at the present time. we may at least be sure that no commercial convulsion is likely to lower it. We have further to remember that in an age like the present, in which science and its applications to the arts are, in all civilised countries, making rapid strides, there exists, in most articles of general consumption (but more particularly in the finished manufactures) a constant tendency to a decline of price, through the employment of more efficient machinery and improved processes of production. Now, taking all these circumstances together, the propitiousness of the seasons, the action of free trade, the absence of war the contraction of credit, and the general tendency to a reduction of cost proceeding from the progress of knowledge, it appears to me that, were there no other cause in operation, we should have reason to look for a very considerable fall of prices at the present time (1858), as compared with (say) eight or ten years ago. Prices however, as the following table will show, have not fallen; they have, on the contrary, very decidedly risen; and the advance has moreover, as the same tables will also show, on the whole proceeded in conformity with the principles which I have in this paper endeavoured to establish. And this is my ground for asserting that the depreciation of our standard money is already, under the action of the new gold, an accomplished fact.'

III. Professor Jevons, taking 1849 as his datum point, and the prices of about forty of the chief commodities from 1789, and of about fifty from 1847, arrived at the following results:—

Average Ratios of the Price of about 40 or 50 of the chief articles of commerce during the past eighty years, i.e. the average ratio of prices to the prices of the year 1849:—

	Ratio		Ratio		Ratio		Ratio		Ratio
1789	133	1847	122	1853	116	1859	120	1865	121
1799	202	1848	106	1854	130	1860	124	1866	128
1809	245	1849	100	1855	125	1861	123	1867	118
1819	175	1850	101	1856	129	1862	124	1868	120
1829	124	1851	103	1857	132	1863	123	1869	119
1839	144	1852	101	1858	118	1864	122		

a. 'Between 1809 and 1849, prices fell in the ratio of 100 to 41, partly from the improvement, extension, and cheapening of production at an accelerated pace, and partly from the production of gold, from 1810 to 1830, having been one-half the previous amount.

b. 'When prices were highest here (Europe), between 1810 and 1815, the prices of eastern produce were not higher than they had been, and consequently, in comparison with the prices of other articles, had fallen.

c. 'The years 1836-39 form a temporary but remarkable exception to the fall of prices from 1810 to 1849. In 1849-52 prices were unprecedentedly low, and, other things being equal, we might have expected that, after another period of speculation, and its corresponding relapse of trade, prices should descend still lower. But prices in 1858 were still 18 per cent. above those of 1852.

d. 'The range of prices since 1853, has always been considerably above the point they attained in 1849. The three great collapses of credit and enterprise occurred in the years 1847, 1857, and 1866; and the depressions of prices thereby occasioned were respectively 22, 14 and 10 per cent. It is perfectly fair, therefore, to compare together the three lowest points thus attained in the years 1849, 1858, and 1867, and we thus learn that there has been a *net* or permanent rise of 18 per cent. accomplished in the prices of about fifty of the chief materials and commodities. The still greater elevation of 32 per cent. in 1857 and of 28 per cent. in 1866 are partly due to the inflated credit and excessive speculation of those periods.

e. 'I cannot help, then, reasserting with the utmost confidence that a real rise of prices to the extent of 18 per cent., as measured by fifty chief commodities, has (May 1869) been established since the year 1849. This is an undoubted depreciation of gold, and one which covers a real depreciation of more than 18 per cent.; for the gold discoveries reversed a decidedly downward course of prices, so that the new gold has both promoted a further fall, and occasioned a rise in its stead.'

IV. Von Dr. E. Lespeyres: Professor T. E. Cliffe Leslie, in the 'Fortnightly Review' for November 1872, wrote—'An eminent German statician has recently published an elaborate analysis of the prices of 312 commodities from 1846 to 1865, in the market of Hamburg. Among the results is a classification of the 312 commodities in eleven groups, with the comparative prices of successive quinquennial periods, indicated in the following table, in which the prices of the first period, 1846-50, are represented by 100.

	No. of Commodities	Each period of five years				Fifteen Years 1851–65
		1846–50	1851–5	1855–60	1861–5	
I. Products of South European plants (wines, fruit, &c.)	28	100	121	143	136	133·7
II. Agricultural products, Continental Europe (corn, beans, peas, &c.) . .	41	100	122	133	128	127·8
III. Hunting and fishing products	10	100	116	135	131	127·8
IV. Products of sylviculture	17	100	109	113	160	127·2
V. Products of European cattle-rearing	29	100	113	137	125	124 1
VI. Edible colonial products	44	100	110	125	129	121·8
VII. Non-edible colonial products	44	100	105	115	123	114
VIII. Fibrous manufactures	12	100	102	107	127	112·2
IX. Chemical manufactures	40	100	111	117	102	109·9
X. Mineral and metal manufactures	22	100	107	111	101	106·4
XI. Products of mining and smelting (coal, iron, &c.).	24	100	107	108	97	104·1
	312	100	111·2	122·1	123·3	118·98

The first seven groups consist of animal and vegetable products, or raw materials; and in them the rise of price has been much greater than in the remaining three groups, which consist of manufactures; thus confirming the conclusions of Professor Cairnes in 1858. The exceptional rise in fibrous manufactures in 1861–5 was from the cotton famine.

V. 'It is computed that the purchasing power of gold has lessened only 25 per cent. instead of 50 from its increased production.'—*Westminster Review*, January 1876.

9. The 'Commercial History and Review' of the 'Economist' gives a table of prices of raw materials, and of some articles of food and drink. Free trade, the repeal of the navigation laws, and a vast increase of tonnage have countervailed the tendency of the increased production of gold and silver to raise the prices of these commodities in particular. The growth of indebtedness of the agricultural countries from which these products come has also, since the great diminution of foreign loans, tended to lower the price of raw materials. The depreciation of gold, as evidenced by the actual figures of the 'Economist,' is to be estimated, therefore, not by those figures, but by a mental

addition thereto, on account of the further reduction below actual prices, which the increased supplies of the precious metals have prevented.

10. The proportions which the prices of subsequent years bear to the average prices of 1845 to 1850 are thus stated by the 'Economist:'

PRICES IN ENGLAND ON 1ST OF JANUARY OF EACH YEAR.

(*Prices in Proportion to the Average Prices in* 1845–50, *taking* 100 *as representing that Average.*)

	1859	1867	1868	1869	1870	1871	1873	1876	1877
I.									
Iron	100	**88**	**86**	**85**	88	87	**141**	125	104
Lead	125	**114**	**111**	**109**	109	103	**124***	131	126
Timber	91	**95**	**94**	**97**	99	115	**127***	128	128
Indigo	117	**145**	**154**	**143**	151	137	**169***	130	173
Leather	116	**128**	**136**	**136**	128	128	**144***	147	144
Sheep's wool	131	**144**	**115**	**104**	96	88	**157**	133	141
Tallow	116	**106**	**98**	**111**	105	102	**98***	120	102
A. Butchers' meat	114	**121**	**112**	**117**	123	133	**144**	153	138
A. Tobacco	166	**200**	**200**	**167**	167	155	**195***	256	211
A. Coffee	129	**149**	**141**	**127**	134	125	**171***	183	178
A. Tea	119	**108**	**104**	**105**	102	100	**100***	100	100
A. Wheat	75	**113**	**127**	**96**	80	100	**104**	84	97
II.									
Sugar (A)	80	**66**	**73**	**72**	83	83	**74**	67	88
Oils	118	**140**	**138**	**127**	126	114	**118**	116	114
Silk, raw	124	**183**	**161**	**183**	174	183	**169**	87	187
Flax and hemp	113	**116**	**121**	**124**	116	116	**118**	105	99
Tin	145	**99**	**112**	**129**	138	160	**171**	99	95
Copper	121	**98**	**96**	**89**	83	81	**105**	100	93
III.									
Cotton	95	**227**	**100**	**155**	173	118	**132**	107	94
Cotton wool, Pernambuco only	97	**191**	**181**	**139**	144	106	**126**	106	82
Cotton yarn	124	**215**	**118**	**149**	154	138	**154**	123	108
" cloth	112	**178**	**114**	**131**	135	118	**126**	111	113
IV.									
Silver	103 9	**102·09**	**101·26**	**101·68**	101·46	101·46	**99·48**	94·13	—

11. The following remarks are suggested by this table:—

I. The prices of articles in the first group, excepting tea, were greater in 1876 and 1877 than in 1859; those in the second group, excepting sugar, were dearer in 1859, from special circumstances to be presently mentioned. The position of cotton is exceptional. On the whole, the table indicates a depreciation of gold in 1876 and 1877, compared with 1859; when, as ascertained by Professor Cairnes,

M. Lavasseur, Professor Jevons, and Von Dr. E. Lespeyres, a considerable depreciation had already taken place.

II. There has been a gradation in the rise of prices of articles in the first group, excepting iron, lead, and tea; prices having been higher in 1867, after the crisis of 1866, than in 1859; and higher in 1876 and 1877, after the American and European crises of 1873, than in 1867. The articles forming exceptions, in the comparison of 1867 with 1859, are—

a. Iron. Low in 1867, from over-production in years before 1866; but after a depression for two years more, or in 1870 and 1871, prices rose inordinately, from the undue extension of foreign railways, to 41 per cent. above the rate in 1859, till the rate gradually fell, after the crisis in 1873, to 25 per cent. in 1876, and 4 per cent. on January 1, 1877, below 1859, over-production having continued, from its own momentum, independently of the reduced demand, owing to the difficulty of closing works which had been established for the excessive demand before 1873.

b. Lead. A slight depression, which was soon followed by an increase, until the price on January 1, 1876, exceeded, and that on January 1, 1877, was about the same as that in 1859.

c. Tea. The reduction of the tea duties has admitted of the importation of inferior kinds, which have been brought within reach of vast additional numbers; and the augmented importations, with an increasing admixture of Indian with Chinese teas, have combined in cheapening the article.

III. The exceptions in the second group to the rise in prices since 1859 are—

a. Sugar; as with tea, the reduction of the sugar duties, and the consequently increased importation of the lower class sugars, including beet-root sugar, explain the diminished price, in the same way as a deficient manufacture of beet-root sugar explains the enhancement of previous prices in 1876.

b. Oils. Decline, from the immense importations of petroleum oil, which have reduced not only its own price, but the prices of other oils, one or other of which it has partially displaced, the displacement causing, among the rest, a competition which has lowered prices. The importations of linseed oil have also been large, whilst the Continental demand must, to a great extent, be now supplied direct.

c. Silk, Raw. The revival of the growth of silk in Europe, particularly of the cheap Italian sorts, has increased the consumption of cheap silks, and has lowered the price of other silk by reducing the demand for it. The competition of foreign manufactured silks in the English markets has also reduced the price of raw silk in the United Kingdom. The failure of the European crop in 1876 caused the great enhancement of price in that year.

d. Flax, Hemp, and Jute. With the revival of the cotton industry, cotton has recovered its position in some of the fabrics in which it had been displaced by flax, jute, &c., during the cotton famine. The Continental demand has also fallen off. On the other hand, the importations have greatly increased.

(*In millions of cwts.*)

	1861	1865	1869	1870	1872	1873	1874	1875	1876
Flax and hemp . . .	2·1	3·	2 6	3·5	3·2	3·5	3·7	3·1	2 6
Jute	·9	2·1	2·5	2·4	4·0	4·0	4·2	3·4	3·8
	3·	5·1	5·1	5·9	7·2	7·5	7·9	6·5	6·4

The total importations in 1871 were 6·3 millions. The abundant supplies since, and the inferior quality of much of the additions, together with the lessened demand from some quarters, as above-mentioned, have reduced prices. The fall in the price of silver also enables exporters from India to sell at a lower gold price in England.

e. Tin. There was a steady rise of prices from January 1, 1867, to January 1, 1873, which shows that the price was affected by the demand. After the panic in the United States, the demand fell off, and prices declined.

f. Copper. A largely-increased importation; the competition of new countries, including Chili and Japan, and the displacement of sailing vessels by steamers, account for the reduced price, as compared with 1859; the price, however, was higher in 1876, and on January 1, 1877, than in 1871.

12. On the whole, where there has been an exceptional increase of production, as of articles in the second group, much exceeding the rate of increase of production of the precious metals, with latterly a lessened demand for the articles, prices have fallen below those of 1859. But in other respects, so far as inferences either way can be drawn from the table, the conclusion seems warranted, that, on the whole, gold was of less value in 1867, after the crisis of 1866, than in 1859,

and was of still less value in January 1877, after three years of depressed trade since the inflation of 1873, than in 1867.

13. It appears also that out of twelve articles in the first group, the prices of eight, on January 1, 1877, were higher than, or as high as on January 1, 1873, notwithstanding the known inflation of prices in 1872 and 1873 from an inflation of credit; thus showing that various circumstances of demand and supply must be considered, before any confident opinion can be formed, from only three or four years' prices, of a rise in the value of gold.

14. Such hesitation would be only prudent when it is considered that nothing occurred from 1872 to 1875, to depreciate gold in 1872 and 1873, when prices were inflated, or to raise its value in 1874 to 1876, when prices fell; the facts, indeed, were all the other way. In 1872 there was a net export of gold from the United Kingdom of 1¼ million, and in 1873 a net import of only 1½ million, and yet prices were excessively high. In 1874 the net importations of gold amounted to 7½ millions, in 1875 to 4¼ millions, in 1876 to nearly 7 millions, and yet prices receded from those of 1873. Throughout this period, the currencies of Germany and France were full to repletion; the inconvertible note paper in the latter was at par, that is, it was as good as gold; and the metallic circulation in the former was excessive; for, with the whole thaler currency raised to gold value, and with the new gold currency circulating in addition, there was a manifest excess of specie. In England, as above shown, there was no depletion of currency. These facts discountenance the theory that gold rose in value from 1873 to 1876.

15. Of late the 'Economist' has selected certain articles for showing the course of prices. Taking the prices of March 1873 as 100, the proportion of the subsequent prices of these articles, to the prices in that month, are as shown in the table on page 324.

16. The following remarks are suggested by this table:—

1. Seven of the eight articles in the first group were dearer in July 1877 than in March 1873, and the eighth was no cheaper than in 1873, thus testifying on the whole to a fall in the value of gold; but on January 1, 1877, three of the articles testified to a rise and five others to a fall in the value of gold. In earlier years their evidence was just the reverse; those articles which on January 1, 1877, indicated respectively a rise or fall, having in the earlier years indicated conversely a fall or a rise in the value of gold. The evidence may be put aside; the fluctuations in the prices of the articles

being too great to be attributable to any circumstances affecting the supply of gold.

II. Of the eight articles in the second group, the prices of five were, in July 1877, 32 to 54 per cent. below, and those of the other three were 23 or 24 per cent. below, the prices in March 1873; that is to say, adopting the inflated prices of 1873 as a standard, gold has risen in value since that year more than it had depreciated since the gold discoveries.

	Actual Price				Ratio of Price to that in March 1873						
	1871	1872	March 1873	July 1877	March 1878	July 1878	June 1874	June 1875	June 1876	Jan. 1877	July 1877
I.	d.	d.	d.	d.							
Beef, inferior . .	52	48	54	40	100	125	97·5	127·5	110	105	100
Sugar, foreign,	s.	s.	s.	s.							
Muscovado . .	—	—	—	—	100	87·2	82·1	88 3	73·1	101·3	101·3
Coffee . . .	50	67	85	87	100	94·2	108·1	104·	98·1	101·7	100·57
Wheat, gazette average . .	52 7/13	55¼	56⅛	64½	100	108·7	109·8	77·7	87·5	94·6	116·74
Wheat, American, Red Spring . .	—	—	—	—	—	100	98·7	80·1	83·4	98·0	110·59
Flour, town made .	—	—	—	—	100	110·6	107·4	76·6	81·9	95·7	110·64
„ New York .	—	—	—	—	—	100	100	84·8	80·0	98·4	104
	d.	d.	d.	d.							
Beef, prime, small .	56	54	58	66	100	109·5	101·6	106·4	100	95·2	105
II.	s.	s.	s.	s.							
Iron, Scotch, pig .	58½	101½	117¼	54¾	100	91·8	81·5	51·3	48·6	47·7	46·23
Coals, Hetton Wallsend . .	19	23¼	40	19	100	86·6	74·6	67·2	62·7	52·7	57·91
	£	£	£	£							
Tin, Straits . .	137	—	147	66	100	89 3	69·4	57·0	50·9	51·5	45·7
Copper, Chili bars .	85	85½	91	69	100	90·5	88·5	91·6	84 9	82·7	77·09
Cotton, middling	d.	d.	d.	d.							
upland . . .	8 5/16	11 3/16	9¼	6 5/16	100	94·6	89 2	80·4	66·9	73·7	68
Pepper . . .	—	6¼	7⅓	4⅞	100	98·9	88·6	85·2	66·5	69·0	66·48
Cotton, No. 40 mule twist . . .	13½	15⅜	14	10	100	90·5	88·5	91·6	84·9	82·7	77·09
Wool, Southdown,	s.	s.	s.	s.							
Hogs . . .	18	21¼	22½	15⅝	100	97·6	76·8	82·9	70·7	82·9	75 61
III.											
Sugar, Mauritius .	30½	31½	29	31½	100	87·9	75·3	71·9	69·1	88 6	87·91
Saltpetre . .	—	30	28	27	100	–	70·3	85·6	79·3	89·2	97·29

III. In the III. group, as in the other two, the circumstances of demand and supply of the articles, and not any deficiency of gold supply, explain the decrease of price below the inflated prices of 1871 to 1873.

IV. In reality the table only confirms the testimony to the depreciation of gold which is afforded by the table in paragraph 10. Down to 1873, the immense borrowings by foreign States, and subscriptions of capital for railway and joint-stock companies abroad, kept up prices, 1st, by sparing the borrowing countries, so long as the loans continued, an export of goods in payment of interest on debt; 2nd, by creating an exceptional demand for exports from the lending countries. With the collapse of credit of most foreign States in 1873, and with the discredit which then overtook railway and other joint-stock enterprise, the circumstances which had restrained exports by the borrowing countries ceased, and those exports multiplied, while the special demand for the goods of the creditor countries, which had been intense down to 1873, collapsed with a suddenness which prevented an immediate decrease of production. The straitened income of the heavily taxed debtor countries also reduced their ordinary purchases. Prices, therefore, should have fallen, not from any scarcity of gold, but from a contraction of demand and of credit; and if, 1st, they have not fallen for a number of articles, or 2nd, with a decrease in production are gradually rising in price, or 3rd, have fallen below the price in 1873 incommensurately with the great contraction of credit since that year; insomuch that, still, they are higher than the prices in 1867 and 1868, the conclusion which the table in paragraph 10 supports, of a continued depreciation of gold since 1859, seems to be confirmed.

17. The course of prices in India is traceable through the prices current of Chambers of Commerce, as regards articles of the seaborne foreign trade of India, and through returns in the local government gazettes, of the prices of food grains in India. These latter are not quite reliable, nor can they be effectively used in the absence of any record, in an accessible form, of the character of the seasons, from year to year, in the several provinces of British India.

18. The rupee quotations for exports in the prices current of the Chambers of Commerce are read at a disadvantage, without their conversion into sterling at the current rates of exchange, at least for the period of low exchange, since the depreciation of silver; and they must be read with the further caution that, down to 1868 or 1869, there was a special external demand, stimulated by a brisk foreign competition; whereas, of late years, the prices of Indian productions have been determined by the greater urgency now laid upon India, through a sluggish foreign demand, of competing in European markets, with other countries, for the sale of her products. Hence, in this later period, the prices in India of her exports were dominated by prices in the London markets, in such manner that the rise or fall in them, if evidencing the action of any of the precious metals, would show a rise or fall in the value of gold in Europe, but would not be satisfactory evidence of any appreciation or depreciation of silver in

India, where the articles concerned are produced principally for export.

19. Taking 100 for the prices of January 1850, the proportions of prices in other years to those of 1850 have been as follows :—

PRICES IN CALCUTTA.

	Imports			Exports							Gold
	Copper, Brazier's	Iron	Spelter	Hides, Buffalo	Indigo, good	Jute, Serajgunge	Sugar, Benares	Silk, Raw, Cossimbazar	Linseed	Rice, Ballam	
Jan. 1844	102	87	198	124	96	98	142	121	65	126	100
" 1847	108	125	126	112	109	100	122	99	71	137	98·9
" 1848	113	130	146	98	96	108	108	98	67	100	100·8
" 1850	100	100	100	100	100	100	100	100	100	100	100
" 1851	93	85	90	102	131	105	104	137	73	121	96·9
" 1852	87	72	76	97	84	87	90	116	49	142	98·3
" 1853	116	115	111	100	140	111	96	140	90	129	97·3
" 1854	129	150	157	104	140[1]	140	101	163	93	147	96·7
" 1856	149	185	174	159	149	116	107	140	159	142	97·5
" 1858	144	155	178	207[1]	—	124	162	—	114	168	97·1
" 1860	129	130	137	268	190	147	124	236	114	221	95·8
" 1862	114	115	111	207	236	129	128	—	120	147	95·9
" 1864	115	112	103	220	168	222	122	187	127	153	97·4
" 1865	104	102	96	182[1]	192	169	128	210	131	221	96·9
" 1867	109	145	205	183	190	173	145	286	155	263	98·5
" 1868	95	130	161	198	208	149	139	247	147	168	98·5
" 1869	99	102	135	244	228	160	128	304	159	221	98·5
" 1870	89	112	109	244	254	180	145	292	155	168	98·3
" 1871	85	112	97	244	236	227	136	286	149	184	98·5
" 1872	93	126	94	237	266	213	130	239	147	189	97·7
" 1873	105	147	96	203	202	142	—	247	157	184	99·6
" 1874	116	210	106	280	240	249	180	245	167	279	100·8
" 1875	119	167	118	244	228	204	122	169	158	247	103·1
" 1876	113	137	144	220	192	200	122	140	131	211	108·9
July 1876	115	132	147	190	N.	191	116	222	133	210	127·1

The following remarks are suggested by the table :—

I. For IMPORTS, silver was depreciated to its lowest, or by 40 to 50 per cent., in 1856 to 1858, the increased importations of the precious metals to double or treble the amount down to 1854–5, having begun in 1855–6.

II. For EXPORTS, prices rose markedly after 1852, and (after fluctuations at high rates) reached the maximum, for one or other of the articles, in 1867 to 1870. The continuous net imports of gold and silver, in amounts ranging from 9½ to 24 millions sterling, and

[1] July.

aggregating 223 millions from 1855-6 to 1869-70, with a yearly average of nearly 15 millions sterling, ended in 1869-70 with a net importation in that year of nearly 13 millions sterling. Measured against prices in 1850, the depreciation of silver was from 50 to 200 per cent. on the several articles, the average being about 100 per cent.

III. On the whole, except for jute, prices have receded below the maximum that was attained in or before 1870—but they still remained in July 1876 at a point which showed a depreciation of silver in India, much greater than the depreciation of gold in Europe. The depreciation of silver in India was both quicker and greater than that of gold, because an amount of silver equal to the whole of the new production of gold since 1848 was exported to the East.

IV. It is not surprising that the increase of exports from India, on account of the reduction of borrowing in England, should correct some of the abnormal depreciation of silver just mentioned; the fact is quite compatible with the recent depreciation of silver in Europe, relatively to gold.

V. Indeed, it is noteworthy that when silver was depreciating in India, its gold price was highest in Europe; and since it has been appreciating in India, its gold price in Europe has declined. The high price of Indian commodities in Europe coincided with the high price of silver in Europe.

VI. But if the price of silver in Europe is in accord with the price of Indian commodities in Europe, then (more especially since the cessation of silver coinage in Europe) silver is degraded there to a mere commodity or article of merchandise in the commerce of the East with the West; that is, to a position in which it has ceased to be a standard of value.

VII. Hence, if it were indeed the case that the decline of prices of commodities in Europe since 1873, and of the price of silver with those commodities, denotes a rise in the value of gold, it shows that silver has become degraded to the same level with commodities, and that accordingly gold is now the sole standard of value.

VIII. It follows also, from the sympathy of the European price of silver with the gold price of Indian commodities in Europe, that the hope of silver regaining its former value through an increase of Indian exports is delusive. The nations have not now—as in the years from 1858 to 1870—to solicit India for her exports. Under an imperious necessity India has to send forward her exports in payment of interest on her yearly increasing debt, or of a tribute to the amount of 15 millions sterling a year; and she must offer them at a lower gold price abroad, to which the sympathetic European price of silver will respond.

Owing to the lack in India of cheap transport over great distances, a favourable season or two may cheapen food grain in some districts so as to reduce the price greatly below the general average. Allowing for this circumstance, the prices of food grains in India seem to confirm the evidence of the prices of articles which are exchanged in the foreign trade. These prices are shown in the following tables :—

Prices of Food Grains in India.

(*Seers per Rupee* (1 *seer* = 2,057 *lbs.*)

BENGAL.										
	RICE									
	Midnapore	Calcutta	Backergunge	Dacca	Chittagong	Dinagepore	Monghyr	Moorshedabad	Cuttack	Budwan
1861	31·96	19·55	24·28	37·50	28 69	32·35	23·73	22 86	38·45	20·53
1862	31·72	19·55	24·26	32 91	19·12	32·55	31·38	18·19	27·40	24·26
1863	32·19	19 32	22·86	27·30	19·12	29·49	26·53	17·08	26·56	29 86
1864	31·49	15·13	22·86	23·22	25·66	27·55	18 62	16·33	31·15	28·00
1865	22·63	12·57	21·46	17·86	18·66	15·20	17·35	14 23	22·50	26·12
1866	9·56	11·40	10·73	11·22	26·36	24·69	21·43	11·43	8 34	9·79
1867	20·06	16·76	15·97	23·22	20·06	33 27	29·08	22·39	15·46	18·66
1868	23·56	14·89	19·36	26·02	22·16	26·94	19·13	21·46	27·88	28·00
1869	20·53	15·13	18·77	19·64	19·13	26·63	22·96	18·66	22·98	25·66
1870	23·33	15·83	22·27	22·96	20·06	26·39	25·26	21·93	30·00	25 19
1871	24·66	20·00	20·87	25·08	23·28	33·90	24·04	23·14	26·98	25·74
1872	23·29	17·80	25·69	30·18	23·65	28·65	18·30	20·47	28·79	21·59
1873	22·72	11·82	24·37	25·38	21·53	22·33	15·39	17·13	28·55	18·97
1874	16·90	11 36	14·97	14·04	12·54	15·01	12·40	12·39	26·27	13·50
1875	17·68	14·25	19·60	20·00	19·33	26·00	17·50	19·08	24·70	19·26
1876	23·53	12·28	18·88	19·44	13·74	21·80	16·96	18·69	24·16	22·24

	WHEAT					JOWAR				
	OUDH			BENGAL		OUDH			BENGAL	
	Lucknow	Fyzabad	Sultanpore	Patna	Mozufferpore	Lucknow	Fyzabad	Sultanpore	Patna	Mozufferpore
1861	20·50	25·00	28·50	23·24	25·51	25·00	32·00	32·00	44·33	15·73
1862	28·75	28·50	28·50	16·21	27·55	34·50	35·75	32·00	44·33	15·30
1863	25·66	27·00	27·00	32·77	25·51	31·00	38·50	33·75	58·86	17·35
1864	18·00	22·00	26·75	16·21	22·45	17·75	26·50	30·00	58·06	15·75
1865	14·50	16·50	16·00	16·89	12·25	19·00	20·25	20·25	26·42	14·28
1866	13·25	13·75	18·00	10·54	10·20	15·25	18·50	30·50	18·37	13·26
1867	18·25	23·50	19·00	15·19	19·29	25·50	33·25	30·50	33·79	18·37
1868	20·00	17·50	20·00	30·61	19·39	29·25	33·25	20·25	37·98	17·35
1869	11·25	13·75	12·75	18·04	14·28	14·00	20·00	16·00	12·61	15·73
1870	15·00	19·00	13·75	12·02	15·73	19·50	24·50	18·50	28·59	15·30
1871	22·81	24 56	23·25	23·94	19·90	28·44	35·78	21·00	33·40	—
1872	15·78	15·30	13·57	18 57	14·80	18·56	25·38	20·62	34·09	—
1873	14·51	14·31	14·15	15·20	11·66	16·64	23·04	19·54	28·32	—
1874	17·34	16·13	17·26	16·88	12·39	20·58	21·02	20·52	20·84	—
1875	24·68	24·43	24·75	23·48	18·34	32·50	34·34	30·00	20·20	—
1876	37·81	25·95	27·90	25·39	19·74	41·53	43·01	40·00	30·00	—

PRICES OF FOOD GRAINS IN INDIA—(continued).

N.W. PROVINCES.

	WHEAT					BAJRA				
	Saharunpur	Bareilly	Agra	Cawnpore	Mirzapore	Saharunpur	Bareilly	Agra	Cawnpore	Mirzapore
1861	9·50	15·00	14·25	17·25	25·00	16·00	20·50	20·00	21 50	31·00
1862	35·00	34·50	26·00	27·50	24·00	38·25	9·75	31·75	35·25	30·00
1863	30·00	28·00	25·25	28·50	24·00	35·00	52·00	27·25	36·00	30·00
1864	24·50	20·00	18·00	19·75	17·00	25.50	15·00	20·00	19·25	22·00
1865	20·50	15·50	15·75	16·75	15·00	24·00	18·25	19·00	20·00	17·00
1866	20·50	14·00	15·50	14·00	13·00	20·00	30·00	25·75	20·50	16·00
1867	22·25	18·00	18·00	16·75	18·75	22·00	20·00	25·00	23·00	26·00
1868	15·00	16·00	18·00	20·00	17·00	14·50	18·75	23·00	23·25	19·75
1869	11·00	9·50	11·25	11·50	11·50	10·50	10·50	15·25	14·25	14·75
1870	17·00	16·00	16·00	15·50	14·75	26·50	20·75	25·25	23·50	20·00
1871	25·56	25·93	22·56	24·11	19·18	30·88	27·01	22·04	25·39	20·82
1872	22·82	19·81	19·02	18·00	15·00	20·91	18·31	16·73	21·52	18·50
1873	18 61	15·99	15·32	15·69	12·98	22·62	18·58	17·49	19·98	15·54
1874	21·29	17·03	16·42	17·35	14·75	20·32	17·19	17·50	21·72	18·79
1875	23 01	21·45	20·55	23 28	19·55	26·89	23·35	25·20	27·09	25·25
1876	24·93	25·06	24·95	25·10	22·17	24·21	31·25	29·89	36·11	29·00

PUNJAB.

	WHEAT					JOWAR				
	Delhi	Amritsur	Rawalpindi	Mooltan	Peshawar	Delhi	Amritsur	Rawalpindi	Mooltan	Peshawar
1861	15·86	17·08	29·04	15·62	22·86	20·58	17·55	27·89	16·32	40·12
1862	29·04	28·45	26·59	20·85	25·89	33·47	35·22	30·55	28·10	47·58
1863	25·60	31·20	29·74	20·81	30·79	29·16	37·32	37·84	31·62	48·87
1864	20·47	26·01	25·42	13·70	24·90	24·61	31·87	37·44	17·84	42·57
1865	17·08	17·78	23·38	13·77	21·92	25·60	26·12	38·87	16·32	33·70
1866	18·48	22·05	22·86	15·86	22·80	25·42	24·87	28·96	18·25	32·07
1867	24·55	19·65	19·36	13·23	16·21	27·40	25·36	33·59	20·06	23·15
1868	25·83	11·19	12·65	18·41	15·51	18·25	12·59	15 04	14·92	20·35
1869	10·55	9·44	13·29	9·68	15 62	14·25	15·04	14·17	13·64	24·31
1870	15·97	16·38	15·09	12·30	14·98	14·11	20·29	25·31	17·72	22·97
1871	23·41	—	17·92	16·49	13·34	31·13	—	31·32	26·75	18·91
1872	20 93	20·87	17·55	18·42	15·31	21·78	19·93	23·26	21·62	19·50
1873	18 76	24·26	17·46	19·46	18·29	25·11	31·97	24·13	24·65	25·68
1874	20·14	24·63	23·56	17·62	21·07	24·94	30·56	26·18	24 23	27·20
1875	22·01	24·39	28·91	19·31	23·59	26·00	30·72	30·82	27·00	29·75
1876	25·71	24·24	32·48	19·76	24·76	32·08	32·26	42·00	25·00	28·28

PRICES OF FOOD GRAINS IN INDIA—(continued).

MADRAS.

	JOWAR					RAGI				
	Ganjam	Bellary	Tanjore	Tinne-velly	Salem	Ganjam	Bellary	Tanjore	Tinne-velly	Salem
1861	32 80	24 70	25 80	20·90	20·70	36·30	27·00	28 50	22·90	21 40
1862	31·60	25·30	25 60	20·60	20·70	35·00	28 70	27·00	21·50	21 70
1863	25 80	20 50	26 60	10·60	22·80	32·60	23 30	30·20	19·80	24·90
1864	32 60	12·00	25 80	16·90	26 60	39 90	14 30	28·70	19 60	28 90
1865	23 00	12 40	18 60	12 60	20 80	29·30	15·10	23 60	13 80	24 40
1866	11·90	10 80	17·00	12 20	16 10	14·40	12 20	20 80	13·50	17 70
1867	14 40	9·20	12 80	20 00	11 50	16 00	10 20	15 20	14 00	12·30
1868	33 40	19·50	18·10	17·20	16·30	38 80	20 70	20·90	20 60	16·80
1869	24·40	28·30	20 00	18 20	18·60	26·10	32 80	24·90	20·60	20·10
1870	22 80	27·30	24·40	20·30	22 30	30 20	32·10	20 00	21·60	25 20
1871	33 61	34·70	34 34	29·38	44·23	38 89	42 40	44 85	30·94	52 67
1872	23·21	30·12	28·90	25·73	42·94	30 66	37·49	37 63	28 33	48·84
1873	34 85	23·22	26·95	—	21 64	36·95	32 60	28 53	20·73	28·16
1874	29 80	28·29	24 32	—	22 29	37·12	34·46	25·12	16·59	26 47
1875	23·90	22·88	28 38	—	24·66	41·05	27 88	29·99	21·11	27 32
1876	27·10	17·63	23·75	—	18 02	37 86	17·71	23·81	20·08	19·13

BOMBAY.

	WHEAT					BAJRA				
	Surat	Khan-desh (Dhulia)	Ahmed-nagar	Karachi	Shikar-pur	Surat	Khan-desh (Dhulia)	Ahmed-nagar	Karachi	Shikar-pur
1861	13·60	19·00	18·50	19·68	19·11	15·26	25·00	30·50	25·43	28·31
1862	12·30	18·00	15·50	15·24	21·16	16·99	19·50	19·75	23·68	26 47
1863	12·67	15·00	13·00	15·00	17·90	16·17	16·00	14·75	21·25	21·66
1864	7·17	8·50	10·00	10·25	11·31	6·80	11·50	15·00	10·06	13·97
1865	6·80	5 50	10·50	11·56	14·32	8·45	9·00	26·50	9·81	19 60
1866	5·62	7·00	10 30	11·75	16·06	18·50	13·00	24·00	14·37	20·62
1867	9·67	7·75	11·75	13·33	18·42	12·21	10·00	17·25	17·50	29·86
1868	8·00	8·25	14·50	13·87	19·06	12·21	11·75	26·00	17·37	25·92
1869	8·45	7·25	10·00	13·62	12·85	11·21	7·50	16·25	14·68	17·37
1870	6·80	9·25	8·75	10·28	9·66	8·99	16·50	20·25	12·06	14·20
1871	9·93	15·16	14·30	11·67	12·80	11·72	18·72	15·92	15·27	23·19
1872	8·98	12·07	12·37	13·27	16 92	13·21	13·63	14·26	16·66	28·97
1873	11·80	13·46	16·90	12·66	15·44	15·49	20·66	24·09	18 88	29·75
1874	13·57	19·76	23·26	13·17	16·05	18·28	24·61	32·58	19·53	28·15
1875	13·07	17·31	17·46	13·71	17·63	16·33	24·25	29·14	18·96	24·55
1876	12·46	16·23	16·95	13·06	18·14	14·20	19·68	18·71	16·17	27·27

These tables do not begin early enough; much of the depreciation of silver occurred before 1861, there having been a considerable rise in prices from 1850 to 1860. Only the further depreciation since 1861 is shown in these tables, from which it appears that generally silver reached its utmost depreciation from 1867 to 1870, or earlier in some places; since the latter year silver has been rising in value in India, whilst its gold price has been falling in Europe, as, conversely, in previous years when silver was falling in value in India, its gold price was high in Europe.

On a review of the conclusions suggested by this summary of prices in Europe and in India the sum of the matter seems to be that, down to 1867 or 1870, the effect of the gold discoveries in raising prices was moderated in Europe by the displacement there, by the new gold, of silver, which was exported to the East. Thereby, the bulk of the addition to the metallic currencies of the world, from the new gold, occurred in the East, and only to a very small extent in the West. In accordance with this course of the precious metals, prices rose in India earlier, and by a much higher percentage than in Europe. Since 1870, the new production of gold has been accumulating in the West, and the result should have been a great rise of prices in Europe. There has been a rise, though not to the extent that might have been expected; a collapse of credit, and the displacement of silver by gold in the German currency and in that of the Scandinavian Kingdoms, having partly counteracted the effects of the block of gold in the West, since 1870.

APPENDIX V.

WAGES.

The depreciation of the precious metals, as estimated by a rise of prices, is also illustrated by an increase of wages, out of which the enhanced prices of food and necessaries are paid.

2. FRANCE.

With a caution that the statistics were applicable only to the chief towns, and were, perhaps, not always carefully verified, the 'Pall Mall Gazette' of December 22, 1874, summarised some of the results given in a recent publication of the *Bureau of General Statistics of France.*

I. *Exclusive of Paris,* the average wages, with board, paid throughout France to labourers of all kinds amounted in 1853 to 96 centimes a day, or very nearly 9½*d.* In 1871 this pay had risen to 1f. 40c. In the eighteen years, therefore, the increase had been slightly over 45 per cent. During the same period the maximum wages had risen from 1f. 23c. to 1f. 82c.; an increase of nearly 48 per cent; and the minimum had risen from 74c. to 1f. 10c., being a little over 48 per cent. The wages of labourers who did not receive board had risen from 1f. 89c. to 2f. 65c.—an increase of only 40 per cent. The maximum increased 32 per cent. and the minimum 43 per cent. The rate of increase has been highest in the case of those who receive board with wages; and the difference of wages, where board was and was not given amounted in 1853 to 93c. or just ninepence a day, and in 1871 to 125c, or exactly a shilling. We may conclude, we presume, that the cost of feeding a man in the two years is represented with tolerable accuracy by these figures. If so, it follows that the *cost of the necessaries of life had risen in the eighteen years, as nearly as possible, one third,* and therefore that the increase of wages was greater than the increase in the cost of living. In other words, the working classes have shared, whether proportionately or not these figures do not enable us to say, in the increased prosperity of France.

II. Another writer in the 'Edinburgh Review' for January 1875 observed—

'There is no country in which the emigration of the rural population of the large towns has been more felt than in France, and it has led to a considerable improvement in the condition of the labourer. To speak generally, the rise in wages has been, on an average, 50 per cent. during the last thirty years, an advance which has been checked only by the stationary disposition engendered by the possession of small plots of land. . . . Of the whole number of agricultural labourers, it is supposed that not less than three-fourths are small proprietors.'

III. Mr. Fred. Brittain, who was employed in 1876 by the associated Chambers of Commerce to visit France, and investigate the comparative condition of the leading trades in that country and the United Kingdom, gives the following as the average annual wages earned in France in coal and iron mines—

	1864.	1869.
	£	£
Coal mines	24	30
Iron mines	30	34

The average rate of wages per day, in what is called the *Petite Industrie*, which includes nearly all but the large works, was given as

	1858.		1871.		1872.	
	s.	d.	s.	d.	s.	d.
Men	1	8½	2	4	2	4½
Women	0	10½	1	2½	1	3

On these figures, the increase since 1858 has been 39 to 43 per cent.

EUROPEAN CONTINENT.

Mr. T. E. Cliffe Leslie, in the 'Fortnightly Review' for June 1874, wrote—

I. In Belgium, where farm wages had been rising for twenty years, they have lately sprung in some districts from 2½ francs to 3½ francs and upwards.

II. In France, M. de Lavergne estimated the general rise in the decade 1855–1865, at 20 per cent; but it was much greater in many places, and continued down to the war. Dr. Baur and Professor von der Goltz put it at 60 per cent. in the north of France, in the last 20 years; and one cannot doubt that the rise throughout the country would have been greater, and would be still going on, but for the late war, the drain of money which has followed it, and the uncertain state of political affairs.

III. In Germany there are four different classes of agricultural labourers, and a calculation of the rise in wages is embarrassed by the difference in the modes of payment, and payments in kind; but for the present purpose we need concern ourselves only with the earnings, measured in money, of the two classes called *Einlieger* and *Hausler* (the latter having cottages of their own, and the former being lodgers) who share the designations of day labourers and free labourers. Dr. F. von der Goltz, Professor of Rural Economy in the University of Königsberg, a writer of great practical experience, in the new edition of his work on the German agricultural labourers' question, measures in money the rise of the wages of the classes of labourers referred to at 100 per cent. in the Rhine province, and from 50 to 60 per cent. in the eastern province of Prussia, in the last ten to twenty years. A table in the last number of the Journal of the Agricultural Society for Rhenish Prussia puts the rise in one district at from 75 to 100 per cent. in the last four years, in another district at 200 per cent. in the last twenty years, and in a third at 200 per cent. in the last ten years. At Tubingen in Wurtemburg, Dr. Gustav Cohn tells me, the rate was 1*s.* 2*d.* a day in 1850–55; 1*s.* 4*d.* in 1860–65; 1*s.* 8½*d.* in 1866–70; and is 2*s.* 0½*d.* in 1874. At Wessen in the Rhine Province, on the border of Westphalia, Mr. W. Wynne, a resident English engineer, states, ten years ago agricultural wages were 1*s.* 2½*d.* a day, measured in money; about that time railway works commenced, and they rose very quickly. At present they are about 2*s.* a day—a fall after the exaggerated rates of last year. Mr. White, British Consul at Danzig, one of the best informed and most intelligent Englishmen in Germany, although remarking (April 27) that the price of labour in Germany has quite lately entered into a retrogressive stage, measures the general rise in the price of agricultural labour at from 50 to 100 per cent. in the last twenty years, and speaks of great alarm on the part of farmers, with respect to the future.

The foregoing estimates (continued Mr. Cliffe Leslie) are in accordance both with facts ascertained by myself in several visits to Germany, and with recent information from authorities as high as Professor Nasse of Bonn, Member of the Prussian Parliament, Mr. W. T. Mulvaney of Dusseldorf, and Herr Bruck, formerly Secretary to an East Prussian Agricultural Society, and now to an important Society in Rhenish Prussia. It may be concluded from these authentic data, that the rise of farm wages in some parts of Germany much exceeds the rise, according to Mr. Caird's estimate, in England.

IV. (The foregoing relates to agricultural labour; in other industries, wages materially lost in 1875 and 1876 the increase which they had gained in 1871 and 1872.)

NAPLES.

According to statistics published in 1874 by the Chamber of Commerce of Naples, wages of skilled workmen had doubled in ten years from 1862 to 1872; but the price of provisions had increased at about the same rate.

AMERICA.

I. Mr. D. A. Wells, Special Commissioner of Revenue, United States, reported in 1868 that

'An examination of the statistics of manufactures shows a clear increase in wages in 1866, of upwards of 60 per cent., as compared with the wages paid in 1860. Allowing for the depreciation of the paper currency, the increase was about 40 per cent.'

In a paper published in 1872, in the second series of the 'Cobden Club Essays,' Mr. Wells observed—

'A recent investigation made in one of the large manufacturing cities of the Atlantic States, of the comparative prices of labour, rents, and commodities, in 1860 and 1871, afforded the following results. The lowest class of unskilled labour, which in 1860 earned one dollar (gold) per day, or *six* dollars per week, received in July 1871 ten dollars currency per week, or in gold at 112 (the average market price) 8$\frac{4}{5}$ dollars, showing an increase on a gold basis, in eleven years, of 46$\frac{3}{5}$ per cent. Labour earning two dollars (gold) per day, or twelve dollars (gold) per week, in 1860, received in 1871 twenty dollars currency, or seventeen dollars (gold) for the same service; showing an increase in eleven years of 46$\frac{3}{5}$ per cent., but with no benefit whatever to the labourer, owing to a corresponding increased price of rents and commodities.'

II. But with the crisis of 1873 there occurred in the United States 'a very decided fall in wages, which continued through 1874 and 1875.' The 'Commercial History and Review' for 1875 quoted McCulloch's 'New York Circular' as follows:—

'1876 is opening with a very general attempt on the part of manufacturers to effect still further reductions of wages. . . . The renewed reduction of wages, following previous ones so quickly, meets with very general opposition from the persons employed, and strikes are resulting; but as the workmen are in no condition to hold out, such resistance can only be temporary.'

The 'Review' for 1876 completes the story.

'In spite of Protection, all the protected industries remain in collapse; and in spite of inconvertible paper money and unlimited land, the working classes are worse off in the United States than in any other part of the world.'

III. In 1877 the railroad companies reduced wages by 10 per cent., or from 1 dollar 50 cents to 1 dollar 35 cents, for a day's labour. The extensive strike of the men, accompanied with violent acts, was put down; and the reduction of wages has been accepted. The large numbers of unemployed men who were available for replacing the men on strike defeated the movement. The 'New York Finance Chronicle' (July 28, 1877) upheld the right of the railway companies to fix the wages which they deem it expedient to pay, but added—

'On the other hand, those who speak flippantly of the matter, saying that there is no hardship, that a dollar a day is enough for bread, and whoever cannot live on bread and water is no man at all, do not show either a wise head or a feeling heart. Hardship undeniably exists. It is a hardship that men should be forced down to such scanty pay, as it is a hardship and a proof of something widely wrong, that men willing and anxious to work can find no work to do.'

UNITED KINGDOM.

I. AGRICULTURAL LABOUR.—Mr. Caird, in a letter published in the 'Times' of January 2, 1874, stated the wages of agricultural labourers in England as follows:—

	1770.		1850.		1873.	
	s.	d.	s.	d.	s.	d.
Average weekly wages:						
In Northern counties .	6	9	11	6	18	0
In Southern counties .	7	6	8	5	12	0

The increase since 1850 has been 56½ per cent. in the north, and 42½ per cent. in the south; and ('Economist,' July 15, 1876) there has been a slight improvement since 1873. In Ireland the increase since 1850 has been 50 to 100 per cent. ('Statistical Journal,' March 1870.

II. WAGES GENERALLY.—*a.* A writer in the 'Westminster Review' for October 1874 estimates the rise in wages since the gold discoveries at 30 per cent.

b. Owing to the crisis in 1857, there was probably in the next two years, a reduction in wages, prices having fallen to their lowest in 1859. It does not appear, however, that there were any strikes up to 1858, inclusive, subsequent to the strike of the amalgamated engineers in 1851, and of the Preston operatives in 1853. In 1859 and 1860 there were strikes among a limited class, namely, in the building trade in London. The notices in the following sections, of the subsequent course of wages, are taken from the 'Economist,' from its 'Commercial History and Review.'

c. In 1861 there was distress in Lancashire, with necessarily a reduction of wages. But with the expansion of trade in 1863, from the growth of joint-stock enterprise, production and wages of all kinds rose, step by step, from 1863 to 1865. In 1865, with a general tendency to further increase, additions of 10 to 15 per cent. were actually allowed in many cases.

d. In 1866 wages fell in several large trades from 10 to 20 per cent; 'and that year will be remembered as the one in which the advancing tide that, for a long period, had promoted the advance of wages, was stopped.'

e. The 'Commercial History and Review' of 1867 observed:—

'Speaking generally, prices and wages are about 15 per cent. lower than in 1865;' (that is, about the same, apparently, as the enhanced rates of 1863, if not 1864). And in the 'Review' for 1868 it was stated that 'wages were much the same as in 1867, that is, about 20 to 25 per cent. below the limits which had been reached early in 1866.' (Thus again describing, apparently, a reversion to the rates in 1863, *plus* a portion of the advance in 1864.)

f. The trade of the years 1869 and 1870 showed a recovery from the depression in 1866 and 1867; and in several trades wages advanced in 1869 by 3 to 7 per cent. In 1871, wages in the silk trade were above 25 per cent. higher than in 1870; in 1872 there was a general and rapid rise in the prices of commodities, and in the wages of labour. In September 1873 occurred the financial crisis in the United States, which was followed by crises in Germany and Austria, and these crises were attended with a very decided fall in wages; but a similar decline in the United Kingdom only took effect in 1874, and continued in progress through 1875 and 1876, which latter year,

'Until quite the close of it, has been marked by dull and limited trade, restricted confidence, the rigorous application of reduction and economies, lessened wages, and the failure of numberless commercial and manufacturing concerns. This description applies with even more force to North America, Germany, Austria, Russia, and Belgium, than to this country.

g. 1877. Trade in England continues very bad, and wages are falling in every direction. There seems to be some prospect of a bad winter, more especially if it should be a severe one; and the working classes are already beginning to cry out.'—*New York Financial Chronicle*, August 18, 1877.

h. But yet the final result is, that a large excess over wages in 1848 still remains with the working classes. Thus:—

'Nor must we mix up with the excess of imports another point of which Mr. Rathbone also speaks, viz., the increased proportion of the income of the country which is said now to go to the working men, and the fear that they may not save so much of it as the capitalist used to do. And no doubt English working men are not as saving as English capitalists, perhaps never will be. No doubt they drank out an immense amount of whatever augmented wages they have received; but this is not a reason for regretting the increased import of food and other invigorating things. These are one of the best ways of saving, for they increase the strength of an increasing population.'—*Economist*, February 10, 1877.

III. Cotton Industry.—*a.* In the cotton trade the advance of wages averaged 10 to 25 per cent. in 1859 compared with 1839. For a spinner the rates of weekly wages were 20*s.* in 1850; 22*s.* in 1853; 27*s.* in 1860; and 30*s.* in 1865, being an increase of fifty per cent. since 1850. The crisis of 1866 did not affect Lancashire operatives, except by a reduction, not of rates, but to short time; but there was distress in Lancashire in 1869; followed, however, by a rapid increase of wages in subsequent years. Part of this increase has ceased, and the operatives endeavoured to regain it in the second half of 1876; but

'The lock-out of operatives in Manchester has been averted, the masters not giving way to the demands of the operatives.'—*Economist*, November 25, 1876.

On July 15, 1876, the 'Economist' published 'returns recently furnished to inquiries on the subject of wages,' in which it was stated of Manchester spinners that—

'Since 1870, the price of wages to the spinning and weaving operative hands in Lancashire has not varied 2½ per cent., if the reckoning of wages is taken by the piece. The great point, however, as bearing on the question, is that machinery has been improved so much that, in some mills, or some districts, the operatives, getting paid on the same basis as in 1870, actually earn more money, that is to say, the machinery turns off a greater weight of yarn or cloth, and so an operative earns more, but there are hardly two mills exactly alike in this respect.'

b. 'In many branches of manufacture a chronic controversy exists between masters and men. It comes to the surface in bad times, and is peculiarly active just at present in several centres of the Cotton Trade, especially at Blackwall and Bolton—in the latter of which towns an extensive strike is at this moment threatened. Trade is dull, demand stagnant; the cotton manufacture in most of its branches is unprofitable or worse; stocks are accumulating, and unsaleable at remunerative prices. Under these circumstances the masters have called upon their operatives to bear their share in the general difficulty, and to submit to a reduction of wages to the moderate extent of 5 per cent. The operatives resist this reduction, and declare they will strike, rather than accept it. There are about 150 mills in Bolton, and from 10,000 to 12,000 persons are under notice.

The workmen plead that as stocks are accumulating, the mills should work short time, whereby (1st) more would be saved to the manufacturer, than by a reduction of wages if the mills continued to work full time; (2nd) over-production, the cause of the existing difficulty, would cease; (3rd) the workmen would forego a larger proportion of the amount of their wages, but without a reduction of rate, than the five per cent. which the masters desire to reduce from the rate. The masters reply that by working their mills short time, with full rate of wages, the cost of production is greater than by working full time, with a reduced rate of wages; because certain fixed charges, viz., interest on capital, depreciation and wear and tear, and the yearly salaries paid to the superior officers, superintendents and overseers, in a factory remain the same, with the diminished production on short time, as with the production on full time. The result of the whole is as follows—as shown by a careful calculation in certain average cases we can vouch for. There are factories which consume a large amount of raw material. The cost of production when working full time (6 days) was 3·75*d.* per lb.; when on short time (4 days) it rose to 4·25*d.*; when working full time, with a reduction of wages to the amount of ten per cent., it fell to 3·5*d.*; that is, short time added a halfpenny per pound to the cost of making the calico, which in the case of the ordinary mill, turning out 48,000 lbs. a week, means a difference of £5,000 a year; while a reduction in wages to the extent of ten per cent. would reduce the cost by a farthing per lb., or economise £2,500. The diminished cost of production, by reducing the selling price, would extend sales. . . . The experience of the operatives might remind them that some ten or twelve years since, wages in their districts rose gradually above 25 or 30 per cent., with no effort and little reluctance; while since 1872 there have been two or three successive reductions, in spite of the most eager struggles to avert them.'—*Economist*, September 1, 1877.

c. On the whole, wages appear to be above fifty per cent. higher than they were in 1848.

IV. Other Textile Manufactures.—The operatives in these manufactures participated in the general rise in wages until 1870, and in the exceptional rise after that year. The rates given in the returns published in the 'Economist' of July 15, 1876, show that wages in 1876, compared with those in 1870, were higher by about ten per cent. in the worsted trade (Bradford) and in the woollen trade (Huddersfield), and even fifty per cent. higher in the woollen trade in Leicester.

V. Coal and Iron.—*a.* There had been an inflated demand for iron in 1864, 1865, and 1866; and there was a large increase of wages in 1864 and 1865. In 1867–8 there were reductions, and in 1868 there was a strike against a reduction of wages. In 1869 wages were increased in Cleveland by two instalments aggregating 15 per cent. to January 1, 1870; but from January 1, 1871, they were reduced five per cent. to ten per cent. in advance of the rate in 1868.

b. Thus wages were, in 1870, fifteen per cent., and in 1871 ten per cent. in advance of the rate in 1868.

c. In 1871 there was a rise in wages of probably 15 to 20 per cent., and compared with 1861 the rise was 25 to 30 and 35 per cent., except for moulders (17 per cent.) and for fitters (12 per cent). In 1872 there was a further increase, which raised the aggregate advance to 50 per cent. since August 1861. In 1873, without a reduction of rate, there were endeavours to work short time, which led to strikes; and in 1874 wages were reduced to what they had been before the increase in 1872, or (as it is stated) to about 25 or 30 per cent. higher than the lowest rate paid in 1871. In 1875 a further reduction was effected, and was under arbitration in others; or, as one of the trade circulars put it, 'speaking generally, it may be said that wages in the coal and iron industries have been brought down to within (i.e. above)' 15 or 20 per cent. of the rates paid in 1868–9.

d. Respecting 1876, Messrs. W. Fallows and Co., of Liverpool, report:—

'The iron trade has passed through a year of extreme adversity and depression. During its course some of the largest and wealthiest manufacturing concerns had to succumb to the severe reaction which succeeded the inflation of 1872 and 1873, whilst the operatives suffered in no small degree by the decreased demand for labour, and greatly diminished wages. During 1876 there has been *a further reduction in the wages paid to puddlers and millmen* of 7½ to 12½ per cent., and *miners* of 10 to 15 per cent. This will bring wages back to about the old level of 1868; but there still remains the question of the *hours of labour* (which were reduced during the last few years), and it may yet be necessary to revert to the old standard in this respect also.'

e. The extent of the late reductions of wages is further illustrated by the following return, which was published in the 'Economist' of July 15, 1876:—

PRICE OF PUDDLING PER TON.

	1868	1870	1873	1876 Jan. to June
	s.	*s.*	*s.*	*s.*
North of England .	8, 7, and 6½	9½ for all mixtures	13¼	8¼
Staffordshire . .	7½	8½	13¼	8¼

f. It appears from the preceding that the rates were about the same in 1868 as in 1861 or 1864; and that in 1874 they were 35 or 40 per cent., and in 1875, 15 or 20 per cent. higher than in 1868; while in 1876 they were brought down to about the same level as in 1868. In March 1877, owing to a fall in the price of iron, of 8*s.* 3*d.* per ton since February 1876, the ironmasters gave notice to their workmen of a proportionate reduction in the rate of wages,[1] but the final report in the 'Economist' of May 12, 1877, does not accord with these results. Messrs. T. W. and J. Walker, of London and Wolverhampton, in their quarterly report on the iron trade, to the end of April 1877, observed:—

'When we consider that coal is about 2*s.* per ton higher in price now than in June 1872, and that workmen's wages are after all but slightly reduced

[1] *Economist*, April 7, 1877.

(in comparison to the above percentage of decrease in price of iron, viz., 46 to 50 per cent.), we can understand the terrible disadvantages that manufacturers are at present labouring under, and the dwindling profits, not to speak of loss.'

So that wages appear to be still in considerable advance of the rates in 1868, 1861, and 1848.

g. In the collieries wages were advanced during 1870 to 1873, beyond the rates in 1869, by about 58 per cent.; but most part of the increase was withdrawn in 1875 and 1876, still leaving, however, some advance beyond the rates in 1869.

It appears from this account of the rise in wages in the United Kingdom, that in the several industries, including the agricultural, the increase has been considerable; and, unlike the state of things on the Continent, where a rise in wages was accompanied by a corresponding rise in the prices of necessaries, the advance of wages in England has been accompanied by a reduction of the price of wheat. Measured by this last fact, the rise in wages has been greater than it seems; and hence, the depreciation of gold, so far as it can be measured by a rise of wages, has been proportionately great.

But the sudden increase of wages in several industries, by more than fifty per cent. from 1870 to 1873, and the summary withdrawal since, of the greater part, or, in some instances, of the whole of that increase, show that the inflation of prices and of wages in those years, and the subsequent decline, are not due to the depreciation or appreciation of gold; they were caused by the expansion and contraction of credit.

APPENDIX VI.

TRADE OF THE UNITED KINGDOM AND OF BRITISH INDIA.

UNITED KINGDOM.

THE annual averages of the trade are as follows :—

(*Millions sterling.*)

	1854 to 1857	1858 to 1860	1861 to 1866	1867 to 1872	1873 to 1875	1876
MERCHANDISE.						
Exports:						
British produce . . .	107·7	127·6	151·8	204·9	239·4	200·6
Foreign and colonial merchandise . . .	21·8	25·7	47·0	50·6	57·4	56·2
Total	129·5	153·3	198·8	255·5	296 8	256·8
Imports	164·	184·7	255·6	309·1	371·8	375·1
BULLION (gross imports).						
Gold	—	19·9	17·7	17·6	20·6	23·5
Silver	—	10·6	9·6	10·1	11·8	13·6
MERCHANDISE.						
Imports:						
Countries not indebted .	—	40·8	51·8	61·9	72·4	75·2
France, Belgium, and Australia	—	25·4	41·0	59·3	78·6	81·1
Indebted countries . .	—	118·6	162·8	187·9	220·8	218·8
Exports:						
Countries not indebted .	—	40·	58·	72·6	86·0	72·4
France, Belgium, and Australia	—	26·1	42·0	48·0	62·9	61·3
Indebted countries . .	—	87·2	108·8	134·9	147·9	123·1

2. The following remarks are suggested by the table:—

I. The countries reckoned as indebted are Russia, Spain, Portugal, Turkey, Wallachia, Moldavia, Austria, Italy, America, the East, and Gibraltar.

II. The trade for the undermentioned years was—

(Millions sterling.)

	1866	1869	1871	1872	1873	1874	1875	1876
Exports:								
British produce .	188·9	189·9	223·1	256·3	255·2	239·6	223·5	200·6
Foreign and colonial .	50·	47·1	60·5	58·3	55·8	58·1	58·1	56·1
	238·9	237·0	283·6	314·6	311·0	297·7	281·6	256·7
Imports .	295·3	295·5	331·0	354·7	371·3	370·1	373·9	375·1

In 1870 the exports amounted to 199·6 millions of British produce, and 44·4 millions of foreign and colonial. The latter has receded a little below the amount in 1871; but it yet greatly exceeds that in 1870, notwithstanding the opening of the Suez Canal. The exports of British produce had declined in 1876 to the amount in 1870, and there has been a further decrease in 1877.

III. While foreign countries were borrowing, and taking part-payment in dear goods, British trade advanced 'with leaps and bounds' which excited the admiration of a statesman and financier who steadily reduced debt. After the collapse of foreign credit in 1873, exports of British produce rapidly declined; but imports have continued to increase.

IV. The trade with countries not indebted shows a greater proportionate and also absolute increase of exports than that with indebted countries.

	Countries not indebted			Indebted countries		
	1860	1867 to 1872	1876	1860	1867 to 1872	1876
Imports .	36·6	61·9	75·2	135·2	187·9	218·8
Exports .	39·3	72·6	72·4	94·3	134·9	128·1

The commerce with countries not indebted is on the sound normal footing of an exchange of equivalents in merchandise; the healthy regulation of which is the province of Political Economy. But the trade with indebted countries forms a chapter in finance, not in political economy. The crises which, at successively shorter intervals, convulse commerce, occur in this part of the trade; and the battle between free trade and Protection rages round this part. The nations which borrow, being obliged to supplement their exchange of equivalents in merchandise, by a further export of produce in payment of interest, endeavour to provide the interest by taxes, which both bring in revenue and increase the excess of exports. The philosopher may call this cutting off the nose to spite the face; but perhaps the practical result is an enforced economy in the borrowing country, which consumes less goods of the kinds that are taxed, and is enabled, by the saving, and from the proceeds of the tax, to pay interest on debt. In theory, the tax should fall entirely on the consumer; but the necessity under which, for some time, British exports have been sent abroad at a loss, in some trades, shows that this is not wholly the case. When a nation combines the functions of banker to other nations and of merchant, it must expect that the debtor countries, with incomes reduced by heavy taxation for meeting the interest due to it as banker, will not be able to buy freely from it as merchant. Disquisitions on free trade are unmeaning platitudes to nations which, whether they will it or not, are forced to sell heavily to the creditor country in payment of interest.

V. It follows that, in the trade of the United Kingdom, imports, which depend so much on the necessity of other countries to sell, independently of an exchange of equivalents in merchandise, should show a steady progress, while exports, which depend more upon their ability to buy, would show less elasticity, and a slower progress, after culmination of the charge for interest, that is, of the amount of taxation, at the end of a long course of borrowing. The statistics of the Board of Trade show a progress of imports and exports which is in accordance with this remark.

VI. The great falling off in exports is partly explained in the 'Economist' by the export of foreign securities, through the discredit into which they have fallen in England; but this only means a diversion of part of the export and import trade to the countries which have bought the securities, and that, but for these sales of securities, the imports into the United Kingdom would have been greater.

VII. Some might consider the United States a notable exception to these remarks. Interest on debt, and the amount of taxation by the Federal Government, have been reduced; and yet the exports to those States have greatly declined; but, first, the taxation of the separate States and municipal taxation are heavy; secondly, the rapid decline of the gold premium necessitates a readjustment (through these diminished imports into the United States, among other ways) of expenditure to income.

VIII. Since 1865, national debts have increased by more than one-fourth; taxation in the indebted countries, exclusive of municipal, by about one-third; deposits have more than doubled; large amounts of capital have been sunk in abortive enterprises; and upon all this has supervened a collapse of commercial credit and of foreign loans, which, with the growth of unemployed deposits, has diminished incomes; even the wages of the poorest among the working classes. At the same time a heavily augmented taxation presses on this diminished income of the mass of consumers with a severity which has reduced their power of purchase beyond the experience of the year or two following former crises. All the causes of commercial depression which prevailed in those years are intensified in the present depression after the crisis of 1873, by the vaster accumulation of debt bearing interest, the more extensive collapse of national and commercial credit, a greater decline of wages below the point reached in the year of crisis, a heavier taxation, and the combination, in the present depression, of all these causes; while in the year or two after the crises of 1857 and 1866, some of these did not operate, and others were not so intense in their operation. Add to this, the rapid reduction of gold premium in the United States, and an accumulation in the West of most of the fresh yearly production of gold since 1867—without the export of a corresponding amount of silver to the East—and we have causes sufficient to account for a discordance between cost of production and market prices of goods; for diminished means of purchase from England; and for a diminished expenditure which is in course of adjustment to a reduced income. Some of these causes will endure for many years; others are removable.

IX. The complacent feeling that England gets a large portion of her imports in return for investments abroad, and not in exchange for equivalents in merchandise, may be pleasant to a nation retired from business, but not to the working bees and captains of industry who have raised England to her present supremacy among the nations. These may be excused if they feel that some better vocation and some dearer interests should attach them to their fatherland, than the defence of creditors of indebted nations, goaded by heavy taxation, who (now become adepts in borrowing) would borrow from the history of the Roman Empire, an easy way of paying old debts, were the strength and manhood of England to be weakened by an emigration to other parts of the earth, from want of remunerative employment at home.

X. But perhaps this feeling of complacency merely disguises a sense of uneasiness. In May 1876, Mr. Bagehot wrote:—

> 'England acts for the United States as produce broker on a vast scale—both sends on the silver to the countries which want it, and pays indirectly for what she buys, to the countries that she buys from. That we are able so to pay is one of the many instances in which, in trade, most is given to those who already have most. Our export trade is so much greater and so much more easily augmented than that of any other country, because we are able to settle any debt in commodities far better than any other nation. If the United States buy of Nation B, B is more likely to want something of England than of any one else; or if, instead, B buys of C, C is so likely, and so on through the alphabet, till at last you come to England. Our predominant international trade (that is, our export trade) gives us, in a business such as this, an assured pre-eminence.'

The shrewdest nation in the world will not be long in finding a way to dispense with the commission of the rich produce broker.

3. The imports are shown in the table on page 347—classing the stimulant of tobacco with food and drink.

4. The following remarks are suggested by the table:

I. The gross and the net imports alike are progressive; though the periods compared are the years of crises, and those preceding or following a crisis. The progress is under every head excepting raw materials (grist for the mill), in which there was a falling off after each year of crisis, but notably after 1873—and excepting 'other articles' which have declined since 1872.

II. The excess of 211 millions in 1876 over 1858 includes 98 millions in articles of food and drink (partly cattle for agriculture and food for cattle), and 60 millions gross, or 45 millions net for raw materials: the latter increase is in a proportion much inferior to that under the other heads.

III. The increased imports of articles of food and drink are principally from agricultural countries which are indebted to England. In one view, they benefit manufactures by reducing the cost of production; in another, they denote diminished markets for manufactures, abroad and at home; abroad, because, to a considerable extent, the imports are received not in exchange for equivalents in merchandise, but in payment of interest, which implies diminished means of foreign consumers: at home, because the largeness of the importations of the products of agriculture indicates a formidable

Imports and Re-exports of the United Kingdom.

(Millions sterling.)

	1858	1860	1865	1866	1869	1871	1872	1873	1876
Imports.									
I. Food and drink:									
Corn and rice . . .	22	33	22	31	40	45	55	55	55
Oxen, bulls, cows, sheep and lambs, and farm and dairy produce .	6	11	19	20	21	23	24	31	38
Fish and groceries . .	24	26	33	32	37	43	47	46	48
Spirits and wine . .	3	6	6	7	7	10	10	12	11
Tobacco	3	2	3	3	2	3	3	4	4
	58	78	83	93	107	124	139	148	156
II. Raw materials:									
Fibres	50	63	101	112	88	96	92	94	79
Other	27	36	40	39	41	47	45	58	58
	77	99	141	151	129	143	137	152	137
III. Manufactures . .	4	7	14	16	19	19	20	21	25
Miscellaneous[1] . .	6	7	8	8	9	10	9	10	11
Other articles . . .	19	20	25	27	31	35	50	40	46
	29	34	47	51	59	64	79	71	82
Grand total	164	211	271	295	295	331	355	371	375
Re-exports.									
Corn and rice	1	1	1	1	1	1	2	3	2
Groceries	2	3	7	6	7	9	9	10	9
Spirits, wine and tobacco .	2	2	2	2	2	2	2	2	2
	5	6	10	9	10	12	13	15	13
Raw materials:									
Fibres	8	11	30	28	22	25	23	20	20
Other	4	5	5	5	5	7	7	7	7
	12	16	35	33	27	32	30	27	27
All other articles . .	6	7	8	8	10	16	15	14	16
Total	23	29	53	50	47	60	58	56	56
Net imports	141	182	218	245	248	271	297	315	319

[1] Petroleum, oils, cotton seed, oilseed cake, and clover and grass seeds.

competition with British agriculture which is a main support of home manufactures. The increase under spirits indicates but imperfectly the increased consumption of liquor which deteriorates the quality of labour, and creates a craving for short hours and short time.

5. In the eight months ended August 31, 1877, the total imports amounted to 264 millions sterling against 251 millions in the corresponding period in 1876; while the re-exports were £1,200,000 less than in the eight months ended August 31, 1876. The picture, unfavourable to the prospects and to the efficiency of British labour, which is presented by the growth of the import trade down to 1876, will be painted in somewhat darker colours by the year 1877.

6. The exports of British produce and manufactures have been as follows:—

(*Millions sterling.*)

	1858	1860	1865	1866	1869	1871	1872	1873	1876
BRITISH PRODUCE AND MANUFACTURES.									
I. Fibres: Yarn . .	16	17	20	22	24	26	28	26	20
Manufactures, piece goods.	49	61	78	93	84	96	108	97	82
Apparel and slops, haberdashery and millinery .	5	6	7	8	7	8	10	10	7
	70	84	105	123	115	130	146	133	109
II. Coals	3	3	4	5	5	6	10	13	9
Machinery and steam engines	4	4	4	4	5	5	5	5	7
	7	7	8	9	10	11	15	18	16
III. Metals: Iron and steel	12	13	15	17	22	26	36	38	21
Other sorts . . .	4	4	4	4	5	5	5	5	5
Telegraphic wire .	—	—	—	—	1	2	—	2	1
	16	17	19	21	28	33	41	45	27
IV. Other articles . .	24	28	34	36	37	49	54	59	49
Grand total . . .	117	136	166	189	190	223	256	255	201
V. Net imports of fibres .	42	52	71	84	66	71	69	74	59
VI. Excess of I. over V. .	28	32	34	39	49	59	77	59	50
Excess of V. over VI. .	14	20	37	45	17	12	—	—	—
,, VI. over V. .	—	—	—	—	—	—	8	15	9

7. The following remarks are suggested by the table :—

I. The total exports in 1876 exceeded those in 1858 by 84 millions sterling, of which 39 millions, or forty-six per cent., occurred in manufactures of fibres, which gave England her commercial supremacy. But these manufactures attained to their largest amounts in 1866, 1872, and 1873. Between 1866 and 1871 they ranged under 100 millions sterling. If 1876 be compared with 1872, the results of the comparison with 1858 are reversed; the total exports show a decrease of 55 millions, including 37 millions in textile manufactures, 14 millions under metals, and the remainder (six millions gross) under articles other than coals, machinery, and steam engines. These last alone show an excess of one million sterling in 1876 over the amount in 1872. It has been found in every country on the Continent, in America, in India, that railways stimulate exports more than imports, the prosperity which they promote by more extended markets for exports, creating or improving various industries for the supply of home markets with manufactures. Partly at England's expense, foreign countries have obtained a full equipment of railways—this effectual handmaid of home manufactures; and hence the exports of iron and steel show a considerable decline. The next stage in which foreign manufacturing industries need help, is in the instruments of manufacture, viz., steam engines and machinery. Accordingly, these show an excess in 1876 over 1872 of two millions sterling, or (including implements and tools), two and one-third millions, notwithstanding the general commercial depression. The position is, that agricultural industries abroad send us more of their produce, and manufacturing industries abroad lead foreign countries to take less from our industries.

II. The exports of textile manufactures exceed the net imports of fibres by amounts which, down to 1871, were greater, but from 1872 have been less than the amount of those imports. The apparent inference is, that the home consumption of manufactures has fallen off of late years; and, in this regard, the increase of imports of foreign textile manufactures is suggestive, viz. :—

(Millions sterling.)

1858	3·38	1866	12·48	1871	14·27	1874	17·19
1860	5·23	1869	15·51	1872	14·67	1875	17·61
1865	10·98	1870	19·65	1873	15·17	1876	18·55

III. The import of the facts in I. and II. is not affected by any consideration that the quantities of exports have increased, though the values have diminished. Where the supply of raw material is limited, as with cotton, an increasing quantity of exports only denotes that less is consumed at home. The railway traffic receipts, indeed, have increased greatly, but perhaps not more than is involved in the increased importation of corn and other bulky goods.

IV. The production of both coal and iron has progressed faster than the export; the consumption depends mainly on a home demand, which perforce slackens when factories and (for one of them) mines are not in full work. But for coal there is a solacing consideration, that with the fall in its price, many collieries on the continent must be closed. And the iron industry too has an advantage, in that the produce of pig iron from British ore was increased by only half a million tons (from 6 to 6·6 millions) in 1871, beyond the production in 1870, of which three hundred thousand tons had been reduced in 1876, so that the correction to be applied here is only the subsidence of the inflation of prices and wages, after the excitement in 1871. And this has nearly been effected, with the result that the continental production, which had been stimulated by the high prices of 1873, has collapsed.

V. On the whole, it appears that coal, iron, and the jute manufacture are, or will soon be, in good condition; but that the prospects of the remaining exports, on which many important industries depend, are discouraging.

8. The average gross imports of gold and silver into the United Kingdom have been—

(*Millions sterling.*)

	1858 to 1860	1861 to 1866	1867 to 1872	1873 to 1876
Gold . .	19·2	17·7	17·6	21·4
Silver . .	10·6	9·7	10·1	12·3
	29·8	27·4	27·7	33·7

These figures do not suggest a dimininished production of gold. The gross imports of silver into the United Kingdom in 1876 amounted to 13$\frac{3}{5}$ millions sterling.

II. Foreign Trade of British India.

9. The trade has been as follows—

(*In millions sterling.*)

	Merchandise													
	Imports			Exports										
	Cotton goods	Other	Total	Cotton, raw	Other	Total	Net Exports	Net Imports of Gold and Silver	Home Government's Bills	Loss by Exchange on preceding	Government Stores purchased in England	Stores for guaranteed Railways exported to India	Annual average rate of drawings by the Home Government	Price per ounce of bar Silver in London
1854–5	6·7	6·3	13	2·4	16·6	19	6	·8	3·7	—	·4	—	21·4	61 1/16
1855–6	6·4	7·6	14	3·3	19·7	23	9	11	1·5	—	·5	—	23·6	61 5/16
1856–7	6·1	7·9	14	4·4	20·6	25	11	13	2·8	—	1·	—	24·1	61 5/16
1857–8	5·7	9·3	15	4·3	22·7	27	12	15	·6	—	1·7	—	24·5	61 1/4
1858–9	9·8	12·2	22	4·1	25·9	30	8	12	·1	—	1·4	—	25·8	61 5/16
1859–60	11·7	12·3	24	5·6	22·4	28	4	15	·0	—	1·4	—	26·0	62 1/16
1860–1	11·0	12·	23	7·3	25·7	33	10	10	·0	—	1·2	2·1	26·0	61 11/16
	50·7	61·3	112	29·0	137·0	166	54	76	5·0	—	7·2		—	—
1861–2	10·2	11·8	22	10·2	25·8	36	14	14	1·2	·0	1·	1·9	23·9	60 13/16
1862–3	9·6	13·4	23	18·8	29·2	48	25	19	6·6	·1	·7	1·7	23·9	60 7/16
1863–4	11·9	15·1	27	35·9	30·1	66	39	22	9·	·0	·4	1·5	23·9	61 3/8
1864–5	13·2	14·8	28	37·6	30·4	68	40	20	6·8	·0	·6	1·2	23·9	61 3/8
1865–6	13·8	15·2	29	35·6	29·4	65	36	24	7·0	·0	1·2	1·9	23·8	61 1/16
1866–7 (11 months)	15·1	13·9	29	16·5	25·5	42	13	11	5·1	·1	1·2	3·3	23·2	61 1/8
1867–8	17·7	18·3	36	20·1	30·9	51	15	10	4·1	·1	1·1	3·8	23·3	60 9/16
1868–9	18·8	17·2	36	20·1	32·9	53	17	14	3·7	·2	1·6	2·2	23·1	60 1/2
1869–70	16·2	16·8	33	19·1	33·9	53	20	13	7·0	·2	1·5	1·8	23·3	60 7/16
	126·5	136·5	263	213·9	268·1	482	219	147	50·5	·7	9·3	19·3	—	—
1870–1	19·	15·	34	19·4	35·6	55	21	3	8·4	·6	1·5	2·	22·6	60 9/16
1871–2	17·5	14·5	32	21·3	41·7	63	21	10	10·3	·4	1·4	·9	23·0	60 1/2
1872–3	17·2	14·8	32	14·0	41·	55	23	3	13·9	·8	1·4	·5	22·8	60 5/16
1873–4	17·8	16·2	34	13·2	41·8	55	21	4	13·3	1·	2·2	·8	22·4	59 1/4
1874–5	19·4	16·6	36	15·3	40·7	56	20	6	10·8	·9	2·6	·9	22·2	58 5/16
	90·9	77·1	168	83·2	200·8	284	106	26	56·7	3·7	9·1	5·1	—	—
1875–6	19·3	19·7	39	13·3	44·7	58	19	3	12·4	1·4	2·3	1·1	21·6	56 7/8
1876–7	18·7	18·3	37	11·7	49·3	61	24	7	12·7	—	—	—	—	—
	38·0	38·0	76	25·0	94·0	119	43	10	25·1	—	—	—	—	—
Trade to Sept. 30														
1875–6	9·0	9·	18	9·4	19·6	29	11	2	—	—	—	—	—	—
1876–7	8·6	8·4	17	7·5	22·5	30	13	1	—	—	—	—	—	—
1877–8	9·5	9·5	19	5·7	25·3	31	12	6	—	—	—	—	—	—

10. The annual averages of the trade are shown in the table on page 352.

11. The following remarks are suggested by these tables:—

I. Imports and exports were doubled in the period from 1854–5 to 1862–3–4, or in nine years; but they were not trebled, on a comparison with 1854–5, until 1875–6, or in a further period of thirteen years, that is, at a diminished rate of development. Since 1875–6 the imports have declined.

II. The increase has been greater in cotton goods than in other imported goods; the former having more than trebled, and the latter only doubled by 1875–6 compared with 1857–8. Excluding government stores, and stores exported to India by the guaranteed railways, the imports, other than cotton goods, have increased by only two or three millions sterling since 1863–4 to 1865–6. If the income of the people may be measured by what they consume of foreign goods, this rate of increased consumption, which includes that of Native States within, and of countries beyond British India, does not promise much for additional taxation.

	1854-5	1855–6 to 1860–1	1861–2 to 1869–70	1870–1 to 1874–5	1875–6 and 1876–7
	d.	*d.*	*d.*	*d.*	*d.*
Rate of exchange on Home Government's bills	21·4	23·6 to 26	23·9 to 23·3	22·6 to 22·2	21·6 to
Price per ounce of bar silver	above $61\frac{1}{4}$	$61\frac{1}{4}$ to $62\frac{1}{4}$	$60\frac{1}{2}$ to $61\frac{3}{8}$	$60\frac{1}{2}$ to $58\frac{5}{16}$	$56\frac{7}{8}$ to
MERCHANDISE.					
Imports:					
Cotton goods	6·7	8·4	14·	18·2	19·
Other	6·3	10·2	15·2	15·4	19·
	13·	18·6	29·2	33·6	38·
Exports:					
Raw cotton	2·4	4·8	23·7	16·6	12·5
Other	16·6	22·8	29·8	40·2	47·
	19·0	27·6	53·5	56·8	59·5
Net exports	6·	9·	24·3	23·2	21·5
Net imports of gold and silver	·8	12·8	16·3	5·2	5·
Home Government's bills on India	3·7	·8	5·6	11·3	—
Government stores purchased in England	·4	1·2	1·0	1·8	2·3
Stores for guaranteed railways exported to India	—	—	2·2	1·	1·

III. The imports of cotton goods reached 19 millions sterling in 1870–1, with exchange at 1*s.* $10\frac{1}{2}$*d.* per rupee. They fell off from that amount for three years, and latterly have exceeded it somewhat, but with a low exchange which diminishes the returns of the importers, insomuch that, for long, Manchester's exports to the East have been unprofitable, and have sometimes entailed loss. The limit to the cotton supply also restricts the importation of cotton goods.

IV. Before the cotton famine, the Government's obligation to remit for the Home charges did not interfere with Manchester's inerests; the imports of cotton goods exceeded the exports of raw cotton by only three millions sterling, and silver was not depreciated. Now they exceed the exports of raw cotton by above six millions sterling, while the Home Government's bills will range henceforth at about 15 millions, and silver has depreciated. In its extremity Manchester has wildly assailed the Indian cotton duties, instead of the Indian currency.

V. The slow progress of the mass of the exports should also check the sanguine expectations of those who hope that a very great expansion of exports will restore the former price of silver. The staple exports are raw cotton, grain, coffee and tea, indigo, jute, hides and skins, seeds and opium; excluding these, the remaining exports have amounted to the following sums in millions sterling—

1856–7	7·2	1869–70	7·4	1873–4	8·6
1861–2	6·9	1870–1	7·4	1874–5	8·9
1865–6	7·4	1871–2	7·7	1875–6	9·1
1867–8	6·7	1872–3	9·0	1876–7	10·8

The drop in the exchange below 23 pence in 1870–1, and again from 1872–3, coincides with the increase of these exports, which had remained at about seven to seven and a half millions sterling, while the exchange was above 23 pence. A similar remark applies to the bulk of the imports other than the staple imports, or those for which there is a special demand. These increased while exchange was high, and fell off with the depression of the exchange.

VI. The export of opium has increased from seven millions in 1856–7 to twelve millions in 1876–7, which last amount was also attained or exceeded in the years 1867–8, 1871–2, and 1874–5. The amount of above one half of the export depends on the quantity which the Government of India chooses to produce in its opium agencies, in the regulation of the opium monopoly.

VII. The exports of raw cotton are detailed in a previous table; from 2½ millions sterling in 1854–5 the export increased to 37½ millions in 1864–5, after which it steadily declined, with but slight recovery in one or two years, to 11¾ millions in 1876–7; while in the six months ended September 30, 1877, the export amounted to only 5¾ millions against 7½ millions in the corresponding period in 1876. Its reversion to at least the amount of six or seven millions sterling, as before the American Civil War, against 13 millions in 1875–6, when the great depreciation of silver began, seems certain.

VIII. Two other staple exports are indigo, and hides and skins. Five-sixths of the imports into the United Kingdom in 1876 consisted of Indian indigo—which, notwithstanding its command thus of the London market, has declined since 1873–4. In 1856–7, the exports amounted to nearly two millions sterling; in 1869–70, to three and one-fifth millions; in 1873–4, to three and three-fifths millions; but since then the amount has ranged below three millions. In hides and skins, the exports increased from three-fifths of a million in 1856–7 to one and three-fifths million in 1869–70, and to nearly three millions in 1872–3. They have since fluctuated about that sum; the exports in 1876–7 amounted to three millions. The six months of 1877–8 show one and seven-tenths million, against one and three-tenths in 1876, and one and four-tenths million in the corresponding period in 1875; but any great expansion of this trade is not probable: the agriculture of India has certainly not an over-abundant supply of cattle; the demand for butcher's meat is but limited; and the development of the American meat trade will give to the United States even a more commanding position in the London market than it now occupies in respect of hides.

IX. The remaining staples are—

(Millions sterling.)

	Jute	Seeds	Coffee	Tea	Rice	Wheat and other grains	Total
1856–7	·3	1·1	·1	—	2·3	·3	4·1
1861–2	·5	1·2	·5	·2	3·6	·1	6·1
1865–6	·8	1·8	·8	·3	4·9	·3	8·9
1867–8	1·3	2·2	·8	·7	3·6	·3	8·9
1870–1	2·6	3·5	·8	1·1	4·1	·3	12·4
1871–2	4·1	2·7	1·4	1·5	4·4	·4	14·5
1872–3	4·1	1·5	1·6	1·6	5·7	·4	14·9
1873–4	3·4	2·4	1·8	1·8	5·5	1·1	16·0
						Only wheat	
1874–5	3·2	3·2	1·3	2·	4·7	·5	14·9
1875–6	3·3	5·5	1·6	2·2	5·3	·9	18·8
1876–7	3·4	5·3	1·3	2·6	5·7	1·9	20·2
To Sept. 30							
1874–5	1·0	2·9	·6	1·0	2·3	·5	8·3
1875–6	1·4	3·3	·6	1·2	2·1	1·	9·6
1876–7	1·4	4·7	·6	1·4	2·4	2·2	12·7

X. The following remarks are suggested by this table:—

a. The Crimean war gave rise to the exports of jute, but the trade was not developed until the cotton famine. The largest amount attained was in 1871–2–3; since then the value of the export has remained stationary at about three and one-third millions sterling, and any tendency to increase will be counteracted by the progress of the jute manufacture in India.

b. In seeds the largest amount attained before 1875–6, viz. in 1870–1, was not exceeded until 1875–6, when there was an increase of two millions sterling. The spurt in 1875 was apparently from the low exchange; and in 1876 additionally from the failure of supplies of linseed and rapeseed from Southern Russia. If the progress gained, with a million sterling more, can be permanently secured, it will be well; but an indefinite development, after Russia shall have resumed her southern exports, is not probable, the consumption of linseed in the United Kingdom showing only a moderate progress, while the increase of imports of rapeseed from 289,000 quarters in 1874 to 460,000 quarters in 1876 into the United Kingdom is only a partial recovery from a depression of the trade, which had reached 665,000 quarters in 1871.

c. In thirteen years after 1854 the consumption of tea in the United Kingdom increased by 49 millions of pounds, or from 62 millions in 1854, when the duty was 1*s*. 6½*d*., to 111 millions in 1867, when the duty was 6*d*. In the nine years since 1867, the increase has amounted to 38 million pounds, that is, at a faster rate than in the earlier period. The increase in value, however, of the imports in those nine years has been only 2⅔ millions sterling. Hence, though the exports of Indian tea have increased by 1·9 million sterling since 1867, the further extension must fall far short of the requirements for correcting the Indian exchanges.

d. The demands for rice for distillation, and for uses inferior to its use as human food, must keep the Indian export somewhere about the present limits. The consumption in the United Kingdom has declined since 1872, when it reached 7 million hundredweights, against six and a half millions in 1876. Japan is appearing as a new competitor for the supply of Europe.

e. In wheat there has been great progress since 1873–4, the increase having amounted to one and three-quarter million sterling; but a rise of local prices from the importation of silver into India, and the circumstance of India not having an abundance of cattle, precludes hope of a very great extension of the trade.

f. On the whole, it is satisfactory that through the exports of the staples which have been passed in review, a great deal of the decline in the export of raw cotton has been compensated; but the next exports from India (para. 9) are still a long way below the amount 1862–3 to 1865–6; and they are now under the disadvantage that every material increase of the exports will reduce the gold price of the staples in Europe, while in 1862–3 to 1865–6 the gold price of Indian cotton was high. It has been shown in another appendix, that there is a sympathy between the prices in London of Indian exports and of silver, their gold prices rising and falling together.

12. As yet, the increase of Indian exports by five millions sterling since 1874–5, and by one million sterling additional in the eight months ended September 30, 1877, beyond the amount in the corresponding period in 1876, has been unavailing to raise the price of silver. Instead of elevating that price, the amount of exports has only been stimulated by its fall. The price of silver was 57$\frac{1}{4}$*d.* in January 1875, 54$\frac{7}{8}$*d.* in January 1876, 57*d.* in January 1877, and 54$\frac{3}{4}$*d.* in October 1877. It would not be enough that the amount of net export in 1862–3 to 1865–6 should be regained, the circumstances being so dissimilar, owing to the increase of the Home Government's bills on India, and to the decline in Europe of the gold price of Indian productions compared with the excessive price of cotton in those years. Indeed, the net export in 1876–7 did amount to 24 millions sterling against 25 millions in 1862–3; but the price of silver was nearly 60$\frac{1}{2}$*d.* an ounce in 1862; against 52$\frac{3}{4}$*d.* in 1876.

13. The course of the Indian trade and of prices since 1854–5 shows that a mere increase of exports from India will not improve the exchange and the price of silver, unless the exports increase from a special foreign demand for them which may raise their gold price in European markets. The figures respecting the net imports of treasure (para. 9) also indicate that the depreciation of silver, as measured by the prices of articles, was completed in India in the period from 1855–6 to 1869–70. In the first six years of that period, the net imports of bullion amounted to 76 millions sterling, or at the rate of nearly 13 millions a year; in the next nine years they amounted to 147 millions, giving a yearly rate of 16 millions; and in the next seven years from 1871 to 1876 to 36 millions, or at the yearly rate of five millions. It does not require any detailed exhibition of prices to show that they reached their highest in or before 1870, and that their subsequent fall simply denotes that silver had depreciated, down to 1870, in India, in a greater degree than gold had depreciated in the same period in Europe, and that silver had since 1871 been regaining a portion of the value which, from extra depreciation, it

had lost in India. This circumstance is quite compatible with the depreciation, since 1870, of the gold price of silver in Europe. In India, silver is a standard of value; in Europe it is mere merchandise, like Indian commodities, and its gold price rises or falls with theirs. Any increase of Indian exports which shall lower their gold price in Europe, as it needs must do, will lower, not raise the gold price of silver.

14. As a circumstance affecting prices, it is useful to note that the sailing vessels and steamers which entered and cleared at ports in the United Kingdom amounted in 1855 to 15 million tons, and in 1875 to 39 million tons. The tonnage has trebled since 1855; and the increase is principally in steamers, only 5 millions of the increase being in the tonnage of sailing vessels. Increase of tonnage, which means diminution of freight, and the attraction of the world supplies to the centres of trade, has counteracted, in a measure, the depreciation of gold.

APPENDIX VII.

COTTON AND THE COTTON TRADE OF THE UNITED KINGDOM.

MANCHESTER is apt to forget a fact which she ought to remember, at least when she clamours for the repeal of the Indian import duty on her manufactures, viz., that the cotton industry and trade are not susceptible of indefinito expansion, because the supply of cotton is limited. The number of spindles and the consumption of cotton are as follows :—

(*Three* 000's *omitted*).

	Spins and Spindles					Consumption				
	Continent	United States	Total	Great Britain	Grand Total	Continent	United States	Total	Great Britain	Grand Total
						Bales	Bales	Bales	Bales	Bales
1846	7,585	2,500	10,085	17,500	27,585	908	491	1,399	1,561	2,960
1861	—	—	—	30,387	—	1,776	843	2,619	2,635	5,254
1870	—	—	—	34,695	—	1,722	928	2,650	2,760	5,410
1876	19,440	9,500	28,940	39,000	67,940	2,605	1,357	3,962	3,017	6,979

Compared with 1846, the spindle power in Great Britain maintains its old preponderance. The superiority over the rest of the world is greater than it seems, the English machinery in 1876 being more efficient than that in 1846, and representing a proportionately smaller outlay of capital. On the other hand, the number of spindles in the United States and in Continental Europe is now only one and a half million less than the number in Great Britain in 1861; whilst their consumption in 1876 was one million bales more than the consumption of Great Britain in 1846. This excess has been gained since 1870, the spindle power of Great Britain having also been increased since that year by 4,300,000 spindles, for, however, not quite 260,000 bales of extra consumption; that is, in great disproportion to the extra consumption. In the hope, among other things, of correcting the effects of this mistake, Manchester desires a repeal of the Indian import duty on cotton.

2. The supply of cotton in the three periods was as follows, stated in thousands of bales :—

	Supply			Consumption				
	United States	Other kinds	Total	Continent	United States	Total	Great Britain	Grand Total
1846	2,170	377	2,547	908	491	1,399	1,561	2,960
1861	3,826	1,058	4,884	1.776	843	2,619	2,635	5,254
1876	4,669	2,306	6,975	2,605	1,357	3,962	3,017	6,979

Of the increased supply of United States cotton in 1861 (season 1860) compared with 1846, viz., 1,656,000 bales, the bulk was for Europe, only 352,000 of the additional bales having been consumed in the States; but of the excess of 843,000 bales in 1876 over 1861, 514,000 bales were retained in the States, and only 329,000 bales were sent to Europe. The supply for 1877 (season 1876–7) is 4,485,000 bales, showing an excess over 1876 of only 184,000 bales, and the quantity retained for consumption in the States is 1,435,000 bales against 1,357,000 in 1876; that is, the States retained 78,000 out of the 184,000 bales, or less than half, but still a considerable proportion, of the additional supply. The crop of the season 1877 is 4,500,000 bales. If, out of this, a larger quantity than the home consumption of 1877 be retained in the States, the supply for Europe will recede.

3. Pursuing the subject in greater detail, the supply of cotton in Great Britain, Continental Europe, and the United States, stated in thousands of bales, is as follows for the cotton seasons from October 1 to September 30 :—

(*In thousands of bales.*)

Season	Supply			Deliveries for Consumption				
	United States crop	Other sorts imported into Europe	Total	United States	Conti-nent	Total	Great Britain	Grand Total
1858–9	3,994	791	4,785	927	1,525	2,452	2,179	4,631
1859–60	4,824	992	5,816	972	1,712	2,684	2,560	5,244
1860–1	3,826	1,058	4,884	843	1,776	2,619	2,635	5,254
1865–6	2,314	3,156	5,470	733	1,588	2,321	2,319	4,640
1866–7	2,204	2,601	4,805	853	1,791	2,644	2,414	5,058
1867–8	2,499	2,554	5,053	884	1,867	2,751	2,822	5,573
1868–9	2,439	3,110	5,549	1,017	2,002	3,019	2,587	5,606
1869–70	3,155	2,479	5,634	928	1,722	2,650	2,760	5,410
1870–1	4,352	2,383	6,735	1,140	2,327	3,467	3,222	6,689
1871–2	2,974	3,680	6,654	1,067	1,779	2,846	3,132	5,978
1872–3	3,930	2,488	6,418	1,214	2,099	3,313	3,335	6,648
1873–4	4,170	2,762	6,932	1,315	2,397	3,712	3,149	6,861
1874–5	3,833	2,717	6,550	1,194	2,369	3,563	3,077	6,640
1875–6	4,669	2,306	6,975	1,357	2,605	3,962	3,017	6,979
Calendar year, 1876	—	—	—	1,362	2,513	3,875	3,145	7,020
Season 1876–7	4,485	—	—	1,435	—	—	—	—
Yearly average from:								
1865–6 to 1869–70	2,522	2,780	5,302	883	1,794	2,677	2,580	5,257
1870–1 to 1875–6	3,988	2,722	6,710	1,214	2,263	3,477	3,155	6,632

4. The following remarks arise from the table:—

I. The bales are not of uniform weight, but the general result is not thereby materially affected, it being much the same as in the following statement of consumption, in bales of the uniform weight of 400 pounds each.

	United States	Continent	Total	Great Britain	Grand Total
1873	1,321	1,970	3,291	3,108	6,399
1874	1,441	2,267	3,708	3,167	6,875
1875	1,306	2,363	3,669	3,076	6,745
1876	1,484	2,545	4,029	3,255	7,284

II. The total supply has increased by two millions of bales since 1860–1, including an excess in the season 1875–6, over the season 1860–1, of 1,500 million bales in the supply of other sorts than United

States cotton. The supply of these other kinds, however, is declining. It never exceeded 3,680,000 bales, even under the stimulus of excessive prices during the cotton famine; their average supply was 2,780,000 bales from 1865-6 to 1869-70, and 2,722,000 bales from 1870-1 to 1875-6, whilst in 1875-6, they amounted to only 2,306,000 bales. After United States cotton regained its supremacy, the other kinds barely maintained the footing they had acquired during the cotton famine; and in 1876 they receded through the low prices induced by the increasing production of American cotton.

III. At the same time, any very great extension of supply from the United States, except in an unusually good season, cannot be predicated; the acres planted having been as follows, according to the statistics of the 'New York Financial Chronicle':—

(*Three 000's omitted*).

	Acres planted	Crop, lbs.	Crop, bales	Pounds per Acre	Pounds per Bale
1869-70	7,833	1,381,800	3,155	176	438
1870-1	9,985	1,906,300	4,352	191	438
1871-2	8,911	1,305,700	2,974	147	439
1872-3	9,560	1,729,400	3,930	181	440
1873-4	10,816	1,830,800	4,170	161	439
1874-5	10,982	1,682,700	3,833	154	440
1875-6	11,635	2,054,360	4,669	177	440
1876-7	11,501	—	4,485	—	—
1877-8	11,825	—	4,500	—	—

The total consumption of cotton in Europe and America has increased by one-third since 1860-1; but the bulk of the increase has occurred in the United States and in Continental Europe. The States' supply has not materially increased since 1870-1, whilst prices have fallen since that year for middling uplands by more than one-third, and for fair Surat by above one-half. The area of average, however, has increased, and falling prices have, since 1875, been met by diminished cost of production, which ('New York Financial Chronicle,' March 17, 1877) has been brought down to 6·60 cents per pound, against a selling price, at the time, of about 9½ cents per pound. This affords a liberal margin for the higgling of the market, between producers and exporters, when the latter lose the advantage of the premium on gold, which already has well nigh ceased. India would need to reduce, similarly, her cost of production, should the low exchange from the depreciation of silver be corrected by an alteration to a gold standard.

5. The imports of the various kinds of cotton into the United Kingdom, and the price of cotton, have been as follows :—

Imports into the United Kingdom.

(*In millions.*)

Calendar Year	United States	Brazil	Egypt	Total	East Indies	Other countries	Total	Exports	Net Imports	Consumption in Great Britain	Average Price of Cotton	
											Middling uplands	Fair Surat
										Bales of 400 lbs. each	d.	d.
1858	833	19	38	890	134	10	1,034	150	885	—	$6\frac{7}{8}$	$5\frac{1}{2}$
1859	962	22	38	1,022	192	12	1,226	175	1,051	—	$6\frac{3}{4}$	5
1860	1,116	17	44	1,177	204	10	1,391	250	1,141	—	$6\frac{1}{4}$	5
1861	819	17	41	877	370	10	1,257	1,298	959	—	$8\frac{9}{16}$	$6\frac{5}{16}$
1862	14·	23	50	96	393	35	524	215	309	1·124	$17\frac{1}{4}$	$12\frac{7}{8}$
1863	6·	23	94	123	434	113	670	241	429	1·191	$23\frac{1}{4}$	$19\frac{1}{4}$
1864	14	38	126	178	506	210	894	245	649	1·403	$27\frac{1}{2}$	$21\frac{1}{2}$
1865	136	55	177	368	446	165	979	303	676	1·796	19	$14\frac{1}{2}$
1866	520	69	118	707	615	55	1,377	389	988	2·227	$15\frac{1}{2}$	12
1867	528	71	126	725	498	40	1,263	351	912	2·386	$10\frac{7}{8}$	$8\frac{3}{4}$
1868	574	99	129	802	494	33	1,329	423	1,006	2·490	$10\frac{1}{2}$	$8\frac{1}{2}$
1869	457	79	161	697	481	48	1,225	274	947	2·347	$12\frac{1}{8}$	$9\frac{1}{4}$
1870	716	64	144	924	341	74	1,339	238	1,101	2·679	$9\frac{15}{16}$	$8\frac{7}{8}$
1871	1,039	86	176	1,301	461	46	1,778	362	1,416	3·014	$8\frac{9}{16}$	$5\frac{13}{16}$
1872	626	112	178	916	443	50	1,409	273	1,136	2·938	$10\frac{9}{16}$	$7\frac{1}{2}$
1873	833	72	205	1,110	367	51	1,528	220	1,308	3·115	9	$6\frac{3}{16}$
1874	884	80	171	1,135	412	28	1,575	259	1,316	3·165	8	$5\frac{5}{16}$
1875	816	68	168	1,052	388	19	1,459	252	1,207	3·076	$7\frac{3}{8}$	5
1876	905	54	199	1,158	287	15	1,460	194	1,266	3·186	$6\frac{1}{4}$	$4\frac{1}{2}$

Pence per lb. in 1877.

	Jan. 26	March 2	April 6	May 4	June 1	July 6	August 3	Sept. 14
Middling uplands .	$6\frac{15}{16}$	$6\frac{5}{8}$	$6\frac{1}{4}$	$7\frac{5}{8}$	$7\frac{7}{8}$	$6\frac{1}{4}$	$6\frac{1}{8}$	$6\frac{13}{16}$
Surat, fair .	$5\frac{13}{16}$	$5\frac{1}{2}$	$5\frac{1}{4}$	$5\frac{3}{4}$	$5\frac{3}{4}$	$5\frac{3}{8}$	$5\frac{1}{4}$	$5\frac{1}{8}$

6. The following remarks are suggested by the table :—

I. The long stapled cottons, viz. United States, Brazilian, and Egyptian, have provided the whole of the increase ; and whilst the competition of United States cotton has greatly reduced imports of the short staples (East Indian and others), the imports of Brazilian and Egyptian have materially increased beyond their amounts in the years of the cotton famine. In 1876, however, the imports of Brazilian fell off from the great decline in price below the prices of 1874 and 1875; but in 1877 there has been a recovery in Brazilian and a decline in Egyptian imports.

II. The increase of net imports of the long staples is still greater:—

(In millions of bales.)

	1867	1868	1869	1870	1871	1872	1873	1874	1875	1876
IMPORTED INTO GREAT BRITAIN.										
American, Brazilian, and Egyptian	1·8	2·1	1·7	2·2	3·	2·4	2·7	2·8	2·6	2·7
East Indian	1·5	1·4	1·5	1·1	1·2	1·3	1·1	1·0	1·1	·8
Others	·2	·1	·2	·2	·2	·2	·1	·1	·0	·1
	3·5	3·6	3·4	3·5	4·4	3·9	3·9	3·9	3·7	3·6
EXPORTS FROM GREAT BRITAIN.										
American, Brazilian, and Egyptian	·3	·3	·2	·2	·4	·2	·2	·2	·2	·1
East Indian	·7	·6	·6	·5	·5	·6	·4	·5	·5	·4
Other kinds	·1	—	—	—	—	—	—	—	—	—
	1·1	·9	·8	·7	·9	·8	·6	·7	·7	·5
NET IMPORTS.										
American, Brazilian, and Egyptian	1·5	1·8	1·5	2·0	2·6	2·2	2·5	2·6	2·4	2·6
East Indian	·8	·8	·9	·6	·7	·7	·7	·5	6·	·4
Other kinds	·1	·1	·2	·1	·2	·2	·1	·1	—	·1
	2·4	2·7	2·6	2.8	3·5	3·1	3·3	3·2	3·0	3·1

Of long staples, the gross imports have increased by only one-half, but the net imports by seven-tenths, since 1867. Of East Indian, the gross and the net imports alike have fallen off by one-half; the proportion of decline in the other kinds is greater.

III. During the cotton famine, the high prices offered by Liverpool drew all the cotton supplies to England; and the factories on the Continent were starved. With the revival of the American supply the exports from the United Kingdom to the Continent increased, until the opening of the Suez Canal diverted direct supplies from India to the Continent. The direct supplies from America to the Continent of Europe have also increased. The total deliveries of cotton on the Continent have been as follows :—

(In thousands of bales.)

	1871	1872	1873	1874	1875	1876
American and Brazilian .	1,325	1,095	1,070	1,197	1,190	1,288
Mediterranean . . .	186	208	195	196	200	270
East Indian . . .	727	806	765	905	984	894
Other	116	94	89	90	72	61
	2,354	2,203	2,119	2,388	2,446	2,513

Another statement by Messrs. Findlay, Muir & Co. gives the following return, in bales, of the exports of cotton from Bombay :—

(In thousands of bales.)

	1871	1872	1873	1874	1875	To Dec. 28, 1876
To Great Britain . .	807	664	736	845	810	585
„ Continent . . .	339	259	227	412	456	412
„ China . . .	53	39	24	19	37	—
	1,199	962	987	1,276	1,303	997

IV. It appears from II. and III. that the United Kingdom manufactures the finer staples, using the short staples or lower kinds for mixing. The Continent receives half its supply of East Indian cotton direct, and the other half from England ; but the total supply to the Continent has been stationary since 1874, and so far as Continental manufactures depend on East Indian cotton, their progress is checked by a limited supply : the limitation being virtually applied by the progress of cotton manufactures in India. The use of long-stapled cotton on the Continent shows, since 1873, a slight progress which would no doubt be accelerated were there more of East Indian cotton to mix with the long staples. Manchester does not see that the Indian cotton manufacture is a better friend to her than the Secretary of State for India would be were he to repeal the Indian cotton duty. While long-stapled cotton is cheap, the production of short staples will be checked, and the supply for Continental factories will be restricted. But were the Indian import duty to be repealed, the displacement of Indian by British manufactures would liberate, for export to the Continent, cotton which is now used up in India; and this additional export would be promoted by a rise in the price of long-stapled cotton from an increase of the British demand for it. With a larger supply of raw material, the Continental manufacture would flourish, prosperity would stimulate improvements, and gradually the Continent, while extending the manufacture of the coarser fabrics from short staples, would resume its competition with Liverpool for the long staples, and with Manchester for the finer fabrics. Manchester, finding in the Continental manufacture a more formidable competitor than the Indian, would assail the Secretary of State for India with sorrowful reproach, for having brought misfortune upon her by the repeal of £800,000 a year of Indian import duty on cotton goods. Mr. Malet, Secretary of Legation at Rome, in his report on the trade of Italy for the five years ending December 31, 1875, quoting statistics, showed that the import of English cotton goods into Italy had decreased by 6 million francs, while that of French cotton goods had increased by seven million francs, in 1875, compared with 1871. 'We must acknowledge that the French manufactures are more welcome in Italy than ours,' and that it is not the Italian import duty any more than the Indian import duty, through which, chiefly, the consumption of British cotton manufactures does not advance.

7. The statistics of the manufacture of cotton in the United Kingdom are shown in the table on p. 366.

8. The following remarks are suggested by the table:—

I. During years of plentiful supply, the waste in spinning is about one-ninth of the cotton consumed; in years of restricted supply, when inferior cotton was accepted, it was somewhat greater. Of the yarn produced, generally one-fifth is exported, and the remainder is made into cloth. Latterly, from disuse or decrease of sizing, more yarn is put into a given quantity or weight of cloth than in former years.

II. The quantities of yarn and piece goods exported have steadily increased; but the quantities retained for home consumption and stock, and the estimated actual home consumption, were less in 1875 and 1876 than in the years 1859 to 1861, and were less than in the prosperous year 1871. Considering the increased numbers and means of the population, the stationary character of the home consumption is singular.

III. The total cotton consumed, and the total manufacture, are greater by one-fourth or one-fifth than in the years 1859 to 1861, and they have steadily increased since 1869.

(In millions.)

	1859	1860	1861	1868	1869	1870	1871	1872	1873	1874	1875	1876
	lb.	lb.	lb.	lb	lb.	lb.	lb.	lb.	lb.	lb.	lb.	lb.
1. Cotton consumed .	978	1,079	1,005	996	939	1,072	1,205	1,175	1,246	1,266	1,230	1,274
2. Less waste in spinning	103	113	105	119	122	129	132	135	168	146	141	143
3. Yarn produced . .	875	966	900	877	817	943	1,073	1,040	1,078	1,120	1,089	1,131
4. Exported in yarn .	192	197	178	174	170	186	193	212	215	221	216	232
5. „ in piece goods and apparel .	501	543	496	549	535	616	680	698	688	726	713	735
6. Retained for home consumption and stocks . . .	182	226	226	154	112	140	200	130	175	174	160	164
7. Total as above . .	875	966	900	877	817	942	1,073	1,040	1,078	1,121	1,089	1,131

VALUE OF MANUFACTURES.

	1859	1860	1861	1868	1869	1870	1871	1872	1873	1874	1875	1876
	£	£	£	£	£	£	£	£	£	£	£	£
8. Yarn exported . .	9·46	9·87	9 29	14 71	14·16	14 67	15 06	16·71	15·88	14 52	13·17	12·78
9. Piece goods . .	43·06	46·25	41·51	57·34	57·66	61·42	63 88	69·90	68·13	65·93	63·97	59·30
10. Estimated value of home consumption .	19·70	24·47	23·53	19·67	14·38	17·05	23·52	15·66	20·60	20·11	18·31	17·78
11. Total value of goods produced . . .	72·22	80·59	74 33	91·72	86·20	93·14	101·96	102·27	104·61	100·56	95·45	89 86
12. Cost of cotton consumed . . .	27·58	28·91	32·20	40·99	43·77	42·14	40·81	48·05	45 44	40 22	36·53	32·85
13. Paid in wages and other expenses . .	30·33	33 60	31·36	34·94	32·05	—	—	—	—	—	—	—
14. Balance left for interest and profit .	14·31	18·08	10·77	15·79	10·38	51·00	61·15	54 22	59·17	60·34	58·92	57·01
15. Total . . .	72·22	80·59	74·33	91·72	86·20	93 14	101·96	102 27	104·61	100·56	95 45	89 86
16. Value of piece goods exported per Board of Trade Returns . .	38·74	42·14	37·58	52·97	53·02	56·75	57 76	63·47	61·47	59·73	58 60	54 55
	lb.	lb.	lb.	lb.	lb.	lb.	lb.	lb.	lb.	lb.	lb.	lb.
17. Yarns and goods exported . . .	693	740	674	723	705	802	873	917	903	947	929	967
18. Estimated actual home consumption .	172	173	174	160	125	140	185	145	160	174	165	170
	d.	d.	d.	d.	d.	d.	d.	d.	d.	d.	d.	d.
Price of middling uplands	$6\frac{3}{4}$	$6\frac{1}{4}$	$8\frac{9}{16}$	$10\frac{1}{2}$	$12\frac{1}{8}$	$9\frac{5}{16}$	$8\frac{3}{16}$	$10\frac{3}{16}$	9	8	$7\frac{3}{8}$	$6\frac{1}{4}$
Price of $8\frac{1}{4}$ lb. shirtings	$13\frac{3}{4}$	$13\frac{3}{4}$	$13\frac{1}{4}$	$14\frac{15}{16}$	$15\frac{11}{16}$	14 [illegible]	$13\frac{1}{16}$	14 [illegible]	$13\frac{5}{8}$	$12\frac{1}{2}$	12	10 [illegible]
Difference on margin .	7	$7\frac{1}{2}$	$4\frac{7}{16}$	$3\frac{7}{16}$	$3\frac{9}{16}$	4 [illegible]	$4\frac{14}{16}$	$3\frac{13}{16}$	$4\frac{10}{16}$	$4\frac{8}{16}$	$4\frac{10}{16}$	$4\frac{3}{16}$

This may be supplemented by the results of a census of cotton manufactures of Great Britain, taken at the close of 1874.

	Number of		Number of hands employed				
	Spindles	Power looms	Males and females under 13	Females above 13	Total	Males above 13	Grand total
1861	30,387,467	399,992	39,788	251,306	291,094	160,475	451,569
1870	34,695,221	440,676	43,281	251,551	294,832	155,255	450,087
1874	37,515,772	463,118	66,900	258,667	325,567	153,948	479,515

IV. Judged by the quantities manufactured, the industry is flourishing, though not materially progressive; but the outlay and returns may show a different result. Certain it is, that the margin for manufacturing expenses and profit, or the difference between the Liverpool price of cotton and the Manchester price of shirtings, was 7*d.* or 7½*d.* a pound in 1859 or 1860, but only 4½*d.* in 1874 to to 1876. The latter figure may, however, be compatible with a flourishing manufacture, for the margin was only 4⅝*d.* in 1871, which is regarded as the most prosperous year of the cotton industry.

V. The discrepant statements of the value of the cotton manufacture interfere somewhat with any estimate of its profitable character. The value of piece goods exported is returned by Messrs. Ellison and Co. in their circulars, and by the Board of Trade, as follows:—

(*Millions sterling.*)

	1859–1869	Yearly average	1874–1876	Yearly average
Messrs. Ellison .	130·82	43·61	189·20	63·06
Board of Trade .	118·46	39·49	173·18	57·73

In the earlier period the excess valuation by Messrs. Ellison was four millions, in the later period, five millions a year. The difference, and the increase of difference, affect an estimate of the probable and comparative profits in the two periods. Probably Messrs. Ellison and Co. give the credit price, while the returns of the Board of Trade are based on cash prices.

VI. Adopting the statistics of Messrs. Ellison and Co., the figures are—

(*In millions.*)

	1859	1860	1861	Total	1873	1874	1875	Total	Yearly average	1876
	lb.	lb.	lb.	lb.	lb.	lb.	lb.	lb.	lb.	lb.
Total manufactures .	875	960	900	2,741	1,078	1,121	1,089	3,288	1,096	1,131
	£	£	£	£	£	£	£	£	£	£
Value of preceding .	72	81	74	227	105	100	95	300	100	90
Cost of cotton consumed . . .	27	29	32	88	46	40	36	122	41	33
Balance left for wages and other expenses, and for interest and profit . . .	45	52	42	139	59	60	59	178	59	57

After paying for cotton, there remained for the expenses of manufacture, in the first period, 139 millions sterling for 2,741 millions of pounds of cotton manufactured, and in the second period 178 millions sterling for 3,288 million pounds; the yearly averages being 46 millions sterling for 914 million pounds in the first period, and 59 millions sterling for 1,096 million pounds in the second period. On the surface, the prosperity of the years 1859 and 1860, and the large profits to manufacturers in 1861, were surpassed in 1873 to 1875; but unfortunately such a conclusion cannot be adopted without a knowledge of the expenses of production in the later period. This information, which is of especial value on account of the rise in wages, is omitted in the circulars from 1870.

VII. We may attempt, however, a rough approximation of the working expenses.

a. In the period from 1859 to 1861, the yearly average paid in wages and other expenses, other than the cost of cotton, was 31¾ millions sterling.

b. In 1874 (table in para. 7) there were 28,000 hands more than in 1861, but the increase was entirely (36,000) among boys and females, who receive about half or less than half the wages of men, the manufacturers having endeavoured thus, by improved machinery which admitted of the freer employment of boys and women, to counteract the effect of a rise in wages; but the decrease in the males above 13, viz. 6,500, was too small to have given substantial relief.

c. The advance of weekly wages averaged 10 to 25 per cent. in 1859, compared with 1839. For a spinner the weekly wages were 20*s.* in 1850; 22*s.* in 1853; 27*s.* in 1860; 30*s.* in 1865; 42*s.* to 50*s.* in 1874. After the crisis in 1866, there was a reduction, not of rates, but to short time; and the distress in Lancashire in 1869 was followed by a rapid increase of wages in subsequent years. Wages in 1874 were 15 shillings in excess of the wages (27*s.*) in 1860, involving an advance of fifty-five per cent. If, on this account, the yearly average sum paid in the first period (*a*), viz. 32 millions, be increased by about one-third (the prices of coal and iron have increased, as well as wages), the yearly average of working expenses in the second period from 1873 to 1875 would be 43 millions, which, deducted from the 59 millions available for working expenses plus profit, would leave 16 millions as the profit, including interest on capital. For 1876, the amount would be 14 millions. In the period from 1859 to 1861, the corresponding amount was 14 millions.

d. The financial result appears, then, not to have improved with the increase of production since the years from 1859 to 1861; and in 1876 there was a positive deterioration; there must also be considerable abatements—

(1) If the increase of one-third beyond the working expenses in 1860–1 be too little for the reduction of full time by one hour, for the rise in wages, and in the prices of iron and coal, since that year.

(2) If Messrs. Ellison's valuation of exports, which greatly exceeds that of the Board of Trade, be an over-estimate.

(3) Interest should be deducted on the additional amount outstanding, for the larger proportion of business, than in 1860, which is done on credit; the bills created by the allowance of credit bearing interest.

e. Another correction remains. The exports of cotton piece goods to the East—that is, to the countries from which, owing to the depreciation of silver, it is difficult to get back returns without heavy loss—are increasing, and they form one-half of the total trade. An abatement of ten per cent. from the value of half the exports would amount to some three and a half millions sterling. If this be deducted from the returns from 1874 to 1876, the results for those three years may be considered poor, and the prospects of the cotton industry to be unpromising. This loss by exchange is recoverable through a higher selling price, but that has not been obtained yet; and with diminished consumption from a higher selling price, the result may be unchanged.

f. In 1877, much of the cotton trade appears to have been conducted at a loss, or without profit; and there has been reduction of wages.

9. Manchester's proper course is to urge the adoption in India of a gold standard, the change to be effected at a valuation between the rupee and sterling, which would correct the injurious effect of the recent depreciation of silver. More relief would be obtained in this way than from the mere five per cent. which Manchester, with a short-sighted policy, seeks from the repeal of the Indian import duty, which protects Manchester more effectually than it protects the local industry. It should not be forgotten that the manufacture of cotton goods is limited, for Manchester, by the supply of fine-stapled cotton, for which the Continental factories would compete in increased measure, if, through the extinction of the Indian manufacture, more of East Indian cotton became available on the Continent for mixing with the fine staples.

APPENDIX VIII.

WHEAT AND THE PROSPECTS OF BRITISH AGRICULTURE.

The depressed condition of the foreign trade increases the dependence of British manufactures on the home trade. The latter is affected by the consumption of the urban working classes, whose wages are falling, and by the prosperity of British agriculture. At the same time, those who are troubled by the effects upon Indian finance of the depreciation of silver cherish a sanguine hope that matters will be righted by a great expansion of the Indian wheat trade.

2. That hope should, however, awaken concern whether the agricultural interests of Great Britain will be able to endure a competition from wheat which India may export, under the stimulus of a low exchange, that for the time operates like a bounty.

3. Mr. Caird observed[1] that the farmers, if driven from the cultivation of wheat by the importation of foreign wheat, would find their advantage in bestowing more attention on oats, barley, dairy produce, meat, and the like:

> 'The steadily advancing price of these articles, and of barley, is the true explanation of increasing rents and agricultural prosperity, notwithstanding receipts of foreign corn. . . . In the production of barley, as in that of long lustrous wool, this country is still without a rival.'

Opportunities for acting on this advice have been afforded, but somehow it has been unavailing, or hard to follow.

4. The agricultural returns give the following statistics for the United Kingdom:—

[1] *Journals of the Statistical Society* for June 1868 and March 1869.

	1870	1871	1872	1873	1874	1875	1876
	(In millions of acres.)						
Corn crops, viz.:							
Wheat	3·77	3·83	3·84	3·67	3·83	3·51	3·12
Barley	2·62	2·62	2·54	2·57	2·51	2·75	2·76
Oats	4·42	4·36	4·34	4·20	4·09	4·18	4·29
	7·04	6·98	6·88	6·77	6·60	6·93	7·05
Rye, beans, and peas	·95	1·02	·98	·98	·93	·96	·89
	11·76	11·83	11·70	11·42	11·36	11·40	11·06
Green crops	5·11	5·27	5·11	4·97	4·96	5·06	4·96
Clover and grasses	6·32	6·24	6·35	6·24	6·28	6·34	6·44
	23·19	23·34	23·16	22·63	22·60	22·80	22·46
Permanent pasture	22·09	22·52	22·84	23·36	23·68	23·77	24·05
	45·28	45·86	46·00	45·99	46·28	46·57	46·51
	LIVE STOCK *(in thousands).*						
Horses for agriculture and for breeding	1,750	1,743	1,748	1,760	1,789	1,820	1,863
Cattle	9,235	9,346	9,718	10,154	10,281	10,163	9,997
Sheep	32,787	31,403	32,247	33,982	34,837	33,492	32,253

	Millions of acres				Thousands	
	Wheat	Barley	Oats	Permanent pasture	Cattle	Sheep
1868	3·95	2·35	4·47	22·16	9,083	35,607
1869	3·98	2·48	4·48	22·81	9,078	34,250

5. The following remarks are suggested by the table :—

I. The area under corn crops has decreased since 1870 by 700,000 acres, including a gross decrease of 650,000 acres under wheat; barley has gained only 140,000 acres; and oats have lost 130,000 acres.

II. Since 1869 the wheat area has decreased by 830,000 acres; and permanent pasture has increased by 1,240,000 acres, or since 1870 by 1,960,000 acres. Inasmuch, however, as the total area under corn crops, green crops, clover and grasses, exclusive of permanent pasture, has decreased since 1870 by only 730,000 acres, the remaining 1,230,000 of excess under permanent pasture arises from the inclusion of new returns. But as new returns must occur also under the other heads, the real decrease of wheat cultivation is probably greater than the apparent decrease.

III. The increase of permanent pasture has not been accompanied by an increase of cattle and sheep. Mr. Caird's crumbs of comfort appear to have been picked up by foreign birds.

IV. Even vegetables give but scant hope; market gardens in Great Britain showing an increase of only 2,000 acres since 1872. In green crops there is a slight decline.

6. Mr. Caird did not anticipate the considerable increase which has occurred of importations of barley, oats, and maize.

	Yearly average in				
	1841 to 1846	1847 to 1853	1854 to 1860	1861 to 1868	1869 to 1876
	(Thousands of quarters.)			*(Thousands of cwts.)*	
Wheat	1,578	3,516	3,962	34,784	48,392
Other kinds of corn .	1,172	4,607	4,866	27,728	47,213
	2,750	8,213	8,828	62,512	95,605
	(Thousands of cwts.)			1 Imperial quarter = 4⅓ cwt. of wheat = 3½ cwt. of wheat flour.	
Wheat meal and flour .	1,324	4,842	3,424		
Other sorts of meal .	34	466	27		

(In millions of cwts.)

	Barley	Oats	Maize	Total	Other	Total of other kinds than wheat	Wheat & wheat flour	Total corn
1868	7·5	8·1	11·5	27·1	4·2	31·3	36·5	67·8
1869	8·0	7·9	17·7	33·6	3·2	36·8	44·5	81·3
1870	7·2	10·8	16·8	34·8	3·6	38·4	36·9	75·3
1871	8·6	10·9	16·8	36·3	4·3	40·6	44·4	85·0
1872	15·0	11·5	24·5	51·0	4·7	55·7	47·6	103·3
1873	9·2	11·9	18·8	39·9	4·4	44·3	51·6	95·9
1874	11·3	11·4	17·7	40·4	4·8	45·2	49·3	94·5
1875	11·0	12·4	20·4	43·8	5·7	49·5	59·5	109·0
1876	9·8	11·2	39·9	60·9	6·2	67·1	53·3	120·4
1877 to Aug. 31	7·6	8·9	—	—	3·7	—	32·7	—
Year from Sept. 1 to Aug. 31								
1874–5	13·1	12·2	17·2	42·5	4·8	47·3	49·7	97·0
1875–6	8·1	11·0	34·3	53·4	5·8	59·2	53·6	112·8
1876-7	13·2	12·8	34·0	60·0	5·9	65·9	45·2	111·1

From 1861 to 1868, which furnished Mr. Caird's latest experience, when he wrote, the imports of wheat exceeded the imports of other kinds of corn; but in the eight years after 1868 the percentage of increase of wheat was considerably less than the proportion of increase in other kinds of corn.

7. The following remarks are suggested by the last table:—

I. Barley, oats, and maize are used respectively for malting or distillation, or as food for cattle and horses, the three being also used as human food, viz: barley to a considerable extent in Wales, Westmoreland, Cumberland, and Scotland; oats in Scotland; Indian corn in Ireland. The last mentioned is also in great demand for distillation, and as food for stock, since it has become cheaper than oats, and cheaper than any other kind of corn, the produce of the United Kingdom.

II. The requirements of malting and distillation have indeed increased, but not in the proportion of the increase in the importations of the three grains. As food for cattle, maize may have partially displaced oats, but only to liberate the oats for use as human food. On the whole, much of the increased importations of barley, oats, and maize must be held, from their use as human food, to modify the usual estimates of requirements of wheat for consumption in the United Kingdom.

III. Mr. Caird's advice notwithstanding, the remunerative character of the cultivation of oats has not prevented a decline of that cultivation from 4·47 million acres in 1868 to 4·29 million acres in 1876, or of the sales reported from 150 towns in England and Wales, from 249,867 quarters in 1867 to 148,878 quarters in 1876, though the importations of foreign oats increased under prevailing prices by three million cwts., or by nearly 40 per cent.

IV. It is held that the charges of transit of Californian wheat to the Atlantic seaboard, and freight thence to England, set off the rent paid by British farmers; the immensely increased importations of cheap maize seem to denote, however, that the expenses of transit are less than is generally supposed. The competition of canals with the railways [1] keeps down the expenses. The shipments of grain from the the United States in 1877 have exceeded those of last year by nearly 40 per cent.; and the crop in those States this year is 25 million bushels greater than in any previous year. The price of wheat which stimulated the cultivation of that crop was 46*s.* 2*d.* in 1876, after

[1] *Economist*, July 7, 1877.

45*s*. 2*d*. per quarter in 1875. In a paper in the 'Statistical Journal' for March 1869, Mr. Caird observed: "When the price of wheat falls below 50*s*., the farmer begins to turn his attention to other crops.' The increase of agricultural wages since 1869 has not lessened the farmer's expenses of cultivation; on the whole, the cultivation of wheat is pursued in the United Kingdom in the face of a very trying competition.

8. The conclusions in section III. of the preceding paragraph have to be so far modified for the present, that the decline of the cultivation of oats and barley has occurred wholly in Ireland, the Agricultural Returns for which country were brought to a state of accuracy some years before the returns for Great Britain were commenced in 1867; in England and Scotland the cultivation shows a slight increase since 1870; but, first, we have seen that an enormous area of permanent pasture has been added for 1876 from new returns which were not included in the earlier year, and the comparison for wheat, barley, and oats, in favour of 1876, may include an over-statement from the same cause; secondly, the use of maize on the large scale on which the importation is now established, and the increasing importations of foreign barley and oats, which have advanced since 1869 at a greater rate than the home production (notwithstanding the diminished cultivation of wheat), must continue to grow.

9. English and foreign writers have been speculating that as the trade of jute was diverted from Russia by the Crimean war, so her trade in grain may be injured by the present war, through the permanent transfer of a part of it to other countries. England has had similar experience in her own agriculture. The bulk of the increased importations of oats and maize in the five years from 1847 to 1853, compared with the five years from 1841 to 1846 (para. 6) occurred in the year of the Irish Famine. The extended footing which foreign oats and Indian corn for human consumption in Ireland then acquired has been permanently maintained; and, in like manner, the second considerable spurt which oats received in 1870, and maize in 1869 (same para.) has been maintained with a steady improvement since, in oats, and with yet another spurt for maize, of which the importations reached 34 million hundredweights in the harvest years 1875–6 and 1876–7, against 12 millions in 1868, and 17 to 18 millions in the subsequent calendar years down to 1874.

10. We must look a little closer into the facts of this foreign competition. The imports of wheat, wheat meal, and flour from the principal foreign countries are as follows:—

(*In thousands of cwts.*, 000's *omitted.*)

	1859	1860	1861	1862	1863	1864	1865	1866	1867
I. Austria and Turkey	384	1,041	1,468	2,591	523	527	1,187	1,919	3,154
Germany	4,561	6,805	6,658	7,931	5,729	6,843	7,224	6,802	7,873
Russia	3.837	5,660	4,540	5,756	4,539	5,129	8,094	9,181	14,166
Egypt	1,634	858	1,474	3,304	2,323	367	10	.34	1,472
	10,416	14,464	14,140	19,582	13,114	12,866	16,515	17,936	26,665
British North America	171	1,311	3.388	5,119	3,198	1,832	528	60	835
United States	430	9,815	15,610	21,765	11,869	10,077	1,498	086	5,092
Chili	—	34	364	347	282	198	170	342	2.098
	601	10,660	19,362	27,231	15,349	12,107	2,196	1,388	8,025
Total of I.	11,017	25,124	33.502	46,818	28,463	24,973	18 711	19,324	34,690
II. France	8,125	4,583	1,360	1,962	1,857	2,854	6,059	8,023	2,141
III. Other countries	2,356	2,185	2,785	1,267	568	1,010	1,073	2,025	2,806
Grand total	21,498	31,842	37,647	50,042	30,888	28,837	25,843	29,372	39,137
	s. d	s. d.	s. d.	s. d	s. d.	s. d.	s. d.	s. d.	s. d.
Price of wheat	43 9	53 3	56 4	55 5	44 9	40 2	41 10	49 11	64 5

	1868	1869	1870	1871	1872	1873	1874	1875	1876
I. Austria and Turkey	4,317	3,133	957	2,258	1,287	732	908	1,733	1,823
Germany	7,224	7,547	4,488	4,259	5.183	3,019	4,012	6,613	3,488
Russia	10,055	9,187	10,327	15,697	17,939	9,694	5,799	10,158	8,912
Egypt	3,237	1,029	107	909	2,361	1,272	298	2,112	2,249
	24,833	20,896	15,879	23,123	26,770	14,717	11,017	20,616	16,472
British North America	798	3,396	3,403	3,783	2,157	4,316	4,298	4,070	2,777
United States	6,753	15,320	15,057	15,625	9,644	21,775	27,206	26,872	22,223
Chili	1,478	580	643	590	1,678	1,837	2,207	903	1,012
	9,029	19,296	19,103	19,998	13,469	27,928	33,711	31,345	26,012
Total of I.	33,862	40,192	34,982	43,121	40,239	42,645	44,728	51,961	42,484
II. France	847	2,153	1,060	182	4,554	3,256	1,125	3,574	1,653
III. Other countries	1,797	2,103	864	1,039	2,820	5,730	3,470	4,012	7,767
Grand total	36,506	44,448	36,906	44,362	47,613	51,631	49.323	59.547	51,904
	s. d.	s. d.	s. d.	s. d.	s. d.	s. d	s. d.	s. d.	s. d.
Price of wheat	63 9	48 2	46 10	56 8	57 0	58 8	55 9	45 2	46 2

11. The following remarks are suggested by the table :—

I. The two competitors for the world's supply of wheat are France and England; the former competing only when her own harvest is deficient, and exporting to England when it is plentiful.

II. The importation of 29 million hundredweights in 1859 was equal to 4·9 million quarters, and that in 1860 was 7·3 million quarters. The yearly averages have been—

	Quarters		Quarters
1841 to 1846	1,956,000	1860 to 1870	8,199,000
1847 to 1853	4,900,000	1871 to 1876	11,697,000
1854 to 1859	6,789,000		

The increase in the seventeen years since 1853 was three and one-third million quarters beyond the annual average in the seven years from 1847 to 1853; while in only six years, from 1871 to 1876, the increase beyond the average in the seventeen years to 1870 has amounted to three and a half million quarters. The yield of British wheat cultivation in 1876 was estimated at 10,600,000 quarters, including 800,000 quarters for seed, which left 9,800,000 quarters for consumption; so that the foreign wheat now exceeds the home produce by nearly one-fifth.

III. The imports from Germany include Hungarian wheat; so that nearly all the imports in section I. of the table are from countries which are indebted to England; their debts have been greater since 1867 than previously; and during the same period there has been a great extension of railways in the indebted countries.

IV. The high wages on the Continent have arrested some of the supplies which used to come from Germany, the people who formerly consumed rye bread now consuming wheat.

V. Among the indebted countries, the supply from Russia is dependent more on the seasons than on the price; as a reference to the importations and prices in 1860 to 1862, and 1870 to 1876 will show. The great expansion of the wheat trade has been with the United States and Canada; the imports from which countries were only fifteen or sixteen million hundredweights in 1861 and 1863. From 1869 to 1871, they ranged at about nineteen millions, and then at a bound reached twenty-six millions in 1873, and thirty-one or thirty millions in 1874 and 1875. In 1877, the United States' crop has greatly exceeded that of any previous year, and the importations of wheat will be proportionately greater.

VI. The permanency of the supply from the United States is assured. Mr. Caird, in his letter to the 'Times' of September 19, 1876, observed that the sudden rise in the imports from the United States and Canada was stimulated by four previous years of high prices. 'More capital was put into the business, chiefly in California and Oregon;' whence it follows that the persons who have sunk capital will be under the necessity of producing and exporting so long as there is the smallest margin of profit. Any endeavour to ascertain that margin from a comparison of the ruling prices of wheat at New York and in London can only mislead. Thus—

	Jan. 1, 1876	Jan. 1, 1877
	s. d.	s. d.
Average price in England per quarter .	45 3	50 6
	$	$
No. 2 Chicago Spring, per bushel . .	1·25	1·38
„ „ per quarter . .	10·	11·04

The intrinsic par of the gold dollar is £1=4·8665 dollars. The price of gold was 112⅞ on Dec. 31, 1875, and 107⅛ on Dec. 30, 1876. It is evident that the differences between the prices in the two periods have no reference to the cost of production. The 'New York Financial Chronicle' of January 27, 1877, from which the figures are taken, observed :—

'It is very probable that many who, last August, when No. 2 spring wheat was selling in Chicago at 85 cents a bushel, were certain it would decline to 75 cents, have latterly been buyers there at $1.30, feeling equally certain of an advance to $1.40. When a great staple like wheat has been abnormally depressed, it reaches, on the reaction, extreme figures in the opposite direction, and *vice versâ.*'

Thus, 12 million hundredweights were imported from the United States in 1863, when wheat was at 44*s.* 9*d.*; 10 millions in 1864, with wheat at 40*s.* 2*d.*, when harvest charges were heavier than now; 15 millions in 1870, 26 millions in 1875, and 22 millions in 1876, with prices at 46*s.* 10*d.*, 45*s.* 2*d.*, and 46*s.* 2*d.* respectively. The lowest paying price, in London, for the importation of American wheat is evidently below 44 shillings, whilst Mr. Caird pointed out in March 1869, that when the price of wheat falls below 50 shillings, the farmer begins to turn his attention to other crops. Hence, Mr. Caird perhaps fell into an inadvertence when he wrote in the 'Times' of September 19, 1876, that the price then ruling, viz., 46*s.* 8*d.* a quarter, left very little more than three shillings profit on Californian and Oregon wheat. Even at that rate, however, the profit was nearly one fourteenth, or seven per cent.

12. During the period from 1847 to 1876, the price of wheat has ranged as follows, viz. :—

(1) From 1847 to 1860:

a. At above 50 shillings a quarter during eight years
„ below „ „ six years

(2) From 1861 to 1876:

b. At above 50 shillings a quarter during eight years
„ below „ „ eight years.

The good and bad seasons were distributed in about the same proportions. In the thirty-six years from 1841 to 1876 there were sixteen bad seasons, of which nine occurred in the first twenty years down to 1860, and seven in the other sixteen years; that is, they occurred in equal proportion to the other seasons in the two periods. Of the other sixteen seasons from 1841 to 1876, eight were very good, namely, four in the first period of twenty years, and four in the other sixteen years down to 1876. The average, or nearly average seasons, were seven in the first and five in the second period. On the whole, the advantage has been in favour of the sixteen years from 1861 to 1876, during which the average price of wheat was 51*s.* 8*d.*, against 53*s.* 11*d.* in the twenty years down to 1860. During the last eight years the average price was 51*s.* 9*d.*, or about the same as in the past sixteen years.

13. The high prices occurred generally in the years of high wages. In the first period from 1847 to 1860, the price was above 69 shilllings in four years; in the second period the highest was 64½ shillings, and in only two years did it exceed 59 shillings. In the eight years from 1869 to 1876 it was below 49 shillings during four years, and it ranged above 55 shillings in other four years, of which three were years of high wages. In 1875 and 1876 (years of depressed trade, but during which wages were still maintained above the level of earlier years since 1861) the price was 45*s.* 2*d.* in 1875, and 46*s.* 2*d.* in 1876. On the whole, the price of wheat has declined, with a tendency to fall during a long term of years.

14. Thus far, we have considered the following circumstances which tend collectively to reduce the price of corn, viz.:—

I. Two countries are the principal competitors for the world's supply of wheat, of which countries the population in one is stationary or declining.

II. Of the several kinds of corn the production of wheat and Indian corn, which occupy the extremes as the best and the coarsest, has largely increased, with the result or tendency necessarily of pulling down, at least eventually, the prices of the intermediate kinds, viz., oats, barley, rye, &c.

III. The cost of carriage from California, a principal source of supply, has been reduced; and the indebtedness of the principal agricultural countries which supply England constrains them to sell at a low price. The inconvertible paper money of some of the countries has tended in the same direction.

IV. The one countervailing circumstance tending to raise prices has been the general increase of wages, which has raised the scale of living of the working classes, but latterly there has been going on a reduction of wages, which has not yet ceased.

15. If, under the influence of the three circumstances first mentioned, the price of wheat has not fallen to the extent which might have been expected, the result must be ascribed to one or all of three causes, viz.: 1st, the depreciation of the precious metals; 2nd, the general increase of population and of that of the United Kingdom; 3rd, to the conversion of wheat lands into other cultivation, or into pasturage, in the United Kingdom.

16. Mr. Jacob, in estimating the consumption of wheat from 1816 to 1827, reckoned it, per head, at 6½ bushels a year. Mr. Caird, adopting the results of an elaborate investigation by Messrs. J. B. Lawes and J. H. Gilbert, published in the 'Journal of the Royal Agricultural Society of England,' in 1868, assumed it in 1869 at about 5·3 bushels for the United Kingdom, viz.: for England and Wales, 6·1; for Scotland, 4·2; for Great Britain, 5·3. Reckoning at 5½ bushels, the extra quantity required for the increase of population since 1858 was as follows, viz.:—

(000's *omitted.*)

	Excess in				
	1868 over 1858	1876 over 1868	Yearly average from 1861 to 1868 over 1858	Yearly average from 1869 to 1876 over 1861 to 1868	1876 over 1858
Population	2,228	2,471	1,383	2,209	4,699
Extra quantity required, at 5½ bushels per head	Qrs. 1,532	Qrs. 1,699	Qrs. 951	Qrs. 1,519	Qrs. 3,231
Imported	3,072	3,527	2,669	3,930	6,599

Writing in 1868, Mr. Caird assumed 27 bushels as the average yield of an acre of wheat land; in the present day, the average is assumed by Mr. Caird and other authorities at 30 bushels or 3¾ quarters per acre; the increase of average implying, it is presumed, that inferior wheat lands have been turned to other uses.

17. The quantity of wheat required for the excess of population in 1876 over that in 1858 was 3,231,000 quarters; but the imports of 1876 exceeded those of 1858 by 6,599,000 quarters, which, at an average yield of 3¾ quarters per acre, was equal to the produce of 1,753,066 acres; or nearly one-half the breadth of wheat cultivation in the United Kingdom in 1868. The 11,978,000 quarters imported in 1876 would, in England, have required an area of 3,194,133 acres, or somewhat more than the total area under wheat in 1876. Mr. Caird, in his letter to the 'Times' of September 19, 1876, stated that the area cultivated has decreased from the highest point, in the last ten years, by 16 per cent in Great Britain, and by more than 50 per cent. in Ireland.

18. In 1869, Mr. Caird regarded the decline of wheat cultivation without uneasiness. The farmer, he considered, would be compensated by the rise in the price of barley (which has fallen since Mr. Caird wrote in March 1869), and by the steady price of oats, which would not remain steady, were additional supplies of oats to be substituted for wheat. It may be doubted whether Mr. Caird still cherishes this confident expectation; for a feeling of uneasiness, as if all was not right, may be traced in his remark, in his letter in the 'Times' of September 19, 1876, that 'the cost and charges from Western America and South Russia amount, on the produce of an acre, to more than the rent of our land.' If this be the case, the great decline of wheat cultivation is inexplicable.

19. And we have seen that the great increase of imports of maize, barley, and oats precludes the cultivation, to any material extent, of barley and oats on the wheat land which is being abandoned, under pressure of foreign competition.

20. But Mr. Caird found a gleam of comfort in dairy produce and meat, and in the increasing value of the farmer's live stock. This last, with the increase of above a million acres of permanent pasture, suggests disquieting ideas of vast grazing farms—the decline of an empire. England, with her energies enfeebled, perchance, by the civilisation of which she leads the van, is to renew her youth by returning to some form of pastoral life.

21. But the youngest born of the nations dispels this hope. The 'Pall Mall Budget' of October 19, 1877, writes:—

'The increased facilities for sending fresh meat to Europe have caused the shipments of beef this year to reach, thus far, a value of 8,082,036 dollars, against only 1,795,101 dollars for the same period of last year; and of mutton 113,500 dollars against none in 1876. The live sheep sent in 1877 are valued at 61,110 dollars; in 1876 at nothing. Live cattle this year at 2,060,950 dollars; in 1876 a comparatively insignificant quantity.'

This is only the second year, and the first was an incomplete year, of the American meat trade. It having proved remunerative on a large scale, it needs but little knowledge of the enterprise and spirit of the Americans to be assured of a rapid development of the trade. But, adds Mr. Caird, there is the farmer's dairy produce. The 'Pall Mall Budget,' already quoted, states:—

'The total shipments of butter from January 1 to September 29 consisted of 12,250,690 lbs., against 5,919,073 lbs. last year; and of cheese 89,650,350 lbs. against 53,706,530 lbs. in 1876. A large trade in live stock and meat is also springing up with South America.'

22. The increase of imported animals to five-fold the number, and of meat and lard to eight-fold the quantity in 1876 as compared with 1858, far exceeds the rate of increase of population. A similar remark is applicable to potatoes, butter, cheese, and eggs. In animals the increase is progressive. That this trade has not developed at the expense of the home trade may be admitted, though some might challenge the concession; but the development discourages any hope that the farmers can find in live stock, meat, and dairy produce an adequate compensation for the loss, actual and impending, of wheat cultivation.

23. And will the throbbings and the agony which distress the City on the exportation of gold be relieved or abated when it runs out, in increasing volume, in payment for vastly augmented supplies of wheat, meat, and live-stock?

24. Mr. M'Culloch stated in his 'Statistical Account of the British Empire,' edition 1837, that 'a great deal of arable land, even of a moderately good quality, lets at from 10 to 15 shillings an acre; and where highest, its rent, exclusive of tithes, poor rates, and other public burdens, seldom exceeds 25 shillings an acre, unless where it enjoys some peculiar advantage.' The author of the article on Agriculture in the 'Encyc. Britannica,' edition 1875, observes that '30 shillings an acre would in England be considered a fair and even a high rate for middling land.' The excess of 15 or 20 shillings an acre over Mr. M'Culloch's 10 to 15 shillings, shows a doubling of the rent and more. The increase was met from the enhanced price of barley and of meat. But can it be long maintained, should the price of wheat fall? Before the increase of agricultural wages, Mr. Caird stated that when wheat falls to 50 shillings a quarter, the farmer

turns his attention to other crops, which now encounter strong competition from foreign oats, barley, and maize. And we have seen that American wheat can be sold under 45 shillings a quarter, about which point the price of wheat fluctuated in England from October 1874 to May 1876. The average yield of an acre being 30 bushels, or $3\frac{3}{4}$ quarters, a permanent reduction in price of five shillings per quarter would mean a loss per acre of $18\frac{3}{4}$ shillings, equal to the increase of rent since 1837. This would be the result, without laying stress on Mr. Caird's opinion, that wheat ceases to remunerate the farmer when the price falls to 50 shillings a quarter.

25. Hence we find the 'Pall Mall Budget' of June 20, 1877, writing:—

'Agriculture in England is passing through a crisis. There is great alarm, and no inconsiderable amount of suffering. Many farmers of late years have been ruined, many farms are vacant, and there is great difficulty in finding tenants. In some districts the difficulty amounts to impossibility, and landowners have been forced to become farmers themselves, and to cultivate their own land. Nay, there are not a few cases in which the offer to give a farm rent-free for some years fails to bribe any one to undertake to pay a moderate rent at a future period. The leaders among the tenant farmers recommend their brethren to bring up their children to any trade but that of agriculture. There are symptoms of a change of which no one can confidently predict the issue, but which, in any case, must certainly be momentous. If it means a permanent depreciation in the value of land, it means a social and perhaps a political revolution. If it means only that new conditions are calling for new developments of capital and skill, it still means that old systems are dying, and that henceforth there will be new relations between the various classes who are interested in "the land."

'One thing is at least clear, that this disturbance in the established order is not due to any temporary or accidental cause. We have had two deficient harvests, but they followed upon one which was very abundant, and even 1875 and 1876 were not to be classed with many black years that have been known.

'. . . The extension of drainage, and the introduction of foreign manures and feeding stuffs, brought up the average returns from the soil to a pitch they had never previously reached. At the same time, the extraordinary development in trade and manufactures raised wages in the manufacturing districts, and carried meat and wool to prices unheard of. These influences in combination not only delivered the British farmer from anticipated ruin, but gave him a prosperity he had never before attained—a result which involved the consequence that rents during the quarter of a century between 1848 and 1873 not only did not fall, but unquestionably tended to rise.

'But in every one of the elements of this prosperity there has now occurred a check. Competition from abroad still assumes new phases. Wheat comes not only from Russia and the Atlantic sea-board, but from India, Australia, and California. Meat itself is now imported from America, and even if this should not be on a scale to depress prices, it will probably, at least, prevent any farther rise. But, in addition to these old sources of apprehension, the farmer has now to encounter a totally new burden. The cost necessary for production has immensely increased. More labour is needed under the new system of farming, than under the old, and the wages of labour have, as a consequence of the movement of which the strikes were only a symptom, risen on an average at least 30 per cent. Machinery has indeed been largely introduced, but machines too are very costly. Again, foreign manures, which are now so much depended on to augment the bulk in the rickyard, are, considering deterioration of quality, 50 per cent. dearer than they used to be. The position on the whole is this—that though produce and prices do not as yet fall off, yet to produce involves a much greater outlay; while there seems no longer any room for expecting that prices will go higher. Therefore matters look very black for those who only think of farming as farming used to be. For such persons, there is only one element of the outlay that can be reduced, and that element is the rent. To spend less on labour, means to grow more weeds; to spend less on artificial manures, means to grow less corn; to spend less on machines, means to get the work worse done; and therefore there is nothing for it but to spend less in the hire of the land.'

26. The writer then mentions large exceptions to the class of districts and farms which have been thus affected, viz., Scotland, large districts in England, and all classes of dairy farms. But this brighter side of the picture should only stimulate a hopeful search for a remedy for the extensively prevalent distress; we should not shut our eyes to the drift of the causes of permanent operation which are affecting the interests of British agriculture, and the tendency of which is to reduce farmers' profits to a point when reduction of rent will become imperative.

27. For the facts which confront us are—a greatly augmented production in the world, and of importation into the United Kingdom, of wheat and maize; increasing imports, in considerable amount, of barley and oats; a nascent, fast-developing trade with the western coast of North America and with South America in meat and dairy produce; a fall in wages which, by reducing the consumption of meat, and the general scale of living, must depress agricultural produce; a vast increase of indebtedness in foreign countries which have no means of paying the interest on their debt, beyond an augmented exportation of cereals to England; and, as emphasising these warnings, a serious decrease of wheat cultivation in the United Kingdom, and a fall in the apparent price of wheat, in the last sixteen compared with the previous fourteen years, which indicates a real decrease that is much greater by reason of the depreciation of gold that has increased rents, and has increased expenses of cultivation, but has only

counteracted a fall, without causing further a commensurate rise, in the price of wheat.

28. As yet, the suffering is not general, because most landlords take less than the proper economic rent; and accordingly their tenants have a margin, more or less wide, for meeting a fall in the price of wheat, and withstanding the effects of foreign competition. But when the causes which this year have temporarily raised the price of wheat shall have passed away, the action of the abiding causes that have been reviewed will revive, and British agriculture must undergo afresh the ordeal of the low prices of 1863 to 1866, 1869 and 1870, 1875 and 1876.

29. When, in the struggle with foreign competition, farmers shall have parted with the difference between their actual rent and their proper economic rent (and many have done so already, as testified by the writer in the 'Pall Mall Gazette'), tenants and landlords will be confronted with questions of tenant right, of compensation for improvements, and of revisions of laws which affect expenses of cultivation, or the free employment of capital in farming. Land is a luxury in England, and it has a very high artificial price as such; but sumptuary laws are enacted when luxury begins to sap vital interests of a nation; and English landlords, who instinctively apprehend their duties, in advance of the prevailing sentiment, will perceive, if they regard the handwriting on the wall, that a true conservatism calls for a comprehensive revision of existing laws, which, to be effectual and beneficial, must be undertaken by themselves.

30. The number of persons engaged in agriculture in England and Wales (excluding persons engaged about animals, who in the census of 1861 were not reckoned) has been as follows:—

	Under 20 years	Above 20 years	Total
Census of 1851 . .	435,367	1,576,080	2,011,447
" 1861 . .	392,820	1,531,290	1,924,110
" 1871 . .	341,390	1,217,647	1,559,037
Decrease in 1871:			
Below 1861 . .	51,430	313,643	365,073
Below 1851 . .	93,977	358,433	452,410

31. The decrease has been chiefly since 1861, partly from the substitution of steam power and machines for hand labour, but mainly from the conversion of arable into pasture land. Those who put on a brave face in regarding the competition of foreign with British agri-

culture, studiously look only at the money aspect of the subject; they solace themselves and the public with the thought that the profits of permanent pasture will keep up rents, and leave the public as gainers from wheat cheapened by foreign importations. But we have seen that the profits from pasturage, on a scale adequate to compensate the decline in the cultivation of wheat, are very doubtful; and the present figures show that the advantage of cheap wheat is purchased by the decay of the manhood of the nation—of that part of the population from which the army of England is recruited, and out of which the larger forces with which England must be prepared to maintain her rank and prestige among the nations would be mobilised.

32. The advantage of cheap wheat must not be sacrificed; but it is intolerable that it should be retained by the decay of the strength of the nation. It rests with the landed gentry to reconcile that instinct of human life with this feeling of a patriotism which, having raised England through sacrifices by their fathers, to greatness among the nations, should maintain her there through similar sacrifices by sons worthy of their ancient ancestry, who lived and moved in days when great ends incited to noble deeds.

But sentiment should be distrusted, unless it is supported by common sense. The average yield of wheat per acre is $12\frac{1}{3}$ bushels in the United States and Hungary, $15\frac{1}{2}$ bushels in France, but 30 bushels in the United Kingdom. Is it reasonable that, with this advantage, English agriculture should sustain, from foreign competition, injury which it has partly experienced, and more of which is impending? And is it consistent with patriotism, and with a proper recognition of the duties of property, in which English landlords are not wanting, that the hindrances which prevent English agriculture from prevailing in the competition with foreign are not removed?

The causes which are depressing the foreign export trade of England will not soon cease. Her manufactures must be sustained by an expanding home market; and the measures which would enable British agriculture to withstand foreign competition would largely promote a demand for home manufactures, raise the scale of living by a widely diffused improvement of small incomes, and reduce pauperism. On the other hand, with manufacturing industries languishing, and wages falling, the price of agricultural produce will decline, urban labourers will be returned on their parishes, poor rates will increase, and their incidence upon an income from land, reduced by falling rents, will be doubly severe.

The agricultural and manufacturing industries of England require bracing up; and the obvious measures to that end would unite them in closer sympathy, bridge a chasm between rich and poor, and remove political dangers of which premonitory signs have not been wanting in the past four or five years.

The economic effects more immediately connected with the present inquiry would be more retail dealings, a greater demand for subsidiary currency, and little or no demand for Indian wheat.

GENERAL LIST OF WORKS

PUBLISHED BY

MESSRS. LONGMANS, GREEN & CO.

HISTORY, POLITICS, HISTORICAL MEMOIRS, &c.

A History of England from the Conclusion of the Great War in 1815. By SPENCER WALPOLE, Author of 'Life of the Rt. Hon. Spencer Perceval.' VOLS. I. & II. 8vo. 36*s.*

History of England in the 18th Century. By W. E. H. LECKY, M.A. VOLS. I. & II. 1700–1760. 2 vols. 8vo. 36*s.*

The History of England from the Accession of James II. By the Right Hon. Lord MACAULAY.

STUDENT'S EDITION, 2 vols. cr. 8vo. 12*s.*
PEOPLE'S EDITION, 4 vols. cr. 8vo. 16*s.*
CABINET EDITION, 8 vols. post 8vo. 48*s.*
LIBRARY EDITION, 5 vols. 8vo. £4.

Critical and Historical Essays contributed to the Edinburgh Review. By the Right Hon. Lord MACAULAY.

CHEAP EDITION, crown 8vo. 3*s.* 6*d.*
STUDENT'S EDITION, crown 8vo. 6*s.*
PEOPLE'S EDITION, 2 vols. crown 8vo. 8*s.*
CABINET EDITION, 4 vols. 24*s.*
LIBRARY EDITION, 3 vols. 8vo. 36*s.*

Lord Macaulay's Works. Complete and uniform Library Edition. Edited by his Sister, Lady TREVELYAN. 8 vols. 8vo. with Portrait, £5. 5*s.*

The History of England from the Fall of Wolsey to the Defeat of the Spanish Armada. By J. A. FROUDE, M.A.

CABINET EDITION, 12 vols. cr. 8vo. £3. 12*s.*
LIBRARY EDITION, 12 vols. 8vo. £8. 18*s.*

The English in Ireland in the Eighteenth Century. By J. A. FROUDE, M.A. 3 vols. 8vo. £2. 8*s.*

Journal of the Reigns of King George IV. and King William IV. By the late C. C. F. GREVILLE, Esq. Edited by H. REEVE, Esq. Fifth Edition. 3 vols. 8vo. price 36*s.*

The Life of Napoleon III. derived from State Records, Unpublished Family Correspondence, and Personal Testimony. By BLANCHARD JERROLD. In Four Volumes, 8vo. with numerous Portraits and Facsimiles. VOLS. I. to III. price 18*s.* each.

The Constitutional History of England since the Accession of George III. 1760–1870. By Sir THOMAS ERSKINE MAY, K.C.B. D.C.L. Fifth Edition. 3 vols. crown 8vo. 18*s.*

Democracy in Europe; a History. By Sir THOMAS ERSKINE MAY, K.C.B. D.C.L. 2 vols. 8vo. 32*s.*

Introductory Lectures on Modern History delivered in 1841 and 1842. By the late Rev. T. ARNOLD, D.D. 8vo. price *7s. 6d.*

On Parliamentary Government in England; its Origin, Development, and Practical Operation. By ALPHEUS TODD. 2 vols. 8vo. price £1. 17*s.*

History of Civilisation in England and France, Spain and Scotland. By HENRY THOMAS BUCKLE. 3 vols. crown 8vo. 24*s.*

Lectures on the History of England from the Earliest Times to the Death of King Edward II. By W. LONGMAN, F.S.A. Maps and Illustrations. 8vo. 15*s.*

History of the Life & Times of Edward III. By W. LONGMAN, F.S.A. With 9 Maps, 8 Plates, and 16 Woodcuts. 2 vols. 8vo. 28*s.*

History of the Life and Reign of Richard III. To which is added the Story of PERKIN WARBECK, from Original Documents. By JAMES GAIRDNER. With Portrait and Map. Crown 8vo. 10*s.* 6*d.*

The Life of Simon de Montfort, Earl of Leicester, with special reference to the Parliamentary History of his time. By G. W. PROTHERO. Crown 8vo. Maps, 9*s.*

History of England under the Duke of Buckingham and Charles I. 1624–1628. By S. R. GARDINER. 2 vols. 8vo. Maps, 24*s.*

The Personal Government of Charles I. from the Death of Buckingham to the Declaration in favour of Ship Money, 1628–1637. By S. R. GARDINER. 2 vols. 8vo. 24*s.*

Popular History of France, from the Earliest Times to the Death of Louis XIV. By ELIZABETH M. SEWELL. With 8 Maps. Crown 8vo. 7*s.* 6*d.*

The Famine Campaign in Southern India, (Madras, Bombay, and Mysore,) in 1876–78. By WILLIAM DIGBY, Secretary of the Madras Famine Committee. With Maps and many Illustrations. 2 vols. 8vo. 32*s.*

A Student's Manual of the History of India from the Earliest Period to the Present. By Col. MEADOWS TAYLOR, M.R.A.S. Third Thousand. Crown 8vo. Maps, 7*s.* 6*d.*

Indian Polity; a View of the System of Administration in India. By Lieut.-Col. G. CHESNEY. 8vo. 21*s.*

Waterloo Lectures; a Study of the Campaign of 1815. By Colonel C. C. CHESNEY, R.E. 8vo. 10*s.* 6*d.*

The Oxford Reformers— John Colet, Erasmus, and Thomas More; a History of their Fellow-Work. By F. SEEBOHM. 8vo. 14*s.*

General History of Rome from B.C. 753 to A.D. 476. By Dean MERIVALE, D.D. Crown 8vo. Maps, price 7*s.* 6*d.*

The Fall of the Roman Republic; a Short History of the Last Century of the Commonwealth. By Dean MERIVALE, D.D. 12mo. 7*s.* 6*d.*

Carthage and the Carthaginians. By R. BOSWORTH SMITH, M.A. With 11 Maps, Plans & Illustrations. Crown 8vo. 10*s.* 6*d.*

History of the Romans under the Empire. By Dean MERIVALE, D.D. 8 vols. post 8vo. 48*s.*

The History of Rome. By WILHELM IHNE. VOLS. I. to III. 8vo. price 45*s.*

History of the Mongols from the Ninth to the Nineteenth Century. By HENRY H. HOWORTH, F.S.A. VOL. I. Royal 8vo. 28*s.*

The Sixth Oriental Monarchy; or, the Geography, History, and Antiquities of Parthia. By G. RAWLINSON, M.A. With Maps and Illustrations. 8vo. 16*s.*

The Seventh Great Oriental Monarchy; or, a History of the Sassanians. By G. RAWLINSON, M.A. With Map and 95 Illustrations. 8vo. 28*s.*

The History of European Morals from Augustus to Charlemagne. By W. E. H. LECKY, M.A. 2 vols. crown 8vo. 16*s.*

History of the Rise and Influence of the Spirit of Rationalism in Europe. By W. E. H. LECKY, M.A. 2 vols. crown 8vo. 16*s.*

The Childhood of the English Nation; or, the Beginnings of English History. By ELLA S. ARMITAGE. Fcp. 8vo. 2*s.* 6*d.*

Sketch of the History of the Church of England to the Revolution of 1688. By T. V. SHORT, D.D. Crown 8vo. 7*s.* 6*d.*

The History of Philosophy, from Thales to Comte. By GEORGE HENRY LEWES. Fourth Edition 2 vols. 8vo. 32*s.*

Introduction to the Science of Religion, Four Lectures delivered at the Royal Institution; with Two Essays on False Analogies and the Philosophy of Mythology. By MAX MÜLLER, M.A. Crown 8vo. 10*s.* 6*d.*

Zeller's Stoics, Epicureans, and Sceptics. Translated by the Rev. O. J. REICHEL, M.A. Cr. 8vo. 14*s.*

Zeller's Socrates & the Socratic Schools. Translated by the Rev. O. J. REICHEL, M.A. Second Edition. Crown 8vo. 10*s.* 6*d.*

Zeller's Plato & the Older Academy. Translated by S. FRANCES ALLEYNE and ALFRED GOODWIN, B.A. Crown 8vo. 18*s.*

Epochs of Modern History. Edited by C. COLBECK, M.A.

Church's Beginning of the Middle Ages, 2*s.* 6*d.*
Cox's Crusades, 2*s.* 6*d.*
Creighton's Age of Elizabeth, 2*s.* 6*d.*
Gairdner's Houses of Lancaster and York, 2*s.* 6*d.*
Gardiner's Puritan Revolution, 2*s.* 6*d.*
——— **Thirty Years' War,** 2*s.* 6*d.*
Hale's Fall of the Stuarts, 2*s.* 6*d.*
Johnson's Normans in Europe, 2*s.* 6*d.*
Ludlow's War of American Independence, 2*s.* 6*d.*
Morris's Age of Anne, 2s. 6*d.*
Seebohm's Protestant Revolution, price 2*s.* 6*d.*
Stubbs's Early Plantagenets, 2*s.* 6*d.*
Warburton's Edward III. 2*s.* 6*d.*

Epochs of Ancient History. Edited by the Rev. Sir G. W. COX, Bart. M.A. & C. SANKEY, M.A.

Beesly's Gracchi, Marius & Sulla, 2*s.* 6*d.*
Capes's Age of the Antonines, 2*s.* 6*d.*
——— **Early Roman Empire,** 2*s.* 6*d.*
Cox's Athenian Empire, 2*s.* 6*d.*
——— **Greeks & Persians,** 2*s.* 6*d.*
Curteis's Macedonian Empire, 2*s.* 6*d.*
Ihne's Rome to its Capture by the Gauls, 2*s.* 6*d.*
Merivale's Roman Triumvirates, 2*s.* 6*d.*
Sankey's Spartan & Theban Supremacies, 2*s.* 6*d.*

Epochs of English History. Edited by the Rev. MANDELL CREIGHTON, M.A.

Browning's Modern England, 1820–1874, 9*d.*
Cordery's Struggle against Absolute Monarchy, 1603–1688, 9*d.*
Creighton's (Mrs.) England a Continental Power, 1066–1216, 9*d.*
Creighton's (Rev. M.) Tudors and the Reformation, 1485–1603, 9*d.*
Rowley's Rise of the People, 1215–1485, 9*d.*
Rowley's Settlement of the Constitution, 1688–1778, 9*d.*
Tancock's England during the American & European Wars, 1778–1820, 9*d.*
York-Powell's Early England to the Conquest, 1*s.*

The Student's Manual of Modern History; the Rise and Progress of the Principal European Nations. By W. COOKE TAYLOR, LL.D. Crown 8vo. 7*s.* 6*d.*

The Student's Manual of Ancient History; the Political History, Geography and Social State of the Principal Nations of Antiquity. By W. COOKE TAYLOR, LL.D. Cr. 8vo. 7*s.* 6*d.*

BIOGRAPHICAL WORKS.

Memoirs of the Life of Anna Jameson, Author of 'Sacred and Legendary Art' &c. By her Niece, GERARDINE MACPHERSON. 8vo. with Portrait, price 12*s.* 6*d.*

Memorials of Charlotte Williams-Wynn. Edited by her Sister. Crown 8vo. with Portrait, price 10*s.* 6*d.*

The Life and Letters of Lord Macaulay. By his Nephew, G. OTTO TREVELYAN, M.P.
CABINET EDITION, 2 vols. crown 8vo. 12*s.*
LIBRARY EDITION, 2 vols. 8vo. 36*s.*

The Life of Sir William Fairbairn, Bart. F.R.S. Crown 8vo. 2*s.* 6*d.* demy 8vo. 18*s.*

The Life of Sir Martin Frobisher, Knt. containing a Narrative of the Spanish Armada. By the Rev. FRANK JONES, B.A. Portrait, Maps, and Facsimile. Crown 8vo. 6*s.*

Arthur Schopenhauer, his Life and his Philosophy. By HELEN ZIMMERN. Post 8vo. Portrait, 7*s.* 6*d.*

Gotthold Ephraim Lessing, his Life and Works. By HELEN ZIMMERN. Crown 8vo. 10*s.* 6*d.*

The Life, Works, and Opinions of Heinrich Heine. By WILLIAM STIGAND. 2 vols. 8vo. Portrait, 28*s.*

The Life of Mozart. Translated from the German Work of Dr. LUDWIG NOHL by Lady WALLACE. 2 vols. crown 8vo. 21*s.*

Life of Robert Frampton, D.D. Bishop of Gloucester, deprived as a Non-Juror in 1689. Edited by T. S. EVANS, M.A. Crown 8vo. 10*s.* 6*d.*

Felix Mendelssohn's Letters, translated by Lady WALLACE. 2 vols. crown 8vo. 5*s.* each.

Autobiography. By JOHN STUART MILL. 8vo. 7*s.* 6*d.*

Apologia pro Vitâ Suâ; Being a History of his Religious Opinions by JOHN HENRY NEWMAN, D.D. of the Oratory of St. Philip Neri. New Edition. Crown 8vo. 6*s.*

Pope Pius IX. By the late J. F. MAGUIRE, M.P. Revised and brought down to the Accession of Pope Leo the Thirteenth by the Right Rev. Monsignor PATTERSON. Crown 8vo. Portraits, 6*s.* post 8vo. 2*s.* 6*d.*

Isaac Casaubon, 1559-1614. By MARK PATTISON, Rector of Lincoln College, Oxford. 8vo. 18*s.*

Leaders of Public Opinion in Ireland; Swift, Flood, Grattan, O'Connell. By W. E. H. LECKY, M.A. Crown 8vo. 7*s.* 6*d.*

Essays in Ecclesiastical Biography. By the Right Hon. Sir J. STEPHEN, LL.D. Crown 8vo. 7*s.* 6*d.*

Dictionary of General Biography; containing Concise Memoirs and Notices of the most Eminent Persons of all Ages and Countries. By W. L. R. CATES. 8vo. 25*s.*

Life of the Duke of Wellington. By the Rev. G. R. GLEIG, M.A. Crown 8vo. Portrait, 6*s.*

Memoirs of Sir Henry Havelock, K.C.B. By JOHN CLARK MARSHMAN. Crown 8vo. 3*s.* 6*d.*

Vicissitudes of Families. By Sir BERNARD BURKE, C.B. Two vols. crown 8vo. 21*s.*

MENTAL and POLITICAL PHILOSOPHY.

Comte's System of Positive Polity, or Treatise upon Sociology :—

VOL. I. **General View of Positivism** and Introductory Principles. Translated by J. H. BRIDGES, M.B. 8vo. 21*s.*

VOL. II. **The Social Statics,** or the Abstract Laws of Human Order. Translated by F. HARRISON, M.A. 8vo. 14*s.*

VOL. III. **The Social Dynamics,** or the General Laws of Human Progress (the Philosophy of History). Translated by E. S. BEESLY, M.A. 8vo. 21*s.*

VOL. IV. **The Theory of the Future of Man**; with COMTE'S Early Essays on Social Philosophy. Translated by R. CONGREVE, M.D. and H. D. HUTTON, B.A. 8vo. 24*s.*

De Tocqueville's Democracy in America, translated by H. REEVE. 2 vols. crown 8vo. 16*s.*

Analysis of the Phenomena of the Human Mind. By JAMES MILL. With Notes, Illustrative and Critical. 2 vols. 8vo. 28*s.*

On Representative Government. By JOHN STUART MILL. Crown 8vo. 2*s.*

On Liberty. By JOHN STUART MILL. Post 8vo. 7*s.* 6*d.* crown 8vo. 1*s.* 4*d.*

Principles of Political Economy. By JOHN STUART MILL. 2 vols. 8vo. 30*s.* or 1 vol. crown 8vo. 5*s.*

Essays on some Unsettled Questions of Political Economy. By JOHN STUART MILL. 8vo. 6*s.* 6*d.*

Utilitarianism. By JOHN STUART MILL. 8vo. 5*s.*

The Subjection of Women. By JOHN STUART MILL. Fourth Edition. Crown 8vo. 6*s.*

Examination of Sir William Hamilton's Philosophy. By JOHN STUART MILL. 8vo. 16*s.*

A System of Logic, Ratiocinative and Inductive. By JOHN STUART MILL. 2 vols. 8vo. 25*s.*

Dissertations and Discussions. By JOHN STUART MILL. 4 vols. 8vo. price £2. 6*s.* 6*d.*

The Philosophy of Reflection. By SHADWORTH H. HODGSON, Hon. LL.D. Edin. Author of 'Time and Space,' and 'The Theory of Practice.' 2 vols. 8vo. 21*s.*

The Law of Nations considered as Independent Political Communities. By Sir TRAVERS TWISS, D.C.L. 2 vols. 8vo. £1. 13*s.*

A Systematic View of the Science of Jurisprudence. By SHELDON AMOS, M.A. 8vo. 18*s.*

A Primer of the English Constitution and Government. By S. AMOS, M.A. Crown 8vo. 6*s.*

A Sketch of the History of Taxes in England from the Earliest Times to the Present Day. By STEPHEN DOWELL. VOL. I. to the Civil War 1642. 8vo. 10*s.* 6*d.*

Principles of Economical Philosophy. By H. D. MACLEOD, M.A. Second Edition in 2 vols. VOL. I. 8vo. 15*s.* VOL. II. PART I. 12*s.*

The Institutes of Justinian; with English Introduction, Translation, and Notes. By T. C. SANDARS, M.A. 8vo. 18*s.*

Lord Bacon's Works, collected & edited by R. L. ELLIS, M.A. J. SPEDDING, M.A. and D. D. HEATH. 7 vols. 8vo. £3. 13*s.* 6*d.*

Letters and Life of Francis Bacon, including all his Occasional Works. Collected and edited, with a Commentary, by J. SPEDDING. 7 vols. 8vo. £4. 4*s.*

The Nicomachean Ethics of Aristotle, translated into English by R. WILLIAMS, B.A. Crown 8vo. price 7*s.* 6*d.*

Aristotle's Politics, Books I. III. IV. (VII.) Greek Text, with an English Translation by W. E. BOLLAND, M.A. and Short Essays by A. LANG, M.A. Crown 8vo. 7*s.* 6*d.*

The Politics of Aristotle; Greek Text, with English Notes. By RICHARD CONGREVE, M.A. 8vo. 18*s.*

The Ethics of Aristotle; with Essays and Notes. By Sir A. GRANT, Bart. LL.D. 2 vols. 8vo. 32*s.*

Bacon's Essays, with Annotations. By R. WHATELY, D.D. 8vo. 10*s.* 6*d.*

Picture Logic; an Attempt to Popularise the Science of Reasoning. By A. SWINBOURNE, B.A. Post 8vo. 5*s.*

Elements of Logic. By R. WHATELY, D.D. 8vo. 10*s.* 6*d.* Crown 8vo. 4*s.* 6*d.*

Elements of Rhetoric. By R. WHATELY, D.D. 8vo. 10*s.* 6*d.* Crown 8vo. 4*s.* 6*d.*

On the Influence of Authority in Matters of Opinion. By the late Sir. G. C. LEWIS, Bart. 8vo. 14*s.*

The Senses and the Intellect. By A. BAIN, LL.D. 8vo. 15*s.*

The Emotions and the Will. By A. BAIN, LL.D. 8vo. 15*s.*

Mental and Moral Science; a Compendium of Psychology and Ethics. By A. BAIN, LL.D. Crown 8vo. 10*s.* 6*d.* Or separately, PART I. Mental Science, 6*s.* 6*d.* PART II. Moral Science, 4*s.* 6*d.*

An Outline of the Necessary Laws of Thought; a Treatise on Pure and Applied Logic. By W. THOMPSON, D.D. Crown 8vo. 6*s.*

Hume's Philosophical Works. Edited, with Notes, &c. by T. H. GREEN, M.A. and the Rev. T. H. GROSE, M.A. 4 vols. 8vo. 56*s.* Or separately, Essays, 2 vols. 28*s.* Treatise on Human Nature, 2 vols. 28*s.*

The Schools of Charles the Great, and the Restoration of Education in the Ninth Century. By J. BASS MULLINGER, M.A. 8vo. price 7*s.* 6*d.*

MISCELLANEOUS & CRITICAL WORKS.

The London Series of English Classics. Edited by JOHN W. Hales, M.A. and by CHARLES S. JERRAM, M.A. Fcp. 8vo.

Bacon's Essays, annotated by E. A. ABBOT, D.D. 2 vols. 6*s.*

Ben Jonson's Every Man in His Humour, by H. B. WHEATLEY, F.S.A. Price 2*s.* 6*d.*

Macaulay's Clive, by H. C. BOWEN, M.A. 2*s.* 6*d.*

Marlowe's Doctor Faustus, by W. WAGNER, Ph.D. 2*s.*

Milton's Paradise Regained, by C. S. JERRAM, M.A. 2*s.* 6*d.*

Pope's Select Poems, by T. ARNOLD, M.A. 2*s.* 6*d.*

Miscellaneous Writings of J. Conington, M.A. Edited by J. A. SYMONDS, M.A. 2 vols. 8vo. 28*s.*

Mesmerism, Spiritualism &c. Historically and Scientifically Considered. By W. B. CARPENTER, F.R.S. &c. Crown 8vo. 5*s.*

Evenings with the Skeptics; or, Free Discussion on Free Thinkers. By JOHN OWEN, Rector of East Anstey, Devon. Crown 8vo. [*Just ready.*

Short Studies on Great Subjects. By J. A. FROUDE, M.A. 3 vols. crown 8vo. 18*s.*

Manual of English Literature, Historical and Critical. By T. ARNOLD, M.A. Crown 8vo. 7*s.* 6*d.*

Lord Macaulay's Miscellaneous Writings:—
LIBRARY EDITION, 2 vols. 8vo. 21*s.*
PEOPLE'S EDITION, 1 vol. cr. 8vo. 4*s.* 6*d.*

Lord Macaulay's Miscellaneous Writings and Speeches. Student's Edition. Crown 8vo. 6*s.*

Speeches of the Right Hon. Lord Macaulay, corrected by Himself. Crown 8vo. 3*s.* 6*d.*

Selections from the Writings of Lord Macaulay. Edited, with Notes, by G. O. TREVELYAN, M.P. Crown. 8vo. 6*s.*

The Rev. Sydney Smith's Essays. Crown 8vo. 3*s.* 6*d.* cloth.

The Wit and Wisdom of the Rev. Sydney Smith. Crown 8vo. 3*s.* 6*d.*

Miscellaneous and Posthumous Works of the late Henry Thomas Buckle. Edited by HELEN TAYLOR. 3 vols. 8vo. 52*s.* 6*d.*

Miscellaneous Works of Thomas Arnold, D.D. late Head Master of Rugby School. 8vo. 7*s.* 6*d.*

German Home Life; a Series of Essays on the Domestic Life of Germany. Crown 8vo. 6*s.*

Realities of Irish Life. By W. STEUART TRENCH. Crown 8vo. 2*s.* 6*d.* sewed, or 3*s.* 6*d.* cloth.

Church and State; their Relations Historically Developed. By H. GEFFCKEN, Prof. of International Law, Univ. of Strasburg. Translated by E. F. TAYLOR. 2 vols. 8vo. 42*s.*

Lectures on the Science of Language. By F. MAX MÜLLER, M.A. 2 vols. crown 8vo. 16*s.*

Chips from a German Workshop; Essays on the Science of Religion, and on Mythology, Traditions & Customs. By F. MAX MULLER, M.A. 4 vols. 8vo. £2. 18*s.*

Language & Languages. A Revised Edition of Chapters on Language and Families of Speech. By F. W. FARRAR, D.D. F.R.S. Crown 8vo. 6*s.*

The Essays and Contributions of A. K. H. B. Uniform Cabinet Editions in crown 8vo.

Recreations of a Country Parson, Three Series, 3*s.* 6*d.* each.

Landscapes, Churches, and Moralities, price 3*s.* 6*d.*

Seaside Musings, 3*s.* 6*d.*

Changed Aspects of Unchanged Truths, 3*s.* 6*d.*

Counsel and Comfort from a City Pulpit, 3*s.* 6*d.*

Lessons of Middle Age, 3*s.* 6*d.*

Leisure Hours in Town, 3*s.* 6*d.*

Autumn Holidays of a Country Parson, price 3*s.* 6*d.*

Sunday Afternoons at the Parish Church of a University City, 3*s.* 6*d.*

The Commonplace Philosopher in Town and Country, 3*s.* 6*d.*

Present-Day Thoughts, 3*s.* 6*d.*

Critical Essays of a Country Parson, price 3*s.* 6*d.*

The Graver Thoughts of a Country Parson, Three Series, 3*s.* 6*d.* each.

DICTIONARIES and OTHER BOOKS of REFERENCE.

Dictionary of the English Language. By R. G. LATHAM, M.A. M.D. Abridged from Dr. Latham's Edition of Johnson's English Dictionary. Medium 8vo. 24*s.*

A Dictionary of the English Language. By R. G. LATHAM, M.A. M.D. Founded on Johnson's English Dictionary as edited by the Rev. H. J. TODD. 4 vols. 4to. £7.

Thesaurus of English Words and Phrases, classified and arranged so as to facilitate the expression of Ideas, and assist in Literary Composition. By P. M. ROGET, M.D. Crown 8vo. 10*s.* 6*d.*

English Synonymes. By E. J. WHATELY. Edited by R. WHATELY, D.D. Fcp. 8vo. 3*s.*

Handbook of the English Language. By R. G. LATHAM, M.A. M.D. Crown 8vo. 6*s.*

Contanseau's Practical Dictionary of the French and English Languages. Post 8vo. price 7*s.* 6*d.*

Contanseau's Pocket Dictionary, French and English, abridged from the Practical Dictionary by the Author. Square 18mo. 3*s.* 6*d.*

A New Pocket Dictionary of the German and English Languages. By F. W. LONGMAN, Ball. Coll. Oxford. Square 18mo. 5*s.*

A Practical Dictionary of the German and English Languages. By Rev. W. L. BLACKLEY, M.A. & Dr. C. M. FRIEDLÄNDER. Post 8vo. 7*s.* 6*d.*

A Dictionary of Roman and Greek Antiquities. With 2,000 Woodcuts illustrative of the Arts and Life of the Greeks and Romans. By A. RICH, B.A. Crown 8vo. 7*s.* 6*d.*

The Critical Lexicon and Concordance to the English and Greek New Testament. By the Rev. E. W. BULLINGER. Medium 8vo. 30*s.*

A Greek-English Lexicon. By H. G. LIDDELL, D.D. Dean of Christchurch, and R. SCOTT, D.D. Dean of Rochester. Crown 4to. 36*s.*

Liddell & Scott's Lexicon, Greek and English, abridged for Schools. Square 12mo. 7*s.* 6*d.*

An English-Greek Lexicon, containing all the Greek Words used by Writers of good authority. By C. D. YONGE, M.A. 4to. 21*s.*

Mr. Yonge's Lexicon, English and Greek, abridged from his larger Lexicon. Square 12mo. 8*s.* 6*d.*

A Latin-English Dictionary. By JOHN T. WHITE, D.D. Oxon. and J. E. RIDDLE, M.A. Oxon. Sixth Edition, revised. 1 vol. 4to. 28s.

White's College Latin-English Dictionary, for the use of University Students. Medium 8vo. 15*s.*

A Latin-English Dictionary for the use of Middle-Class Schools. By JOHN T. WHITE, D.D. Oxon. Square fcp. 8vo. 3*s.*

White's Junior Student's Latin-English and English-Latin Dictionary. Square 12mo.

ENGLISH-LATIN DICTIONARY, 5*s.* 6*d.*
LATIN-ENGLISH DICTIONARY, 7*s.* 6*d.*
COMPLETE, 12*s.*

M'Culloch's Dictionary of Commerce and Commercial Navigation. Re-edited by HUGH G. REID, Assistant-Comptroller H.H. Stationery Office. With 11 Maps and 30 Charts. 8vo. 63*s.*

Keith Johnston's General Dictionary of Geography, Descriptive, Physical, Statistical, and Historical; a complete Gazetteer of the World. Medium 8vo. 42*s.*

The Public Schools Atlas of Ancient Geography, in 28 entirely new Coloured Maps. Edited by the Rev. G. BUTLER, M.A. Imperial 8vo. or imperial 4to. 7*s.* 6*d.*

The Public Schools Atlas of Modern Geography, in 31 entirely new Coloured Maps. Edited by the Rev. G. BUTLER, M.A. Imperial 8vo. or imperial 4to. 5*s.*

ASTRONOMY and METEOROLOGY.

Outlines of Astronomy. By Sir J. F. W. HERSCHEL, Bart. M.A. Latest Edition, with Plates and Diagrams. Square crown 8vo. 12*s.*

Essays on Astronomy. A Series of Papers on Planets and Meteors, the Sun and Sun-surrounding Space, Star and Star Cloudlets. By R. A. PROCTOR, B.A. With 10 Plates and 24 Woodcuts. 8vo. 12*s.*

The Moon; her Motions, Aspects, Scenery, and Physical Condition. By R. A. PROCTOR, B.A. With Plates, Charts, Woodcuts, and Lunar Photographs. Crown 8vo. 10*s.* 6*d.*

The Sun; Ruler, Light, Fire, and Life of the Planetary System. By R. A. PROCTOR, B.A. With Plates & Woodcuts. Crown 8vo. 14*s.*

The Orbs Around Us; a Series of Essays on the Moon & Planets, Meteors & Comets, the Sun & Coloured Pairs of Suns. By R. A. PROCTOR, B.A. With Chart and Diagrams. Crown 8vo. 7*s.* 6*d.*

Other Worlds than Ours; The Plurality of Worlds Studied under the Light of Recent Scientific Researches. By R. A. PROCTOR, B.A. With 14 Illustrations. Cr. 8vo. 10*s.* 6*d.*

The Universe of Stars; Presenting Researches into and New Views respecting the Constitution of the Heavens. By R. A. PROCTOR, B.A. Second Edition, with 22 Charts (4 Coloured) and 22 Diagrams. 8vo. price 10*s.* 6*d.*

The Transits of Venus; A Popular Account of Past and Coming Transits. By R. A. PROCTOR, B.A. 20 Plates (12 Coloured) and 27 Woodcuts. Crown 8vo. 8*s.* 6*d.*

Saturn and its System. By R. A. PROCTOR, B.A. 8vo. with 14 Plates, 14*s.*

The Moon, and the Condition and Configurations of its Surface. By E. NEISON, F.R.A.S. With 26 Maps & 5 Plates. Medium 8vo. 31*s.* 6*d.*

Celestial Objects for Common Telescopes. By T. W. WEBB, M.A. With Chart and Woodcuts. New Edition in the press.

A New Star Atlas, for the Library, the School, and the Observatory, in 12 Circular Maps (with 2 Index Plates). By R. A. PROCTOR, B. A. Crown 8vo. 5*s.*

Larger Star Atlas, for the Library, in Twelve Circular Maps, with Introduction and 2 Index Plates. By R. A. PROCTOR, B.A. Folio, 15*s.* or Maps only, 12*s.* 6*d.*

Dove's Law of Storms, considered in connexion with the Ordinary Movements of the Atmosphere. Translated by R. H. SCOTT, M.A. 8vo. 10*s.* 6*d.*

Air and Rain; the Beginnings of a Chemical Climatology. By R. A. SMITH, F.R.S. 8vo. 24*s.*

Air and its Relations to Life, 1774–1874; a Course of Lectures delivered at the Royal Institution. By W. N. HARTLEY, F.C.S. With 66 Woodcuts. Small 8vo. 6*s.*

Schellen's Spectrum Analysis, in its Application to Terrestrial Substances and the Physical Constitution of the Heavenly Bodies. Translated by JANE and C. LASSELL, with Notes by W. HUGGINS, LL.D. F.R.S. 8vo. Plates and Woodcuts, 28*s.*

A Treatise on the Cycloid, and on all forms of Cycloidal Curves, and on the use of Cycloidal Curves in dealing with the Motions of Planets, Comets, &c. and of Matter projected from the Sun. By R. A. PROCTOR, B.A. With 161 Diagrams. Crown 8vo. 10*s.* 6*d.*

NATURAL HISTORY and PHYSICAL SCIENCE.

Professor Helmholtz' Popular Lectures on Scientific Subjects. Translated by E. ATKINSON, F.C.S. With numerous Wood Engravings. 8vo. 12*s.* 6*d.*

Professor Helmholtz on the Sensations of Tone, as a Physiological Basis for the Theory of Music. Translated by A. J. ELLIS, F.R.S. 8vo. 36*s.*

Ganot's Natural Philosophy for General Readers and Young Persons; a Course of Physics divested of Mathematical Formulæ and expressed in the language of daily life. Translated by E. ATKINSON, F.C.S. Third Edition. Plates and Woodcuts. Crown 8vo. 7*s.* 6*d.*

Ganot's Elementary Treatise on Physics, Experimental and Applied, for the use of Colleges and Schools. Translated and edited by E. ATKINSON, F.C.S. Eighth Edition. Plates and Woodcuts. Post 8vo. 15*s.*

Arnott's Elements of Physics or Natural Philosophy. Seventh Edition, edited by A. BAIN, LL.D. and A. S. TAYLOR, M.D. F.R.S. Crown 8vo. Woodcuts, 12*s.* 6*d.*

The Correlation of Physical Forces. By the Hon. Sir W. R. GROVE, F.R.S. &c. Sixth Edition, revised and augmented. 8vo. 15*s.*

Weinhold's Introduction to Experimental Physics; including Directions for Constructing Physical Apparatus and for Making Experiments. Translated by B. LOEWY, F.R.A.S. With a Preface by G. C. FOSTER, F.R.S. 8vo. Plates & Woodcuts 31*s.* 6*d.*

A Treatise on Magnetism, General and Terrestrial. By H. LLOYD, D.D. D.C.L. 8vo. 10*s.* 6*d.*

Elementary Treatise on the Wave-Theory of Light. By H. LLOYD, D.D. D.C.L. 8vo. 10*s.* 6*d.*

Fragments of Science. By JOHN TYNDALL, F.R.S., Latest Edition. Crown 8vo. 10*s.* 6*d.*

Heat a Mode of Motion. By JOHN TYNDALL, F.R.S. Fifth Edition nearly ready.

Sound. By JOHN TYNDALL, F.R.S. Third Edition, including Recent Researches on Fog-Signalling. Crown 8vo. price 10*s.* 6*d.*

Researches on Diamagnetism and Magne-Crystallic Action; including Diamagnetic Polarity. By JOHN TYNDALL, F.R.S. With 6 Plates and many Woodcuts. 8vo. 14*s.*

Contributions to Molecular Physics in the domain of Radiant Heat. By JOHN TYNDALL, F.R.S. Plates and Woodcuts. 8vo. 16*s.*

Six Lectures on Light, delivered in America in 1872 and 1873. By JOHN TYNDALL, F.R.S. Second Edition. Portrait, Plate, and Diagrams. Crown 8vo. 7*s.* 6*d.*

Lessons in Electricity at the Royal Institution, 1875–6. By JOHN TYNDALL, F.R.S. With 58 Woodcuts. Crown 8vo. 2*s.* 6*d.*

Notes of a Course of Seven Lectures on Electrical Phenomena and Theories, delivered at the Royal Institution. By JOHN TYNDALL, F.R.S. Crown 8vo. 1*s.* sewed, or 1*s.* 6*d.* cloth.

Notes of a Course of Nine Lectures on Light, delivered at the Royal Institution. By JOHN TYNDALL, F.R.S. Crown 8vo. 1*s.* sewed, or 1*s.* 6*d.* cloth.

Principles of Animal Mechanics. By the Rev. S. HAUGHTON, F.R.S. Second Edition. 8vo. 21*s.*

Text-Books of Science, Mechanical and Physical, adapted for the use of Artisans and of Students in Public and Science Schools. Small 8vo. with Woodcuts, &c.

Abney's Photography, 3s. 6d.
Anderson's Strength of Materials, 3s. 6d.
Armstrong's Organic Chemistry, 3s. 6d.
Barry's Railway Appliances, 3s. 6d.
Bloxam's Metals, 3s. 6d.
Goodeve's Mechanics, 3s. 6d.
——— Mechanism, 3s. 6d.
Gore's Electro-Metallurgy, 6s.
Griffin's Algebra & Trigonometry, 3/6.
Jenkin's Electricity & Magnetism, 3/6.
Maxwell's Theory of Heat, 3s. 6d.
Merrifield's Technical Arithmetic, 3s. 6d.
Miller's Inorganic Chemistry, 3s. 6d.
Preece & Sivewright's Telegraphy, 3/6.
Shelley's Workshop Appliances, 3s 6d.
Thomé's Structural and Physiological Botany, 6s.
Thorpe's Quantitative Analysis, 4s. 6d.
Thorpe & Muir's Qualitative Analysis, price 3s. 6d.
Tilden's Systematic Chemistry, 3s. 6d.
Unwin's Machine Design, 3s. 6d.
Watson's Plane & Solid Geometry, 3/6.

Light Science for Leisure Hours; Familiar Essays on Scientific Subjects, Natural Phenomena, &c. By R. A. PROCTOR, B.A. 2 vols. crown 8vo. 7s. 6d. each.

The Comparative Anatomy and Physiology of the Vertebrate Animals. By RICHARD OWEN, F.R.S. With 1,472 Woodcuts. 3 vols. 8vo. £3. 13s. 6d.

Kirby and Spence's Introduction to Entomology, or Elements of the Natural History of Insects. Crown 8vo. 5s.

A Familiar History of Birds. By E. STANLEY, D.D. Fcp. 8vo. with Woodcuts, 3s. 6d.

Homes without Hands; a Description of the Habitations of Animals, classed according to their Principle of Construction. By the Rev. J. G. WOOD, M.A. With about 140 Vignettes on Wood. 8vo. 14s.

Wood's Strange Dwellings; a Description of the Habitations of Animals, abridged from 'Homes without Hands.' With Frontispiece and 60 Woodcuts. Crown 8vo. 7s. 6d.

Wood's Insects at Home; a Popular Account of British Insects, their Structure, Habits, and Transformations. With 700 Woodcuts. 8vo. 14s.

Wood's Insects Abroad; a Popular Account of Foreign Insects, their Structure, Habits, and Transformations. With 700 Woodcuts. 8vo. 14s.

Wood's Out of Doors; a Selection of Original Articles on Practical Natural History. With 6 Illustrations. Crown 8vo. 7s. 6d.

Wood's Bible Animals; a description of every Living Creature mentioned in the Scriptures, from the Ape to the Coral. With 112 Vignettes. 8vo. 14s.

The Sea and its Living Wonders. By Dr. G. HARTWIG. 8vo. with numerous Illustrations, price 10s. 6d.

Hartwig's Tropical World. With about 200 Illustrations. 8vo. 10s. 6d.

Hartwig's Polar World; a Description of Man and Nature in the Arctic and Antarctic Regions of the Globe. Chromoxylographs, Maps, and Woodcuts. 8vo. 10s. 6d.

Hartwig's Subterranean World. With Maps and Woodcuts. 8vo. 10s. 6d.

Hartwig's Aerial World; a Popular Account of the Phenomena and Life of the Atmosphere. Map, Chromoxylographs, Woodcuts. 8vo. price 10s. 6d.

Rocks Classified and Described. By BERNHARD VON COTTA. An English Translation, by P. H. LAWRENCE (with English, German, and French Synonymes), revised by the Author. Post 8vo. 14*s.*

The Geology of England and Wales; a Concise Account of the Lithological Characters, Leading Fossils, and Economic Products of the Rocks. By H. B. WOODWARD, F.G.S. Crown 8vo. Map & Woodcuts, 14*s.*

Keller's Lake Dwellings of Switzerland, and other Parts of Europe. Translated by JOHN E. LEE, F.S.A. F.G.S. New Edition, enlarged, with 206 Illustrations. 2 vols. royal 8vo. 42*s.*

The Primæval World of Switzerland. By Professor OSWAL HEER, of the University of Zurich. Edited by JAMES HEYWOOD, M.A. F.R.S. With Map, 19 Plates, & 372 Woodcuts. 2 vols. 8vo. 28*s.*

The Puzzle of Life and How it Has Been Put Together; a Short History of Praehistoric Vegetable and Animal Life on the Earth. By A. NICOLS, F.R.G.S. With 12 Illustrations. Crown 8vo. 3*s.* 6*d.*

The Origin of Civilisation, and the Primitive Condition of Man; Mental and Social Condition of Savages. By Sir J. LUBBOCK, Bart. M.P. F.R.S. 8vo. Woodcuts, 18*s.*

The Ancient Stone Implements, Weapons, and Ornaments of Great Britain. By JOHN EVANS, F.R.S. With 2 Plates and 476 Woodcuts. 8vo. 28*s.*

A Dictionary of Science, Literature, and Art. Re-edited by the late W. T. BRANDE (the Author) and the Rev. Sir G. W. COX, Bart., M.A. 3 vols. medium 8vo. 63*s.*

The History of Modern Music, a Course of Lectures delivered at the Royal Institution of Great Britain. By JOHN HULLAH, LL.D. 8vo. price 8*s.* 6*d.*

Dr. Hullah's 2d Course of Lectures on the Transition Period of Musical History, from the Beginning of the 17th to the Middle of the 18th Century. 8vo. 10*s.* 6*d.*

Loudon's Encyclopædia of Plants; comprising the Specific Character, Description, Culture, History, &c. of all the Plants found in Great Britain. With upwards of 12,000 Woodcuts. 8vo. 42*s.*

De Caisne & Le Maout's System of Descriptive and Analytical Botany. Translated by Mrs. HOOKER; edited and arranged according to the English Botanical System, by J. D. HOOKER, M.D. With 5,500 Woodcuts. Imperial 8vo. 31*s.* 6*d.*

Hand-Book of Hardy Trees, Shrubs, and Herbaceous Plants; containing Descriptions &c. of the Best Species in Cultivation. With 720 Original Woodcut Illustrations. By W. B. HEMSLEY. Medium 8vo. 12*s.*

The Rose Amateur's Guide. By THOMAS RIVERS. Latest Edition. Fcp. 8vo. 4*s.* 6*d.*

CHEMISTRY and PHYSIOLOGY.

Miller's Elements of Chemistry, Theoretical and Practical. Re-edited, with Additions, by H. MACLEOD, F.C.S. 3 vols. 8vo.

PART I. CHEMICAL PHYSICS. 16*s.*
PART II. INORGANIC CHEMISTRY, 24*s.*
PART III. ORGANIC CHEMISTRY, New Edition in the press.

Animal Chemistry; or, the Relations of Chemistry to Physiology and Pathology: a Manual for Medical Men and Scientific Chemists. By CHARLES T. KINGZETT, F.C.S. 8vo. price 18*s.*

A Dictionary of Chemistry and the Allied Branches of other Sciences. By HENRY WATTS, F.C.S. assisted by eminent Scientific and Practical Chemists. 7 vols. medium 8vo. £10. 16*s*. 6*d*.

Supplementary Volume, completing the Record of Chemical Discovery to the year 1877. [*In the press.*

Select Methods in Chemical Analysis, chiefly Inorganic. By WM. CROOKES, F.R.S. With 22 Woodcuts. Crown 8vo. 12*s*. 6*d*.

The History, Products, and Processes of the Alkali Trade, including the most recent Improvements. By CHARLES T. KINGZETT, F.C.S. With 32 Woodcuts. 8vo. 12*s*.

Health in the House: Twenty-five Lectures on Elementary Physiology in its Application to the Daily Wants of Man and Animals. By Mrs. BUCKTON. Crown 8vo. Woodcuts, 2*s*.

The FINE ARTS and ILLUSTRATED EDITIONS.

In Fairyland; Pictures from the Elf-World. By RICHARD DOYLE. With a Poem by W. ALLINGHAM. With 16 coloured Plates, containing 36 Designs. Folio, 15*s*.

Lord Macaulay's Lays of Ancient Rome. With Ninety Illustrations on Wood from Drawings by G. SCHARF. Fcp. 4to. 21*s*.

Miniature Edition of Macaulay's Lays of Ancient Rome, with Scharf's 90 Illustrations reduced in Lithography. Imp. 16mo. 10*s*. 6*d*.

Moore's Lalla Rookh. TENNIEL's Edition, with 68 Woodcut Illustrations. Fcp. 4to. 21*s*.

Moore's Irish Melodies, MACLISE's Edition, with 161 Steel Plates. Super-royal 8vo. 21*s*.

Lectures on Harmony, delivered at the Royal Institution. By G. A. MACFARREN. 8vo. 12*s*.

Sacred and Legendary Art. By Mrs. JAMESON. 6 vols. square crown 8vo. price £5. 15*s*. 6*d*.

Jameson's Legends of the Saints and Martyrs. With 19 Etchings and 187 Woodcuts. 2 vols. 31*s*. 6*d*.

Jameson's Legends of the Monastic Orders. With 11 Etchings and 88 Woodcuts. 1 vol. 21*s*.

Jameson's Legends of the Madonna. With 27 Etchings and 165 Woodcuts. 1 vol. 21*s*.

Jameson's History of the Saviour, His Types and Precursors. Completed by Lady EASTLAKE. With 13 Etchings and 281 Woodcuts. 2 vols. 42*s*.

The Three Cathedrals dedicated to St. Paul in London. By W. LONGMAN, F.S.A. With numerous Illustrations. Square crown 8vo. 21*s*.

The USEFUL ARTS, MANUFACTURES, &c.

The Art of Scientific Discovery. By G. GORE, LL.D. F.R.S. Author of 'The Art of Electro-Metallurgy.' Crown 8vo. price 15*s*.

The Amateur Mechanics' Practical Handbook; describing the different Tools required in the Workshop. By A. H. G. HOBSON. With 33 Woodcuts. Crown 8vo. 2*s*. 6*d*.

The Engineer's Valuing Assistant. By H. D. HOSKOLD, Civil and Mining Engineer, 16 years Mining Engineer to the Dean Forest Iron Company. 8vo. 31*s.* 6*d.*

Industrial Chemistry; a Manual for Manufacturers and for Colleges or Technical Schools; a Translation (by Dr. T. H. BARRY) of Stohmann and Engler's German Edition of PAYEN'S 'Précis de Chimie Industrielle;' with Chapters on the Chemistry of the Metals, &c. by B. H. PAUL, Ph.D. With 698 Woodcuts. Medium 8vo. 42*s.*

Gwilt's Encyclopædia of Architecture, with above 1,600 Woodcuts. Revised and extended by W. PAPWORTH. 8vo. 52*s.* 6*d.*

Lathes and Turning, Simple, Mechanical, and Ornamental. By W. H. NORTHCOTT. Second Edition, with 338 Illustrations. 8vo. 18*s.*

Hints on Household Taste in Furniture, Upholstery, and other Details. By C. L. EASTLAKE. Fourth Edition, with 100 Illustrations. Square crown 8vo. 14*s.*

Handbook of Practical Telegraphy. By R. S. CULLEY, Memb. Inst. C.E. Seventh Edition. Plates & Woodcuts. 8vo. price 16*s.*

A Treatise on the Steam Engine, in its various applications to Mines, Mills, Steam Navigation, Railways and Agriculture. By J. BOURNE, C.E. With Portrait, 37 Plates, and 546 Woodcuts. 4to. 42*s.*

Recent Improvements in the Steam Engine. By J. BOURNE, C.E. Fcp. 8vo. Woodcuts, 6*s.*

Catechism of the Steam Engine, in its various Applications. By JOHN BOURNE, C.E. Fcp. 8vo. Woodcuts, 6*s.*

Handbook of the Steam Engine, a Key to the Author's Catechism of the Steam Engine. By J. BOURNE, C.E. Fcp. 8vo. Woodcuts, 9*s.*

Encyclopædia of Civil Engineering, Historical, Theoretical, and Practical. By E. CRESY, C.E. With above 3,000 Woodcuts. 8vo. 42*s.*

Ure's Dictionary of Arts, Manufactures, and Mines. Seventh Edition, re-written and enlarged by R. HUNT, F.R.S. assisted by numerous contributors. With 2,604 Woodcuts. 4 vols. medium 8vo. £7. 7*s.*

Practical Treatise on Metallurgy. Adapted from the last German Edition of Professor KERL'S Metallurgy by W. CROOKES, F.R.S. &c. and E. RÖHRIG, Ph.D. 3 vols. 8vo. with 625 Woodcuts. £4. 19*s.*

The Theory of Strains in Girders and similar Structures, with Observations on the application of Theory to Practice, and Tables of the Strength and other Properties of Materials. By B. B. STONEY, M.A. M. Inst. C.E. Royal 8vo. with 5 Plates and 123 Woodcuts, 36*s.*

Railways and Locomotives; a Series of Lectures delivered at the School of Military Engineering, Chatham, in the year 1877. *Railways,* by JOHN WOLFE BARRY, M. Inst. C.E. *Locomotives,* by F. J. BRAMWELL, F.R.S. M. Inst. C.E. [*In the press.*

A Treatise on Mills and Millwork. By the late Sir W. FAIRBAIRN, Bart. C.E. Fourth Edition, with 18 Plates and 333 Woodcuts. 1 vol. 8vo. 25*s.*

Useful Information for Engineers. By the late Sir W. FAIRBAIRN, Bart. C.E. With many Plates and Woodcuts. 3 vols. crown 8vo. 31*s.* 6*d.*

The Application of Cast and Wrought Iron to Building Purposes. By the late Sir W. FAIRBAIRN, Bart. C.E. With 6 Plates and 118 Woodcuts. 8vo. 16*s.*

Anthracen; its Constitution, Properties, Manufacture, and Derivatives, including Artificial Alizarin, Anthrapurpurin, &c. with their Applications in Dyeing and Printing. By G. AUERBACH. Translated by W. CROOKES, F.R.S. 8vo. 12*s.*

Practical Handbook of Dyeing and Calico-Printing. By W. CROOKES, F.R.S. &c. With numerous Illustrations and specimens of Dyed Textile Fabrics. 8vo. 42*s.*

Mitchell's Manual of Practical Assaying. Fourth Edition, revised, with the Recent Discoveries incorporated, by W. CROOKES, F.R.S. Crown 8vo. Woodcuts, 31*s.* 6*d.*

Loudon's Encyclopædia of Gardening; the Theory and Practice of Horticulture, Floriculture, Arboriculture & Landscape Gardening. With 1,000 Woodcuts. 8vo. 21*s.*

Loudon's Encyclopædia of Agriculture; the Laying-out, Improvement, and Management of Landed Property; the Cultivation and Economy of the Productions of Agriculture. With 1,100 Woodcuts. 8vo. 21*s.*

RELIGIOUS and MORAL WORKS.

An Exposition of the 39 Articles, Historical and Doctrinal. By E. H. BROWNE, D.D. Bishop of Winchester. Eleventh Edition. 8vo. 16*s.*

A Commentary on the 39 Articles, forming an Introduction to the Theology of the Church of England. By the Rev. T. P. BOULTBEE, LL.D. New Edition. Crown 8vo. 6*s.*

Historical Lectures on the Life of Our Lord Jesus Christ. By C. J. ELLICOTT, D.D. 8vo. 12*s.*

Sermons preached mostly in the Chapel of Rugby School by the late T. ARNOLD, D.D. Collective Edition, revised by the Author's Daughter, Mrs. W. E. FORSTER. 6 vols. crown 8vo. 30*s.* or separately, 5*s.* each.

The Eclipse of Faith; or a Visit to a Religious Sceptic. By HENRY ROGERS. Fcp. 8vo. 5*s.*

Defence of the Eclipse of Faith. By H. ROGERS. Fcp. 8vo. 3*s.* 6*d.*

Nature, the Utility of Religion and Theism. Three Essays by JOHN STUART MILL. 8vo. 10*s.* 6*d.*

A Critical and Grammatical Commentary on St. Paul's Epistles. By C. J. ELLICOTT, D.D. 8vo. Galatians, 8*s.* 6*d.* Ephesians, 8*s.* 6*d.* Pastoral Epistles, 10*s.* 6*d.* Philippians, Colossians, & Philemon, 10*s.* 6*d.* Thessalonians, 7*s.* 6*d.*

Conybeare & Howson's Life and Epistles of St. Paul. Three Editions, copiously illustrated.

Library Edition, with all the Original Illustrations, Maps, Landscapes on Steel, Woodcuts, &c. 2 vols. 4to. 42*s.*

Intermediate Edition, with a Selection of Maps, Plates, and Woodcuts. 2 vols. square crown 8vo. 21*s.*

Student's Edition, revised and condensed, with 46 Illustrations and Maps. 1 vol. crown 8vo. 9*s.*

The Jewish Messiah; Critical History of the Messianic Idea among the Jews, from the Rise of the Maccabees to the Closing of the Talmud. By JAMES DRUMMOND, B.A. 8vo. 15*s.*

Evidence of the Truth of the Christian Religion derived from the Literal Fulfilment of Prophecy. By A. KEITH, D.D. 40th Edition, with numerous Plates. Square 8vo. 12*s.* 6*d.* or post 8vo. with 5 Plates, 6*s.*

The Prophets and Prophecy in Israel; an Historical and Critical Inquiry. By Prof. A. KUENEN, Translated from the Dutch by the Rev. A. MILROY, M.A. with an Introduction by J. MUIR, D.C.L. 8vo. 21*s.*

The History and Literature of the Israelites, according to the Old Testament and the Apocrypha. By C. DE ROTHSCHILD & A. DE ROTHSCHILD. 2 vols. crown 8vo. 12*s.* 6*d.* 1 vol. fcp. 8vo. 3*s.* 6*d.*

Mythology among the Hebrews and its Historical Development. By IGNAZ GOLDZIHER, Ph.D. Translated by RUSSELL MARTINEAU, M.A. 8vo. 16*s.*

Bible Studies. By M. M. KALISCH, Ph.D. PART I. *The Prophecies of Balaam.* 8vo. 10*s.* 6*d.* PART II. *The Book of Jonah.* 8vo. 10*s.* 6*d.*

Historical and Critical Commentary on the Old Testament; with a New Translation. By M. M. KALISCH, Ph.D. Vol. I. Genesis, 8vo. 18*s.* or adapted for the General Reader, 12*s.* Vol. II. Exodus, 15*s.* or adapted for the General Reader, 12*s.* Vol. III. Leviticus, Part I. 15*s.* or adapted for the General Reader, 8*s.* Vol. IV. Leviticus, Part II. 15*s.* or adapted for the General Reader, 8*s.*

Ewald's History of Israel. Translated from the German by J. E. CARPENTER, M.A. with Preface by R. MARTINEAU, M.A. 5 vols. 8vo. 63*s.*

Ewald's Antiquities of Israel. Translated from the German by H. S. SOLLY, M.A. 8vo. 12*s.* 6*d.*

The Trident, the Crescent & the Cross; a View of the Religious History of India during the Hindu, Buddhist, Mohammedan, and Christian Periods. By the Rev. J. VAUGHAN. 8vo. 9*s.* 6*d.*

The Types of Genesis, briefly considered as revealing the Development of Human Nature. By A. JUKES. Crown 8vo. 7*s.* 6*d.*

The Second Death and the Restitution of all Things; with some Preliminary Remarks on the Nature and Inspiration of Holy Scripture. By A. JUKES. Crown 8vo. 3*s.* 6*d.*

History of the Reformation in Europe in the time of Calvin. By the Rev. J. H. MERLE D'AUBIGNÉ, D.D. Translated by W. L. R. CATES. 8 vols. 8vo. price £6. 12*s.*

Commentaries, by the Rev. W. A. O'CONOR, B.A. Rector of St. Simon and St. Jude, Manchester.

Epistle to the Romans, crown 8vo. 3*s.* 6*d.*
Epistle to the Hebrews, 4*s.* 6*d.*
St. John's Gospel, 10*s.* 6*d.*

Supernatural Religion; an Inquiry into the Reality of Divine Revelation. 3 vols. 8vo. 38*s.*

The Four Gospels in Greek, with Greek-English Lexicon. By JOHN T. WHITE, D.D. Oxon. Square 32mo. 5*s.*

Passing Thoughts on Religion. By ELIZABETH M. SEWELL. Fcp. 8vo. 3*s.* 6*d.*

Thoughts for the Age. by ELIZABETH M. SEWELL. New Edition. Fcp. 8vo. 3*s.* 6*d.*

Preparation for the Holy Communion; the Devotions chiefly from the works of Jeremy Taylor. By ELIZABETH M. SEWELL. 32mo. 3*s.*

The Ritual of the Altar, or Order of the Holy Communion according to the Church of England. Edited by the Rev. O. SHIPLEY, M.A. Second Edition, revised and enlarged, with Frontispiece and 70 Woodcuts. Small folio, 42*s.*

Bishop Jeremy Taylor's Entire Works; with Life by Bishop Heber. Revised and corrected by the Rev. C. P. EDEN. 10 vols. £5. 5*s.*

Hymns of Praise and Prayer. Corrected and edited by Rev. JOHN MARTINEAU, LL.D. Crown 8vo. 4*s.* 6*d.* 32mo. 1*s.* 6*d.*

One Hundred Holy Songs, Carols and Sacred Ballads, Original and Suitable for Music. Square fcp. 8vo. 2*s.* 6*d.*

Spiritual Songs for the Sundays and Holidays throughout the Year. By J. S. B. MONSELL, LL.D. Fcp. 8vo. 5*s.* 18mo. 2*s.*

Lyra Germanica; Hymns translated from the German by Miss C. WINKWORTH. Fcp. 8vo. 5*s.*

The Temporal Mission of the Holy Ghost; or, Reason and Revelation. By HENRY EDWARD MANNING, D.D. Crown 8vo. 8*s.* 6*d.*

Hours of Thought on Sacred Things; a Volume of Sermons. By JAMES MARTINEAU, D.D. LL.D. Crown 8vo. Price 7*s.* 6*d.*

Endeavours after the Christian Life; Discourses. By JAMES MARTINEAU, D.D. LL.D. Fifth Edition. Crown 8vo. 7*s.* 6*d.*

The Pentateuch & Book of Joshua Critically Examined. By J. W. COLENSO, D.D. Bishop of Natal. Crown 8vo. 6*s.*

Lectures on the Pentateuch and the Moabite Stone; with Appendices. By J. W. COLENSO, D.D. Bishop of Natal. 8vo. 12*s.*

TRAVELS, VOYAGES, &c.

A Voyage in the 'Sunbeam,' our Home on the Ocean for Eleven Months. By Mrs. BRASSEY. Sixth Edition, with 8 Maps and Charts and 118 Wood Engravings. 8vo. 21*s.*

A Year in Western France. By M. BETHAM-EDWARDS. Crown 8vo. Frontispiece, 10*s.* 6*d.*

One Thousand Miles up the Nile; a Journey through Egypt and Nubia to the Second Cataract. By AMELIA B. EDWARDS. With Plans, Maps & Illustrations. Imperial 8vo. 42*s.*

The Indian Alps, and How we Crossed them; Two Years' Residence in the Eastern Himalayas, and Two Months' Tour into the Interior. By a LADY PIONEER. With Illustrations. Imperial 8vo. 42*s.*

Discoveries at Ephesus, Including the Site and Remains of the Great Temple of Diana. By J. T. WOOD, F.S.A. With 27 Lithographic Plates and 42 Wood Engravings. Medium 8vo. 63*s.*

Through Bosnia and the Herzegovina on Foot during the Insurrection, August and September 1875. By ARTHUR J. EVANS, B.A. F.S.A. Map & Woodcuts. 8vo. 18*s.*

Illyrian Letters, from the Provinces of Bosnia, Herzegovina, Montenegro, Albania, Dalmatia, Croatia & Slavonia, during the year 1877. By A. J. EVANS, B.A. F.S.A. Post 8vo. Maps. 7*s.* 6*d.*

Over the Sea and Far Away; a Narrative of a Ramble round the World. By T. W. HINCHLIFF, M.A. With 14 full-page Illustrations. Medium 8vo. 21*s.*

Guide to the Pyrenees, for the use of Mountaineers. By CHARLES PACKE. Crown 8vo. 7*s.* 6*d.*

The Alpine Club Map of Switzerland, with parts of the Neighbouring Countries, on the scale of Four Miles to an Inch. Edited by R. C. NICHOLS, F.R.G.S. 4 Sheets in Portfolio, 42*s.* coloured, or 34*s.* uncoloured.

The Alpine Guide. By JOHN BALL, M.R.I.A. Post 8vo. with Maps and other Illustrations.

The Eastern Alps, 10*s.* 6*d.*

Central Alps, including all the Oberland District, 7*s.* 6*d.*

Western Alps, including Mont Blanc, Monte Rosa, Zermatt, &c. Price 6*s.* 6*d.*

On Alpine Travelling and the Geology of the Alps. Price 1*s.* Either of the 3 Volumes or Parts of the 'Alpine Guide' may be had with this Introduction prefixed, 1*s.* extra. The 'Alpine Guide' may also be had in 10 separate Parts, or districts, 2*s.* 6*d.* each.

How to see Norway. By J. R. CAMPBELL. Fcp. 8vo. Map & Woodcuts, 5*s.*

Memorials of the Discovery and Early Settlement of the Bermudas or Somers Islands, from 1615 to 1685. By Major-General Sir J. H. LEFROY, R.A. VOL. I. imperial 8vo. with 2 Maps, 30*s.*

Eight Years in Ceylon. By Sir SAMUEL W. BAKER, M.A. Crown 8vo. Woodcuts, 7*s.* 6*d.*

The Rifle and the Hound in Ceylon. By Sir SAMUEL W. BAKER, M.A. Crown 8vo. Woodcuts, 7*s.* 6*d.*

WORKS of FICTION.

Novels and Tales. By the Right Hon. the EARL of BEACONSFIELD, K.G. Cabinet Editions, complete in Ten Volumes, crown 8vo. 6*s.* each.

Lothair, 6*s.*	Venetia, 6*s.*
Coningsby, 6*s.*	Alroy, Ixion, &c. 6*s.*
Sybil, 6*s.*	Young Duke &c. 6*s.*
Tancred, 6*s.*	Vivian Grey, 6*s.*

Henrietta Temple, 6*s.*
Contarini Fleming, &c. 6*s.*

The Atelier du Lys; or an Art-Student in the Reign of Terror. By the author of 'Mademoiselle Mori.' Third Edition. Crown 8vo. 6*s.*

Whispers from Fairyland. By the Right Hon. E. H. KNATCHBULL-HUGESSEN, M.P. With 9 Illustrations. Crown 8vo. 3*s.* 6*d.*

Higgledy-Piggledy; or, Stories for Everybody and Everybody's Children. By the Right Hon. E. H. KNATCHBULL-HUGESSEN, M.P. With 9 Illustrations. Cr. 8vo. 3*s.* 6*d.*

Stories and Tales. By ELIZABETH M. SEWELL. Cabinet Edition, in Ten Volumes, each containing a complete Tale or Story:—

Amy Herbert, 2*s.* 6*d.* Gertrude, 2*s.* 6*d.* The Earl's Daughter, 2*s.* 6*d.* The Experience of Life, 2*s.* 6*d.* Cleve Hall, 2*s.* 6*d.* Ivors, 2*s.* 6*d.* Katharine Ashton, 2*s.* 6*d.* Margaret Percival, 3*s.* 6*d.* Laneton Parsonage, 3*s.* 6*d.* Ursula, 3*s.* 6*d.*

The Modern Novelist's Library. Each work complete in itself, price 2*s.* boards, or 2*s.* 6*d.* cloth.

By Lord BEACONSFIELD.

- Lothair.
- Coningsby.
- Sybil.
- Tancred.
- Venetia.
- Henrietta Temple.
- Contarini Fleming.
- Alroy, Ixion, &c.
- The Young Duke, &c.
- Vivian Grey.

By ANTHONY TROLLOPE.

- Barchester Towers.
- The Warden.

By the Author of 'The Rose Garden.'

- Unawares.

By Major WHYTE-MELVILLE.

- Digby Grand.
- General Bounce.
- Kate Coventry.
- The Gladiators.
- Good for Nothing.
- Holmby House.
- The Interpreter.
- The Queen's Maries.

By the Author of 'The Atelier du Lys.'

- Mademoiselle Mori.

By Various Writers.

- Atherstone Priory.
- The Burgomaster's Family.
- Elsa and her Vulture.
- The Six Sisters of the Valleys.

The Novels and Tales of the Right Honourable the Earl of Beaconsfield, K.G. Complete in Ten Volumes, crown 8vo. cloth extra, gilt edges, price 30*s.*

POETRY and THE DRAMA.

Lays of Ancient Rome; with Ivry and the Armada. By LORD MACAULAY. 16mo. 3*s.* 6*d.*

Horatii Opera. Library Edition, with English Notes, Marginal References & various Readings. Edited by Rev. J. E. YONGE, M.A. 8vo. 21*s.*

Poems by Jean Ingelow. 2 vols. fcp. 8vo. 10*s.*

FIRST SERIES, containing 'Divided,' 'The Star's Monument,' &c. Fcp. 8vo. 5*s.*

SECOND SERIES, 'A Story of Doom,' 'Gladys and her Island,' &c. 5*s.*

Poems by Jean Ingelow. First Series, with nearly 100 Woodcut Illustrations. Fcp. 4to. 21*s.*

Festus, a Poem. By PHILIP JAMES BAILEY. 10th Edition, enlarged & revised. Crown 8vo. 12*s.* 6*d.*

The Iliad of Homer, Homometrically translated by C. B. CAYLEY, Translator of Dante's Comedy, &c. 8vo. 12*s.* 6*d.*

The Æneid of Virgil. Translated into English Verse. By J. CONINGTON, M.A. Crown 8vo. 9*s.*

Bowdler's Family Shakspeare. Genuine Edition, in 1 vol. medium 8vo. large type, with 36 Woodcuts, 14*s.* or in 6 vols. fcp. 8vo. 21*s.*

Southey's Poetical Works, with the Author's last Corrections and Additions. Medium 8vo. with Portrait, 14*s.*

RURAL SPORTS, HORSE and CATTLE MANAGEMENT, &c.

Annals of the Road; or, Notes on Mail and Stage-Coaching in Great Britain. By Captain MALET. With 3 Woodcuts and 10 Coloured Illustrations. Medium 8vo. 21*s.*

Down the Road; or, Reminiscences of a Gentleman Coachman. By C. T. S. BIRCH REYNARDSON. Second Edition, with 12 Coloured Illustrations. Medium 8vo. 21*s.*

Blaine's Encyclopædia of Rural Sports; Complete Accounts, Historical, Practical, and Descriptive, of Hunting, Shooting, Fishing, Racing, &c. With 600 Woodcuts. 8vo. 21*s.*

A Book on Angling; or, Treatise on the Art of Fishing in every branch; including full Illustrated Lists of Salmon Flies. By FRANCIS FRANCIS. Post 8vo. Portrait and Plates, 15*s.*

Wilcocks's Sea-Fisherman: comprising the Chief Methods of Hook and Line Fishing, a glance at Nets, and remarks on Boats and Boating. Post 8vo. Woodcuts, 12*s.* 6*d.*

The Fly-Fisher's Entomology. By ALFRED RONALDS. With 20 Coloured Plates. 8vo. 14*s.*

Horses and Riding. By GEORGE NEVILE, M.A. With 31 Illustrations. Crown 8vo. 6*s.*

Horses and Stables. By Colonel F. FITZWYGRAM, XV. the King's Hussars. With 24 Plates of Illustrations. 8vo. 10*s.* 6*d.*

Youatt on the Horse. Revised and enlarged by W. WATSON, M.R.C.V.S. 8vo. Woodcuts, 12*s.* 6*d.*

Youatt's Work on the Dog. Revised and enlarged. 8vo. Woodcuts, 6*s.*

The Dog in Health and Disease. By STONEHENGE. With 73 Wood Engravings. Square crown 8vo. 7*s.* 6*d.*

The Greyhound. By STONEHENGE. Revised Edition, with 25 Portraits of Greyhounds, &c. Square crown 8vo. 15*s.*

Stables and Stable Fittings. By W. MILES. Imp. 8vo. with 13 Plates, 15*s.*

The Horse's Foot, and How to keep it Sound. By W. MILES. Imp. 8vo. Woodcuts, 12*s.* 6*d.*

A Plain Treatise on Horse-shoeing. By W. MILES. Post 8vo. Woodcuts, 2*s.* 6*d.*

Remarks on Horses' Teeth, addressed to Purchasers. By W. MILES. Post 8vo. 1*s.* 6*d.*

The Ox, his Diseases and their Treatment; with an Essay on Parturition in the Cow. By J. R. DOBSON, M.R.C.V.S. Crown 8vo. Illustrations, 7*s.* 6*d.*

WORKS of UTILITY and GENERAL INFORMATION.

Maunder's Treasury of Knowledge and Library of Reference; comprising an English Dictionary and Grammar, Universal Gazetteer, Classical Dictionary, Chronology, Law Dictionary, Synopsis of the Peerage, Useful Tables, &c. Fcp. 8vo. 6*s.*

Maunder's Biographical Treasury. Latest Edition, reconstructed and partly re-written, with above 1,600 additional Memoirs, by W. L. R. CATES. Fcp. 8vo. 6*s.*

Maunder's Scientific and Literary Treasury; a Popular Encyclopædia of Science, Literature, and Art. Latest Edition, partly re-written, with above 1,000 New Articles, by J. Y. JOHNSON. Fcp. 8vo. 6*s.*

Maunder's Treasury of Geography, Physical, Historical, Descriptive, and Political. Edited by W. HUGHES, F.R.G.S. With 7 Maps and 16 Plates. Fcp. 8vo. 6*s.*

Maunder's Historical Treasury; Introductory Outlines of Universal History, and Separate Histories of all Nations. Revised by the Rev. Sir G. W. COX, Bart. M.A. Fcp. 8vo. 6*s.*

Maunder's Treasury of Natural History; or, Popular Dictionary of Zoology. Revised and corrected Edition. Fcp. 8vo. with 900 Woodcuts, 6*s.*

The Treasury of Botany, or Popular Dictionary of the Vegetable Kingdom; with which is incorporated a Glossary of Botanical Terms. Edited by J. LINDLEY, F.R.S. and T. MOORE, F.L.S. With 274 Woodcuts and 20 Steel Plates. Two Parts, fcp. 8vo. 12*s.*

The Treasury of Bible Knowledge; being a Dictionary of the Books, Persons, Places, Events, and other Matters of which mention is made in Holy Scripture. By the Rev. J. AYRE, M.A. Maps, Plates & Woodcuts. Fcp. 8vo. 6*s.*

A Practical Treatise on Brewing; with Formulæ for Public Brewers & Instructions for Private Families. By W. BLACK. 8vo. 10*s.* 6*d.*

The Theory of the Modern Scientific Game of Whist. By W. POLE, F.R.S. Tenth Edition. Fcp. 8vo. 2*s.* 6*d.*

The Correct Card; or, How to Play at Whist; a Whist Catechism. By Captain A. CAMPBELL-WALKER, F.R.G.S. New Edition. Fcp. 8vo. 2*s.* 6*d.*

The Cabinet Lawyer; a Popular Digest of the Laws of England, Civil, Criminal, and Constitutional. Twenty-Fifth Edition, corrected and extended. Fcp. 8vo. 9*s.*

Chess Openings. By F. W. LONGMAN, Balliol College, Oxford. Second Edition. Fcp. 8vo. 2*s.* 6*d.*

English Chess Problems. Edited by J. PIERCE, M.A. and W. T. PIERCE. With 608 Diagrams. Crown 8vo. 12*s.* 6*d.*

Pewtner's Comprehensive Specifier; a Guide to the Practical Specification of every kind of Building-Artificer's Work. Edited by W. YOUNG. Crown 8vo. 6*s.*

A Handbook on Gold and Silver. By an INDIAN OFFICER. 8vo. 12*s*. 6*d*.

The English Manual of Banking. By ARTHUR CRUMP. Second Edition, revised and enlarged. 8vo. 15*s*.

Modern Cookery for Private Families, reduced to a System of Easy Practice in a Series of carefully-tested Receipts. By ELIZA ACTON. With 8 Plates and 150 Woodcuts. Fcp. 8vo. 6*s*.

Hints to Mothers on the Management of their Health during the Period of Pregnancy and in the Lying-in Room. By THOMAS BULL, M.D. Fcp. 8vo, 2*s*. 6*d*.

The Maternal Management of Children in Health and Disease. By THOMAS BULL, M.D. Fcp. 8vo. 2*s*. 6*d*.

Economics for Beginners By H. D. MACLEOD, M.A. Small crown 8vo. 2*s*. 6*d*.

The Elements of Banking. By H. D. MACLEOD, M.A. Third Edition. Crown 8vo. 7*s*. 6*d*.

The Theory and Practice of Banking. By H. D. MACLEOD, M.A. 2 vols. 8vo. 26*s*.

The Resources of Modern Countries; Essays towards an Estimate of the Economic Position of Nations and British Trade Prospects. By ALEX. WILSON. 2 vols. 8vo. 24*s*.

Willich's Popular Tables for ascertaining, according to the Carlisle Table of Mortality, the value of Lifehold, Leasehold, and Church Property, Renewal Fines, Reversions, &c. Also Interest, Legacy, Succession Duty, and various other useful tables. Eighth Edition. Post 8vo. 10*s*.

INDEX.